I0644186

COMPLETE WORKS

OF

PIR-O-MURSHID

HAZRAT INAYAT KHAN

ORIGINAL TEXTS:

LECTURES ON SUFISM

1924 I: January - June 8

"Work for the work; not for success.

"Forget the Past; think not of the Future; mind the Now."

INAYAT KHAN.

1924.

	JANUARY.						FEBRUARY.						MARCH.					
S	...	6	13	20	27	...	...	3	10	17	24	...	...	2	9	16	23	30
M	...	7	14	21	28	...	...	4	11	18	25	...	...	3	10	17	24	31
T	1	8	15	22	29	...	...	5	12	19	26	...	...	4	11	18	25	...
W	2	9	16	23	30	...	...	6	13	20	27	...	...	5	12	19	26	...
T	3	10	17	24	31	...	...	7	14	21	28	...	...	6	13	20	27	...
F	4	11	18	25	...	...	1	8	15	22	29	...	...	7	14	21	28	...
S	5	12	19	26	...	...	2	9	16	23	...	...	1	8	15	22	29	...

	APRIL.						MAY.						JUNE.					
S	...	6	13	20	27	...	...	4	11	18	25	...	1	8	15	22	29	...
M	...	7	14	21	28	...	...	5	12	19	26	...	2	9	16	23	30	...
T	1	8	15	22	29	...	...	6	13	20	27	...	3	10	17	24	...	...
W	2	9	16	23	30	...	...	7	14	21	28	...	4	11	18	25	...	...
T	3	10	17	24	...	...	1	8	15	22	29	...	5	12	19	26	...	...
F	4	11	18	25	...	...	2	9	16	23	30	...	6	13	20	27	...	...
S	5	12	19	26	...	...	3	10	17	24	31	...	7	14	21	28	...	...

	JULY.						AUGUST.						SEPTEMBER.					
S	...	6	13	20	27	...	...	3	10	17	24	31	...	7	14	21	28	...
M	...	7	14	21	28	...	...	4	11	18	25	...	1	8	15	22	29	...
T	1	8	15	22	29	...	...	5	12	19	26	...	2	9	16	23	30	...
W	2	9	16	23	30	...	...	6	13	20	27	...	3	10	17	24	...	...
T	3	10	17	24	31	...	...	7	14	21	28	...	4	11	18	25	...	...
F	4	11	18	25	...	...	1	8	15	22	29	...	5	12	19	26	...	...
S	5	12	19	26	...	...	2	9	16	23	30	...	6	13	20	27	...	...

	OCTOBER.						NOVEMBER.						DECEMBER.					
S	...	5	12	19	26	...	...	2	9	16	23	30	...	7	14	21	28	...
M	...	6	13	20	27	...	...	3	10	17	24	...	1	8	15	22	29	...
T	...	7	14	21	28	...	...	4	11	18	25	...	2	9	16	23	30	...
W	1	8	15	22	29	...	...	5	12	19	26	...	3	10	17	24	31	...
T	2	9	16	23	30	...	...	6	13	20	27	...	4	11	18	25	...	...
F	3	10	17	24	31	...	...	7	14	21	28	...	5	12	19	26	...	...
S	4	11	18	25	...	...	1	8	15	22	29	...	6	13	20	27	...	...

Pir-o-Murshid Inayat Khan

1882-1927

COMPLETE WORKS

OF

PIR-O-MURSHID

HAZRAT INAYAT KHAN

ORIGINAL TEXTS:

LECTURES ON SUFISM

1924 I: January - June 8

Source Edition

Omega Publications
New Lebanon

Previous volumes in this series:

Biography of Pir-o-Murshid Inayat Khan (1979)

Complete Works of Pir-o-Murshid Hazrat Inayat Khan, Original Texts:

Sayings, Part I (*Gayan, Vadan, Nirtan*, 1982, revised edition 1989)

Sayings, Part II (*Bowl of Saki*, *Aphorisms*, unpublished sayings, etc., 1982, rev. ed. 1989)

Lectures on Sufism:

1922 I: January-August (1990)

1922 II: September-December (1996)

1923 I: January-June (1989)

1923 II: July-December (1988)

Edited by Prof. Sharif Graham, Rev. Berthi van der Bent Hamel, and Mrs. Mary Jane Parrish; published by the Nekbakht Stichting.

© 2004 by the Nekbakht Stichting

This book and CD-ROM are copyrighted under the Berne Convention. Enquiries should be addressed to Fondation Nekbakht, 34 rue de la Tuilerie, 92150 Suresnes, France.

No part of this book may be reproduced in any form, by print, photoprint, microfilm, electronic reproduction, or by any other means without written permission from the copyright holder.

ISBN 0-930872-33-9

Table of Contents

PREFACE

The present volume is the seventh in the series *Complete Works of Pir-o-Murshid Hazrat Inayat Khan.* It covers the period from the beginning of 1924 up through June 8; on June 13 began the Summer School (an annual event from 1921-1926) for that year, which will appear in a separate volume. During this period eighty-six lectures or lessons are known to have been delivered by Inayat Khan, and there are usable written records of sixty-six of them[1]. These records range from the very thorough shorthand of Miss Sakina Furnée (for fifteen lectures) to single typed copies of unknown provenance. In each case, what is considered to be the oldest and/or best text (i.e. the closest to what was actually said) is presented as the basic text, and all other early relevant manuscripts, including first publication when that occurred early, are included in the extensive footnotes.

Background Information on Lectures

Pir-o-Murshid Inayat Khan's travels during this period were restricted to western Europe. At the beginning of the new year he went to the Netherlands, where he had a large and increasing number of followers. On his way he stopped in Brussels to greet the Belgian mureeds. During his three weeks in the Netherlands he gave a lecture or class almost every day, and sometimes two in the same day. Many of these were taken down by Miss Toni de Ridder, a well-known Dutch writer who had become an initiate. The great majority of the missing lectures come from this period, especially from January 4-10, when apparently no one was taking them down. Some of the lectures preserved from this period were public lectures, and thus have a much more general frame of reference than the lessons given to initiates. Of the latter, a number of the classes given in this period have become highly treasured by initiates in the various Sufi organizations in which these are still used as teaching material. However, several of these classes have never been distributed even to initiates, and appear in print for the first time in the present volume.

---

1. Please see Appendix C "Missing Lectures" for indications of the twenty missing lectures; during the period in England there must have been classes for mureeds given, but there is no record of time and place for any of these, let alone any texts.

He next went from the Netherlands to England, where he had lived from 1914 to 1920, and where he had a very solid group of followers and helpers. During his two week stay in England, he is known to have given nine lectures, most of them public (though he may have given closed classes for initiates which are not recorded). Because publication of the teachings of Inayat Khan in their original English was naturally most advanced in England, most of the lectures given in this period were soon published and have remained well-known.

He then returned to his home in Suresnes, near Paris. He gave some public lectures at the Sorbonne, and a series of private lectures and lesson for initiates in Paris and Suresnes. Generally, this period from February 11 until the end of March appears to have been a quiet time.

He then went to Geneva, where the International Headquarters of the Sufi Movement had been established, for meetings with the officers of the organization. While there, he also gave several talks.

From Geneva he went directly to Italy for his second visit there. In Florence he gave several talks, none of which has been preserved. Then he went to Rome, where he gave three talks at the university which have been preserved in their Italian translation only. It was also on this occasion that he met Maria Montessori. An account of his time in Rome has come down to us from Mrs. Munira Craig, who was present:

> Hazrat Inayat Khan came back to Rome in the glory of the following spring, to offer to his followers of the precious gift of the altar of universal worship. He spoke then at our university on "The Inner Life", "The Freedom of the Soul" and "The Culture of the Heart". His inspired words were heard by many.
>
> On this occasion I had the pleasure of introducing him to my teacher and friend Maria Montessori. It was a wonderful exchange of thoughts between these two personalities. The Sufi master told her that for her children she employed the method he applied for the souls of his disciples and that he admired her reform which was aiming at peace in a time when the word "reform" suggested agitation. Signora Montessori invited him to her home. There she illustrated practically the principal theories of her teaching, and her grandchildren demonstrated her method by different exercises chosen by themselves. She told him that the only collective lesson in her school was "silence". When the little ones got up spontaneously to close the window shutters to make the room dark, and sat down, remaining silent for some minutes, Hazrat Inayat Khan expressed his greatest admiration.
>
> And then a Signora Montessori led us to her garden. As we were saying goodbye, she hesitatingly plucked a red rose, saying,

"Perhaps the master does not approve of taking away the life of a flower, but I would like my granddaughter to give him this rose." And the rose passed from her loving hands to the innocent ones of the child, and thence to the blessed ones of the mystic.

Early in May he returned to Suresnes, and again there is a quiet period with only occasional lectures. On May 21 he went to Brussels, and gave a lecture each day for four days. He continued on to the Netherlands again, and gave a few talks up through June 8. He then returned to Suresnes for the annual Summer School, which began on June 12. The numerous lectures from June through September will be presented in another volume of this series.

In summary, Pir-o-Murshid Inayat Khan's travels in this period:

Jan. 3-25	The Netherlands (Brussels en route)
Jan. 25-Feb. 11	England
Feb. 11-Mar. 31	Suresnes (Paris)
April 1-10	Geneva
April 11-30	Italy (Florence, Rome)
May 1-21	Suresnes
May 22-26	Brussels
May 26-June 8	The Netherlands
June 12 on	Suresnes (Summer School)

Notes to Lectures

For each lecture, the basic printed text is the one closest to the actual words of Pir-o-Murshid Inayat Khan. Its origin is indicated in the upper right-hand corner. When there is a shorthand record taken down by Miss Sakina Furnée, this always constitutes the basic text, as these are by far the most accurate records of Inayat Khan's speaking. In the present volume, fifteen lectures were taken down by Sakina. All differences from this earliest text in other early documents, up to and including first publication (if any), are indicated in the notes. An abbreviated title is assigned to each document. A complete list of the documents compared, along with specific information about each document for that particular lecture, appears before the beginning of the notes. Where one or more of the listed documents is not cited in the notes, this indicates a text identical to the basic text.

Over the course of years, different typewritten copies and stencils were prepared at International Headquarters in Geneva for distribution among *mureeds*. In many cases, the earliest Headquarters' stencils (in earlier years called "cyclostyled copies") show very extensive editing, and often, therefore, were considered by Sakina Furnée to be incorrect; however, sometimes they show originally spoken words which were lost in later edited copies of the lecture. However, on the whole, later stencils show a return to something closer to the original reporting[2], apparently reflecting an editorial decision by Murshida Sherifa Goodenough, who was primarily responsible for these documents. Many Headquarters' stencils are found in the archives, on which Sakina Furnée noted the differences as compared to her shorthand reporting, writing the original words in the margin. In certain cases, however, she did not write the original word(s) in the margin, apparently indicating that she accepted the change.

There exists an extensive *errata* list on which Sirdar van Tuyll and Sakina Furnée exchanged comments as to the revisions which had been made in the texts, dating from the 1950s. Although this list does not cover all the lectures, it is mentioned in the notes, particularly for the lectures with shorthand originals, since the work they were doing then is so similar to, and therefore entirely relevant to, the work of comparison done in the preparation of these books. In many instances Sirdar suggested accepting editorial changes made by Sherifa Goodenough, while Sakina's choices in the revision of the text always inclined toward what was said by Pir-o-Murshid Inayat Khan, which to her was more important than the correctness or refinement of the English, in keeping with the Pir-o-Murshid's often expressed wish that his words be preserved as exactly as possible (please see Preface to 1922 I, pp. xiv-xv). Since it was Sakina who was doing or supervising the typing, naturally she made the final decision.

The footnote numbers in the text have been repeated in the following instances:

1. When the note refers to a lengthy set of words rather than just a few, the note number appears both at the beginning and the end;
2. When the same information applies to more than one place.

References to the various works of ancient Sufis and to scriptures, particularly the Bible and the Qur'an, have been included whenever they could be found. Many works of ancient Sufis still await translation into English or other European languages. Where Biblical references begin with "See", the quotation does not correspond exactly to standard translations. Often citations of the Qur'an are difficult or impossible to identify precisely.

---

2. The word "reporting", a rare but established usage (see OED), is used in this series to indicate a text taken down as the speaker is speaking.

The Shorthand Records

Various descriptions of the shorthand process have already been given in the prefaces of the previously published books of 1922 (I and II), 1923 (I and II). Pir-o-Murshid Inayat Khan's own statements, such as: "I have my own English in which I can best express my feelings....", prompted the need for a shorthand recording of his discourses in order to preserve them exactly.

The first and main stenographer chosen by Pir-o-Murshid Inayat Khan was Miss Sakina Furnée from the Netherlands. She applied the Pont System (a Dutch sound system) and started to take down Pir-o-Murshid Inayat Khan's discourses beginning in 1922.

During a consultation of the current transcriber (B.v.d.B.) with a stenographer[3] of the Gregg Shorthand System (U.S.A.), the same genre as the Pont System (i.e., a sound system), some additional observations became clear:

- if the shorthand reporter does not know or does not recall a shorthand composition for one word, the reporter writes it immediately in longhand.
- furthermore, there is no time for crossing out words, for the speaker goes on talking and the shorthand reporter needs to keep up with the speaker and cross-outs are done afterwards. From this it follows that, most likely, what was written down first, underneath a crossed out word, is the original spoken communication. Crossing out could be done if there was a pause; however, a lecturer generally continues talking without discussing such changes. In light of the above, the crossing out of a word belongs to the editing process. In this publication all cross-outs are noted as they appear by a footnote.

"On the whole Sakina's reportings were very complete and exact. No copies of Sakina's original transcripts of her reportings, which she sent to the administrative office of all Sufi activities, the International Headquarters of the Sufi Movement in Geneva, have been found in the archives. Sakina only kept her shorthand Notebooks." (Preface, 1923 II, xii) It is from these notebooks that the current shorthand transcriber (B.v.d.B.) makes transcriptions for the basic text of 1924 I.

For particulars on the Questions and Answers the reader is again referred to the Preface of 1923 II, Question and Answer section (p. xxii): "The exact reporting of question and answers often appears to have been

---

3. Mrs. R. Schweitzer, Bartonsville, Pennsylvania, U.S.A. (see Acknowledgements).

more difficult than the reporting of the lectures . . . . presumably the questions were not always written very clearly. In any case, several omission and uncertainties in Sakina's shorthand show that the reporting of this part of Pir-o-Murshid Inayat Khan's teaching was not an easy task. The questions do not, of course, represent the words of Pir-o-Murshid Inayat Khan; therefore, to make this evident, the questions have been reprinted in italics."

In addition, the reader's attention is directed toward the fact that the text, although printed here, was spoken without a script. Therefore "in the transcript of the lectures, here and there we find that Pir-o-Murshid Inayat Khan changes a word, or begins a phrase and then, part way through, decides to replace it with another." So also one finds at times a word being repeated, at times for emphasis, but also during the prompting of train-of-thought development, etc.

As has already been mentioned, Sakina Furnée "was very accurate in taking down the spoken word just as she heard it. Even foreign words, unknown to her, she would take down phonetically, which often allows us to discern how Pir-o-Murshid pronounced these words." (Preface, 1922 I, xii)

In order to introduce the reader somewhat to the mode of speech used by Pir-o-Murshid Inayat Khan, here follow some sentences with the speech patterns just alluded to:

- From "the Aim of Life", May 22nd, 1924:

"He gets such a patience the, when he has, he is on the way to his object that whatever unfortunate happens, it does not discourage him."

And also:

"When it are his clothes he feels comfortable, they are his. Real thing therefore is to give freedom to every soul, ..."

- From "Ancient Music", February 16th, 1924:

"What is which reason?"

- From "Intellect and Wisdom", February 25th, 1924:

"The very reason he knows it, he is so satisfied that that satisfaction does not give him that hunger that, as that person who argues."

- From "My Mureeds", May 22, 1924:

"The wrong doer has his own wrong as his worst enemy. Besides us being hard on him, his own wrong is his enemy, he is himself in a trouble. He is his own enemy, the conditions, the circumstance, the people he will meet; from every side he will receive a hate sooner or later."

- From "The Inner Life", June 3rd, 1924:

"What this wakening is?"

Table of Contents

In the Table of Contents the lectures have been listed under the title which appears on the basic text. Many lectures bear the same title; in some cases, in order to distinguish them, the first few words have been added following the title in quotation marks. In the absence of any title, a selection from the first few words of the lecture appears in quotation marks.

When lectures were given without any title, one was usually added later by those using the lecture in their Sufi Centres. In several cases the title was changed at International Headquarters in documents prepared for use in the Centres, and the chapter headings in the books in which the lectures were published also show changes.

As far as books and classified series of lectures are concerned, these later titles can be found by consulting Appendix A.

Appendix A

Appendix A is designed to show what a particular lecture may have become later on. One use, of course, was as a chapter for a book. Another very common use was as a lesson to be distributed to Sufi Centres, which included several different series for different purposes. The *Gatha*s, *Githa*s, *Sangatha*s, and *Sangitha*s were texts for *mureed*s of particular levels of initiation. The various *Gatheka* series were for a more general use. Those in possession of the books or copies of the lessons will be able to use this appendix to discover the source of the material, and then to compare the edited versions with the original lectures.

Explanation of Abbreviations

This list, which follows this preface, offers the general meaning of each abbreviation. For this volume, the abbreviations have been adjusted so that generally each reference consists of two letters. This changes the abbreviations from previous volumes in this series, where they had one, two, or three letters. The list of documents preceding the notes for each lecture indicates a more specific meaning of the abbreviation for that particular lecture. For information about the *mureed*s who took down or later edited the lectures, please refer to the List of Persons, etc.

Glossary

Even though explanations of foreign (non-English) terms are generally given only in the glossary, in some instances an immediate understanding of a term is so essential to understanding the statement that a brief explanation has been included in the notes. When Inayat Khan seems to have used a term with a special, personal sense, the usual accepted meaning is given first, and his special meaning afterwards. Standard reference sources have been used to make these entries, but especially Dr. M. C. Monna's *Short Dictionary of the Foreign Words in Hazrat Inayat Khan's Teachings* (revised edition, Alkmaar, 1991). Because of occasional errors in this dictionary, all entries have been checked in standard sources. In addition, the Glossary and List have benefited from the careful examination by Shaikh-ul-Mashaikh Mahmood Maheboob Khan and his wife, Harunnisa, who is a native speaker of Gujerati and Urdu, as was Pir-o-Murshid Inayat Khan.

List of Persons, Places and Works

Of the names of deities, persons, peoples, geographical locations, works, etc., mentioned in the lectures in this volume, a short explanation has been given following the Glossary. In many cases, these might appear to be so well-known or readily available in reference works that no explanation is required. However, these *Complete Works* are intended for wide distribution to preserve the precise contents of the teachings of Pir-o-Murshid Inayat Khan wherever there may be an interest in them. In some cases this may be far from seemingly readily available reference works, so an attempt has been made to make these volumes as complete in themselves as reasonably possible.

Index

The extensive analytical index at the end of the book may prove useful for private study, for preparing lectures, as well as for scholarly purposes in general. The intent has been to be inclusive and to provide some idea of the content of each reference.

Illustration of Documents

The illustration of documents section shows photocopied samples of document types which have not been illustrated in previous volumes.

In the work on the present volume, the division of labour has been as follows: Berthi van der Bent has transcribed Sakina Furnée's shorthand into regular English; Mary Jane Parrish has compared these transcriptions to all other early manuscripts and created the extensive footnotes; Sharif Graham has transcribed the lectures in other handwriting, and has prepared the footnotes for the other lectures. All three of us have proofread each other's work repeatedly. For the others who have participated in the work, please see Acknowledgements. And we all work under the inspiration of the example left to us by Munira van Voorst van Beest, the founding editor.

In conclusion, the objects of this book, and indeed of the whole series, may be summed up as threefold:

— to safeguard for posterity the teachings of Pir-o-Murshid Inayat Khan gathered in the Biographical Department;
— to serve as the basis of future publications and translations;
— to make the earliest source materials of Pir-o-Murshid Inayat Khan's words available to scholars, researchers, students, and the many persons interested today in finding authentic texts of Sufi spiritual teachings.

Donald A. "Sharif" Graham
Rev. Berthi van der Bent Hamel
Mary Jane Parrish
Editorial Staff of the Nekbakht Stichting

34, rue de la Tuilerie
92150 Suresnes, France

Explanation of Abbreviations

Those persons or places mentioned in this list about whom there is further information in the List of Persons, Places, Works, etc., are indicated by (L).

a.o.d. - all other documents

an. - annotation(s)

AP. - the Anna Paulownastraat in the Hague (L)

B.v.d.B. - the Rev. Berthi van der Bent Hamel, transcriber of the shorthand of Sk.

bk. - book

cr. - correction

ed. - editing, edited version

er. - early (generally, before 1927)

Fm. - Murshida Fazal Mai Egelink (L)
Fm.hw. - a handwritten document from Fazal Mai

Gd. - Murshida Sherifa Goodenough (L)
Gd.hw. - a handwritten document by Sherifa Goodenough, sometimes taken down as P-o-M. was speaking
Gd.tp. - a typewritten document, typically on Sherifa Goodenough's large-letter typewriter, made from her own or someone else's reporting

Hq. - International Headquarters, Geneva (L)
Hq.tp. - a typewritten document prepared at Hq., sometimes in multiple carbon copies for distribution to Sufi centres
Hq.st. - a stencilled document produced at Hq. for distribution to Sufi centres

hw. - handwriting, handwritten document

Lb. - Mrs. E. Leembruggen
Lb.hw. - a document in the handwriting of Lb., taken down as P-o-M. spoke in the Netherlands

Lf. - Mlle Henriette Lefèbvre, a French mureed
Lf.hw. - a handwritten record of the French translation of P-o-M.'s lectures as he spoke in Paris

MD. - Dott. Prof. Antonio Mendicini, a Roman psychiatrist
MD.hw. - a handwritten record of the Italian translation of P-o-M.'s lectures in Rome

P-o-M. - Pir-o-Murshid Inayat Khan (L)

q.a. - question(s) and answer(s)

SF. - *Sufism*, a Sufi journal (L)

sh. - shorthand

Sk. - Miss Sakina Furneé (L)
Sk.sh. - Sakina Furnée's shorthand reporting, taken down as P-o-M. spoke
Sk.tp. - a typewritten copy prepared by Sakina or under her supervision from her own or some else's reporting, or occasionally from another typescript when no reporting was available to her

SQ. - *The Sufi Quarterly*, a Sufi journal (L)

Sr. - Shaikh Sirdar van Tuyll (L)
Sr.Sk. - a written exchange discussing editorial changes in P-o-M.'s text between Sirdar and Sakina in the 1950s and '60s

SR. - *The Sufi Record*, a Sufi journal (L)

st. - stencil, a stencilled ("cyclostyled") document

Sz. - Mr. Edgar (Shabaz) Mitchell, an English journalist
Sz.hw. - a handwritten reporting taken down as P-o-M. spoke

tp. - typed, typescript

TR. - Miss Toni de Ridder (L)
TR.hw. - Toni de Ridder's handwritten reporting, taken down as P-o-M. spoke

Acknowledgements

The team which has worked together to produce this book has received help from a number of persons, and we wish to express our gratitude.

First of all, thanks to Koré Salvato, who did the final proofreading on every document in the book, and whose eagle eye saved us from many errors overlooked in repeated proofreadings. Inevitably, in a book of this kind, there are errors, but there are far fewer thanks to the careful attention Koré gave to this tedious task. She also gave many helpful suggestions for refining the editorial process.

Secondly, Shaikh-ul-Mashaikh Mahmud Maheboob Khan most kindly reviewed the entries in the Glossary and the List, and provided many most helpful suggestions for improvements. His wife Mashaikha Begum Harunnisa also gave attention particularly to the linguistic accuracy and, as a native speaker of Urdu and Gujerati, was able to shed light on Pir-o-Murshid Inayat Khan's phraseology. We are most grateful for their expertise and their willingness to help, even at short notice.

Third, we have benefited from the long experience of Dr. Michel Guillaume in French translations of Pir-o-Murshid Inayat Khan's lectures. He carefully transliterated the difficult handwriting of Mlle Lefèbvre (whom he actually knew long ago) into usable French texts. Many of the words might otherwise have proven indecipherable. For the three lectures in Italian, Mrs. Dahnya Bozzini-van Gelder carefully transcribed the Italian handwriting and made a rough translation into English; Mme Alessandra Chiaverini, a native speaker of Italian, checked the final text.

Fourth, we have had the frequent consultations of the Secretary of the Board of the Nekbakht Foundation, Ir. Wali Folkersma, which has helped us to resolve a number of difficult questions. His suggestions have been particularly helpful in the area of reducing the number of unnecessary footnotes, which always threaten to get out of hand.

Fifth, the Rev. Virginia Roger Black of Storrs, Connecticut, USA, helpfully entered thirty-six lectures into computer format early in our work on this book.

Finally, two persons we have consulted have given valuable indications about our work. Mrs Reggie Schweitzer of Bartonsville, Pennsylvania, USA, an experienced stenographer (in the Gregg system), reviewed the situation when a speaker makes corrections during a shorthand dictation, which helped to understand the revisions Sakina Furnée made in her own shorthand. Dr. Bruce Metzger, one of the main editors of The New Revised Standard Version and the New Oxford Annotated Bible, gave valuable indications on the methods of textual work.

Without this willing help, and that of a few other friends who prefer to remain anonymous, our work would have been much harder, and in some cases impossible. Our gratitude therefore is genuine, though the responsibility is of course ours.

Sakina's shorthand reporting

January 3, 1924
Chez Mlle Graeffe[1]

[2]

I have today broken my journey to visit Brussels, chiefly with the view that I may personally greet my friends at the beginning of the new year. A personal meeting[3] in the beginning of the year was meant and desired. And now I would like to say an answer to a question which is very often put to me by friends and by strangers, that: What do we expect from our work in the Sufi esoteric school?[4]

In answer to this I will say that our esoteric school does not wish to give to friends ideas which they cannot understand and beliefs which are not supported by reasons. Now the[5] desire of our friends to become interested in the wonder workings and phenomenas[6] of life, nor we wish them to become so good that it would be difficult for them to live in the world, or to

---

Documents:

Sk.sh. = Sakina Furnée's shorthand reporting, on loose-leafed (larger paper than the shorthand books) paper folded inside the 1923-1924 shorthand book. Apparently Sakina had traveled to Brussels without her shorthand notebook. The shorthand is newly transcribed by B.v.d.B.

Sk.er.tp. = an early typescript, made by Sakina or under her supervision, from an unknown source, on long, fine paper, double-spaced. Sakina corrected it in ink, indicated in the notes as "(Sk.er.tp.)Sk.cr.", making it nearly identical in wording to the sh.

Hq.tp. = a typescript made at Headquarters, Geneva ("No. 70"), of unknown origin, with several unique differences, some of which are corrected in an unknown handwriting.

Sk.tp. = a typescript prepared by Sakina or under her supervision from "(Sk.er.tp.)Sk.cr.", with two corrections by Sakina in ink.

Notes:

1. Sk.sh.: Indicating that this talk was given at the house of Mlle Graeffe, one of the mureeds in Brussels; Hq.tp., Sk.er.tp.: "for mureeds in Brussels." added; later "Brussels" crossed out by Sk.
2. Sk.sh.: "I have today broken my journey . . . . What do we expect . . . in the Sufi esoteric school" later added in lh. above the text; Sk.tp.: "Private Lecture" typed at upper left, then crossed out; "FOR MUREEDS." typed below; title omitted; Hq.tp.: "No. 70" added at upper left, and the title added: "What do we expect from our work in the Sufi esoteric school?"
3. Sk.sh.: actually Sk. wrote the sh. symbol "year" instead of "meeting"; a.o.d.: "meeting"
4. Sk.sh.: underlined "Sufi esoteric school"; Hq.tp.: "what do we expect from our work in the Sufi esoteric school" underlined in lh. as the title
5. Sk.sh.: "nor" inserted after "Now"; "the" in sh. traced over to read "we"; a.o.d.: "Nor we" instead of "Now the"
6. A.o.d.: "phenomena" instead of "phenomenas" (P-o-M. characteristically used "phenomena" as a singular, and here apparently added an "s" to make it plural)

be so pious that they would need[7] out of the world. Our work is to learn to[8] and to practice[9] how to make the best of our life in the world, how to develop that strength which is necessary for us to keep firm and steady through[10] the continual jarring influences of everyday life, how to look after the condition of our physical body, our moral[11] upon which our life's success or failure, our happiness or unhappiness depends. It is these questions that we are concerned with, and if spirituality comes in and if God-ideal comes in, and if religion comes in, it is pertaining to this particular question: the question that how to make the best of our life. Now those who are initiated[12], they must not think that they belong to an order of monks or hermits or something out of ordinary; or that they belong to some secret order; there is nothing secret in it. The truth, call it secret or call it anything. Our initiation is of[13] mutual trust given to the pupil by the teacher and to the teacher by the pupil. When the pupil says: I will take your directions without any wall between us; I shall walk in the path that I have not trodden before, as a little child with trust and confidence for all that I do not know and have not seen. You say that you will lead me[14] towards it; I have the confidence to go with you at a gain or a loss.

Leaving here my subject for a moment, I wish[15] tell you of my conversation with a man yesterday, a man who was once[16] a great believer, a Frenchman. And then from that believer[17] he turned into an unbeliever and last night[18] he came to see[19] me. In conversation he told me that there was a time when he had such a belief, but there came something which had[20] taken away his belief. I said: "I am sorry for your loss". I said: "I would rather lose and trust than distrust[21] and gain". He said: "What do you mean then by faith?" I said: "Trust". He said: "Trust in what?" I said: "First trust in yourself. No one can trust in another if one has not the trust in oneself". He said: "If[22] in trusting someone you were[23] disappointed, would you still

---

7. A.o.d.: an empty space added after "need"; (Sk.tp.)Sk.cr.: "(to go)" inserted in the blank
8. Sk.sh.: "to" crossed out, and omitted in a.o.d.
9. Hq.tp.: "to" added after "practice", then crossed out
10. Sk.er.tp.: "to" instead of "through"; (Sk.er.tp.)Sk.cr.: "to" changed back to "through"
11. Sk.sh.: although "moral" is written in sh., P-o-M. may have said "morale"; a.o.d.: "moral"
12. Sk.er.tp.: "inclined" instead of "initiated"; (Sk.er.tp.)Sk.cr.: "initiated" reinstated
13. A.o.d.: "a" instead of "of"
14. Sk.er.tp.: "my" instead of "me"
15. A.o.d.: "to" inserted after "wish"
16. Sk.er.tp.: "one" instead of "once"; (Sk.er.tp.)Sk.cr.: "once" reinstated
17. A.o.d.: "belief" instead of "believer"
18. Hq.tp.: "at last" instead of "last night"; changed to "last night" in unknown hw.
19. Sk.er.tp.: "visit" instead of "see"; (Sk.er.tp.)Sk.cr.: "see" reinstated
20. Hq.tp.: "has" instead of "had"
21. Sk.er.tp.: first typed "trust", then typed "dis-" above to read "distrust"
22. Sk.er.tp.: "In" instead of "If", followed by "in" again, probably a typographical error
23. Ibid.: "have" crossed out in type, followed by "were"

trust?" I said: "After hundred[24] fooled[25] [26] I would continue to trust. For there is no greater loss than the breaking of the trust and the power that the trust gives is a power which can be equal with nothing".

The golden words of my *murshid*[27] which I remember, when he blessed me every day I met him, he said: "May your faith be strengthened". I was a young man at that time; I doubted if my faith was little, therefore my murshid says it. I sometimes wondered why he does not say: "May you be prosperous, healthy, may you live long. May you make a success, may you be happy, may you attain a very high spiritual attainment". Why does he say such a simple thing: "May your faith be strengthened"? And it is now that I am beginning to see what really it[28] meant. It was everything [29] of [29] . In the strength of the faith there is everything. And in the absence of that there is nothing. Nothing in anything. And where is a faith, then in everything there is all that is necessary. You see, the presence of God and the absence of God both are the conditions of the[30] faith: He is present when our faith allows us to see him present. He is absent when our faith fails us to feel his presence. And what is God? God is all: wealth and health and prosperity and inspiration and success and progress and spirituality and goodness and peace and happiness and wisdom and all. Therefore Christ has said: "Seek ye the kingdom of God first and all else will be added"[31]. I wish that my friends will realize every day[32] more and more what is meant by our Sufi idea. The more they will realize, the more they will feel that it is more than a religion, more than a philosophy, [33]a mysticism, [34]for it is the very truth, which is our ideal and which we wish to attain.[34]

One should not expect that by the initiation one should at once become a most inspirational person. It is possible, yet it is not promised. Nor is it[35] promised[36] that immediately after initiation a person will be as good as a saint, nor that he will see or do wonderful things; only it is promised that a helping hand will be given to him in seeking the truth for himself.

Now there comes a question: Is it expected of every person who is

---

24. Sk.sh.: Sk. wrote "100" in digits; it is unclear whether P-o-M. said "a hundred" or "one hundred"; a.o.d.: "hundred"
25. A.o.d.: "fooled" omitted
26. Sk.sh.: originally a blank, later Sk. added "disappointments" above in lh.; a.o.d.: "disappointments" included here
27. Sufis use the word *murshid* to refer to a spiritual guide (see Glossary)
28. Hq.tp.: "is" instead of "it"
29. Sk.sh.: a blank before and after "of"; a.o.d.: end with "everything."
30. A.o.d.: "the" omitted
31. See Matthew 6:33
32. Hq.tp.: "every day" omitted; reinstated in unknown hw.
33. Sk.sh.: "more than" inserted above in sh., and included in a.o.d.
34. Sk.er.tp.: omitted, then inserted in type: "For it is . . . wish to attain."
35. Hq.tp.: "it is" instead of "is it";changed back to "is it" with an indication in ink to reverse the words
36. Sk.er.tp.: "the promise" instead of "it promised"; (Sk.er.tp.)Sk.cr.: "it promised" reinstated

initiated to work for the cause? Not at all. If it would be expected it would be like giving pearls for pebbles: You take the truth and you serve the cause. No, it should come from the heart of the person who is attaining the truth, the desire that it is a beautiful work, it is a laudable[37] object; I have a little time spare, [38] I can be of service. But the initiation does not force a person that he is obliged to serve the cause.

Nevertheless, it must be understood that it is the answer of the cry of humanity just now; it must spread and it must reach every corner of the world. The help of every kind, as it is needed, it will come, it must come. At times it will seem difficult, but every moment it will become easier. It is therefore our privilege, some of us who can offer to serve the cause in whatever manner, in whatever little way it is possible to bring about that result which is destined, which must be fulfilled. I have come again in Br.[39] also with a wish that the fire started here may be blown every now and then by me personally, by these *mureed*s[40] of mine, who have taken up[41] themselves leaving their own country to come here and do what little they can, and have gone through what little sacrifice they could, to do some service. Also by those of you who are here, if every now and then a little blowing is given to the fire you will all keep it alive. It is not necessary that one should leave one's duties at home, in the world, but whenever one can do some little work to keep the fire going, no doubt it will be appreciated greatly by your murshid and by God, whose cause it is and for whose service we are all ready, and it is our privilege.

42

---

37. Sk.sh.: "loadabbe" in lh., which Sk. heard for "loadable", which actually should be "laudable"; Sk.er.tp., Hq.tp.: "loadable" instead of "laudable"; Sk.tp.: "loadable"; changed by Sk. to "laudable"; the re-typed copy uses "laudable"
38. Sk.sh.: a blank
39. Sk.sh.: "Br." in lh. abbr. for Brussels; written out in a.o.d.
40. Sufis use the word *mureed* to refer to an initiate (see Glossary)
41. A.o.d.: "upon" instead of "up"
42. A.o.d.: sentence added: "God bless you."

Miss Toni de Ridder's handwritten text

1

Amsterdam, Jan 10th, '24 2

The Power of Breath

Since the last fifty years there seems to be an increasing desire on the part of Western nations to know and study the science of breath. When the Theosophical ideas were introduced to the Western mind they, like the Buddhist religion, based their teachings upon the science of breath. Only in the commercial part of the world the desire to know more about breath took expression in a material sense and lost its deeper meaning, which it had in India, where the science of breath was even more serious than religion, more sacred than anything else. In the East, which much more than the West considers the unity of life in all different aspects, there is no difference between God and life and breath, which is something sacred. As there is no separation between life and dream.

In a great many books about Yoga-practices people were taught to study this science without a teacher, in this way playing with the most delicate thing there is. Nevertheless it has helped in a certain direction. It was the moving of the matter. They began to understand breath in its deepest sense. And yet, how little do people realize that the beauty and fineness of the strength of the voice, its volume, depended entirely upon breath. And thinking further on breath, one will find that breath is in a person's life as important as a tick in the clock. When the tick is in the clock, the clock is going. When the tick stops, the clock stops. If the tick in the clock is not regular, the clock gives no regular time. If breath in a person is not rhythmical, that person's health is not well. The circulation of the blood, the position of head and heart, the secret power, the divine battery behind it all is breath. When nothing more than breath is in disorder, or lacking, many diseases creep up.

Not long ago I met a man whose family brought him to ruin and it

---

Document:

TR.hw. = Miss Toni de Ridder's handwritten manuscript, taken down as P-o-M. was speaking, or copied from such a document. The corrections appear to have been made as the document was being written, and are therefore included in the text and explained in the footnotes.

Notes:

1. TR.hw.: "N. 102" added, apparently an archive number
2. Ibid.: note "(Reported by Miss Toni de Ridder.)" added in Gd.'s hw.

looked as if he was losing his balance. The physician could not find what was the matter and so he came to me and I told him to go to the physician and ask him whether his breathing was in order; and then, there was found that, as he could only breathe through one nostril, his breath was not free, which caused the disease, in case his loss of balance. And so there are a thousand cases. In India there are living and have been living Yogis, Sufis, whose life's occupation it is to bring their breathing in order. Hardly one upon 1000[3] mystics suffer from chronic diseases, diseases of the breath. Their health is better than of those who live in balance.

And now, leaving this physical aspect and coming to the deeper thoughts, we see that man is not only body, though the greatest illusion man has is about himself. He is not aware of the greatness of his own being; there is no such thing as mortality—all this is an illusion. What happens is this: a man holds and values that part of his being of which he is conscious; the rest he forgets. You ask a man: what is your being, the first thing he ~~answers~~ can think[4] of is his body, which is the only thing he has to show. From a mystical point of view man is a different, a spiritual being. Man's body is like an overcoat covering the soul. But man is so taken up with the colour and form of the overcoat, that the whole life of man upon earth, he is living upon the body overcoat.

Breath is the holiness which binds the body with the mind. What is breath?

This knowledge opens a world of thought and surpasses the deepest aspect of metaphysics. The air we breathe is not breath. It is that living current, which causes the ~~motion~~ motion[5] in there. A current inexpressible, beyond explanation. It is a living power everywhere manifest. It is more skilled a[6] than electricity. All the power of electricity breath possesses: warmth, heat of the body, even of the mind. In the breath one does not only express the condition of the body, but the condition of man's heart manifests through it. It is why we feel better near a warmhearted person. Very often a person comes into the room without speaking a word, and yet he troubles everybody in the room, and that is the mystery which we might call the lack of life, which cools down everything; it is the breath. And so it is also in the opposite way. Hindu and Sanskrit scriptures call this *prana*—which means life. The different ways of healing are all connected with breath, which is the secret of life.

The electricity has power of motion, so has the breath power over

---

3. Ibid.: written as a numeral in the manuscript, so it cannot be determined whether P-o-M. said "one thousand" or "a thousand"
4. Ibid.: in the manuscript, "answers" is crossed out, and "can think" is written above
5. Ibid.: in the manuscript, the word "motion" is written twice, the first one crossed out
6. Ibid.: the manuscript clearly reads "skilled a", but one or more words seem to be missing

the mind. Who knows the right way of breathing, his mind would be brilliant, balanced, his memory clear—his thoughts developed. Besides that: what we call a self-controlled person, he shows it by the way in which he controls his breath. If he loses his temper, his breath comes in an irregular way and he is no longer able to do anything. The great mystics, Yogis, sages and saints had known the science of breath by which to control their breath and have control over every action and motion.

Our lives are so absorbed in worthless things; very little time has been left to us to think about life and the mystery of it. Absorbed as we are in worldly things, all these will take away all our lives and thoughts. But a fuller life should be lived.

At the back of all the misfortunes of humanity, the lack of patience, of self control, of consideration and equilibrium, the one reason is: the lack of self-discipline. Wherefore all mystics say: the medicine of all diseases is this, to be master of life. Behind all disappointments, all difficult situations, which they are not able to fight, seem to stand several causes, the only cause in reality being: not to be able to rise above it.

The old mystic symbol of the East is the serpent, the snake, which rises without wings, without being a bird. The snake can go forward sooner than feet can, yet it has not got any feet: without feet it digs into the ground, it walks; without wings it ~~flies~~ rises[7], without food it can remain for many days, and yet its strength remains ~~and~~ always the same. It is the most intelligent creature known to mankind. Be wise as the serpent, the Bible says. The serpent is in ~~the~~ its[8] stillness a symbol of wisdom. It can rest its body for hours together without moving. How difficult it is for man to be motionless for a quarter of an hour. We can hardly be still for one moment if the photographer tells us so.

So man has no control over his own life, and as long as he has no control over his body and mind he cannot gain that control over his spiritual life, he can never attain to that inner vision which is the benediction of life.

---

7. Ibid.: "flies" is crossed out, and "rises" written above
8. Ibid.: "the" is crossed out and "its" follows

Toni de Ridder's handwritten reporting

Amsterdam, Jan 11th 24[1]

The Inner Meaning of the Sufi Order

The word[2] Sufi Order is used to define the esoteric school of our movement. Initiation is given to those who come and want[3] this, [4]and [5]one enters the Order, which[6] opens the door to the esoteric school[4]. There are no obligations of[7] discipline[8] as would make it difficult for anyone to follow it.

Now about what is taught in the esoteric school. In a few words: it is the raising of the consciousness from the [9]limitations of our person[9]. How is this done? By [10]way of concentration and meditation. How is this to be done? By the sacred word, the elementary explanation of which Coué[11] has been giving. Coué says, by repeating a certain number of times to yourself that your health is well[12], you can regain that[13] health. He has been opposed very much, and has been very successful. Now when a person is

---

Documents:

TR.hw. = Toni de Ridder's handwritten reporting, taken down as Pir-o-Murshid Inayat Khan was speaking or copied from such a document. Later, Murshida Sherifa Goodenough made handwritten changes on one copy of this document, indicated by "(TR.hw.)Gd.ed."

er.tp. = an early typewritten copy of the lecture of unknown origin which appears to have been made before the Gd.ed., as it does not incorporate those alterations. A second typescript from the collection at the Anna Paulownastraat centre in The Hague is evidently a copy of the er.tp., showing minor variations, and is therefore not included in the notes.

Notes:

1. Er.tp.: heading moved to below the title, reading: "Amsterdam, Friday-afternoon, Jan. 11th, 1924."
2. (TR.hw.)Gd.ed.: "word" crossed out, and "name" written above
3. Ibid.: "come and want" crossed out, "desire" written above
4. Er.tp.: "and one enters the Order, which opens the door to the esoteric school" altered to read: "and by this the door is opened to the esoteric school, and one enters the order"
5. (TR.hw.)Gd.ed.: "when" written above, to precede "one"
6. Ibid.: "which" crossed out, and "this" written above
7. Ibid.: "of" crossed out, and "or" written above
8. Ibid.: "such" inserted after "discipline"
9. Ibid.: "of our person" crossed out, and "personal" written above before "limitations"
10. Ibid.: "the" inserted before "way"
11. Émile Coué (see List)
12. (TR.hw.)Gd.ed.: "well" crossed out, and "good" written above
13. Ibid.: "that" crossed out

using the word and its repetition in order to regain his[14] health, very few things are[15] accomplished, and compared with the spiritual attainment it is still small. But, intellectually, Coué is explaining the same thing the Sufi Order explains for the higher attempt[16]. [17]No comparison can there be between those[18] two things.[17] There are pebbles and[19] stones, but all are called stones.

Man[20] seems to have lost all[21] this time a[22] communication with himself by the tremendous of impossibilities[23] of everyday of[24] life. The Sufi Order by its[25] initiation helps one to come in communication with oneself. This opens the door to the heart. All the mysteries and wonders of life are got[26] when one has got in communication with one's own heart. It is therefore that we in the Sufi Order do not occupy ourselves with the[27] wonder-working or any other sort of communication; we only pay attention to communicating with ourselves in order[28] to find our deeper self.

What is the difference between the work a Sufi does and [29]another mystic? [30]In the East the Yogi mystics are the best[31] known[30], and it is worth while to consider what difference there is. The Yogi tries to touch the infinite by diving deep into his innermost being; and the process he takes is to close himself and move away[32] as far away[33] from the world as he can. And by doing this he reaches that depth which is the goal everyone is seeking. The methods of the Sufi differ herein[34] from those of the Yogis[35] that the Sufi opens[36] himself to all that is good and successful[37]. He says that

---

14. Ibid.: "his" crossed out, but then restored
15. Ibid.: "few things are" crossed out, and "little has been" written above
16. Ibid.: "attempt" crossed out, and "attainment" substituted
17. Ibid.: brackets and numbers added to indicate this should read: "There can be no comparison between those two things."
18. Er.tp.: "these" instead of "those"
19. (TR.hw.)Gd.ed.: "there are precious" inserted above
20. Er.tp.: "of this time" inserted here
21. (TR.hw.)Gd.ed.: "all" crossed out, and "at" written above
22. Er.tp.: "all this time a" omitted here
23. Er.tp: "responsibilities" instead of "of impossibilities"; (TR.hw.)Gd.ed.: "tremendous of impossibilities" crossed out, and "ever increasing responsibilities" written above
24. Er.tp.: "of" omitted; (TR.hw.)Gd.ed.: "of" crossed out
25. (TR.hw.)Gd.ed.: "its" crossed out
26. Ibid.: "got" crossed out, and "gained" written above
27. Ibid.: "the" crossed out
28. Er.tp.: "in order" omitted
29. (TR.hw.)Gd.ed.: "that of" inserted before "another"
30. Ibid.: rewritten to read: "The Yogis in the East are very well known,"
31. Er.tp.: "most" instead of "best"
32. (TR.hw.)Gd.ed.: "move away" crossed out, and "remove" written above
33. Er.tp.: "away" omitted here, but later written in ink
34. (TR.hw.)Gd.ed.: "herein" crossed out
35. Er.tp.: "Yogi" instead of "Yogis"; (TR.hw.)Gd.ed.: the final "s" in "Yogis" crossed out, and "in this" inserted above
36. TR.hw.: the word "opens" is underlined in the hw., perhaps indication that P-o-M. emphasized the word while speaking
37. (TR.hw.)Gd.ed.: "successful" crossed out, and "beautiful" inserted above

to go back to the infinite without[38] all that is beautiful here is absurd. He wants to love[39] all the beauty of the earth, and so he opens himself. Therefore his part[40] is very difficult—to love and yet not to be attached; to be in the crowd, and yet in the solitude; to be in the world and yet be above it. [41]And by this process the Sufi reaches in thousands of years what the Yogi reaches in one year.[41] He sees[42] in opening himself to the beauty of the world.

Self-denial to a Sufi is different [43]to those who deny themselves all things of life. Self-denial for the Sufi is the denial of the false self [44]which one had in its own[45] conception. His whole concentration and meditation mean[46] to get rid of that false conception of himself. A Sufi says: Man's very being is truth. It cannot be taught nor learned[47]. It exists. It[48] must come by itself. There are no doubt some studies to go through, but that is not the main thing. Meditation and concentration are only taught to make it easy for a person to advance. Truth is not an object to be given, it is one's own being. One can realize the truth by communicating with oneself.

In what way are we Sufis doing our work[49] in the Western country[50]? Sufis always have adopted the ways of the different people they were living among and of the countries they were staying in. Here in the Western world we give it[51] partly in the form of the Christian religion and partly in the form of [52]modern terminology. Truth is truth and [53]who understand it, to them it does not make any difference in what outer form it shows itself.

The path that we tread is a delicate path. The less spoken of it the better. We cannot keep it too sufficiently[54] in a humble garb. For the more

---

38. Ibid.: "having known" inserted above
39. Ibid.: "love" crossed out and "know" written above, but then "know" crossed out and "love" restored
40. Ibid.: "part" crossed out, and "path" written above
41. TR.hw.: above this sentence TR. wrote: "(I am not sure if this is right)"; Er.tp.: this entire sentence omitted
42. Er.tp.: "God" inserted after "sees"; (TR.hw.)Gd.ed.: "sees" crossed out, and "believes" written above
43. (TR.hw.)Gd.ed.: "from what it is" inserted before "to"
44. Ibid.: "of" inserted before" "which", but then crossed it out
45. Ibid.: "as the conception of self" instead of "in its own conception"
46. Ibid.: "is meant" in place of "mean"
47. Er.tp.: "learned and taught" instead of "taught nor learned"
48. (TR.hw.)Gd.ed.: "It" replaced by "The realisation"
49. Ibid.: rewritten to read, "In what way is the Sufi work being done", but then crossed out; it is unclear how Gd. meant this sentence to read
50. Er.tp.: "world" instead of "country"; (TR.hw.)Gd.ed.: "country" crossed out and "part" written above but then crossed out, and then "the world?" written after; it is not clear how this was meant to read
51. (TR.hw.)Gd.ed.: "it is given" in place of "we give it"
52. Er.tp.: "the" added before "modern"
53. (TR.hw.)Gd.ed.: "those" inserted before "who"
54. Ibid.: "too" crossed out, and brackets and numbers added to indicate this should read "sufficiently keep it", but then "too" restored, apparently indicating to leave it as written originally

we keep[55] it, the more it is necessary to keep it humbly[56]. Nor do we argue[57] our ideas upon others. Our service is a most delicate one and therefore we have a great responsibility, and we must not force our ideas upon any earnest seeker after truth. Our task is difficult, but by realizing it every day more, you understand my difficulty from your own difficulties[58]. [59]Our sacrifices a thousand times are blest in the service of humanity and the blessing of light, of God.[59] [60]We must surpass[61] the feeling of physical weakness.[60]

The secret is one[62], which is: to try and to maintain harmony in every situation. It is a very difficult task to begin with, but in time one will get accustomed to it. The first thing to be thought of is whether it will bring harmony, as God asks from us to do his higher work. You can only live in the world in [63]two conditions: either being a peacemaker or a fighter, but one must be a good fighter in order to win every battle. Life is a continual battle, but warfare does not only ask strength, it requires some sense also. And to be a peacemaker [64]one must be friends with everyone. How[65] insignificant the person is[64], you must harmonize, else it would be impossible to live. This strain to harmonize causes a strain upon one every day. But still, in trying to harmonize his life becomes easy[66] and easier. And then it's[67] like a[68] wonder-working. It is not only a story that Daniel tamed lions. It is much more difficult to tame human beings; [69]one must understand the psychology of human nature. There is a slang expression, [70]which says: They've rubbed him wrong[70,71]— it takes a long time of getting over this little error of rubbing wrong[72].

People think that there is an art to study or practise, but I say: Life itself is an art and if one can learn how to live, one has learned the only thing one really wants. Besides if you know[73] the psychology of human nature, one

---

55. Ibid.: "keep" crossed out, and "value" written above
56. Er.tp.: "that it should be humbly kept" instead of "to keep it humbly"
57. (TR.hw.)Gd.ed.: "argue" crossed out, and "urge" written above
58. Er.tp.: "difficulty" instead of "difficulties", and the whole sentence put in parentheses
59. Ibid.: this sentence rewritten to read: "Our sacrifices in the service of humanity and of God are a thousand times blessed."
60. Ibid.: this entire sentence omitted
61. (TR.hw.)Gd.ed.: "surpass" crossed out, and "overcome" written above
62. Ibid.: rewritten to read, "There is one secret"
63. Ibid.: "one of" inserted before "two"
64. Er.tp.: the first part of the sentence, "And to be a peacemaker" omitted, and the last part reads: "One must be a friend with everyone, how insignificant the person is."
65. (TR.hw.)Gd.ed.: "ever" written above to read "however"
66. Ibid.: "easy" changed to "easier"
67. Er.tp.: "it is" instead of "it's"
68. (TR.hw.)Gd.ed.: "a" crossed out
69. Ibid.: "for this" inserted before "one"
70. Ibid.: "which says: They've rubbed him wrong" crossed out, and "to rub the wrong way" substituted
71. Er.tp.: "wrong" later crossed out and "raw" written in ink
72. Er.tp.: again "wrong" later crossed out, and "raw" written in ink; (TR.hw.)Gd.ed.: "the" inserted before "wrong" and "way" after, to read: "the wrong way"
73. Er.tp.: "one knows" instead of "you know"

sees how very often one overlooked an act of human[74] kindness to be done. Some natures there are who only need a word of human[73] sympathy and of comfort, of kindness. If we do not listen to people at the right moment, very often we lose a battle which we might have won by having listened to him and having understood his wants. No strength is needed, only tact.

It is this wonder-working of a person[75] which has done miracles. There is no greater miracle to perform than to create harmony in one's life, one's home, one's office, one's work. The more you advance in life, the more you will see people like children. If you rise above it, you will be able to create harmony. You must feel grown-up yourself; you must feel the power of the grown-up[76]. No grown-up[76] will fight with a child. The best thing to do is to wake[77] in everybody the good that is in everyone. Very often a proud person, as you have touched[78] his pride, feels his pride melt away at once. As soon as your pride stands against the proud person—then there will be a battle.

It is the continual desire to create harmony which creates the greatness in life.

---

74. (TR.hw.)Gd.ed.: "human" crossed out
75. Ibid.: "a person" crossed out, and "the prophets" inserted above
76. Ibid.: "person" inserted after "grown-up"
77. Ibid.: "wake" changed to "waken"
78. Er.tp.: "overlooked" instead of "touched"

1

[2]Mysticism

(Introduction to the lecture[3] on Sufi mysticism)[2]

[4]I wish to speak this evening on the subject of the Sufi mysticism.[4] There is one God and one truth, one religion and one mysticism; call it Sufi mysticism[5], [6]Christian mysticism, [6]Hindu mysticism, [6]Buddhist mysticism, whatever you may. As God cannot be divided, so mysticism cannot be divided.

It is an error when a person says ~~that~~[7]: My mysticism[8] is different from your mysticism[9]. He has not yet known[10] what mysticism[8] means. [11]There cannot be many mysticisms[12]; there is one mysticism. There can only

---

Documents:

TR.hw. = Toni de Ridder's longhand reporting of the lecture, taken down as Pir-o-Murshid Inayat Khan was speaking, or copied from such a document. Later this document was lightly edited by Murshida Sherifa Goodenough, indicated by "(TR.hw.)Gd.ed."

Hq.st. = a stencilled (cyclostyled) copy of the lecture prepared at Headquarters, Geneva, for distribution to Sufi Centres; it was probably edited by Murshida Sherifa Goodenough, though the editorial changes are different from those in "(TR.hw.)Gd.ed."

Sk.tp. = a typescript prepared by Sakina Furnée or under her supervision, based on Hq.st. and showing only minor differences, probably copying errors. Included in the footnotes only where it differs from Hq.st.; a few corrections are indicated by "(Sk.tp.)Sk.cr."

A highly edited version of this lecture was published in the series *The Sufi Message of Hazrat Inayat Khan*, volume X, *Sufi Mysticism*, chapter III, "Realization" (London, 1964); it is not mentioned in the notes.

Notes:

1. Hq.st.: above the title appears in the centre the word GATHEKA (a classification of the teachings of P-o-M., see Glossary) and to the right margin "Number 7", indicating its place in the series. Below that is the Sufi Invocation (see List), and then the title, "Sufi Mysticism." The Sk.tp. adds "I" after the title. The date, 15 January 1924, is known only from the list of lectures P-o-M. gave in the Netherlands.
2. Hq.st.: this title and the parenthetical subtitle do not appear
3. (TR.hw.)Gd.ed.: "s" inserted to read "lectures"
4. (TR.hw.)Gd.ed.: this sentence crossed out; Hq.st.: this sentence omitted
5. Hq.st.: "Sufism" instead of "Sufi mysticism"
6. Ibid.: "or" added before "Christian", "Hindu", and "Buddhist"
7. TR.hw.: "that" crossed out, and omitted in Hq.st.
8. Hq.st.: "religion" in place of "mysticism"
9. Ibid.: "yours" instead of "your mysticism"
10. Ibid.: "does not know" instead of "has not yet known"
11. Ibid.: "For" added before "There"
12. Ibid.: "as there cannot be many wisdoms; there is" instead of "; there is one mysticism. There can only be"

be[12] one wisdom. It is the[13] error of mankind that there[14] is Eastern and [15]Western wisdom[16]. [17]As long as Eastern and Western is attached to wisdom, it is not wisdom. If that is passed, he touches wisdom, the inheritance of mankind.[17]

It is the divine heritage[18] that man has, no matter to what part he belongs[19]. It is also an error when [20]man distinguishes between occultism and mysticism. [21]This error is made by limited man who does not know what he says. The one who wishes to think he knows, he does not know.[21] When a person pictures mysticism as a branch of the[22] tree which is truth, he is mistaken[23], and when he[24] says that mysticism is a branch [25]and all other things are branches[25], he is mistaken[26]. [27]Mysticism is the stem [28]to which all others are attached[28].

[29]Now coming to the question, what really[30] mysticism is. Mysticism is the way by which to realize the truth. Jesus Christ has said: "I am the truth and[31] I am the way"[32]. He has not said: "I am the truths and [33]the ways", for there are not many ways[34], there is only one way. If[35] there is another way, it[36] is the wrong way. There are many religions[37], but not many wisdoms. There are[38] many houses of worship for[39] God[40], but only[41] one God. There are[38] many scriptures, but only[41] one truth. So there are many methods, but only[41] one way.

---

13. Ibid.: "the" omitted
14. Ibid.: "to say: this" instead of "that there"
15. Ibid.: "that is" added before "Western"
16. Ibid.: "wisdom" omitted
17. Ibid.: these two sentences replaced with the phrase added to the previous sentence, "which only shows lack of wisdom"
18. Ibid.: "truth" instead of "heritage"
19. Ibid.: "what part of the world he belongs to" in place of "to what part he belongs"
20. Ibid.: "a" added
21. Ibid.: instead of these two sentences, the following: "It is an error to say: this is my eye and that is yours. The two eyes belong to one soul."
22. Ibid.: "a" instead of "the"
23. Ibid.: "he is mistaken" eliminated here
24. Ibid.: "when he" omitted
25. Ibid.: "and all other things are branches" omitted
26. Ibid.: "wrong" in place of "mistaken"
27. Ibid.: "For" added before "Mysticism"
28. Ibid.: ", which unites all branches" instead of "to which all others are attached"
29. Ibid.: "And" added
30. Ibid.: "really" moved to after "mysticism"
31. Ibid.: just a comma instead of "and"
32. See John 14:6: "I am the way, and the truth, and the life."
33. Hq.st.: "I am" added
34. Ibid.: "there are not many ways," omitted
35. Ibid.: "If" omitted
36. Ibid.: "which" instead of "it"
37. Ibid.: "many religions" moved to before "There are"
38. Ibid.: "There are" omitted
39. (TR.hw.)Gd.ed.: "for" changed to "of"
40. Hq.st.: "the Lord for worship" instead of "worship for God"
41. Ibid.: "only" omitted

But for either man taking[42] the right or the wrong way, the methods of attaining[43] that[44] realization are many. But principally[45] there are[46] four methods[47]: by the heart, by the head, by action, and[48] by repose. A person might[49] choose from[50] four different methods to develop[51] himself and prepare[52] himself to journey on the way, the only way, which is called mysticism. No religion can call it its own;[53] it is the way of all religions. No church can say that it belongs to it; it is the way of[54] all churches. No person can say that[55] this is the way, that[56] he has shown to man[57]. All have journeyed[58] by the same way.

Often people have imagined that to be[59] a mystic means to be[59] an ascetic, that a mystic is someone who dreams, a person who talks[60] ~~with~~ in the air, someone who does not live here on the earth, a person who is not practical, who is an ascetic[61], a hermit. But that[62] is not the case in reality. [63]Very often people want to see a[64] mystic in a peculiar[65] man, and if there is someone peculiar, they [66]think that this is a mystic[66]. But that[67] is a wrong conception. That is not proper mysticism, but[68] exaggeration; it is[69] one-sidedness. A real mystic must show [70]equilibrium; a true mystic strikes [71]balance in his life, his head in heaven,[70] his feet on the earth. [72]He is the knower of both worlds, this world and the next. It does not mean that a

---

42. Ibid.: "And either it is" instead of "But for either man taking";
    Sk.tp.: "And either is it"; (Sk.tp.)Sk.cr.: later corrected in ink to "it is"
43. Hq.st.: "gaining" instead of "attaining"
44. Ibid.: "way of" added
45. Ibid.: "principally" omitted
46. Ibid.: "mainly" added
47. Ibid.: "methods" omitted
48. Ibid.: ", and" omitted
49. Ibid.: "must" in place of "might"
50. Ibid.: "among these" added
51. Ibid.: "of developing" instead of "to develop"
52. Ibid.: "preparing" instead of "prepare"
53. Ibid.: ", but" instead of semi-colon
54. Ibid.: ", for it belongs to" instead of "; it is the way of"
55. Ibid.: "that" eliminated and quotation marks put around "This is the way"
56. Ibid.: "which" added
57. Ibid.: "chosen" instead of "shown to man"
58. Ibid.: "others are getting there" instead of "have journeyed"
59. Ibid.: "to be" omitted
60. Ibid.: "dwells" instead of "talks"
61. Ibid.: "that a person who is an ascetic must be" instead of "who is an ascetic,"
62. Ibid.: "Now this" instead of "But that"
63. Ibid.: "And" added
64. Ibid.: "the" instead of "a"
65. Ibid.: "as a peculiar sort of" instead of "in a peculiar"
66. Ibid.: "say that is he" in place of "think that this is a mystic"
67. Ibid.: "Now this" instead of "But that"
68. Ibid.: "an" instead of "That is not proper mysticism, but"
69. Ibid.: "it is" omitted
70. Ibid.: "equilibrium, balance. He will have his head in the heavens," instead of "equilibrium; a true mystic strikes balance in his life, his head in heaven,"
71. (TR.hw.)Gd.ed.: "the" inserted
72. Hq.st.: "The real mystic" instead of "He is the knower of both worlds, this world and the next. It does not mean that a mystic is absent from this world. He"

mystic is absent from this world. He[72] is as wide awake in this world as in the other. A mystic is not someone who does not possess intellect. [73]Intellect is his weapon.[73] He is not someone who dreams; he is wide awake. Yet a mystic is someone who is capable to dream[74] when others cannot[75], and a mystic[76] is capable to keep[77] awake when others[78] cannot keep awake. A mystic strikes [79]balance between two things, power and beauty. Neither does he[80] sacrifice power for beauty, nor beauty for power. He possesses power and enjoys beauty.

As to the restrictions in the life of a mystic, there are no restrictions[81]. There is balance, reason, love, harmony and beauty[82]. The religion of the mystic is every religion, all religions, and yet he is above what people consider[83] religion. In the[84] point of fact [85]his religion is the[86] religion[85], for it is not any religion, it is all[86] religions. The moral of the mystic[87] is reciprocity, beneficence and self-sacrifice[88]: to reciprocate all the kindness he receives[89] from others; to do an act of kindness to the[90] others without meaning[91] to have an[92] appreciation or [93]return for it; and to make every sacrifice, however great, for love, harmony and beauty.

The God of the mystic is to be found in the depth of[94] his own heart; the truth of the mystic is beyond words. People discuss ~~over~~[95] things of little importance[96]. [97]~~For~~ To a mystic it is not a discussion, it is a passion.[97] People want to talk, therefore they talk[98]. Very often it is not the one who knows who talks[99], it is the one who does not know who talks. But by

---

73. Ibid.: this sentence omitted
74. (TR.hw.)Gd.ed.: "to dream" changed to "of dreaming"; Hq.st.: "of dreaming"
75. Hq.st.: "are not" instead of "cannot"
76. Ibid.: "a mystic" omitted
77. Ibid.: "of keeping" instead of "to keep"
78. Ibid.: "the rest" instead of "others"
79. (TR.hw.)Gd.ed.: "the" inserted; Hq.st.: "the" added
80. Hq.st.: "He does not" instead of "Neither does he"
81. Ibid.: "is no restriction" instead of "are no restrictions"
82. Ibid.: "and beauty" omitted
83. Ibid.: "call their" instead of "consider"
84. (TR.hw.)Gd.ed.: "the" crossed out; Hq.st.: "the" omitted
85. Hq.st.: "he is religion" in place of "his religion is the religion"
86. TR.hw.: the words "the" and "all" are underlined in the hw., perhaps indicating that Pir-o-Murshid Inayat Khan emphasized these words while speaking; Hq.st.: the first phrase altered as indicated in the previous note, and the "all" not underlined
87. Hq.st.: "all religion" instead of "the mystic"
88. Ibid.: ", beneficence and self-sacrifice" omitted
89. Ibid.: "we receive" in place of "he receives"
90. Ibid.: "the" omitted
91. Ibid.: "intending" in place of "meaning"
92. Ibid.: "an" omitted
93. Ibid.: "a" added
94. Ibid.: "the depth of" omitted
95. Ibid.: "argue and debate about" in place of "discuss ~~over~~"
96. Ibid.: "but mysticism is not to be discussed" added
97. Ibid.: this sentence, "~~For~~ To a mystic it is not a discussion, it is a passion." omitted
98. Ibid.: "in order to know, and then they forget all" instead of ", therefore they talk"
99. Ibid.: "much, but" instead of ", it is the one who does not know who talks. But by discussing"

discussing[99] he [100]wants to know. Yet he is not sure.[101] The one who knows needs no discussion[102]. [103]He knows. His happiness is his own.[103] Besides to put the truth[104] into words is like putting[105] the ocean in a bottle[106].

Yes,[107] there is a wine the mystic drinks and that wine is ecstasy, a wine so powerful that the presence of the mystic becomes like[108] wine for everyone who comes in his presence—[109]the wine of the real sacrament. [110]In the church they only have the symbol of it.[110] One may[111] ask: [112]Where does it come from, what is it made of? Call it power or life[113] which comes through the mystic, through spheres every man is attached to. The mystic by his attachment to this sphere[114] drinks the wine which is the sustenance of human souls[115]. That wine is ecstasy[116]. That intoxication is the love which manifests itself in [117]the form of charity, in all manner of gentleness, of humbleness, of modesty. It springs up by itself and yet that wine makes the mystic independent and indifferent to things people of the world are so attached to.[117] Once a mystic drinks[118], what does it matter [119]to him ~~if~~ whether he lives in the wilderness or in a palace? To him[120] it is all the same. Neither the palace deprives[121] him of it, nor the wilderness takes[122] it away. [123]Once his kingliness is realized, he himself becomes[126] the kingdom of God[124] about which Jesus Christ has said, "Seek ye the kingdom first and all things will be added"[125].

---

100. Ibid.: "who" added
101. Ibid.: this sentence, "Yet he is not sure." omitted
102. Ibid.: "but does not discuss is the mystic" instead of "needs no discussion"
103. Ibid.: "He knows the happiness in his own heart" instead of "He knows. His happiness is his own"
104. Ibid.: "it" in place of "the truth"
105. Ibid.: "to put" instead of "like putting"
106. Ibid.: "drop of water" instead of "bottle"
107. Ibid.: "Yet" instead of "Yes,"
108. Ibid.: "has become" instead of "becomes like"
109. Ibid.: "This wine is" added
110. Ibid.: ", the symbol of which is in the church." instead of "In the church they only have the symbol of it."
111. Ibid.: "might" instead of "may"
112. Ibid.: "What is it," added
113. Ibid.: "You may call it a power, a life, a strength" in place of "Call it power or life"
114. Ibid.: "these spheres" instead of "this sphere"
115. Ibid.: "the human soul" instead of "human souls"
116. Ibid.: ", the mystic's intoxication" added
117. Ibid.: "the human heart." instead of "the form of charity, in all manner of gentleness, of humbleness, of modesty. It springs up by itself and yet that wine makes the mystic independent and indifferent to things people of the world are so attached to."
118. Ibid.: "that wine" added
119. Ibid.: "if he is sitting on rocks" instead of "to him ~~if~~ whether he lives"
120. Ibid.: "To him" omitted
121. (TR.hw.)Gd.ed., Hq.st.: "the palace deprives" changed to "does the palace deprive"
122. Ibid.: "the wilderness takes" changed to "does the wilderness take"
123. Hq.st.: "He has found" instead of "Once his kingliness is realized, he himself becomes"
124. Ibid.: "on earth" added
125. Ibid.: the quotation altered to: "Seek ye first the kingdom of God and all these things will be added unto you" (Gospel of Matthew 6:33), making it closer to the text of the Authorized Version of 1611

There are many persons who[126] strive for many [127]things in this world. [128]The one says, In the end I will try and find the path, and there are others who say, We have much time before us, and others say, When we are in the wheel of death and birth, when will the time come? A mystic does not wait. First he seeks the kingdom of God and all things come afterwards; he gives great importance to this.[128]

[129]But do you mean to say that by attaching himself to the[129] realization of God he neglects his duty[130] in the world? It is not necessary. As I have said,[131] there is nothing a mystic should renounce to come to[132] the realization of truth[133]. The only thing necessary is[134] to give [135]importance to the things others give no importance to. It is in this that he differs from the ordinary man. He gives first importance to things others give ~~the last~~ importance to last of all.[135]

One may ask: Is the life of a mystic meditative? [136]Meditation for a mystic is like winding the clock[137]. [138]It does not mean that a mystic is in meditation all the time. It is like winding up the clock; it goes on and you need not trouble about it.[138] A Shah of Persia used to sit at[139] night vigils[140], [141]and one day his prime minister said, "After all day's working, all the night's meditation, that is too much for you. You are already doing a lot of good. Do not meditate at night".[141] [142]The Shah answered, "Don't say so, for

---

126. Ibid.: "people" instead of "There are many persons who"
127. Ibid.: "different" added
128. Ibid.: the rest of this paragraph altered to read: "And there are some indifferent ones who say, 'There is a long life before us and when the time comes that I must awake I shall awake'. But the mystic says: 'That is the one thing I must attend to, all other things come after that'. It is of the greatest importance in his life."
129. Ibid.: "Should he by working for" instead of "But do you mean to say that by attaching himself to the"
130. Ibid.: "neglect his duties" instead of "he neglects his duty"
131. Ibid.: "As I have said," omitted
132. Ibid.: "in order to have" instead of "to come to"
133. Ibid.: "life" instead of "truth"
134. Ibid.: "It is only" in place of "The only thing necessary is"
135. Ibid.: "the greatest importance to what is of the greatest importance in life. For every man gives it the least importance. The mystic gives it the first importance." instead of "importance to the things others give no importance to. It is in this that he differs from the ordinary man. He gives first importance to things others give ~~the last~~ importance to last of all."
136. Ibid.: "Yes, but" added
137. Ibid.: "the winding of a clock" instead of "winding the clock"
138. Ibid.: "It is wound for a moment, and all day long it goes by itself. It does not mean that he must think about it all day long. He does not trouble about it." instead of "It does not mean that a mystic is in meditation all the time. It is like winding up the clock; it goes on and you need not trouble about it."
139. (TR.hw.)Gd.ed.: "at" changed to "in"
140. Hq.st.: "up at night for his night vigils, and prayers" instead of "at night vigils"
141. Ibid.: "And a visitor coming to pay him a visit, wondered at his meditating and that after all day's work. 'It is too much', he said. 'You do not need meditation'." instead of ", and one day his prime minister said, 'After all day's working, all the night's meditation, that is too much for you. You are already doing a lot of good. Do not meditate at night'."
142. Ibid.: "'Do not say so', was the answer. 'You do not know.'" instead of "The Shah answered, 'Don't say so, for you don't know.'"

you don't know.[145] During the[143] night I pursue God and during the day God follows me." A few moments'[144] meditation make[145] the whole mechanism [146]of one's being in a running order as a stream running to the ocean[146]. It does not [147]take him away in the least from his duties[147]. It only blesses [148]the work he does because in all he does is a perfume of God. That becomes a healing, a blessing.[148]

[149]A mystic who becomes thoughtful, kind and sensitive[150], how does he get on amidst the[151] everyday life, [152]for the rough edges of daily life break against his heart and[152] must necessarily make it sore[153]? Certainly they do. The heart of the mystic is more sore than the heart of anyone else[154]. [155]For the reason is where there is give and take in the roughness of daily life, the heart is not sensitive; it gives blow for blow. But when the heart is always patient and kind and full of sympathy, then it only takes all the roughness and never gives it back.[155] [156]It cuts the heart to become a cut diamond.[156] And by being cut it[157] becomes brilliant and when it is[158] sufficiently cut, it[159] becomes a flame, [160]illuminating the life of himself and the lives of others[160].
[161]

---

143. Ibid.: "For at" instead of "During the"
144. Ibid.: "Your moments of" instead of "A few moments'"
145. Ibid.: "set" instead of "make"
146. Ibid.: "in running order as a stream running in the ocean" instead of "of one's being in a running order as a stream running to the ocean"
147. Ibid.: "in the least take away the mystic from his duty" instead of "take him away in the least from his duties"
148. Ibid.: "every word he speaks with the thought of God. In all he thinks or does is a perfume of God, that becomes a healing, a blessing." instead of "the work he does because in all he does is a perfume of God. That becomes a healing, a blessing."
149. Ibid.: "And now there comes the question," added
150. Ibid.: "kind and helpful" instead of "thoughtful, kind and sensitive"
151. Ibid.: "crowd in" added
152. Ibid.: "The rough edges of everyday life rubbing against him" instead of "for the rough edges of daily life break against his heart and"
153. Ibid.: "him heartsore" instead of "it sore"
154. Ibid.: "that of anybody else" instead of "the heart of anyone else"
155. Ibid.: "And where there is only kindness, only patience, then it takes all the thorns." instead of the two sentences, "For the reason . . . . gives it back."; Sk.tp.: "And where there is only kindness, only patience, the heart takes all the thorns."; (Sk.tp.)Sk.cr.: "the heart" later crossed out and "then it" added in ink
156. Hq.st.: "It is like the diamond being cut." instead of "It cuts the heart to become a cut diamond."
157. Ibid.: "So the heart being cut" instead of "And by being cut it"
158. Ibid.: "The heart, being" instead of "and when it is"
159. Ibid.: "it" omitted
160. Ibid.: "which illuminates the life of the mystic and also that of others" instead of "illuminating the life of himself and the lives of others"
161. Ibid.: "To be circulated among the candidates for Initiation in the Sufi Order." added; Sk.tp.: "To be read before Candidates for Initiation in the Sufi Order."

A stencil prepared at Headquarters, Geneva

GATHEKA. Number 10[1]

Toward the One, the Perfection of Love, Harmony and Beauty, the Only Being, united with All the Illuminated Souls, who form the Embodiment of the Master, the Spirit of Guidance.[2]

SUFI MYSTICISM. II.

[3]

I would like to speak of[4] the knowledge a mystic attains by the head which[5] prepares him to find his way to the truth. Reasoning is a faculty which the mystic uses, and which he may develop like any man of common sense, a practical man; for the difference is only that the mystic does not stop at the first reason, but he wishes to see the reason behind them all. Therefore in everything, whether right or wrong, the mystic inquires the reason. But the immediate answer to that is a reason that is not satisfaction[6], for he sees that behind that reason there is another reason. And so he goes on in the knowledge of all things, which is far greater than the knowledge gained by one thing. It is therefore that neither wrong nor right, neither good nor evil excites the mystic too much, nor does it give him a great shock or surprise. For everything seems to have its nature, and it is understanding which makes him feel at one with all things existing. And what can one wish more in life than understanding? It is understanding that gives one harmony in the home

---

Documents:

Hq.st. = a stencil prepared at Headquarters, Geneva, for inclusion in the "Gatheka" series for distribution to Sufi centres.

Sk.tp. = a typescript prepared by Sakina Furnée or under her supervision, showing a few omissions and changes.

A highly edited form of this lecture appeared in *The Sufi Message* series, vol. 10 (London, 1964), *The Path of Initiation, Sufi Mysticism*, as part of chapter iv, "The Nature and Work of a Mystic", not included in the notes.

Notes:

1. Hq.st.: later "Bis" (meaning "second") added in ink; Sk.tp.: "bis" typed; date added later in pencil, "15/16 Jan. 1924", with "15/" later erased
2. Hq.st.: this is the Sufi Invocation, which appears at the beginning of many stencils from Hq. (see List)
3. Sk.tp.: "The Knowledge a Mystic attains by the Head." added as a title
4. Ibid.: "I would like to speak of" omitted
5. Ibid.: "which" omitted
6. Ibid.: "satisfactory" instead of "satisfaction"

with those near and dear to one, and peace outside home with so many different natures and characters. If one lacks understanding, one is poor with all that one possesses of the goods of this world, and it is understanding which gives a man riches.

If life could be pictured, one would say that it reminds one of a sea in the storm, and the waves coming and going; such is life. And it is this understanding which gives man that weight which can endure through the rain and the storm and all the vicissitudes. Without understanding he is like a jolly-boat on the sea which cannot go on through the storm. By understanding a mystic learns. He learns tact; he is tactful under all circumstances. And his tact is like a ship with a heavy load, which the wind cannot move and which stands still in the midst of the storm on the sea.

The nature of life is such that it easily excites the mind and makes man unhappy in a moment's time. It makes man so confused that he does not know where to take the next step. Contrary to this, the mystic stands still and inquires of life its secret, and from every experience, every failure or success, the mystic learns a lesson. Therefore, failure and success both are profitable to a mystic.

The ideal of a mystic is never to think of disagreeable things. What one does not want to happen one must not think of. All disagreeable things from the past, a mystic erases them from his mind. He collects and keeps his happy experiences and makes out of them a paradise. Are there not many unhappy people, who keep a part of the past before them which causes them pain in their heart? Past is past, it is gone. There is eternity before you. If you want to make your life as you wish, do not think of disagreeable thoughts and of painful experiences and memories that make you unhappy.

It is therefore that life becomes to some extent easy for a mystic to deal with, for he knows every heart, every nature; whereas there are others, untouched by the mystic's secret, who suffer from their difficulties at home and difficulties outside. They dread the presence of people. They do not understand, they want to run away from them, and if they cannot escape, they feel as if they are in the mouth of a dragon. And perhaps they are placed in a situation which cannot easily be changed. The consequence is that they heap confusion upon confusion. And how very often one sees that where two people do not understand one another, a third comes and helps them to understand each other, and the light thrown upon them[7] causes greater harmony. The mystic says, whether it be agreeable or disagreeable, if you are in a certain situation, make the best of it; try to understand how to deal with such a situation. Therefore, a life without such understanding is like a dark room which contains everything you wish. It is all there, but there is no

---

7. Ibid.: "then" in place of "them", possibly a copying error

light.

The world after all is a wonderful place, in spite of so many souls wishing to leave this world. For there is nothing which is not to be obtained in this world. It is all there; all things good and beautiful, all things precious and worth-while, they are all there if one knows their nature, their character, and how to obtain them.

If you ask a person what is the nature of life, he will say: The further we go in the strife for happiness, the further we are removed from it. This is true. But he takes the wrong way who does not know that unhappiness does not exist. Besides happiness is more natural than unhappiness, as good is more natural than evil, and health than illness. And yet man is so pessimistic. If you tell him the good of anyone he cannot believe this to be true. But if you tell him the bad of a person, he says: Yes, that is really true.

The work of the mystic therefore is to study life. For the mystic, life is not a stage play or an amusement. For the mystic it is a school, to learn every moment of life; it is a continual study. Therefore the scripture of the mystic is human nature. Every morning he turns a new page of this scripture. And the great ones, who have brought the message to the world from time to time, and whose books have become scriptures to the world (which has kept such scriptures for thousands of years, [8]from which generations of people have taken their spiritual food), [9]is their interpretation that they have given. And therefore the sacred scriptures are always with the same sacred feeling, always behind.

The mystic has a respect for all religions and he understands all the different and contrary ideas, for he understands everyone's language. The mystic can agree, without having to dispute, with the wise and the foolish, the simple one. For he sees that the nature of facts is such that they are true in their places; he understands every aspect of their nature. The mystic sees from every point of view. He sees from the point of view of each person, and that is why he is harmonious with all. A man comes to a mystic and says: I cannot believe in a personal God, it means nothing to me. Then the mystic answers: You are quite right. Another man says: The only way of making God intelligible is in the form of man. The mystic says: You are right. And another man says: How foolish of these people to make of this man a God; he is above comprehension. And the mystic says: You are right. For a mystic understands the reason behind all the opposing arguments. Once a missionary came to a Sufi in Persia, as he had desired to make a discussion and prove his point of view to be the right one about the Sufi

---

8. Ibid.: "and" added
9. Hq.st., Sk.tp.: a grammatical element is missing from this sentence

teachings. The Sufi, in his silent, quiet attitude of rest, was sitting, and his two and three pupils by his side. And the missionary asked some questions. The mystic answered: You are right. But the man went on to dispute and the Sufi said only: That is quite true. Then he took another turn and put his questions in an eloquent manner. The man was very disappointed as there was no opportunity for argument. The Sufi saw the truth in all.

The truth is like a piano: the notes may be high or low, you may strike a C or an E, but they are all notes. And so the difference between the ideas is like that between notes. So in daily life with the right and the wrong attitude. If we have the wrong attitude, all things are wrong; if we have the right, all things are right. The man who mistrusts himself will mistrust even his best friend. The man who trusts himself will trust everyone.

Things which seem to be apart, such as right and wrong, light and darkness, form and shadow, before the mystic, then, come so close that it is only a hair's breadth that divides right and wrong. Before the mystic there opens out an outlook on life, an outlook in which there is the purpose of life. The question which the mystic puts to himself is: Which is my being? My body? No. This body is my possession. I cannot be that which I possess. He asks himself: Is it my mind? The answer comes: No. The mind is something I possess, it is something one witnesses. There must be a difference between the knower and the known. By this in the end the Sufi comes to an understanding of the illusionary character of all the things he possesses. It is like a man who has a coat made; it is his coat, it is not he himself.

Then the mystic begins to think: It is not myself who thinks, it is the mind. It is the body which suffers, it is not myself. It is a kind of liberation for him to know: I am not my mind. For man wonders: One moment I have a good thought, another moment a bad thought, a right thought or a wrong, one moment an earthly thought, the other moment a thought of heaven. It is like a moving picture, and it is I who see, who am dancing there.

By seeing this the mystic liberates his self, which, owing to his illusion, was buried under mind and body. What men call a soul, that was lost; it was a soul not aware of the mystical truth that body and mind are the vehicles by which to experience life. And it is in this way that the mystic begins his journey towards immortality.

To be circulated among the[10] Candidates for Initiation in the Sufi Order.

---

10. Sk.tp.: "read before" in place of "circulated among the"

[1]

January 16th
The Hague
private

Beloved Ones of God,

I am asked by the kindness of our hostess to speak a few words telling about the service the Sufi Movement is rendering to humanity[2]. Friends, if I explain the history of the Sufi idea, I should like to say that it has existed in all ages and we can very well trace up[3] to the time of Abraham the esoteric school of the Sufi Movement. Even now there exist in different parts of the East different schools promoting the Sufi idea which trace their origin as far[4] as the time of Abraham.

And now coming to the subject how Sufism has developed in the past, I should like to say that in India[5], Palestine, Syria it passed its childhood. Its youth passed in Persia. And in India it came to its fullest development.

And now to tell you what Sufism is. It only means "wisdom". Wisdom not in the ordinary sense of the word, but wisdom which comes from within, which is not dependent on the exteriors[6] of life. A knowledge

Documents:

TR.hw. = a handwritten manuscript by Miss Toni de Ridder, taken down as P-o-M. was speaking or copied from such a document.

Lm.hw. = a handwritten document by Mrs. E. Leembruggen, written as P-o-M. was speaking, but too fragmentary to transcribe as a separate document. In some places the text, where it can be made out, seems fuller and/or more accurate than the text in "TR.hw.", and therefore extensive footnotes indicate these differences. In this case, however, there are no notes to indicate the many words and passages in TR.hw. which do not appear in Lm.hw.

Hq.tp. = a typewritten document which is clearly an attempted transcription of "TR.hw." As it contains several obviously mistaken transcriptions, and offers no further evidence of what P-o-M. said, it is not included in the notes.

Notes:

1. TR.hw.: in an unknown hand, "N. ~~99~~ 98" (apparently referring to a manuscript number) and "Gatheka. 1924"; later Murshida Sherifa Goodenough wrote "This reporting of doubtful accuracy"
2. Ibid.: "the service the Sufi Movement is rendering to humanity" underlined to indicate its possible use as a title
3. Lm.hw.: "back" instead of "up"
4. Ibid.: "back" added
5. Ibid.: "Arabia" (certainly correct in context) instead of "India"
6. Ibid.: "external experiences" instead of "exteriors"

which [7]is perfected by the inner illumination and this outer . . . of sight.[7]

In Islam, in Buddhism[8], and in all occult philosophical and mystical ideas, it is there where Sufism flourished and so to speak became finished. If one would[9] travel to inquire what Sufism has done in India ~~and~~ one may[10] easily find that in every village there is either a tomb of Sufis or a little cottage[11], where Hindus and Muslims and Christians[12] all rest[13]; its door is opened to all. At the tomb of the Sufi, people of all different creeds and religions go and pay homage to a personality who did not work throughout his life for a particular creed or religion or sect, but who worked for mankind whatever his religion[14]. It was the thing[15] that out of that school a message came forth[16], an answer to the cry of humanity at this judgment. At this time when it started, a [17]hatred existed between nations and had upset the whole of humanity. [18]Thinking of all the misery humanity has gone through, one may not deny the fact that humanity stands before a similar . . . It is good that life actually has thrown such an intoxication upon mankind.[18]

The service of this Universal Worship[19] will bring the warning in the world to ~~make~~ awake people[20] to a greater idea, a deeper truth of life beyond the idea of a purpose[21]. No doubt the object is laudable, most difficult nevertheless. [22]And the service of all persons must bless, must be blest by all powers whom we render our humble service to.[22]

In 1910 the movement[23] started—first in America, beginning from

---

7. Ibid.: "perfects even wisdom's outer experience in life." instead of "is perfected by the inner illumination and this outer . . . of sight."
8. Ibid.: "India being motherland of Vedanta and Buddhism" instead of "In Islam, in Buddhism"
9. Ibid.: "will" instead of "would"
10. Ibid.: "will" instead of "may"
11. Ibid.: "college of Sufism" instead of "cottage"
12. Ibid.: "and Jews" added
13. Ibid.: "meet" instead of "rest"
14. Ibid.: "for the good of mankind, whatever that man may be" instead of "mankind whatever his religion"
15. Ibid.: a word which could be "destined" instead of "the thing"
16. Ibid.: "should rise" instead of "came forth"
17. Ibid.: "wars" added before "hatred"
18. Ibid.: "If one only could [indecipherable] conditions hum[anity] has gone through, one cannot deny suffered most any time of history can sh[ow]. It is good that own life thinks little about conditions of world." instead of "thinking of all the misery humanity has gone through, one may not deny the fact that humanity stands before a similar . . . It is good that life actually has thrown such an intoxication upon mankind."
19. Ibid.: "movement therefore" instead of "Universal Worship"
20. Ibid.: "nations, races, creeds" instead of "people"
21. Ibid.: "of life on earth" added
22. Ibid.: instead of "And the service . . . our humble service to.", Lm.hw. has : "It is the service of the One all Powerful. Service of all powerful must bless, must be blessed by all power [indecipherable] Although few in number ~~to~~ indiv to all [indecipherable] best way we possibly can."
23. The name of the organization was changed in October of 1923 from Sufi Order to Sufi Movement, and therefore the word "movement" is capitalized only after that date.

California[24], where a very small number[25] of students in the Sufism was—[26]a community was formed thereof and started to work[26], after which for ten years the Sufi centre flourished and began to spread in England. The wartime was the worst time for the work of peace, because the name of peace was a horror, it was a great crime to mention the word.[27]

And our work? Had not there been difficulties? There was no end of it. [28]And if you wish to do a work which you consider the greatest and you're thwarted by mankind's skepticism—it is hard lines upon that work. Commercialism, materialism, are everywhere increasing[29]. Competition ever takes on—there were a great many difficulties to endure[30]—but we went on. There were the faithful workers, who sacrificed themselves and brought the enthusiasm of work which was waiting for its time and Sufism began to be made known.[31]

You know the real peace has not yet come; therefore, the working in the movement is still continued to establish that peace, that real peace.

The movement has existed in France and is the established international[32] in Geneva and now has spread as far as Italy.[33]

And now to the question, what is the different plan of work of the Sufi Movement? We have three activities which have been principally working in the Movement.

Firstly is the work of Brotherhood[34], to try and make the sense and feeling of brotherhood understood among people. One might object that there are many institutions working for brotherhood. Does the Sufi do anything special in that line of work and thought? The answer is, there are many differences, but as a central scheme is the brotherhood with God in God, our source and goal; a brotherhood which nothing else, money or position or whatever else[35], can give. This is done by holding meetings in different places and in whatever ~~ways~~[36] we can to find the ways and the means to help suffering humanity[37]. We do not touch politics, thinking that

---

24. P-o-M. arrived in New York in 1910, but it was in California that he initiated his first student from the West; he made a few other initiates in America before going to England
25. Lm.hw.: "group" instead of "number"
26. Ibid.: "found together and began the work" instead of "a community was founded thereof and started to work"
27. Ibid.: "during war to say peace" instead of "to mention the word" and then adds: "Thanks to God that we lived through it all."
28. Ibid.: adds "Life is diff[icult] on earth"
29. Ibid.: "competitive spirit is progressing" instead of "materialism, are everywhere increasing"
30. Ibid.: "has not been easy task" instead of "there were a great many difficulties to endure"
31. Ibid.: adds "greater scope peace treaties"
32. TR.hw.: the word is written "international" though perhaps it should say "internationally"
33. Lm.hw.: adds "and is spreading [indecipherable] and in United States."
34. Ibid.: "World Brotherhood"[a branch of the Sufi Movement] instead of "work of Brotherhood"
35. Ibid.: "things on earth" instead of "whatever else"
36. TR.hw.: it appears "ways" was written, but then a line put through the "s"
37. Lm.hw.: adds "new reform education" and "social life" after "humanity"

the work we are doing[38] just now, trying to harmonize the heart of everyone we come in contact with, will help to bring about purer[39] politics too in the end.

The other aspect of the work is the Devotional Side. There are just now in the Western world three classes of people[40]. The first class of those (and they are the smallest in number) who have their own particular [41]religion[42]. And then there is another class of people who believe in God and who think that there must be something hereafter and they look out for the secret of life[43]. Then there is a third class of people and their number is slight[44], who do not believe in anything, neither in God nor in hereafter. At this time our Movement has forced[45] all these classes into one form, and the form is: the Universal Worship, wherein the respect is shown to all the great ones who have come to the earth from time to time[46]. A regard is shown for all the scriptures, which millions of people have received and find their most sacred possession. The practice of tolerance[47], we try to realize this among ourselves. In every form it is possible to try to live and express it in everyday life. This may be called the symbol of our churches.

And the third aspect[48] and the most important one[49] is the Esoteric School. It is not everybody who is interested in it, nor is ready for it, nor has the patience for it. And therefore it is not open for anyone.[50] ~~Very rel~~ In this school an initiation is given and as the patient must have trust in the doctor and the doctor must trust the patient, so the pupil trusts the teacher and the teacher trusts his pupil—else the teaching would be nothing and of no avail[51].

[52]What is taught? No one has ever taught the truth to anyone. It is impossible to give the truth. Truth is [53]already there in the deepest of one's heart[53]. Taught can be only the way to reach it[54]. It is not something one can

38. Ibid.: "sufficient to occupy our life" added after "doing"
39. TR.hw.: "purer" is written in ink on top of another word impossible to read
40. Lm.hw.: adds "concerned with religion"
41. Ibid.: "faith or" added
42. Ibid.: adds "not concerned about others"
43. Ibid.: "may not belong to any particular church seekers after truth" instead of "and they look out for the secret of life"
44. Ibid.: "other class largest" instead of "Then there is a third class of people and their number is slight"
45. Ibid.: "been called to serve" instead of "forced"
46. Ibid.: "to waken humanity" added
47. Ibid.: "to followers of all churches" added
48. Ibid.: "of Sufi work" added
49. Ibid.: "although it is for some few" added
50. Ibid.: "For among 100 which [indecipherable] who come barely 1 wholehearted. Mostly tendency to look curiosity human nature" added
51. Ibid.: "training will be broken" added
52. Ibid.: "One may ask" added
53. Ibid.: "so deeply in every heart" instead of "already there in the deepest of one's heart"
54. Ibid.: adds "realize it for oneself"

give or which can be put into words[55]. If there is any [56]science of God, anything divine—it is this in itself[56].

Therefore, those who seriously wish to probe the depth of life and realize the life which is their innermost life[57], it is for those the school is meant[58]. But beyond all this the message is given every day to those who listen, is given as a warning[59] to waken for the higher ideal, to the greater truth, and it does not matter if those who have heard the message once do not come back to us, for the message is spoken. If one word the person takes home[60] and if he is going to practise it in his daily life and that word he listens to—he is working for, he has received the message too.

---

55. Ibid.: adds "beyond words"
56. Ibid.: "sign it is God, it is truth" instead of "science of God, anything divine—it is this in itself"
57. Ibid.: "self" instead of "life"
58. Ibid.: "for those doors are open" instead of "it is for those the school is meant"
59. Ibid.: "a call" instead of "a warning"
60. Ibid.: finishes this last sentence from this point on with "certainly the message is to be found."

Toni de Ridder's handwritten manuscript

Rotterdam at Mrs. van Stolk's
Jan. 17th '24

[1] [2]

Beloved Ones of God,

I ask your attention as with a few words I am going to speak on the subject of the Sufi Movement. The word Sufi has its origin in the Greek word *sophia* or *sufia*[3], wisdom. Therefore neither can wisdom be Eastern or Western, it neither belongs[4] to a particular race, nation or creed. Wisdom is universal and it is the heritage of mankind, a heritage divine.

We often confuse the word wisdom with intellect. Sometimes we call an intellectual person a wise person and sometimes a wise person a clever person. And yet the wise person is different from the clever person. The clever person is worldly-wise. He is partly wise, but there is one part of ~~the~~ wisdom he lacks, that part which cannot be acquired by learning, by inquiry[5]; what can be acquired by study or learning is the intellectual part of wisdom. But there are other ways of obtaining wisdom, and that is the drawing it from within. No doubt the person who thinks that there is only the wisdom to obtain, to him it has no meaning. But the one who sees behind the physical way something of a secret hidden for our physical eyes, that person understands. He can learn from without and from within. Human nature seems to have an inclination of being one-sided, either for the material or for the spiritual, and by doing this he finds something incomplete in his whole life. In the same way in things that come from outside, the knowledge gained by books and from experiences. And however advanced that person may be, he feels at times an obscurity and the void of a certain knowledge which could have completed him to his soul's satisfaction.

Documents:

TR.hw. = a handwritten manuscript by Miss Toni de Ridder, taken down while P-o-M. was speaking, or copied from such a document.

Hq.tp. = a typescript from the archives of Headquarters, Geneva, showing some editorial changes from "TR.hw."

Notes:

1. TR.hw., Hq.tp.: later "N. 98 bis" written in another hand, apparently an archive number
2. TR.hw.: in another hand (Gd.?) "Gatheka" written, and below that in yet another hand, "not printed"; Hq.tp.: across the top, "Rotterdam, January 17, 1924, Gatheka" typed; above, "?" and "not printed" written in hw.
3. Hq.tp.: "or Sufia" omitted
4. Ibid.: "belongs neither" instead of "neither belongs"
5. Ibid.: "enquiry" instead of "inquiry"

During my travelling in East and West I came in contact with numberless souls, every one requiring knowledge which may be gained from the world without, but I always found something in them which was continually searching for another form of knowledge, the want for which was either known or not.

Does there exist such knowledge? What is the nature, the character of that knowledge? Where does it come from? The answer is: where language comes from. Does it come from a person? Is there one person who has invented any language at all? No one. It is a natural outcome of several people talking together which made a systemized[6] language of it. It has become richer and has been vocalized for a long time and so is this also.

Not the outer knowledge, but even the inner knowledge is also a collection of experiences of ages; it is in the Divine Mind. And how does one draw it? The answer is: In the same way as a branch of a tree draws the sustenance from the roots. If you picture our souls as branches of that tree, there is one root, the Divine Mind. Every drop of rain that falls upon the leaves and the sun which makes an effect upon leaves and branches, all these have their collective result upon the root that is the heart of it, and so it is all collected in one mind, the Divine Mind. And it is from that mind that man can draw either consciously or unconsciously that knowledge which is in some degree different from the knowledge to be acquired from the outer world.

The proof of this is not very difficult to be found. Intuition is not something uncommon. In women's[7] nature intuition is better than the intuition of men. The reason is that woman also thinks from the heart, not only from the head. It becomes easy for her, if the knowledge does not come from the head, to draw it from within, from the heart.

A[8] numberless proofs have been found in different countries in Europe among the mothers of soldiers, who had long lived in conditions of fear. Many wives and mothers of soldiers and sometimes the innocent children of those who were fighting on the field of battle, perceived different signs of their dear ones'[9] condition in[10] the battlefield. Who has affection, who knows what love means, what devotion means, or tenderness of heart, he cannot misunderstand for one moment; there comes a knowledge to such a person, which he could not receive by other, outer ways.

And when looking at the problem from another point of view, we shall come to confirm that, as it is two eyes that make the sight complete, and

6. TR.hw., Hq.tp.: an attested American variant of "systematized"
7. Hq.tp.: it appears that originally "women's" was typed, but then changed in ink to "woman's"
8. TR.hw.: There appears to be a majuscule "A" before "numberless"; Hq.tp.: no "A", sentence begins with "Numberless"
9. Hq.tp.: "one's" instead of "ones'"
10. Ibid.: "on" instead of "in"

two ears which complete the hearing, so it is the knowledge from within and without that makes wisdom complete.

Yet there are a good many who are so absorbed in realizing the knowledge from within that they dream in their lives and live in the clouds and talk about imagination, but that is not our idea; this again would be one-sided. Wisdom comes from equilibrium. Truth comes from balance. A person who is wide-awake to the light within and the light without, he can be of greater use and it is that person who lives a fuller life.

Now if we ask ourselves what has brought to the modern ~~mind~~ world this state of unrest and this state of equilibrium[11] that we have been seeing for the last years (wars[12] and disasters), what reason is there behind it all, we shall get the answer sooner or later that humanity has lost its equilibrium in spite of all progress.

Some few there are who have kept their own spiritual beliefs. Some have gone in a material[13] direction—and are they happy? No! That what makes one happy does not exist on the earth. It exists in space; call it, it exists in the heavens. It is something one has to reach up to. And what helps one to reach up to it? Man has lost the value of the[14] imagination, the value of thought.

What are we to reach up to in this world, we give so great importance to? We imagine a pebble costs a penny and a diamond 1000[15] pounds. That is our imagination. The one thing is brighter than the other, but our imagination has made one thing so precious. In the end of keen observation we see it is nothing but imagination. There are times we think certain things worth so much, and at different times other things—it is again our imagination after all. Only we occupy our imagination[16] with things of the earth to our intelligible mind.

And the other thing we do is to be careless about it, we say: It may be or may not be—what does it all matter? <u>But it matters in the long run.</u>[17] It matters when questions of life and death come. For at that time all things around us matter less than ourselves. And then perhaps comes the search for self. And man asks: What is my self[18] that death can take away? If the self is more important and greater, I want to find out what self is and waken to that self more and more and come to that knowledge which can be gained

---

11. TR.hw.: only "equilibrium" is written, but it seems likely that "disequilibrium" may have been said; Hq.tp.: a space left before "equilibrium"
12. Hq.tp.: "war" instead of "wars"
13. Ibid.: "national" instead of "material" (probably a transcription error)
14. Ibid.: "the" omitted
15. TR.hw., Hq.tp.: both the hw. and the tp. write this in numerals, so it cannot be determined whether P-o-M. said "one thousand" or "a thousand"
16. Hq.tp.: "imaginations" instead of "imagination"
17. TR.hw.: this sentence underlined in hw., perhaps indicating that P-o-M. emphasized it while speaking; Hq.tp.: sentence also underlined in tp.
18. Hq.tp.: "myself" instead of "my self"

from within.

And now the question is: How can that be brought about? The answer[19]: By looking within. Our habit is to look without. When a person's eyes are open all that there is attracts his attention, but he is not conscious of all within himself. And when he gets tired of all that is without, he closes his eyes, and then all that which is collected in his mind comes before his eyes. And so, by only closing his eyes, the inner world of his eyes comes before his eyes. If that is true, ~~the~~ one can easily see that in order to dive deep in oneself, one must get deeper within. So the wisdom which the Sufi message presents to the world is acquired by this method of getting in communication with within.

The Sufi message is not giving great principles or doctrines to the world; it is not bringing a new idea to the West. It is only helping them in finding themselves, in striking a balance through them, in getting an equilibrium in all what may happen. There is no promise given of wealth or health, it does not lead to miracles, phenomena, wonder-workings, it does not bring a new way of piety or spirituality, it is not a community nor a new religion. It is a wider outlook on life, a point of view, an attitude.

In the end, I think that happiness which can be acquired within oneself is the best way to that peace which is the fulfilment of one's life.

---

19. Ibid.: "is" added

A typescript prepared by Sakina Furnée or under her supervision

---

1

[2]The Hague,
Friday, four o'clock, Jan. 18th, 1924

Attitude towards the *Murshid*[3] and towards the Cause.[2]

[4]I would like to speak to my *mureeds*[5] about in what relation they stand to their murshid.[4]

[6]As soldier[7] to their general, or as pupils to their professor? They stand much more close[8] to their murshid than words can explain. Mureeds to their murshid are just like the veins of his own body, through which the blood of his message runs continually. And in that way the murshid not alone[9] gives the message, but all the mureeds together with him. I wish my mureeds to understand what responsibility they have in the world, that by realizing this they [10]feel what is their duty in the cause. As they become more and more serious and keen as channels to the message, so they become as the lungs through which the word comes, the lungs of the murshid through which the message comes. And what if there is something wrong with the lungs? It has its effect upon the whole life. The more you will think of this, the more you realize that you [11]not only have become mureeds[11] for your own

---

Documents:

Sk.tp. = a typescript made by Sakina Furnée or under her supervision, copied from an unknown reporting or other early document.

Hq.tp. = a typescript made at Headquarters, Geneva, as part of the *Sangatha* (see Glossary) I series, probably edited by Murshida Sherifa Goodenough, where it appears on pages 61-63.

Hq.st. = a stencilled copy of Hq.tp., identical except for one change near the end, and therefore mentioned only in note 52.

Notes:

1. Sk.tp.: later Sakina wrote "340.4" (one of her archive numbers) at the top
2. Hq.tp., Hq.st.: the place, time, date and title omitted, and the heading "Nasihat" (a category applied to the teachings of P-o-M.; see Glossary) added
3. The word "*murshid*" is the title Sufis use for a spiritual guide (see Glossary)
4. Hq.tp.: "I would like to speak to my mureeds about in what relation they stand to their murshid" replaced with "The Relation In Which the Mureeds Stand to Their Murshid", and used as a title
5. The word "*mureed*" is used by Sufis to indicate an initiate (see Glossary)
6. Hq.tp.: "Do they stand" added
7. Ibid.: "soldiers" instead of "soldier"
8. Ibid.: "closer" instead of "more close"
9. Ibid.: "not alone" omitted
10. Ibid.: "may" added
11. Ibid.: "have not become mureeds only" in place of "not only have become mureeds"

spiritual development; then you might as well have become a member[12] of any esoteric society. If destiny has brought you in the Sufi Movement, then your responsibility is different. If one does not realize this, one has not yet come to the consciousness of one's mureedship. He has been received, but is not yet conscious of his responsibility. In order to have that, all the energy that is needed must be put to[13] the cause of the message. Every mureed has to share its burden; concerning this[14] every mureed is counted, however humble his work. A mureed one does not see for the whole year, that mureed has something to do with the message. That mureed is part of the[15] particle[16] of the body of the cause, and his attitude, his life, his work, his feelings, his thoughts have an effect upon the whole cause. It is not only that the mureeds depend upon the cause, [17]it is also the cause which is dependent upon the mureeds. The best thing, therefore, for my mureeds is[18] to realize this, to realize their responsibility to God and humanity in this cause.

When[19] only they do not think: what am I?, because they are not known perhaps, or are not doing any particular work, either known or unknown. In the abstract world you all have [20]part in the plan.[21] [22]In the abstract world you have it,[22] you all have your part to play in the message. The Sufi cause is a temple for this time built[23], a temple built for the worship of the future. And some will have to be[24] the pillars of the temple, and some will have to serve in the making of the walls, and some must help the position in the dome and minarets. [25]In truth all this is needed[25]; this[26] all must be provided and supplied. By what? By the devoted hearts of the mureeds. This[27] temple built in the abstract will be undestructable[28]. Everything else will follow sooner or later. Every mureed contributes to the making of this temple in the abstract, a duty which is most sacred. The more you are conscious, the more you [29]make the temple. Never mind if your means do not allow you, or your everyday work, or your work,[30] never mind

---

12. Ibid.: "members" in place of "a member"
13. Ibid.: "into" instead of "to"
14. Ibid.: "concerning this" omitted
15. Sk.tp.: later "the" crossed out and "a" added in ink
16. Hq.tp.: "particles" instead of "particle"
17. Ibid.: "but" added
18. Ibid.: "is" moved to before "for my mureeds"
19. Ibid.: "If" instead of "When"
20. Sk.tp.: later "your" added in ink
21. Hq.tp.: "a place." instead of "part in the plan."
22. Ibid.: "In the abstract world you have it," omitted
23. Ibid.: "built" moved to before "for this time"
24. Ibid.: "built" [sic] added, later altered in ink from "be built" to "build"
25. Ibid.: "All that is needed is the truth" instead of "In truth all this is needed"
26. Ibid.: "that" instead of "this"
27. Ibid.: "The" instead of "This"
28. Ibid.: "indestructable" instead of "undestructable", which, although not an established usage, may have been said by P-o-M.
29. Ibid.: "will" added
30. Ibid.: "or your work," omitted

if your life's situation will[31] not allow you opportunity, as long as you intend to do [32]best for the best[33]. If the result is[34] not for today, then it[35] will be for tomorrow. It is your intention which values most[36] in this cause.

No doubt over-enthusiasm upsets a person's balance. So I would not ask you for an[37] over-enthusiasm on your part, although I must appeal to your deepest hearts[38], that we sorely need ten thousand [39]workers to begin our movement. Until[40] we have not got this, we have not developed.[41] I do not consider that we have made a beginning. A cause which is for the whole humanity at least[42] needs the number I have mentioned. And this I[43] will tell you, you must come and do[44] every effort possible to make the number which is wanted just now to serve God and humanity.

Your devotion is really the only consolation I have in the difficulties which are endless and which I can never explain in this world, difficulties which are endless and beyond imagination. As parents I think, who do not think it necessary to bring the troubles before their children. They bear it for themselves. It is that which is the case of your murshid. Yet I am quite well aware that if your murshid were in need, and I was[45] in trouble, you would all gladly help me. But this is my greatest need.

One might ask whether in any cases[46] quality is not more than quantity. This might be true for an esoteric school, but not for a world cause. If it were for an esoteric school it would be quite a different thing. But it is the world service, and we can never have enough work done—it can never be enough[47]. And there is a large part of the world which should be touched, which is still untouched. When we look at the map, how poor we stand for a world message, with all the riches from above that we have at the back of us. No doubt it is true that the message of God must reach all people, must reach all parts of the earth[48], but human efforts are necessary as our part. It is necessary that some people will come out from the mureeds, who will be able to take up the work in other lands, in other parts of the world where the message has not yet spread. Some will have to go before the message and try

---

31. Ibid.: "does" instead of "will"
32. Sk.tp.: later "your" inserted in ink; Hq.tp.: "your" added
33. Hq.tp.: "cause" instead of "best"
34. Ibid.: "results are" instead of "result is"
35. Ibid.: "they" instead of "then it"
36. Ibid.: "is really of most value" instead of "values most"
37. Ibid.: "an" omitted
38. Ibid.: "the depth of your heart" instead of "your deepest hearts"
39. Ibid.: "good" added
40. Ibid.: "as long as" instead of "Until"
41. Ibid.: "we have not developed." omitted
42. Ibid.: "at least" moved to after "needs"
43. Ibid.: "I" omitted
44. Ibid.: "make" instead of "do"
45. Ibid.: "or I were" instead of "and I was"
46. Ibid.: "case" instead of "cases"
47. Ibid.: "—it can never be enough" omitted
48. Ibid.: "world" instead of "earth"

to awaken interest and prepare the ground. And others will go in places where the movement has started, to blow the fire and keep it blowing[49]. Our ideal is so high; our work, our service need[50] a number of souls. But our congregation is so little.[51] This we must realize every day more and more, and find[52] out every day more and more what can be done for this want in order to promote the cause, so dear to our hearts and so sacred to our souls.

---

49. Ibid.: "going" instead of "blowing"
50. Sk.tp.: "s" added in ink to make "needs"; Hq.tp.: "needs"
51. Hq.tp.: "!" instead of "."
52. Hq.st.: "found" instead of "find", evidently a typing error

A stencil prepared at Headquarters, Geneva

1

GATHEKA[2] Number 11.

Toward the One, the Perfection of Love, Harmony and Beauty, the Only Being, united with All the Illuminated Souls, who form the Embodiment of the Master, the Spirit of Guidance.[3]

SUFI MYSTICISM III.

The method by which a mystic prepares his heart to tread the spiritual path

In the first place one asks: What is the heart? Where is the heart? And man is accustomed to say that the heart is in the breast. Yes, that is true. There is a nerve centre in the breast of man which has so much to do with the feelings that always the heart is pictured in the breast, that centre which is most sensitive to our feelings. When a person is feeling a great joy it is in that centre that one feels something lighted up, and by the lighting up of that centre the whole person seems light. The person feels as if he flew, there is a great joy in his life. And again, if depression or despair has come into his life this has an effect upon the centre. Man feels his throat choked and his breath is laden heavily with a load; it again means that it is that centre that feels.

But it is not that only which is the heart. It is like a mirror standing before the heart, focussed to the heart, and every thing, every feeling is reflected in this mirror in the physical being of man. As man is ignorant of his soul, so he knows not where his heart is, nor where the centre is where his feelings are reflected. This is a fact which is known by the scientists, as

Documents:

Hq.st. = a stencil prepared at Headquarters, Geneva, for distribution to Sufi Centres. A note in the archive file in Suresnes says, in Dutch, that the lecture "exists in version E. van Leembruggen", which would indicate a handwritten reporting; however, no such manuscript has been found to date.

Sk.tp. = a typed version made by Sakina Furnée or under her supervision, which closely follows Hq.st.

Notes:

1. Sk.tp.: the date, 19 January 1924, is added in pencil on the typescript
2. A category of the teachings of P-o-M. (see Glossary)
3. This is the Sufi Invocation, which appears at the top of many documents distributed from Hq.

well as that it is the heart which is the beginning of the formation of a child. But if one comes to a mystic's conception one will see that it is in the heart, which is the beginning of form, which is also the beginning of the spirit, which makes man individual. The depth of that spirit is in reality what we call the heart. By this we understand that there is some such thing as a heart which is the deepest depth of man's being, and if one knows something of it first, it is from the impression which he receives in this nerve centre, which is in the breast of man, and therefore man calls it the heart.

In these days people give less importance to sentiment. They rely more upon the intellect. The reason is that when they meet two sorts of people, the intellectual and the sentimental people, they find in an intellectual man greater balance than in the one with sentiment. This is no doubt true. But the lack of balance is for the very reason because there is a greater power than the intellect, which is the sentiment. The earth is fruitful, but not so living and powerful as the water. [4]The intellect is creative, yet not so powerful as the water.[4] The intellect is creative, yet not so powerful as the heart and the sentiment. In reality the intellectual man in the end will prove unbalanced too if he has no sentimental side attached to it.

Are there not many people of whom their surroundings say: I like him, love him, admire him, but he closes his heart? The one who closes his heart neither fully loves others nor allows others to love him fully. Besides, the person who is only intellectual, in time becomes sceptical, doubting, unbelieving, destructive, as there is no power of the heart to balance it. The Sufi considers the devotion of the heart as the best thing to cultivate for spiritual realization. It might seem quite different from what many think, but the one who closes his heart to man, closes his heart to God. Jesus Christ did not say: God is the intellect; he said: God is love[5]. And if, therefore, there is a peace[6] of God that can be found anywhere, it[7] is not in any church on the earth, nor in heaven above, it is in the heart of man. The best place where you are sure to find God is the loving heart of a kind man.

It may be said that by the help of reason man will act according to a certain standard of morals, but that does not make a person good. If they are good or righteous, they are artificially made good. All the prisoners in the gaol[8] can be righteous. But if a natural goodness and righteousness can be found anywhere, it is to be found in the spring of the heart from which life rises, a springing virtue and every drop of this is a living virtue. That proves that goodness is not man-made, it is his very being. And if he lacks goodness

---

4. Sk.tp.: this sentence omitted, probably accidentally
5. I John 4:8 (these words are not actually presented as words of Christ)
6. Although the typescripts have "peace", it is possible that P-o-M. said "piece", which sounds the same.
7. Hq.st.: "if" typed instead of "it" by mistake; Sk.tp.: "if" corrected to "it" in ink
8. Hq.st.: by mistake, "goal" was typed instead of "gaol" (British spelling of "jail"); Sk.tp.: also "goal"

it is not the lack of training, nor training which is very often wanted most; it is because he has not yet found his self. Goodness is natural. For a normal person it is necessary to be good. No one needs teaching to live a good or a[9] righteous life. If[10] love is the torch on his path, it shows him what fairness means, the honour of the word, charity of heart, righteousness. Do we not see sometimes a young man, who with all his boisterous tendencies finds a girl, whom he begins to love, and if he really loves her, he begins to show a difference in his life, he becomes gentle, for he must train for her sake; he leaves off things he was never before willing to leave off. And in the same way forgiveness, where there is love, is not a very difficult thing. A child coming before his mother, having offended her a thousand times, asks her forgiveness. There is no other to go to. It does not take a moment for the heart of the mother to forgive. Forgiveness was waiting there to be manifested. One cannot help being kind when there is feeling. A person whose feeling goes out to another person, he sees in his child the want of his feeling. He strikes a note of sympathy in every person, because he finds that point of contact in every soul he meets, because he has love.

There are people who say: But is it[11] not unwise to give oneself in an outgoing tenderness to everyone, because people are not trustworthy? But I should say: If a person is good and kind, this goodness ought to be manifested to everyone; the doors of the heart should not be closed.

A mystic like Jesus Christ said, "Love your friend," and he went as far as to say, "Love your enemy."[12] It is the same path the Sufi treads. In his charity of heart to his fellow-men he considers it is the love of God, and in showing love to everyone, he considers this as giving love to God. In this the method of the Sufi and the Yogi differ. The Yogi is not unkind. He says: I love you all, but I had better keep away from you, for your souls are always groping in darkness, and my soul is in the light. With your friendship I shall spoil my soul. So I had better keep away and love you from afar, from a distance. The Sufi says: It is a trial, but it is to be tried. I shall take up my everyday duties as they come to me. Although knowing how little important the things of the world are, and not giving too much value to these things, he is attentive to his duties towards those who love him, like him, depend upon him, follow him. For those who dislike, despise him, he tries for the best way of meeting them all. He lives in the world and yet he is not for the world. In this way the Sufi considers loving man as the main principle in the fulfilment of the purpose of his life.

How true it is that those who love their enemies and yet lack

---

9. Sk.tp.: "a" omitted, but added in ink
10. Hq.st.: actually "It" is typed, clearly an error, corrected to "If" in ink
11. Sk.tp.: "it is", corrected in ink to "is it"
12. See Matthew 5:43-45

patience, remind one of this picture of their life, which is like a burning lantern with little oil. It cannot endure. In the end the flame becomes faded. The oil in love is patience. Besides this, in the path of love, what is the oil? From beginning to end: unselfishness, self-sacrifice from beginning to end. And he who says, give and take, does not know love; he knows business.

One says: I have loved dearly once, but I was disappointed, as if a man would say: I dug in the earth, but when the mud came I was disappointed. It was true that mud came. But with patience he would have reached the water one day. Only patience can endure. Only endurance makes great. The only way of greatness is endurance. It is endurance which makes things valuable and men great.[13]

The imitation of gold can be as beautiful as real gold, the imitation of the diamond as bright as a real diamond. The difference is that the one fails in the test of endurance, and the other can stand it. Yet man must not be compared to objects. Man has something divine in himself, and he can prove this by his endurance in the path of love.

And the idea is now, whom should one love, how should one love? Whatever one loves, whether duty, human beings, art, friends, an ideal, his fellow-creatures[14], he has certainly opened that door through which to pass in order to reach that love which is God. The beginning of love is an excuse; it leads to that ideal of love[15] which is God alone. [16]Many say: I can love God, but not the human beings. It would be the same if we said to God: I love you, but not your image. Can one hate the human creatures in which God's image is to be found and yet claim love of God? If one is not tolerant, not willing to sacrifice, can he claim the love of the Lord? The first thing to teach is the broadness of the heart and the awakening of the heart is the inner feeling. If there is a sign for saintliness it is not the power of words, not the high position, either spiritual or intellectual, not magnetism that can prove that saintly spirit which only expresses itself in the love of their creatures. It is the continuous spring of love from that divine fountain situated in the heart of man. Once that fountain is open, it purifies the heart, it makes the heart transparent to see the outer and the inner world. The heart becomes the vehicle for the soul to see all within and without; man not only communicates with another person, but also with God.

To be circulated among the[17] Candidates for Initiation in the Sufi Order.

---

13. See *Gayan*, Bolas: "Endurance makes things precious and men great." (*Complete Works of Pir-o-Murshid Hazrat Inayat Khan*, Sayings 1 (London and The Hague, 1989), p. 75)
14. Hq.st.: actually "follow-creatures" is typed by mistake
15. Hq.st.: actually "os lofe" is typed, corrected to "of love" in ink
16. Sk.tp.: an "A" typed here, then crossed out in type
17. Sk.tp.: "read before" instead of "circulated among the"

Miss Toni de Ridder's handwritten reporting

The Hague, Jan. 20th, 1924

Church of All Sermon

Faith [1]

[2]I should like to speak a few words on the subject of faith.[2] Faith is higher than religion[3], and prayer[4] is higher than church[5]. For the church[5] is on the earth as religion[3] is on the earth, but their prayer[6] goes to the depth of a[7] man.

And now, what is faith? Faith is something which is not dependent upon religion[3] and that person whose faith is dependent upon religion[3], his is no faith, his is only religion[3]. But that does not mean that faith has no religion[3]. Faith is a light thrown upon [8]mind, which sooner or later creates the[9] reason to support it. Yet faith is not dependent on religion[3].

A Moslem asked a Brahman, who was worshipping the idol of a god, he said[10]: "How can this god listen to your prayers or realize your worship? This god of stone! I never can bow to such a god. My God is far beyond comprehension." The Brahman said: "If one has faith, even[11] the

---

Documents:

TR.hw. = a handwritten reporting by Miss Toni de Ridder, apparently taken down as P-o-M. was speaking. Later Murshida Sherifa Goodenough did extensive editing on this document, indicated by "(TR.hw.)Gd.ed." in the notes.

Hq.st. = a stencil prepared by Headquarters, Geneva, and included in a collection of "Addresses to Sirajs and Cherags of the Universal Worship" distributed privately in 1976. It includes only part of this talk, apparently made from TR.hw. and including much of the editing done thereon by Murshida Sherifa Goodenough.

Notes:

1. (TR.hw.)Gd.ed.: later Gd. wrote near the title "Religious Gatheka" (although this talk was not included in that series), "rep. by: Miss de Ridder", and in the margin "Very imperfect report"; in another unidentifiable hw. is added "Not Faith Gatheka no. 31"
2. (TR.hw.)Gd.ed.: this sentence crossed out
3. Ibid.: crossed out "religion" and wrote "reason" above
4. Ibid.: crossed out "prayer" and wrote "faith" above
5. Ibid.: the word "church" capitalized, then boxes drawn around both and a question mark (?) written above
6. Ibid.: "their prayer" crossed out and "faith" written above
7. Ibid.: crossed out "a" (which had possibly been crossed out already by TR.)
8. Ibid.: added "the" above
9. Ibid.: crossed out "the"
10. Ibid.: crossed out "he said"
11. Ibid.: added "from" above, then crossed it out

god of stone loves[12] and will listen[13] to his prayers." The one who lacks[14], for him even the God [15]in the heart of man is a formless God[15].

[16]Before the birth of the soul, it is faith which prepares the soul for the birth on earth. The man who says: I cannot [17]believe because I do not see him[18], it[17] is the man who only believes[19] and therefore he will keep his eyes open and his heart closed. If in order to gain faith he depends upon reason, he will be disappointed, because the reason of today will not be the reason of tomorrow. With every step which evolution takes reason will change, but nothing can change faith, for it stands firm. [20]The intellectual man thinks that [21]he will see the light rise, but he does not know that faith is the horizon of religion and that faith is the summit. It is the highest top.[20,21]

As[22] reason is the outcome of the experience on earth, a person's reason will be one day contradictory[23]. When you say: I believe he is good, another may come and say: I can prove he is not good. But when a person says: I believe my friend is good in all conditions—that is faith. [24]Faith in God, therefore, is not to believe[25] in God, which is dependent upon reason—because God is wise, the creator, the sustainer. Faith in God is not dependent on reason at all.

Perhaps one might think that we should not use reason at all. Certainly we should for all things on[26] the earth. But things from[27] heaven and heavenly life, they[28] belong to faith.[24]

This Universal Worship, which is laid[29] before you here, is

---

12. Ibid.: crossed out "loves" and wrote "lives" above
13. Ibid.: crossed out "and will listen" and wrote "the answer will come" above, then crossed that out and restored "and will listen"
14. Ibid.: added "faith"
15. Ibid.: crossed out "in the heart of man is a formless God" and wrote "in Heaven is as a rock", then crossed that out and restored "in the heart of man is a formless God"
16. Hq.st.: the Headquarters stencil begins here
17. (TR.hw.)Gd.ed.: crossed out "believe because I do not see him, it" and wrote above "have faith in what I do not see", but then crossed that out, restoring only the word "believe" to read: "The man who says: I cannot believe is the man . . ."; Hq.st.: only "it" omitted
18. Hq.st.: "how" instead of "him" (the crossed-out word is difficult to read in TR.hw., and the unknown transcriber may have misread it)
19. (TR.hw.)Gd.ed.: "what he sees" added above
20. Hq.st.: the two following sentences omitted and replaced by an ellipsis (. . .)
21. (TR.hw.)Gd.ed.: crossed out "he will see the light rise" and "It is the highest top" and wrote on a separate slip "that by reason he will reach the highest summit and see the horizon.", apparently intending that this should replace the passage from "he will....highest top."
22. Hq.st.: "As" changed to "The"
23. (TR.hw.)Gd.ed.: replaced "contradictory" with "contradicted"; Hq.st.: "contradicted"
24. Hq.st.: the next five sentences, to the end of the following paragraph, omitted, replaced by an ellipsis (. . .), starting again at "This Universal Worship..."
25. (TR.hw.)Gd.ed.: replaced "to believe" with "the belief"
26. Ibid.: changed "on" to "of"
27. Ibid.: crossed out "from" and wrote "of" above
28. Ibid.: "they" altered to "these"
29. Ibid.: crossed out "laid" and wrote "placed" above

representing[30] that one teaching brought to the earth by different servers of humanity who come from time to time, either recognized or not recognized[31] in this world, which is the martyrdom of the loving heart and the living soul. They have been exposed to more endurance[32], they have been put to a greater test than to their[33] life on earth. This service represents their teaching, their self-sacrificing service, without trying to compare them or hold the one over[34] the other. These candles represent the names of the great servers who have come to the earth in order to awake[35] the souls in it. The price they paid for this serving of humanity was their life, their comfort, their happiness. All was given to the children of the earth, and in this way they gave people consolation in their deepest needs.

One might ask: Are there only a few servers which[36] have been sent to the earth? The answer is: Many more than we know of; think of all the centuries and then of the few names known therein. All we can do is to represent the names of those who came to the earth and show a[37] respect for the memories[38] of those whose memories[38] are[39] as dear to their followers as ours are to our memory[40] and to the memory[41] of all. By this we see that the master and the Lord are one and the same, that it is one divine light which manifests itself, which takes form, the form of service, when man begins to forget himself, when the burden of [42] whole humanity one bears in one's consciousness and one's every moment is taken in order to help humanity.

A great many have come, many of which[43] are known, many of which[43] are not known at all. The candles represent their lives and names. For in whatever name they served, it is all one truth and at the back of it all was the source of all.[44] We therefore try to read their scriptures with perfect, equal tolerance for all. It is this which was a[45] prayer of Moses and the desire of Jesus Christ—that a day should come when communities and creeds

---

30. TR.hw.: it appears that "representant"(?) was first written, and then the "-ant" was crossed out by TR. and "-ing" written above, indicating a reassessment of what she heard; (TR.hw.)Gd.ed.: changed "is representing" to "represents"; Hq.st.: "represents"
31. (TR.hw.)Gd.ed.: crossed out "not" and changed "recognized" to "unrecognized", but then crossed out "un" and restored "not"
32. Ibid.: crossed out "endurance" and wrote "trials of endurance" above
33. Ibid.: added "others" after "than", then crossed both out and changed "to their" to "in the"; Hq.st.: "in the"
34. (TR.hw.)Gd.ed.: crossed out "over" and wrote "above" above; Hq.st.: "above"
35. Ibid.: added an "n" to read "awaken"
36. Ibid.: changed "which" to "who"; Hq.st.: "who"
37. Ibid.: crossed out "a"; Hq.st.: "a" omitted
38. Ibid.: changed "memories" to "memory"
39. Ibid.: changed "are" to "is"
40. Ibid.: crossed out "our memory" and added "us" above
41. Ibid.: "-y" replaced by "-ies", then changed back to "-y"
42. Ibid.: added "the"
43. Ibid.: corrected "which" to "whom"; Hq.st.: "whom"
44. Hq.st.: ends here
45. (TR.hw.)Gd.ed.: changed "a" to "the"

and castes should be overbridged[46] and the religion of every soul should be performed in the service of the Universal Worship, as here are all the different aspects of life grouped together in one worship.

---

46. This form is rare but attested; combinations with "over-" occur freely in English; (TR.hw.)Gd.ed.: crossed out "overbridged" and wrote "united" above

Toni de Ridder's handwritten text

1 The Hague, Jan. 20th, '24

Initiation Mureeds

Allow me to say a few words to the new *mureeds*[2] who have had today[3] their initiation[3] to tread the path towards the spiritual life, who have come with their faith and trust. And I would like to tell you, my new[4] mureeds: [5]What does initiation mean?

You must understand by this that from this very moment all your experiences of the past, all your troubles, all your sorrows[6], all your errors must be forgotten. All disagreeable sensations you might have had in your life, more or less, from the moment of your initiation they are far behind you. You have taken a new step forward in life, you have turned a new page in your life. There is no reason for anyone for grievances[7] or complaining—all[8], all is forgiven, all the past. A new life has begun—with new, clear hope and new courage, and the feeling of single-mindedness

Documents:

TR.hw. = Miss Toni de Ridder's handwritten text, taken down as P-o-M. was speaking, or copied from such a text.

Sk.tp. = a typescript prepared by Sakina Furnée or under her supervision, showing a number of differences from TR.hw.

Hq.st. = a stencil made at Headquarters, Geneva, for distribution to Sufi Centres as the first part of number 33 in the Gatheka series; it incorporates most of the text of this lecture, apparently following TR.hw., without the changes in Sk.tp. Gatheka 33 also incorporates material from the lecture of 22 January 1924 (q.v.).

Notes:

1. Later, in another hand (not Gd.), the word "Initiation" written at top below "Initiation Mureeds"; Gd. added the word "Gatheka", and on the right the number "33" was written, indicating the number in the series of *Gatheka*s (see Glossary) of which part of this address formed the first part; Sk.tp.: a new title, "ADDRESS GIVEN BY PIR-O-MURSHID TO NEW MUREEDS, AFTER THEIR INITIATION"; Hq.st.: location and date omitted; at the top, "GATHEKA." and to the right "Number 33.", followed by the Sufi Invocation (see List), and then the title "Initiation."
2. The word *mureed* is used by Sufis to indicate an initiate (see Glossary)
3. Sk.tp.: "today" omitted, but later added in ink after "initiation"
4. Ibid.: "new" omitted
5. Hq.st.: from this point on, this address was used as the first part of Gatheka 33; the words up to this point omitted
6. Sk.tp.: "all your sorrows" omitted
7. Ibid.: "grievance", with the "s" added later in ink
8. Ibid.: first "all" omitted

which trusts[9] is going to be developed in you.

What your *murshid*[10] asks of you is not sincerity; that has been shown by you by your coming here. This[11] has been proved already and shown. What I ask from you is your patience, which nothing must shorten, nothing must make waver. You are not asked to renounce anything. You are only helped in your good intentions, helped along by your murshid and your co-mureeds.

You all belong now to one large family which forms a caravan for a long journey on the spiritual path here and in the hereafter. To realize your duty to one another, how to make the lives of ourselves and those around us harmonious, and at the same time realize your oneness with God. And to realize this: that nothing in the world should keep you back until you have reached the fulfilment of your desire, which is the spiritual ideal of every soul.[12]

---

9. Ibid.: "with trust" instead of "which trusts"; Hq.st.: "which trust" instead of "which trusts"
10. The word *murshid* is used by Sufis to indicate a spiritual guide (see Glossary)
11. Sk.tp.: ", that" instead of "This"
12. Hq.st.: Gatheka 33 continues from this point with material from the lecture of 22 January 1924.

Mureeds' Class[1]. I

The Hague, Monday, Jan. 21st, 1924

Attitude towards the Practices and towards the Movement

I wish to speak to my *mureeds*[2] a few words about their practices. The prescription-papers[3] given, it is something which must be kept as a sacred trust, something that must not be shown either to the non-members nor[4] even to the members. For each prescription is for that particular person, and may only be presented to *Murshid*[5]. And if there are any questions to be made, the most preferable thing is to ask Murshid by letter; if it is so pressing that you could not do without any explanation, you ask the leader of a certain group of the Sufi Order[6]. If the leader is not there, then the conductor of a certain group.

Now there are three things, besides all other practices, which are most serious:

1stly: The twenty breaths of purification, which are given to all mureeds, because this is a kind of air-ablution which prepares every person going through the spiritual path for his every activity which he is going to take in daily life, and as necessary as one's every day's ablution. And by this I can promise you that if you will keep up the prescription of purification regularly and steadfastly, it will become as a guarantee of [7]our health. Besides this it prepares to keep your intuition-factor clear, so as to think rightly and to act rightly. Therefore, spiritually and physically both, it is the most valuable prescription for you to keep up.

Document:

Sk.tp. = a typescript made by Sakina Furnée or under her supervision for her inclusive set of the teachings of P-o-M. This must have been made from an original reporting, probably by Miss Toni de Ridder (like the classes given before and after this one), which is no longer in the archives. The noted corrections in ink appear to have been made by Sakina Furnée.

Notes:

1. "Class" altered in ink to "Classes"
2. The word "*mureed*" is used by Sufis to indicate an initiate (see Glossary)
3. By "prescription-papers" P-o-M. refers to a paper given to each mureed on which was written a specific set of spiritual practices to be done daily by that person
4. The "n" in "nor" later crossed out in ink
5. The word "*murshid*" is used by Sufis to indicate a spiritual guide; here it refers to P-o-M. himself (see Glossary)
6. In October, 1923, Sufi Movement became the name of the overall organization, and from that time on Sufi Order refers to the esoteric school of the Movement
7. Later "y" added in ink at the beginning of "our" to make "your"

2ndly: The prayers Saum[8] and Salat[8] are the prayers which are meant to be the prayers for today, for this time; therefore their power is much greater than can be imagined. It is a battery itself, by which a great activity is developed. It is the prayer which the spheres repeat, and someday will reach every part of the world; no part of the world will be left without. These prayers will touch every soul one day or other, either directly or indirectly. By seeing and knowing this more and more, you will realize the powers[9] of these prayers a thousand times more than ever. One may say them more times a day than is prescribed. And if you say them more than once, it is better. And if you are able to do them with the movements in all humility, it is best.

There are two ways of saying them; one way is standing, the other bending, bowing, prostrating. It is not a subject which should be considered as secondary, for the movements have a great power. No one who has the slightest idea of the occult laws will for one moment think less of the power of the movements. Yet if behind the movement there is no sense, the whole movement is a lost movement. When that movement comes with a great thought, it has a great power, it is dynamic.

No doubt the Sufi Order keeps all mureeds free to do one kind of movement or the other, or to do no movement at all. This is the Order in which freedom is considered. No mureed is forced to do, no one is urged to follow. You all follow freedom, and freedom is our rule. Only I must tell you what great opportunity you have, what can be of great benefit in your life.

3rdly: When one unites with Murshid in thought at the end of one's practices, it is only in order to feel that we are receiving the divine inspiration and blessing of God, that we are open, that we do not close our hearts to our Murshid who has taken our life's interests in his heart, who can only be happy in our happiness, and who sorrows in our sorrow. Besides this, if your devotion makes you feel inclined that you might help your Murshid in thought, to be in thought with Murshid's task, it will make your work easier.

The continuation of the practices without break, every day, is the very best thing, and if one drops them one day, that does take away some kind of sustenance of the practices. Regularity in practices is a great thing.

But now coming to the practical questions of life. There might be mureeds who think: I am quite willing to do work for the cause, but Murshid does not depend upon me for something fixed. You must never allow such

---

8. "Saum" and "Salat" are titles given by P-o-M. to two of the prayers he gave. For the texts, see *Complete Works of Pir-o-Murshid Hazrat Inayat Khan*, Sayings I (London and The Hague, 1989), pp. 199-205.
9. The "s" on the end of "powers" later crossed out in ink

thoughts to come into your mind. The initiation has appointed you for the work, and to do all the things you can for our cause. Besides this, you can always help those who have the responsibility of the work. This is a work of love and sacrifice. You can all work. By partaking of the responsibility of all, you can do so much.

For ourselves, what we can bring is love, harmony, beauty. Therefore the first experience in ourselves is to forgive one another, thinking that all human beings have their shortcomings. But the main thing which is in our mind, must be this: that all the troubles and difficulties should not hinder our Movement, because we shall stand firm.

And can you imagine what battle it is for your Murshid, a continual battle, and to what extent does it hurt? And if it were only a battle with the adversaries, it was not so bad. But if mureeds should make battle among themselves, what difficulties there will be. It is not the battle outside which gives the greatest fight, but the battle in ourselves which is the hardest.

What I ask my workers is to have understanding for the sacrifice their Murshid has to go through and to understand that they share his sacrifice by their devotion. One great hope I have—that I have not the slightest doubt about your devotion and faith, and I know there are souls who will stand by me through all my strife, and through all my life.

1

The Hague, Jan. 22nd, 24[2]

Mureeds' Class[3]

Now I would like to tell my *mureeds*[4] something about the Gathas[5] which they read in the sacred readings. [6]It is the privilege of the initiated in the Sufi Order to read the Gathas first. No doubt a time will come when these Gathas will be given to a larger population, but just now this privilege my mureeds will appreciate, and instead of speaking about the Gathas will live them in their own lives, and show the others, without trying to correct them or teach them, the example in your own life worked out.

No serious work might succeed if it is not tried. Your privilege it is to receive this, and that will make the message a real message to others. And please remember that truth is the share of the sincerest. The more sincerity is developed, the greater share of truth you will have. And however much sincerity a person may have, there is always a gap to fill, for we live in the midst of falsehood, and we are always apt to be carried away by this world of falsehood.

Therefore we must never think we are sincere enough and we must always be on [7]guard against influences which may carry us away from that

---

Documents:

TR.hw. = a handwritten reporting by Miss Toni de Ridder (see List), taken down as P-o-M. spoke. Later, Murshida Sherifa Goodenough did light editing on this document, indicated by "(TR.hw.)Gd.ed." in the notes.

Sk.tp. = a typescript prepared by Sakina Furnée or under her supervision, showing a few differences of wording from TR.hw. There are a few corrections, indicated by "(Sk.tp.)Sk.cr." in the notes.

Hq.st. = a stencilled document, part of the Gatheka series (see List), prepared at Headquarters, Geneva, for distribution to Sufi Centres. The text of the present lecture constitutes the second half of the Gatheka (see note 6).

Notes:

1. Hq.st.: at the top "GATHEKA" (a category in the teachings of P-o-M., see List and Glossary) and by the right margin "Number 33." followed by the Sufi Invocation, and then the title "Initiation" (see the address of 20 January 1924), omitting "Mureeds' Class" and the place and date
2. (TR.hw.)Gd.ed..: later Gd. wrote "Gatheka" after the date; Sk.tp.: adds "Tuesday" before "Jan. 22nd"
3. Sk.tp.: instead of "Mureeds' Class" has "Attitude towards the Sacred Readings" as the title
4. The word "*mureed*" is used by Sufis to indicate an initiate (see Glossary)
5. The "Gathas" are a part of the teachings of P-o-M. for initiates (see List and Glossary)
6. Beginning at this point, the text of this talk was incorporated into Gatheka 33 as the second half; the address of 20 January 1924 (q.v.) formed the first half
7. (Sk.tp.)Sk.cr.: "our" added later in ink

sincerity which is the bridge between ourselves and our ideas[8]. No study, no meditation are[9] more helpful than sincerity itself. It is by the love of truth that truth can be realized. Your respect for *Murshid*[10], your devotion to the message you will show in your esteem for the teachings given to you. If you find them simple, you must think that all things of real value are simple. If you find them complex, you may know that the truth will not ~~be~~ take[11] very long to be understood. For we will all agree that it is best that in our sacred readings all arguments are kept out, in order to follow the path of truth.

There must be harmony between the mureeds and Murshid[12]. And the[13] harmony is to be realized by your patience in the teachings[14] given to you. You need not be impatient as to[15] the progress you make on the spiritual path, for you must be sure of the fact that your Murshid is more enthusiastic[16] and more keen about your progress than you yourself are. If he does not push you forward too quickly, it is not from[17] lack of interest, nor is it [18]lack of fair dealing on his part. What could be more pleasing to the parents than the progress of their own children? So it is with your Murshid. If you progress in advancement, it is to my content[19], to my credit, it is my great benefit.

In the path of truth you have to have the same tendencies as the ~~passengers~~ travellers[20] in[21] the ship [22]to the captain—towards their captain—[22]the sure trust that he is doing his duty to his best. If anyone should go to the captain and say: I think you are going more to the north than to the south, this is not the place I want to go to, that poor captain would be so confused that he should not know what to do. Shall he go backward or forward? I hope this my mureeds will understand.

And now coming to our attitude as far as the message is concerned.

---

8. Sk.tp.: "ideal" instead of "ideas"
9. (TR.hw.)Gd.ed.: "are" crossed out and "is" substituted; Sk.tp., Hq.st.: "is"
10. The word "*murshid*" is used by Sufis to indicate a spiritual guide; here it refers to P-o-M. himself (see Glossary)
11. TR.hw.: first "be" was written, then crossed out and "take" written above, apparently as TR. was taking down the lecture, perhaps indicating that P-o-M. corrected himself while speaking;
Sk.tp., Hq.st.: "take"
12. Sk.tp.: "between the mureeds, between mureeds and Murshid" instead of "between the mureeds and Murshid", perhaps a typographical copying error
13. (TR.hw.)Gd.ed.: "the" crossed out;
Sk.tp.: "this" instead of "the";
Hq.st.: "the" omitted
14. Hq.st.: "teaching" instead of "teachings"
15. Sk.tp.: "for" instead of "as to"
16. (Sk.tp.)Sk.cr.: "enthusiast" typed, and "-ic" added at the end later in ink
17. Sk.tp.: "the" instead of "from"
18. Ibid.: "the" added
19. (TR.hw.)Gd.ed.:"-ment" added to the end of "content" to make "contentment"; Sk.tp., Hq.st.: "contentment"
20. TR.hw.: first "passengers" was written, then crossed out and "travellers" written above, perhaps indicating that P-o-M. corrected himself while speaking; Sk.tp., Hq.st.: "travellers"
21. Sk.tp.: "on" instead of "in"
22. Ibid.: "towards the captain—" instead of "to the captain—towards their captain—"

I believe without doubt that the message is not only for some certain nation or some certain class of people. The message is for all nations and for every soul living on the earth. Not one soul there is, either of friend[23] or sinner[24], that has nothing to do with the message, nor one nation in the world which will be kept untouched by it. And if this is true, it is absurd on our part to say that this person must come to us and the other person not, or that this particular place is for the Message and the other place not. When a worker who is working in another country writes to me that that place is difficult to work in and that people are not ready yet, I think that that particular mureed-worker[25] is not yet ready himself and the difficulties surpass his faith. If I were dwelling in the forest where no man was to be seen, I would still have worked among the animals and have dug deep into the rocks in order to bring out the spirit.

What attitude then must we have? We must not allow ourselves to become discouraged. We must not allow any pessimistic feeling to rise in our souls[26]. If the whole world stood against us, we shall still stand firm without being disappointed, for the message is the promise of God, and its domain is all the domain which belongs to God, and is in every heart. And its work is in every nation. No people are to be left out. And you, my mureeds, who stand by my side in this world[27] at this moment when it has not yet begun, your response[28] must be great; you must realize this every day and be ready to do all in your power to make the message of God spread, and to make your Murshid's task easy.

God bless you![29]

[30]

---

23. (TR.hw.)Gd.ed.: "friend" crossed out and "saint" substituted; Hq.st.: "saint"
24. Sk.tp.: "friend or foe, saint or sinner" instead of "friend or sinner"
25. (TR.hw.)Gd.ed.: "mureed-" crossed out, and omitted in Hq.st.
26. Hq.st.: "soul" instead of "souls"
27. (TR.hw.)Gd.ed.: "world" crossed out and "work" substituted; Sk.tp., Hq.st.: "work"
28. Sk.tp.: "-s" added to make "responses", but crossed out in type
29. Ibid.: "God bless you!" omitted
30. Hq.st.: "To be read before candidates for initiation in the Sufi Order."

Sakina Furnée's typescript

Jan. 26th, 1924

Divine Impulse

1

Beloved ones[2] of God,

My subject this evening is divine impulse. The first question to be considered in reference to this subject is: Where does every impulse come from? Every movement, every vibration, every motion has one source. One sees a hint in the Bible on this subject, where it says: "The word was God."[3] The word means vibration, and vibration[4] means movement. [5]Among the Hindus in the Vedanta[6] [7] means sound.[5] Vibration was the first or original aspect of Brahma or Creator. [8]In the *Qur'an*, [9]"'*Kun* (?) (Be) he said, and it became.'"[8,9] Every impulse, every action on any plane of existence, has its origin in the one source.

[10]I will quote another *sura*[11] of[10] the *Qur'an* where[12] it is said: "God

---

Documents:

Sk.tp.1 = a typescript prepared by Sakina Furnée or under her supervision, probably made from the handwritten manuscript of Kefayat LLoyd or a typescript made from it, not found in the archives.

Sk.tp.2 = another typescript prepared by Sakina Furnée or under her supervision, made to correct some errors in Sk.tp.1, and introducing further changes.

SF. = an article in the journal *Sufism* for June, 1924, pp. 3-7. The journal, and therefore presumably this article, was edited by Murshida Sophia E.M. Green.

Sk.an. = separate handwritten annotations by Sakina Furnée.

This lecture was published in a highly edited form in the *Sufi Message* volumes, Vol. VIII (London, 1963), pp.145-149; this version is not included in the notes.

Notes:

1. SF.: date omitted, and "An Address by Inayat Khan" added under the title
2. Sk.tp.2: "one" in place of "ones", probably a typographical error
3. John 1:1
4. Sk.tp.2: "vibrations" instead of "vibration"
5. SF.: this sentence omitted
6. See Glossary
7. Sk.tp.1, Sk.tp.2: a space, into which later was written in ink "Nada Brahma" (see Glossary)
8. SF.: this sentence omitted
9. Sura 2:11 of the *Qur'an* contains the words "*kun fayakūn*" ("Be, and it became"); Sk.tp.1: "'*Kun* (?) (Be) he said, and it became.'" crossed out, and "it is said, '*Kun faya kun*', when God said 'Be', it became" substituted at bottom of page in ink; Sk.tp.2: "'. . . be He said, and it became.'" instead of "'*Kun* (?) (Be) he said, and it became.'"
10. SF.: "In" instead of "I will quote another *sura* of"
11. A chapter of the *Qur'an*
12. SF.: "where" omitted

is all power. There is no other power but God's."[13] In all that is done, all is done by his power. And now the question comes: If all the [14] scriptures say this, where does Satan come in? What is the meaning behind the power of Satan? Another power is suggested besides[15] the power of God, and sometimes the power attributed[16] to Satan seems mightier than the power attributed[16] to God. This is a puzzle to many, who wonder, Where does the action of Satan come in?

The explanation is to be found in the understanding of metaphysics and of the laws of nature. There is one law called the natural law, and all that comes directed by nature's law is harmonious. The gardens that man has made [17]seem for the moment to improve upon the forests, but in the end of[18] examination the garden with its artificial structures[19] proves limited in beauty and harmony. The inspiration one gets in the forests, in the wilderness, is much greater than in the garden man has made, for here man has made inspiration limited, for the life he radiates is limited.

Man makes a law, and finds he cannot keep [20]the law, so he makes another law, and is never satisfied, for he takes no account of nature's law of peace and harmony. Men say that nature is cruel; yes, but man is far more cruel than the animals. Animals have never destroyed so many lives as man has. Nature with all its apparent cruelty cannot compare with the cruelty, ignorance, and injustice[21] of man.

Jesus Christ said: "Thy will be done."[22] There is much for us to learn in this saying. Man makes another world in which he lives, different to the plan of God, to the laws of nature, and so the will of God is not done. The prayer teaches man that he must find out what is the will of God. It is not necessary for the animals and birds to find out the will of God, for they are directed by nature's impulse, they are closer to nature than man. The life of man is so far removed from the life of nature, and so every movement is difficult. We do not see this now. With all our knowledge we make life more and more complicated, and so the strife becomes greater and greater. For every person old or young, rich or poor, life is a difficult struggle, for we go further and further from the impulse which comes direct from the source from[23] whence every impulse comes.

---

13. Although God's power is mentioned frequently in the *Qur'an*, it is not clear which instance P-o-M. referred to here
14. Sk.tp.2: "meaning behind" typed here by mistake, then crossed out in type
15. Ibid.: "as well as" in place of "besides"
16. Ibid.: "attributes" instead of "attributed", probably a typing error
17. Sk.tp.1: "may" added in ink; Sk.tp.2, SF.: "may"
18. SF.: "on" in place of "of"
19. Sk.tp.2: "structure" instead of "structures"
20. Sk.tp.1: "to" added in ink; Sk.tp.2: "to"
21. Sk.tp.2: "unjustice" instead of "injustice"; corrected to "injustice" in ink
22. Matthew 6:10
23. Sk.tp.1: "from" later crossed out, and omitted in Sk.tp.2

From the metaphysical point of view there are different rhythms describing the condition of man, spoken of in the Vedanta as *sattva*, *rajas*, and *tamas*.[24] Sattva is a harmonious rhythm. Rajas is a rhythm which is not perfectly in harmony with nature, and tamas is a rhythm which is chaotic by nature, destructive, and every impulse that comes to man while in this chaotic rhythm is followed by destructive results. Any impulse coming when the person is in the impulse of rajas[25] is accomplished, but the impulse that comes when he is in the rhythm of sattva is inspired, and is in harmony with the rhythm of the universe.

The active life of man gives little time for concentration and for putting mind and body in the condition in which he can experience the rhythm which gives inspiration and meets with the will of God. This[26] experience comes in[27] answer to the prayer of Christ, "Thy will be done on[28] earth as it is in heaven." By producing this condition of mind and body, one tunes oneself to a certain pitch which is harmonious and heavenly, and in which the divine will is easily done, as it is in heaven. It is in this rhythm alone[29] that the will of God can be done.

It was not any prejudice against the world that made the great ones leave the world and go to the forests and caves. They went in order to tune themselves to that rhythm in which they could experience heaven. Heaven is not a country [30]or a continent; it is a state, a condition within oneself,[30] only experienced when the rhythm is in perfect working order. If one knows this, one realizes that happiness is man's own property. Man is his own enemy; he seeks for happiness in the wrong direction, and never finds it. It is a continual illusion. Man thinks: If I had this or this I should be happy for ever, and he never arrives because he pursues an illusion instead of the truth. Happiness is only to be found within, and when man tunes himself he finds all for which his soul yearns within himself.

The nature of every impulse is such that it goes through three stages, and after the process of three stages, it is realized as a result. [31]Whether it is right or wrong, beneficent or disadvantageous, as soon as the impulse springs from within.[31] There is no impulse which in its beginning is wrong or purposeless or inharmonious[32], for in the total sum of all things every

---

24. See Glossary
25. Sk.tp.2: "tamas" apparently typed by mistake, later changed in ink to "rajas"
26. Ibid.: "His" instead of "This"
27. Ibid.: "as an" instead of "in"
28. Ibid.: "in" instead of "on"
29. Ibid.: "alone" omitted
30. Ibid. Sk.tp.2: " or a continent; it is a state, a condition within oneself," omitted, but later added in ink
31. A grammatical element is missing from this sentence
32. Sk.tp.2: "unharmonius" [a rare but attested form] instead of "inharmonious", later changed in ink to "inharmonious"

impulse has its purpose. It is our limited outlook that[33] judges. The justice behind is so great that in the ultimate result everything fits into its proper place. But in the process through which the impulse passes, it becomes right or wrong; not in the beginning or the end, for the beginning has a purpose, and the end has answered the demand.

This is a question of metaphysics, and one must study it from different points of view, or one will be very much confused. Man with his little knowledge is ready to condemn or to admire, and thousands of times he finds[34] he fails in judging rightly. All great souls who have attained have realized this. Christ says: "Judge not, and ye shall not be judged."[35] Then tolerance comes, and when one realizes what is behind the impulse, one says very little.

The first process through which the impulse rises is in the region of feeling, and in this region the impulse is either strengthened or destroyed. The feeling may be love or hatred, or kindness, or fairness[36], but whatever the feeling may be, where[37] the impulse rises it gains strength to go forward, or it is destroyed. For instance, a person may have a great feeling of kindness, then the impulse of revenge may rise, but it is destroyed. Another person has a great feeling of bitterness, but if the impulse is to forgive, it will be destroyed before it ever[38] touches the reason. [39]Or a person is most kind, and when the impulse towards revenge has arisen, he feels most uncomfortable.[39] He will not [40] call on thought to judge, for his feelings[41] will destroy it. Or a person has a great feeling of bitterness, and the impulse of doing a service of kindness comes; it will be destroyed before it reaches the realm of thought[42], or if the impulse rises till it reaches the region[43] of thought, there[44] one reasons: Why should I help, why should I serve? Does he deserve it, will he benefit by it, is it right? All these problems are settled in this region.

Then third comes the realm of action. If the mind consumes[45] it, it goes no further; but if the mind allows it, it comes into the region of action and is realized as a result.

And now one questions how sages and thinkers have distinguished divine impulse among the different impulses that rise in the heart of man. First we must understand what the word divine means. Divine means in a

---

33. Ibid.: "which" instead of "that"
34. SF.: "he finds" omitted
35. See Matthew 7:1; SF.: "and ye shall not be judged" omitted from the quotation
36. SF.: "bitterness" instead of "fairness"
37. Sk.tp.2: "when" instead of "where"
38. Sk.tp.2: "even" instead if "ever"
39. SF.: this sentence omitted
40. Ibid.: "have to" added
41. Sk.tp.2, SF.: "feeling" in place of "feelings"
42. Thought is the second phase of the process: feeling, thought, action
43. SF.: "realm" instead of "region"
44. Ibid.: "then" in place of "there"
45. Sk.tp.2: "conserves" instead of "consumes"; Sk.an.: "conserves"

state of perfection. This state is experienced by God through man; in other words, when man has risen to the stage of development when[46] he can be the perfect instrument of God, when nothing of his own being stands in the way[47] against the direct impulse that comes from within, that spirit may be called perfect. That which is most precious, that which is the purpose of man's life, is to arrive at that state[48] of perfection when he can be the perfect instrument of God. When once a man has risen to this stage, he first begins to realize[49] at moments; then, as he develops, for a longer time; and those who develop further still[50] pass most of their time in that realization; then the feeling and thought no longer hinder the[51] divine impulse, for it rises freely and results in a divine purpose. [52]The message of the prophets and teachers of all times has been to teach man how to make peace with God. The fulfilment of life's purpose is in harmonizing with God, and this is done by distinguishing divine impulse.[52]

The question: How can one distinguish divine impulse, is answered in[53] that it is[54] just as in music one can distinguish the true note from the false, the harmonious chord from the chord of[55] discord. It is only a matter of ear-training. When the ear is trained, one can find out the slightest discord; the greater the musician, the more capable is he of finding out harmony and discord, the true and the[56] false note. Many think that what we call right or wrong, good or bad, is something we learn or acquire. That is true when it is man-made right or wrong, but of nature's right or wrong every little child has a sense. The child feels a wrong vibration at once. The infant feels if its surroundings are harmonious or inharmonious[57]. But man confuses himself so that he can no longer distinguish clearly. For man to learn to know for himself is a great advance along the spiritual path. When man is clear as to the feeling he gets from every impulse, he has advanced far. There are some who say after the result, I am sorry; but it is too late then. It was not true ear-training.

The divine impulse is an impulse full of love, it gives happiness, it is creative of peace. The difficulty is that every man does not observe the beginning of the impulse, he only observes the result. He is like an intoxicated person, and so in time, as in the condition of a drunken man, he

46. Ibid.: "that" instead of "when"; SF.: "where" instead of "when"
47. Ibid.: "in the way" omitted
48. Ibid.: "stage" instead of "state"
49. SF.: "God" added
50. Ibid.: "still further" in place of "further still"
51. Sk.tp.2: "the" omitted
52. Ibid.: these two sentences, "The message of . . . . distinguishing divine impulse." omitted
53. Sk.tp.2, SF.: "in" omitted
54. Sk.tp.2: "it is" omitted
55. SF.: "chord of" omitted
56. Sk.tp.2: "the" omitted
57. Ibid.: "unharmonious" instead of "inharmonious"

becomes confused and depressed, and there is struggle and strife; but man was not born for this. He is born for happiness. Peace, love, kindness and[58] harmony, are parts of his own being, and when a person is unhappy it means that he has lost himself, he does not know where he is.

Man is seeking for phenomena; he wants wonder-working, communication with ghosts or spirits. He is looking for something complex, and yet the simplest thing, and the most valuable thing in life, is to find one's true self.

---

58. Ibid.: a comma instead of "and"

Sakina Furnée's typescript

Jan. 28th, 1924

1

Spiritual Circulation through the Veins of Nature

Beloved ones of God,

My subject this evening is spiritual circulation through the veins of the universe. [2]When one observes keenly the nature of this life of variety by a close observation[3], one finds that behind the world[4] of variety is one life, the source and goal of all things. It is that life which may be called the blood of the universe, circulating through the veins of the universe. It is substance, or spirit, or life; something out of which all that is seen and all intelligence is moulded and kept alive and in working order. It is this life which is, so to speak, the veins of the universe and this we know and term intelligence. No doubt we often confuse the word intelligence with intellect, but intelligence is something which is to be found even in the lower creation. It can be traced in plant life, and sensed even in the heart of the rock.

The difference between modern psychology and ancient thought is

Documents:

Sk.tp.1 = a typescript prepared by Sakina Furnée or under her supervision, indicated as coming from "different papers handed down by Murshida Green", and probably made from Murshida Green's handwritten reporting or a typed copy of that reporting, not found in the archives.

Sk.tp.2 = a carefully typed copy, double-spaced on fine paper, prepared under Sakina Furnée's supervision, evidently from a source different from the one used for Sk.tp.1. This was separately copied for Sakina Furnée's set of typescripts and given a different number; this copy is identical to Sk.tp.2 except for very minor copying errors, and is therefore not included in the notes.

SF. = a published version of the lecture, appearing in *Sufism*, a Sufi journal, for September, 1924, on pp. 4-7. The journal, and therefore presumably this article, was edited by Murshida Sophia E. M. Green, who took down the lecture originally. This text is very similar, but not identical, to Sk.tp.2.

An edited form of this lecture was published in *The Sufi Message* series in volume 14 (London, 1998), "The Smiling Forehead"; it is not included in the notes.

Notes:

1. Sk.tp.1: on a copy of this typescript, the words "Rep. Mda. Green" (meaning reported by Murshida Green) written in ink, and then "has been copied in slightly alterated [sic] form as No. 155" (indicating its placement in Sakina Furnée's set of typescripts); Sk.tp.2 : on top, written in pencil, "Private Lecture", but "Private" crossed out and "Public" substituted; on the "set" copy, "For Mureeds" typed at top, later crossed out in ink and "Public Lecture" substituted
2. Sk.tp.2 begins here
3. Sk.tp.2, SF.: "by a close observation" omitted
4. Sk.tp.2: "wall" instead of "world"

that modern psychology says[5] the intellect is a development which manifests in the life of man as mind. But animals[6] have no mind, [7]it is a development of matter, a work of[8] the brain. The idea of the mystics of all times[9], the prophets, and all meditative souls differs; they say, what was is, and will be,[10] and if it is the same substance or[11] life, it is not subject to change, nor does it develop; it is the different grades[12] which we are capable of grasping which gives[13] us the feeling that it is a development rising from matter. The great ones, the meditative souls who sat in the wilderness and the forests and communicated with the life around them, realized this truth, and very often they experienced a greater harmony and peace and upliftment if[14] there was no visible life. Life is intelligence even in the rock[15], and the more one communicates with life, the more one feels that even the rock is not without life, that through it pulses the blood of the universe.

Someone once said to a Brahmin: "O Brahmin, how absurd it is for you to worship a god made of stone, an idol; the true God is the[16] formless one, the one above all things of this world." The Brahmin said: "Do you know the phenomenon of faith? If you have faith in the one[17] God of the rock, you will get your answer, but if you have no faith in your formless God, even he will not communicate with you."

Life seen from this point of view tells us that there is no place, no object which is not sacred, that even in a rock one sees the source and goal of all things in that particular form. Many who are experienced in the life of the plant know how responsive plants are to the sympathy of the man who loves nature[18] and looks after them. I was so[19] interested[20] in meeting a modern scientist in California (Mr. B.)[21]; he[22] devotes his life to the[23] research into plant life. How true it is that through whatever channel one pursues the truth, he arrives at an experience which shows the[23] truth. I was

---

5. Sk.tp.2, SF.: "claims that" instead of "says"
6. Ibid..: "; but says that the lower animals" instead of "But animals"
7. Ibid..: "that" added
8. Ibid..: "depending upon" instead of "a work of"
9. Sk.tp.1: the "-s" crossed out in ink; Sk.tp.2, SF.: "time"
10. SF.: The words "was", "is" and "will be" italicized for emphasis
11. Sk.tp.2: "of" instead of "or"
12. Ibid.: "a different grade" instead of "the different grades"
13. Sk.tp.2, SF.: "give" instead of "gives"
14. Ibid..: "where" instead of "if"
15. Ibid..: "everywhere" instead of "even in the rock"
16. Sk.tp.2: "a" instead of "the"
17. Sk.tp.1: "one" later crossed out in ink;
    Sk.tp.2, SF.: "one" omitted
18. Sk.tp.2, SF.: "nature" omitted
19. Ibid..: "much" instead of "so"
20. Ibid..: "lately" added
21. Sk.tp.1: "(Mr. B.)" was Luther Burbank (see List), whom Pir-o-Murshid Inayat Khan had met in the spring of 1923 in Santa Rosa, California, during his visit to America; Sk.tp.2, SF.: "(Mr. B.)" omitted
22. Sk.tp.2, SF.: "who" instead of "he"
23. Ibid..: "the" omitted

especially interested in the statement of the[24] scientist who said: "I regard plants as really living beings. I work with them always feeling that they are living creatures, they have their own trend of mind; they show obstinacy, they feel your sympathy, and if you learn to understand them, you can manage to derive a great deal of benefit from them. All through my life I have talked to plants as I would talk to man". Here again is the blood of the universe in circulation in a higher grade than in the rock.

. . . [25], the scientist of Bengal, has devoted much time and thought to prove that plants breathe; and if breath is to be found in the[23] plant life, certainly there is intelligence there[26]. I once happened to see a stone [27]a person possessed; he called it a magic stone, but in reality it was quite an ordinary stone[28]. It changed its colour often, and especially when in the hand of a particular person it showed a different colour and shade. So the stone can respond to the person's mind. This teaches that there is a great deal to explore in the mineral kingdom. This is not a discovery of today; it has been known by the people[29] of ancient times. We read in Persian poetry[30] of Jalal-ud-Din Rumi[31], who lived 700 years ago,[32] that God slept in the mineral, dreamed in the vegetable, became[33] conscious in the animal, and realized himself in the human being.

But this one life is to be seen more pronouncedly[34] in human beings, in the intellect they show, in the work they do, in the magnetizing of the atmosphere, in the thought power they exercise, in the influence of healing; all this shows that though[35] one person is separated from another, that[36] there may be no outer connection, yet even from a distance the influence of thoughts and feelings are felt. There were many instances of this during the war, when the mothers and wives of soldiers in times of sorrow, illness and[37] death, felt the trouble without any outer[38] source of communication. How often, when people are in close touch, each feels the other's condition, not

---

24. Sk.tp.2: "this" instead of "the"
25. Sk.tp.1: later the name "Jagadish Chandra Bose" (see List) written by Sk. in ink in the ellipsis;
    Sk.tp.2, SF.: "Another scientist, Prof. Bose," instead of ". . . , the scientist"
26. Sk.tp.2, SF.: "also" instead of "there"
27. Ibid..: "that" added
28. Sk.tp.2: instead of "quite an ordinary stone", "quit ordinary", where the "quit" is a typographical error for "quite"; SF.: "quite ordinary"
29. SF.: "peoples" instead of "people"
30. Sk.tp.2, SF.: "poems" instead of "poetry"
31. Jalal-ud-Din Rumi (see List)
32. Sk.tp.2, SF.: "who lived 700 years ago," omitted
33. Sk.tp.2: "becomes" instead of "became"
34. Sk.tp.2, SF.: "pronounced" instead of "pronouncedly"
35. Ibid..: "although" instead of "all this shows that though"
36. Ibid..: "although" instead of "that"
37. Ibid..: "or" instead of "and"
38. Sk.tp.2: "other" rather than "outer"

only by thought waves, but in the realm of feeling[39]; this shows that there is one body, and in that body there is one life, which as blood continually circulates[40].

This gives a logical explanation of the law of cause and effect. A wrongdoer may escape earthly witness, but he cannot escape this one life in which he lives and moves and has his being. A person who has done good to another perhaps never sees that one again, yet good must return to him again, because there is one body and one life. As with the circulation in the physical body all[41] one eats is absorbed as essence in the blood, so our every thought, word, and action affects the one life. Often people wonder and ridicule certain superstitions. They say[42]: Why[43] can the[44] past, present, and future be read from cards? This, and the science of astrology, and crystal-gazing, may be explained by this, that there is one life in which the circulation is always pulsing, one music, one rhythm; one[45] only needs to be acquainted with the theme of the music, then one[46] can read and understand.

But not only by cards and crystal-gazing, but by all means one can read the past, present, and future; if one is able to communicate with even one vein of this one life, then one is in touch with [47]the veins of all the universe.[47] Some means are better, some are worse, but through a[48] medium one can understand, thus proving that there is one life behind it[49] all. Man may be taught to do good, to learn righteousness, but this is virtue forced on him as the result of a certain teaching; real virtue only comes by understanding the oneness[50] of life, [51]binding man with friend or enemy[52].

Jesus Christ teaches: "Love your enemies."[53] [54]When it is often difficult to love one's friends, one is not able to love one's enemies unless one realizes the secret of the one life behind all, in spite of the world of variety continually creating[55] illusion.

If by religion, philosophy, or mysticism this is attained, then the

---

39. Sk.tp.2: "also" added; SF.: "also" added before "this" at beginning of next part of the sentence
40. Sk.tp.2, SF.: "continually circulates as does the blood in the veins" instead of "as blood continually circulates"
41. Ibid..: "that" added
42. Sk.tp.2: "as" (probably a typographical error for "ask") instead of "say"
43. Sk.tp.2, SF.: "How" instead of "Why"
44. Sk.tp.2: "the" omitted
45. Sk.tp.2, SF.: "a person" in place of "one"
46. Ibid..: "he" instead of "one"
47. Sk.tp.2: "all the veins of the universe." instead of "the veins of all the universe."
48. Sk.tp.2, SF.: "any" in place of "a"
49. Sk.tp.1: "it" crossed out in type (possibly indicating it was typed by mistake); Sk.tp.2, SF.: "it" omitted
50. Sk.tp.2: the word "oneness" underlined for emphasis; SF.: "oneness" in italics
51. Sk.tp.2, SF.: "thus" added
52. Ibid..: "and enemy alike" instead of "or enemy"
53. Matthew 5:44
54. Sk.tp.2, SF.: the previous sentence continued with ", and when" instead of ". When"
55. Ibid..: "which continually creates" instead of "continually creating"

secret of life is touched, and almighty[56] power is gained without any wonder-working. This lesson is easy to learn intellectually, but this is not enough; this truth can be taken as a food in a moment, but to digest it, all[57] life is not sufficient, for truth is mixed with facts. [58]When truth becomes a fact it has no importance. Absorbed in the world of variety, we are apt to forget truth, for we are always absorbed in facts. Therefore, meditative people who spend much time in meditation try to think of the oneness of being, try to meditate on the ultimate truth of being. It works like winding a clock; it only takes a minute to wind, and all day long it goes on. So in meditation the same thought goes on, and in everything one does or says one uses this same truth.

What effect is caused by the lack of understanding of this truth? All disasters, such as wars, floods, earthquakes, famines; all the things that cannot be helped by man come from disorder in the body, the only body which exists. When the blood is disordered all goes wrong, and though sometimes it seems as though[59] what is disadvantageous to one part is advantageous to another, yet in the long run one sees that all suffer. The after-effect is felt by the whole world as strain and pain, and all kinds of suffering.

The soul of the whole creation is one; the life behind all these ever-moving phantoms is one. Meditation on this, and awakening to this truth, will harmonize the condition of the world.

The prophets and great mystics have come to the world from time to time as the physician comes to help the patient who is in disorder, and each time the great ones have come, they have brought to the world another life, a new life brought[60] to the whole[61] organism of the universe to help it to run smoothly. The Sufis, who have existed in all times as mystics, whose lives have been devoted to meditation and spiritual practices, what have they learnt from these meditations?

They have learnt the essence of all, [62]and have called it: . . . , meaning unity,[62] and in thinking unity, in realizing it, and in living it, one[63] fulfills the purpose of life.

---

56. Ibid..: "a mighty" instead of "almighty"
57. Ibid..: "the whole of" instead of "all"
58. Ibid..: the previous sentence continued with ", and when" instead of ". When"
59. Sk.tp.2: "as though" omitted
60. Sk.tp.1: "brought" crossed out in ink, and "see p. 4ª 1) Given" written in margin (the reference is unclear); Sk.tp.2, SF.: "given" instead of "brought"
61. Sk.tp.2: "whole" omitted
62. Sk.tp.2, SF.: "the Oneness, or Unity;" instead of "and have called it: . . . , meaning unity,"
63. Ibid..: "man" instead of "one"

An article in the magazine *Sufism*

---

[1] January 30th, 1924

The Kingship of God

[2]Beloved ones of God,

My subject this evening is the kingship of God.[2] The God ideal has been regarded by different men differently. Some have idealized God as the king of earth and heaven. Some have a conception of God as a person, others think of God as an abstraction. Some believe in God, others do not. Some raise the ideal of the deity to the highest heaven, others bring it down to the lowest depth of earth. Some picture God in paradise, others make an idol and worship it. There are many ideas and many beliefs, different names, such as pantheism, idolatry, belief in a formless God, of belief in many gods and goddesses. But all are striving after something in one way or another.

If I were asked how many conceptions there are of God, I would say, as many as there are souls, for all, whether wise or foolish, have some conception of God. Everyone[3] knows God in some way, and has his own picture of him, either as a man, as the absolute, as goodness, as something beautiful or illuminating; everyone has some conception, and for the one who does not believe in God, even for him the name exists. Very often the unbeliever is an unbeliever because of his own vanity, though this is not always so. He says that only simple people believe in God; he sees that there are millions of simple souls who worship God, and yet it does not raise them

---

Documents:

SF. = an article in the magazine *Sufism* for December, 1924, pp. 1-5. The magazine, and therefore presumably this article, was edited by Murshida Sophia Green, who may also have taken down the talk originally, as it was given in London.

Sk.tp. = a typed copy of the article, prepared by Sakina Furnée or under her supervision. Two minor corrections to the typing are indicated by "(Sk.tp.)Sk.cr."

Hq.tp. = a stencilled copy prepared at Headquarters, Geneva, for distribution to Sufi centres as a part of the Religious Gatheka series. This seems to have been made from the article, and shows only minor differences. In the files is also a typed copy of this Religious Gatheka, identical in wording and therefore not included in the notes.

Notes:

1. Hq.st.: "RELIGIOUS GATHEKA." and "Number 41." at the top, followed by the Sufi Invocation (see List).
2. Ibid.: this opening sentence omitted
3. All documents: the word "Everyone" is written (in this sentence only) as two words ("Every one")

higher, and so he sees no virtue in the worship of God. Others believe in the God-ideal so long as they are happy, but when their condition changes, when sorrow and trouble comes, they begin to doubt whether there really is a God. I have often met people who had had a great belief in God, but having lost a dear one, and having vainly prayed and implored God that they might keep him, they had lost their belief. I once met a most unhappy mother who had given up her belief in God after the death of her only child. It grieved me to think that a soul so religious, tender and fine, by that one great sorrow in life had given up her faith; I told her, that while I sympathized with her most deeply, at the same time in giving up her faith she had brought to herself a much greater loss for which nothing could make up. In the Bible we read, and in the other scriptures, that we should glorify the name of God.

There is a question: Is God raised higher by man's worshipping him; or is he made greater by man's belief in him? The answer is that God is independent of all that man can do for him. If man worships[4] God, believes in him and glorifies him, it is for man's own good; for belief in God serves the greatest and only purpose in life, for the fulfilment of which man was born, and that purpose is the attainment of that perfection which may be called divine.

Why must God be called a king? Why not any other name? The answer is that it is impossible for words to explain or define God, but all that man can do is use the best word for the greatest being, the supreme being, and he uses this word because language is poor and he can find no other or better one.

Again comes the question of the metaphysician or the philosopher when he reads all is God and God is all. He says: If God is goodness, what then is the opposite of goodness? Is it outside God? If so, God is limited. Then something else exists as well as God. Are there two powers, rival[5] powers? What is the power called evil? It is true that God is all, but you would not call a man's shadow the man. What is evil then? It is only a shadow. What is illness? It is another illusion. In reality there is only life, real existence; illness is lack of life, it is a shadow, an illusion.

The being of God is recognized by his attributes. Therefore man speaks of God as the just God, he sees all power, all goodness in God; but when the situation is changed, when he sees God as injustice, he begins to think that God is powerless and to judge the action of God. But one must look at this from a different point of view. Human beings are limited, imperfect, and from our own imperfect standpoint we try to judge the perfect being, or his perfect action. In order to judge, our vision must become as wide as the universe, then we might have a little glimpse of the justice which

4. Sk.tp.: "worship" instead of "worships" (probably a typographical error)
5. Hq.st.: "rivals" instead of "rival" (probably a typographical error)

is perfect in itself. But when we try to judge every action by limiting God and by attaching the responsibility of every action to God, we confuse our faith, and by our own fault we begin to disbelieve. The error is in man's nature. From childhood we think all we do and say is just and fair, and so when man thinks of God he has his own conception, and by that he tries to judge God and his justice. If he is forgiving, he tries to overlook God's apparent injustice and find goodness in God and to see the limitation of man. This is better, but in the end man will realize that every movement is controlled and directed from one source, and that source is the perfection of love, justice and wisdom, a source where nothing lacks. But it is so difficult for man to have a perfect conception of the God-ideal, and he cannot begin in a first lesson to conceive of God as perfect. So the wise must be tolerant of all the forms in which souls picture their God.

There is a story told of Moses. One day he was passing through a farm and he saw a peasant boy sitting quietly and speaking to himself and saying, "O God, I love you so, if I saw you here in these fields, I would bring you soft bedding and delicious dishes to eat, I would take care that no wild animals could come near you. You are so dear to me and I so long to see you; if you only knew how I love you I am sure you would appear to me." Moses heard and said, "Young man, how can you dare to speak of God so? He is the formless God and no wild beast or bird could injure him who guards and protects all." The young man bent his head sorrowfully and wept. Something was lost for him and he felt most unhappy. And then revelation came to Moses as a voice from within which said, "Moses, what have you done? You have separated a sincere lover from me. What does it matter what I am called or how I am spoken to? Am I not in all forms?" This story throws a great light, and teaches that it is only the ignorant who accuse another of a wrong conception of God. Everyone thinks the other person must believe in and worship his God. Everyone has his own conception of God, and this conception makes the stepping stone to the true ideal of God.

Then there are others who believe in God, but do not show their belief in any outward religious tendency. People often misunderstand them, and yet there is something very beautiful hidden in their heart, not understood, not known. There is a story told in the East of a man who used to avoid going to the house of prayer, who showed no outward sign, so that his wife often wondered if he had any belief in God, and she thought a great deal about this, and was very anxious about it. Then one day she said to her husband, "I am very happy today." The man was surprised, and asked what made her happy, and she said, "I was under a false impression, but now I have found out the truth I am glad." He asked: "What has made you glad?" and she replied, "I heard you saying the name of God in your sleep." He said, "I am very sorry." It was too precious, too great for him to speak of, and he felt it was a great blow after having hidden this secret in the deepest part of his being because it was too sacred to speak of. He could not bear it, and he died.

We cannot say from the outward appearance who believes and who does not believe. One person may be pious and orthodox and it may mean nothing, and another may have a profound love for the deity and a great knowledge of him and no one may know it.

What benefit does man receive from believing in the kingship of God? How does he derive real help from his belief? He must begin by realizing the nobility of human nature. Not that one must expect everything to be good and beautiful, and if one's expectation is not realized, think there is no[6] hope of progress, for man is limited, his goodness is limited. No one has ever proved to be your ideal; you may make an ideal of your imagination and whenever you see goodness to be lacking, you may give from your own heart and so complete the nobility of human nature. This is done by patience, tolerance, kindness, forgiveness. The lover of goodness loves every little sign of goodness. He overlooks the faults and fills up the gaps by pouring out love and filling up that which is lacking. And this is real nobility of soul. Religion, prayer, worship are all intended to ennoble the soul, not to make it narrow, sectarian, bigoted. One cannot arrive at true nobility of spirit if one is not prepared to forgive imperfect human nature. For all, worthy or unworthy, require forgiveness, and only in this way can one rise above the lack of harmony and beauty, until at last one arrives at the stage when one reflects what one has collected.

All the riches of love, kindness, tolerance, good manners, a man then reflects and he throws the light on to[7] the other person and brings out those virtues[8] in that other, just as watering a plant makes the leaves and buds open and the flowers blossom. This brings one nearer to the perfection of God in whom alone one sees all that is perfect, all that is divine. As it is said in the Bible, "Be ye perfect, even as your Father in heaven is perfect."[9] [10]

[11]

---

6. (Sk.tp.)Sk.cr.: "no" skipped in the typing, later added in ink
7. Ibid.: "to" skipped in the typing, later added in ink
8. Sk.tp.: "virtue" instead of "virtues" (probably a typographical error)
9. Matthew 5:48
10. Sk.tp. "December, 1924." added, indicating the publication date
11. Hq.st.: "To be read at the Service of the Universal Worship." added

1

The Practice of the Presence of God

Beloved ones of God,

My subject this evening is the practice of the presence of God, a subject which is the central theme of the Sufi message.

There are many believers of the God-ideal in the world, and yet all believers do not profit fully by their belief for the reason that the belief which must help them to go forward is the belief which keeps them backward, standing in one place. Then they do not get the full benefit of it. It is, therefore, that many people in the world, after having believed in the God-ideal, once they meet with disappointment or some distress, some heart-breaking, then they feel that if there was God such things would not happen. And in that way they lose their belief because they have a belief but nothing to strengthen it.

Belief in God begins with the idea. One begins because someone has told one to believe; from the parents one has heard, from one's relative, or teacher, or clergyman one has heard there is a God and one believes, and so long as it is in the imagination it is something, yet it has not become a true belief. True belief comes when from an imagination it becomes a reality. And no one can claim to be a true believer in God, but one can practise. And it is this practice which from beginning to end is the breath of religious life. And in the perfection of this belief is the fulfilment of the purpose of life. One may learn metaphysics and philosophy and mysticism and occult powers, and one may work wonders, but if one has not developed that belief in God, one has not fulfilled the life's purpose.

And now one wonders how a person should set to work to develop his belief. The first step is to depend upon God more than one depends upon outer things. One becomes so accustomed to depend upon the outer things that one depends only upon them, and God is only in one's belief.

There is a story told in India of a peasant who had once seen a king,

---

Document:

Sk.tp. = exceptionally, the typescript prepared by Sakina Furnée or under her supervision is the only document known for this lecture. P-o-M. is known to have given a lecture with this title in London on 1 February and in Southampton on 10 February. The source of the text is unknown (see note 1).

Notes:

1. Later Sk. wrote "handwriting unknown" in ink at the top, and also "Public Lecture"

who was disguised as a traveller, and did not see he was a king. He visited this poor man's house and was warmly welcomed; and when the disguised king was leaving this peasant's home, he said, "If at any time in your life you are in need you must come to me", and he gave him a certain sign to show in the city so that they would bring him to the king. The peasant never thought about it, but famine came and he was in a difficult position. The children began to starve and there was a great need felt of help from somewhere. In this time of difficulty, he thought of some traveller having come to his house and having said to him that if he would come and find him he would be helped. So this peasant went to the city and was taken to the court. He was very much astonished to think that it was a king who called him. And yet he went there, and as he entered the room he saw that the king was engaged in his prayers. This man waited till the king finished his prayers, and as he finished his prayers and got up, he asked of this peasant, "I am very glad to see you. Is there any thing you wish to ask?" And this peasant, instead of telling him his difficulty, asked him as his first question, "Tell me, please, why you who are a king had to bow your head to someone else?" The king said, "He is the King of Kings and I also must bow before him, for we owe our power to him." The peasant understood with his limited understanding and said, "If this is so I must not tell you all my difficulty. I have found the King of Kings whom I will tell." The king was so touched by this belief and the strength of the belief of this peasant that he thought his whole life's prayers could not compare with this one moment's belief which gave him strength and understanding to tell the king, "I will not tell you my difficulty."

What does it show? It shows a simple belief but a living belief. When the belief becomes living it performs miracles. As long as the belief is only in the imagination, it is only a belief; it is an imagination, it is floating in the air. But when that belief becomes a conviction, then it takes root; something which is in the air takes root in the earth, and the plant rises as far as the heavens. Its root is in the ground. It is solid, dependable.

This belief is developed by believers in God in different ways. They begin to study the laws of nature, and by this study they do not lose their belief; on the other hand, their belief is strengthened. As Rumi says in his *Masnavi*[2], "When looking at these same germs, and worms, and insects, what small and tiny little things they seem to be; one might think they would be forgotten by God. Yet do not they receive their food?" They find what perfect wisdom can be found in providence. The hand of providence can support every living creature on the earth, the smallest insect, germ, or worm. And yet man becomes anxious about himself, and becomes worried about the morrow and troubles himself and gives way to anxiety and loses the sense of

2. For Jelal-ud-din Rumi and his *Masnavi*, see List

justice in him, gives up that kindness, that mercy, that compassion, that love which is the element of God in him, which is for his daily bread. And when he cannot get it and does not see any source to get it from, then he worries over it and troubles himself. Sa'di[3] says in connection with this idea that man worries over his daily bread because it is a disease. [4]Yet for the one who works, for him always are busy all the things of his needs.[4] But when a man worries so, it is his disease. He cannot help it.

Man has made his life so complicated! Yet all the beasts and birds live fully and happily and all depend for their life's sustenance on nature's wisdom and never worry about it. It is man who worries because man makes his life more complicated. Besides that, with illness and with other troubles of life, all different kinds, man always seeks for things from the outside world which might help him. And by doing so he always forgets that source which is within himself and so, becoming more and more material, he loses his faith. Whatever be his outward religion, that strength which might be given to the faith, that becomes less. Now the medicine of the birds and animals which live in the forest is the open air and the herbs they eat and the pure water they drink. All the medicine they receive in their trouble is that, and they become well.

What does it show? It shows that nature provides man with everything that he needs, in his illness, in his trouble, in his difficulty, and it is all there, within him and without him. Within him is the source of all things. Without him appear things in name and form, and therefore, to get the essence of all things, one has to find it in God. When once God becomes a reality, man shows in his life great fulness.

The Christian religion has from the beginning taught to appreciate the daily bread given to us. Every religion has gratefulness as the central truth in it and the appreciation of all beauty, and so one develops in oneself that belief by appreciating all that comes. If there was nothing else to thank for, to live under the sun is something that one could thank for over and over, and it is never enough. How much there is that one could appreciate and thank God about and be grateful.

Sa'di, the great poet of Persia, writes in Hindustani[5] an account of his life where he says, "Once I was walking in the sun barefooted and I thought, 'Oh, how miserable I am to be without shoes!' And after having walked like this for a few moments, I saw a lame person who had no shoes and I thanked God that I had no shoes, but that my feet were all right."

If one could appreciate life there is much to appreciate, but everyone

---

3. Sa'di (see List)
4. This sentence, though oddly worded, is as it appears in the typescript
5. Sa'di actually wrote in Farsi; P-o-M. might have been familiar with a Hindustani or Urdu translation

will not see that everyone can appreciate, but will only see things which one can make complaints about. There is a lot to make complaints about, and so one becomes so complaining that one sees nothing but complaining and everything is horrible and everything is a trouble and so one goes on from morning to evening; and where there is no appreciation, there is no God. One has not time to think of God; one only thinks how miserable one is in one's own life. And so one has no time to develop that belief in God.

This tendency to thank God does give a person a habit to thank God and to remember God in every little thing one does from morning to evening, and by doing so one develops that gratefulness and appreciation in one's nature and in the people one comes in contact with from morning to evening. It is grateful to thank people for their little courtesy and kindness, and in this way the blessing multiplies and becomes greater and greater every day.

It is the one who does not appreciate the blessing of his life who becomes worse and worse every day and more and more miserable, until the whole life becomes miserable. It is not that there is nothing to appreciate in his life, but he only looks at the miseries and so becomes more and more miserable. People create greater and greater miseries for themselves and for others, and if they believe in God and if they do not believe in God, in both cases they do not profit by it.

The belief in God is profit and the profit is gained by the development of this tendency. As one goes further in the belief of God, one begins to realize a sense, so to speak, opening a sight which can appreciate beauty in all its different forms. So long as the heart is closed that sense is closed. When the heart is open that sense is open, the senses which shows man beauty in all its different forms, of all different faiths, the beauty of all conditions. And when that sense is opened, then whether in the home or outside of the home, whether in the open air in the country, whether looking up or down, whether with the eyes closed or open, there is always something to admire, there is always something beautiful to suggest, to remind one of the God, the Lord of beauty.

By doing this it is like a person developing appreciation for art. For it is not everyone who can appreciate art. It is the one whose sense of art has developed to appreciate. And when once a person begins to appreciate the art, it is that person who knows the artist. There will come a thousand persons who will look at the piece of art, but there will be perhaps one among the thousand who really understands the soul of the artist, who understands the beauty of the art, who understands what is behind it. And it is that person who is the real friend of the artist because he knows the soul of the artist, and so is the believer of God. When the believer of God has opened his heart, then the believer of God is beginning to see the beauty of creation and to communicate with the beauty; and then he comes to know the artist who is behind this beauty. It is then that he is the true friend of God because he not only believes in God, but sees his signs with open eyes.

In every work of art, be it poetry, be it painting, be it music, you can be a friend of the artist (you can come closer to the artist) by understanding his art; and so one comes closer to God by understanding, by appreciating more and more all he has made. And then what happens? Then a person develops in his nature that sight which sees God in all things, which reminds him of the artist in his art everywhere, in human nature which is very often most jarring and most trying, trying one's patience and most troublesome to deal with. And yet there is a beautiful side to it, which is the same if one can open one's eyes to look at it.

There is a beauty in the infant, there is a beauty in the child's simplicity, there is a beauty in the youth. In every age there is a beauty. There is a certain development of manner, of thought and of experience. It becomes possible in every age, in all situations. If once a person has begun to look at beauty, one sees a beauty reflected in every form, and the only thing which lacks beauty is the shadow. It is non-existent. When one sees beauty, one sees beauty; one does not look at the shadow. But there are others who will look at the shadow. And these who look at the shadow of this illusion, they see and they do not see. Their eyes are open and yet they are closed.

But now there is a step further. A person goes and sees that: All this beauty which I see which is outside, and all this power and goodness and wisdom, the sign of which I see in everything and in all things, where is the source of it? Where can I find the one source in which all this unites and becomes one? And that naturally comes when that person with his opened heart, who has seen beauty outside and has closed his eyes and is one with his heart, sees all this reflected in his own heart. He can sit by the lake of his own heart and see therein the whole beauty reflected. And it is from this point that mysticism begins.

From this point a man begins to realize that: All that I saw before me is manifestation, but within me is something more wonderful hidden, and when my heart is open it becomes as a door for me to look into, something which stands as the source and goal of all this. From that time one begins to meditate, one begins to make a silence. If a person is not prepared for this, tell him to sit quiet and he will feel restless, and if he were to try to make his mind restful, his mind will go on from one thing to another. But once the heart is open and prepared, as soon as a man has closed his eyes he still finds another door open, a door which leads to the heavens, the unearthly joy which may be called the greatest ecstasy. One sees what is to be found there. Is there any form? Is there any name? It is so difficult to explain. What the prophets have said is, when people liked fairies and ghosts and spirits, that there are fairies, ghosts, and angels and delicious dishes. It is all there in paradise. They picture paradise because they cannot explain it more than this, but really speaking it is more than paradise. Paradise is really only for the imagination of the one who wants to please himself by thinking of the things he loves most. This is more than paradise, this is the essence of all beauty, the essence of all understanding, the essence of all justice, all love, all peace; the essence of all that one seeks outwardly is there.

But you may ask: Essence? The essence is not very interesting. I would not like to have all things in their essence. But I shall answer: The essence is certain, is more interesting, even in the ordinary sense of the word. It is the essence of grapes which is wine, which one loves more than grapes; it is the essence of milk which is butter, which is the need of every person in the world. The essence is such a thing that even in the material things, such as the essence of flowers, which is honey, it is more desirable. The essence in its every aspect must be more valuable and more interesting if one only knew what it is, if one only experienced it. The essence of wisdom is not only wisdom but it is the result of wisdom, the sum total of it.

There are five things which man seeks after: light, life, power, happiness, and peace. And all these five things are to be attained in one thing, and that is the essence. It is this essence which is called in religious words a wine. It is this essence which is perfection. It is this essence of which it is spoken in the Bible: "Be ye perfect even as the Father is perfect in heaven."[6] It is towards this perfection that by the help of the belief in God we must make our way, and at the end it is this perfection which we must attain to, which is the ideal goal of all happiness.

God bless you.

---

6. Matthew 5:48

Febr. 2nd 1924[1]

Through Limitation To Perfection

Beloved ones of God,

My subject this evening is through limitation to perfection. Limitation is the condition of man, and perfection is his hope. Limitation is what he experiences, and perfection is what he longs for. Limitation it is to which all the tragedy of life belongs, and perfection is the place where limitation ends. Therefore there is no one in the world, whether wise or foolish, who does not long for perfection. The difference is that the one does not know what he longs for while the other does, but to attain perfection is the true longing of every soul.

And how does he see perfection? Generally as a traveller may see from the ship the horizon, which shows limitation, and yet as one goes further the horizon moves further on, and so it is with perfection. The one who feels the need of the things of the material world, he thinks these things are what he should aim after, and this attainment brings about contentment, but only for the moment. It does not last, and he says: This is not enough. And this is so not only with worldly possessions, but power, strength; he wants more and more and is never satisfied, because limitation still remains, and what happens is that as he gains all things he feels more and more limited. The treasures of earth, which cost more than they are worth, man thinks will bring him satisfaction, but there is no satisfaction. Man strives after power, possessions, rank, or influence, and when he has gained them he finds that all these things need fuel, and that that fuel takes out of him all that he has, and yet he is still far from the perfection for which his soul longs.

Very often after long disappointment a man begins to wonder: Is there anything, anywhere, that will bring peace, the touch of happiness, satisfaction?, and at last he learns that if he finds it, it can only be found within himself. So through mysticism, religion, philosophy, or whatever method the wise ones employed, they had only one object and that was to

---

Document:

Sk.tp. = a typescript prepared by Sakina Furnée or under her supervision; for the probable source, see footnote 1.

Notes:

1. Underneath the date, Sakina typed "Handwriting Kefayat Lloyd.", indicating that the lecture was taken down by Kefayat G.I. LLoyd (see List); however, no such reporting has been found to date

attain to the perfection of which Christ spoke when he said, "Be ye perfect even as your Father in heaven is perfect"[2]. Many will ask: Is it possible for mankind to arrive at perfection?, and it is difficult to answer, for the answer stands above the comprehension of the generality. They say these are the words of Christ, so one listens to them, but if any other had said them one could not listen. How can one believe that man could be perfect? It is like comparing the bubble with the ocean; it is like saying that the glittering atom in the air is to be compared with the sun. But yet we see in everything expansion, progress. The artist may begin his work in a small way, and at last arrives at a stage when his work is so beautiful that he cannot believe that it is his. The musician composes or plays a piece that is so great and so wonderful that he cannot imagine that he did it. Something great is being expressed through him. He is the channel and he forgets himself entirely. Or the great inventor may seem to be occupied with material things, and yet he arrives at a point where he has invented something so wonderful that he cannot say what is the source from whence he learnt it. He can only say that something has sprung from somewhere and has expressed itself through him. No doubt the reason is that man is the slave of the mind. Every time a person asks "why", reason stands by his side and says so and so, but the time comes when the reason can give no explanation and then the soul feels it is because it must be; there is no question any longer of why.

What is reason? It is a collection of experiences that man has gathered, the knowledge of names and forms. There is one stage in every art and science, in every occupation when one feels: I am doing it, it is my production; there is another stage when the person begins to think: It is not I who am doing it, but it is the art which inspires me, and so he forgets himself in his work, in his art that lives.

The third stage is the stage when there is upliftment, intoxication. When something that the art suggests, whether music, poetry, painting, gives such great exaltation—no reason, no definite suggestion—but a great upliftment, and when a person arrives at this stage he forgets everything in a divine intoxication which the Sufis call *wajd*[3], meaning ecstasy. This is something which is experienced by those who have touched the depths of the art to which they have devoted their lives. One might think that musicians are accustomed to meditation and in using their music for the upliftment of the soul they experience ecstasy. But poets also write verses, and the suggestion they express is so beautiful that it makes their souls dance; they are lifted above the earth. A person who has touched such perfection in whatever form begins to show it at times even in the everyday life.

I have always had a desire to see the great devotees of art and

---

2. Matthew 5:48
3. The Sufi word for ecstasy, literally meaning "finding" (see Glossary)

science, considering it my privilege to do so. Once in the city where I lived in India I was told that a wrestler of great fame was coming and though wrestling was not a thing in which I was interested, I felt that he had such a great name that I would like to see him. I had a curiosity, and when I saw him I did not see the wrestling but the childlike innocence of the man. He had no conceit, no pride, he was a man who never knew that he was great. This shows that in whatever line perfection is touched, whether on the material or spiritual plane, it shows itself in some form.

When travelling in the U.S.[4] I saw the celebrated scientific botanist, Mr Burbank[5], a man who had devoted all his life to the science of botany. I found that his life had taught him philosophy, what he did was his religion, and he talked like a sage and mystic. He said, "I work with trees and plants as though they were human beings. I love them, and they feel my sympathy". Does not this show that perfection in whatever form changes the attitude of man, as the philosopher's stone turns into gold? So when man has touched perfection it turns his personality into gold. It may be touched in quite a small way, in science or art, in boxing or wrestling. For perfection is so vast and there are stages of perfection, but even just touching blesses man with something which is beyond explanation.

But spiritual perfection consists of all aspects of perfection. Spiritual perfection is the perfection to which every soul is attracted. Through whatever channel, the destination is spiritual perfection; all other aspects are only stepping stones. Is there any sincere soul that is not entitled to this perfection? No, every earnest desire has an answer. No one has ever truly striven in pursuit of perfection and has not touched it. The difficulty is that man does not believe in himself, he becomes so pessimistic that he disbelieves in himself, in others, in perfection, and even in God. Tell someone that a person is bad and foolish and stupid, and he at once believes it, no proofs are needed; but tell him that someone is good and fine and he says: No, I cannot believe it, it is not possible. Man has lost faith in his fellow beings, in God, and in truth.

Today man is so afraid of the word spiritual, mystical, philosophical, or religious, that he runs away because he has been so often disappointed. He says: I must make money, that is the need of my life; if I can get money the cares of life will be off my mind! The word perfection is too great to mention, and yet is there one soul who will be satisfied without? A man may live in a palace surrounded by all the pleasure and luxury that life can give, and yet he is not happy, because he lacks the main thing in life.

One wonders how to attain spiritual perfection. Is it by being good, pious, or religious, by mystifying others? Nothing of this is of great

---

4. A common abbreviation for the United States of America
5. Luther Burbank (see List)

importance; what is necessary is sincerity in searching after truth, the easiest and the most difficult thing in the world. Few really search after truth. Truth is man's very being, it is the deepest self of man. Truth is self-revealing; it is the only thing which saves, and will save.

Whether we speak of salvation, in whatever language, by whatever people it is sought, they are all seeking one thing, and that is spiritual perfection. What holds man back? It is his love of complexity. Life makes for man a puzzle, and like a child he enjoys the puzzle. Truth is too simple for him; he attaches importance to what he cannot understand. If he is told that there is a sacred mountain a thousand miles away he will walk to it. In the ancient days the people were told that if they walked in a circle round the temple a hundred times they would gain much, and they went and felt they had made a pilgrimage. Such is human nature. Man longs for truth, he searches for truth, and yet he wants to escape from truth. Man wants mystery. He wants something that can be put into words. So long as the seeker has that desire he will remain in a puzzle, but for the one who wishes to come out the door is open. The heart of man is the abode of God. Christ said, "Seek ye first the kingdom of heaven, and all these things shall be added unto you"[6]. Solomon says, "There is nothing new under the sun"[7]. It is the same old way, there is only one way and the same way will remain, and this is the way that man runs away from.

Very often I feel amused when people say: There are so many different things, one looks from one angle and one from another, and we all see part of the truth. Truth is one and the same, it has no angles. There is only one truth in you and in me. Some say there is one way, and others there is another way. Yes, on earth there are many ways, but for the soul there is only one way. There are many names and forms. Some are attached to one church, some to another. What is a name? It is only for purposes of convenience. There is only one truth, and that is nameless; either you see it whole, or you see nothing. What keeps us back from perfection is that man is afraid that he will lose something, but he will lose nothing; by losing himself he gains himself, his true self. After that perfection is not very far away. It is only the next step.

Man has accustomed himself to think of things that are far from truth. Even in religion as well as in everyday life he is continually denying truth, and so he wanders far away because he becomes accustomed to everything but truth. If there is a meditation or spiritual practice by which man gets into communion with himself, it is only to make him accustomed to that one mainspring of life, which is in itself life's mystery.

---

6. Matthew 6:33
7. Ecclesiastes 1:9

Sakina Furnée's typescript

1

February 4th, 1924

Mureeds' Class

I wish to say a few words to my *mureeds*[2] that they will find useful in the path.

My mureeds must consider that the initiation given in the Sufi Order is a most secret and sacred trust, something too sacred to be spoken of before anyone. We must try, when speaking with friends, whether they sympathize with our ideals or not, to refrain from discussing our beliefs and principles, not to speak of phenomena or wonder-working, for the less we discuss, the more easy is the path. It is not the path for everyone; everyone does not care to tread it, and you will be discouraged and detained if you show yourself different from others. It is the humble who will go forward. The more humble we are, the more we shall progress. Our sacred religion is very near to our heart and soul; we cannot put it into words, and by trying to do so we lower it instead of raising it. We must hold fast to tact and wisdom as the most useful things on the path.

Secondly, we have a greater responsibility in our lives than the responsibility of the one who only leads the worldly life. We have two responsibilities, worldly responsibility and spiritual responsibility, and we can only carry the burden if we observe the rules, rules to enable us to strike the note of harmony in word[3], speech and action. We must first think and then act, and we must see that our thoughts, words and actions are harmonious. We must be harmonious not only with the one who is powerful, but with he[4] who is meek; not only with the wise, but also with the foolish and ignorant. Our burden is a double burden, the burden of the life in the world and of our high ideal, and we cannot carry it if we do not make harmony the keynote of our life.

If my mureeds prophesied, worked wonders, and performed

Document:

Sk.tp. = a typescript prepared by Sakina Furnée or under her supervision, which is the only document in the archives. The class was given in London, and the source of the text would appear to be Kefayat LLoyd's handwritten reporting (see Note 1), not found.

Notes:

1. At the upper left, Sk. wrote "Mureeds' Classes II" indicating the inclusion of this class in a series; below the date is typed "Handwriting Kefayat LLoyd"
2. The word *mureed* is used by Sufis to indicate an initiate (see Glossary)
3. Sk.tp.: later Sk. crossed out "word" and wrote "thought" in ink
4. Sk.tp.: later Sk. modified "he" to "him" in ink

miracles, that would not make me proud of them; but what will make me proud is if they will fulfil the duties of everyday life, be they great or small, satisfactorily; if they will think rightly, speak rightly and do right, thus giving an example to others and making life harmonious.

If we discuss doctrines and principles nothing is accomplished. Arguments become a kind of passion to which there is no end. If we endeavour to force our views on others, it makes us bigoted, narrow; our outlook must be tolerant. If our ideals are true and living, they will express themselves in our lives as a living phenomenon. If our soul has touched truth, we shall live the truth in which we believe. Instead of preaching to others we must serve others. There is no greater way of serving God than by serving our fellow-man in love. It is such a simple thing to remember, the attitude of friendliness, the thought of harmony in every little thing, and if we act thus then our success is sure.

The meditations and practices given to you must be done regularly, without break, and without any doubt as to their effects, for results come not only by the practices but by the faith in which they are done. The result is not often quick in coming, but if it is slow it is not the fault of the practice, but some fault in our own life. The practices will be as valuable as we consider them valuable.

There is no religion taught in the Sufi message which hinders you in your own faith. What is taught will deepen your own religion more and more, and those who have no religion will find in the Sufi message their belief in God. Our ideals are great, though it is true that our numbers are as yet small, in spite of the spread of the message in the United States, in Holland and Belgium, France, Italy, and Switzerland, and in other parts; but I do not consider that we have yet begun. When there are a thousand workers ready and willing to give their service in answer to the call, that day our work will begin. The difficulties in building up the work are great, numberless and without end, and though many things have straightened out in the last few years, and though the message has progressed, yet with the growth of the organization for the service of humanity the difficulties increase also. But we look not at the difficulties; there is no difficulty that cannot be surmounted, and remember that nothing can prevent us from rendering service to God and to humanity in this, our sacred task. If I were alone, and everyone was against me, to my last breath I would stand firm. My consolation is that there are truly devoted souls whom I can trust and depend on standing by my side ready to serve at every cost.

Realize your great responsibility and be conscious of your duty towards the furtherance of the message in the fulfilment of which we all shall accomplish the purpose of our life.

Sakina Furnée's typescript

[1]

Brighton, February 6th, 1924[2]

Mureeds' Class

The Religion of the Sufi

I wish to speak a few words to my mureeds on the subject of the religion of the Sufi. The religion of the Sufi is the religion of the heart. The principal moral of the Sufi is to consider the heart of others, so that in the pleasure and displeasure of his fellow-man he sees the pleasure and displeasure of God. It is so simple, and yet so difficult to practise. This teaching is the central theme of all religions. It is the thing which no one in the world does not know, and yet the practice of it is never enough.

What generally happens is that there are three intoxications which cover the tendency for considering the feelings of others and keep man ignorant [3] of that which is his own.

The first intoxication is produced by oneself; it is the consideration of one's own interest which covers the feeling of consideration for another. One is so absorbed in one's own interests in life that one is intoxicated by them and so does not see the importance of considering the feelings of others.

The second intoxication is that which comes from another person. If a person does not come up to one's ideal, if he does not act towards one as one wishes, if he does not answer one's expectation, if he jars upon one's fine feelings, if he is irritable, disagreeable, or of coarse vibrations, all this causes another intoxication which keeps one from feeling for another and sets one against him.

The third intoxication comes from conditions. There are conditions which offer temptations or which cause anxiety, fear, doubt, or confusion. Then there are conditions which promise profit or benefit, things which one desires in life, and under these circumstances another intoxication comes as

---

Document:

Sk.tp. = a typescript prepared by Sakina Furnée or under her supervision, which is the only document in the archive. It indicates a handwritten original (see Note 2), but as the class was given in Brighton, it is not certain whose handwriting would be referred to in this case.

Notes:

1. Later Sk. wrote "Mureeds' Classes II" indicating the inclusion of this class in a series
2. After the date, "In handwriting." is typed
3. Sk. inserted "of the knowledge" in ink at this point

a third cover over the heart.

A person may be wise, learned, and thoughtful, and yet these covers may keep him from seeing clearly the way of seeking the pleasure of every person he meets. This is the tragedy which causes much pain, even though it appears to have come from this or that source.

It matters little what church, faith, or religion a person belongs to, what doctrines or principles he believes in; what counts is that man is sincere. If he thinks and feels sincerely, he certainly is religious. The world does not need so much religious or philosophical people, it needs living hearts ready to serve and to feel the pain of others. If there is a religion, it is the religion of the heart. This religion is best lived if one offers prayers at every moment in the form of thoughtfulness and consideration towards our fellow-men.

The question is, How are we to learn this? Whatever be the condition[4] in our home or outside, we are always presented with opportunities to practise with those who love us, and those who hate us, those who understand us and those who misunderstand us, indeed with all. Life is an opportunity, and by realizing this we learn to make the most of it. Every time we lose an opportunity of consideration towards another we have lost a chance of worshipping a living God.

I do not expect my mureeds to become so clever in their studies that they will win in every argument, nor do I wish them to acquire such occult power that they will work wonders. If they told fortunes, drove away devils, if they tell things of which no one has ever heard, none of these things will give one[5] any pleasure. But I shall be proud of the mureed about whom I hear from another that he has been kind, thoughtful, sincere, and considerate; in this my mission will be fulfilled.

---

4. Sk. added an "s" at the end in ink, but then crossed it out
5. Originally "one" was typed, but then Sk. changed it to "me" in ink

Sakina's shorthand reporting

[1]

Paris, Sorbonne, February 16, 1924

[2]

My subject this evening is "The Ancient Music".[3]

From the Eastern p.o.v.[4] when one looks at this subject, one finds that Eastern idea of music is originated from intuition. But the tradition of any art, of[5] even science will tell[6] us the same thing. It is afterwards that man begins to believe in the outer things and forgets its origin, which is intuition. Music, according to the ancient people, it[7] was not a mechanical science or[8] art; music was the first language. The proof of this can be found even now in the language of the animals and birds, who express their emotions[9] and passions to one another. At which[10] same time there are no words, only sounds. It is the combination of the different sounds of the animals and birds which combined together have also an effect upon the[11] multitude of the lower creation. If music was the first expressive thing in the

---

Documents:

Sk.sh.	=	Sakina Furnée's shorthand reporting of the lecture, newly transcribed by B.v.d.B.
Lf.hw.	=	a handwritten reporting of a simultaneous French translation while the lecture was being given, made by Mlle H. Lefèbvre, an early French mureed living in Paris. This source is not mentioned further as it is fragmentary and provides no further evidence as to the English text.
Hq.tp.	=	a typescript made at Headquarters, Geneva ("N.71") from an unknown source. Sakina's corrections in ink are indicated in the notes as "(Hq.tp.)Sk.cr."
Sk.tp.	=	a typescript prepared by Sakina or under her direction, apparently using Hq.tp. as well as an unknown source, possibly her shorthand. Her corrections in ink are indicated in the notes as "(Sk.tp.)Sk.cr." A nearly identical typed copy of this document is mentioned only in footnote 8.
Sk.an.	=	some corrections made by Sakina on a separate list.

Notes:

1. Sk.tp.: "Public Lecture" typed in upper left corner
2. Sk.sh.: "The Ancient Music" in lh. in margin; a.o.d.: title added, "The Ancient Music"
3. A.o.d.: introductory sentence omitted: "My subject...Music."
4. Sk.sh.: "p.o.v." abbr. for "point of view"; written out in a.o.d.
5. A.o.d.: "or" instead of "of"
6. Sk.tp.: "tells" instead of "will tell"
7. A.o.d.: "it" omitted
8. Sk.tp.: "of" instead of "or"; (the typed copy of Sk.tp. reinstates "or")
9. Hq.tp.: "emotion" instead of "emotions"; (Hq.tp.)Sk.cr.: changed back to "emotions"
10. A.o.d.: "the" instead of "which"
11. Sk.sh.: a partially legible sh. symbol with "numberless" in margin lh., "numerous" may be an alternate sh. reading; a.o.d.: "numberless"

lower creation, so it was[12] in humankind also and since it was the first expression of the emotions and passions of the heart, it is the last expression also of the emotions and passions. For what art cannot express, poetry explains; and what P.[13] cannot express, that is expressed by music. And therefore music in all ages to a thinker will stand on the highest pedestal of the expression of the deepest of oneself. When the ancient music compares[14] with the modern, one will find no doubt which is too vast to gulf. But if there is anything can[15] by which one can have some little idea of the music of the human race, that is from the Eastern music, which has still traces of the ancient music in it. And the reason is, if it was kept by them as music perhaps it would not have been kept intact by them as it has been. But the reason is that it has been kept as a part of the religion and that is the reason why it has been kept on for thousands of years through the tradition. One might ask: How can a music of the ancient times be kept pure? Because always there is a tendency in the human nature to alter things. The thing is this, that it was difficult always with the human race to change religion. Anything else may be changed, but there was one thing that was always kept, and that was religion. The religion of the Hindus consequence[16] was Vedanta. Of[17] the Vedanta [18] the fifth aspect was music, which was called *Sama Veda*.

In the Western world there came a time when translations of these *Vedas* was[19] given. [20] It ought that fifth translation was to be found.[20] The reason is that it is,[21] that being musical it[22] could not very well be regarded as language. But one can trace back in traditions by the study of the music of the Hindus that there was a time before thousands of years, when they knew as fine a difference[23] of tones as quarter tones.

But it was not only the degree of the sound that was considered in that way, but also the nature and character of the sound was analyzed just like chemistry. We can find today in ancient traditions the different effects attached to the different notes; whether dryness or liquidity, whether cold or

---

12. Sk.sh.: illegible sh. symbol traced over to read "was"
13. Ibid.: "P." crossed out and "poetry" in lh. above; "poetry" in a.o.d.
14. Ibid.: "compare<u>d</u>" in lh. added above; "compared" [sic] in a.o.d.
15. Ibid.: "can" crossed out; omitted in a.o.d.
16. Ibid.: "consequence" crossed out; omitted in a.o.d.
17. A.o.d.: "In" instead of "Of"
18. Sk.sh.: a blank
19. Sk.tp.: "were" instead of "was"
20. Sk.sh.: in the margin: "and if there is a part that is not to be found it is that 5th *Veda*"; Hq.tp.: "and if there is a part that is not to be found, it is that fifth *Veda*." instead of "It ought that fifth translation was to be found."; (Hq.tp.)Sk.cr.: "that" (after "part") changed to "the translation of which"; Sk.tp.: "and if there is a part the translation of which is not to be found, it is that fifth *Veda*."
21. A.o.d.: "that it is," omitted
22. Hq.tp.: "they" instead of "it"; Sk.tp.: "they" instead of "it"; (Sk.tp.)Sk.cr., Sk.an.: changed back to "it"
23. Hq.tp.: "difference" crossed out and "distance" typed above; Sk.tp.: "distance" instead of "difference"

heat. No doubt, to distinguish these sounds which express these different effects is today difficult, because the distinguishing is now from the instruments and then[24] it was only from the nature.

And yet it is most interesting to know that we find today in Sanskrit scriptures the different pitch of sound distinguished in the ancient times. In the absence of pianos[25] or in the absence of tuning forks, they had to determine the pitch to the sound of different animals and birds and also the sound was distinguished from different ages[26].

One thing particularly, that scientific aspect developed in the same way as the art of the ancient Hindu[27]. One might wonder that it is perhaps natural that the art should develop, because they were near to the nature. But for that time for science to develop in a way is more interesting to know. One might ask in what way the art developed among the ancient people, the remembrance[28] of which is to be found even now in the East. The idea was that they attached different themes of music to different seasons, different strains[29] of music to different times of the day and night. And as there is nothing in the world which is without reason, also that was not only an imagination or fancy, there was a reason behind, which was a logical reason to find and[30] attribute certain melodies to certain times. If it was a poetic fancy it would have lasted for a little period and would have only influenced a little circle. But it has lasted for ages and[31] till now and influences[32] the whole country. A[33] usage which is[34] carried out for thousands of years and which continued and today[35] to be found East [36], North or South. That a[37] same *raga* sung in[38] the same time, when sung out of that time then it is not appealing. When [39]from the point of view,[40] metaphysic's point of view[39], we shall find that the realization that today the sciences make[41] and will ever

---

24. Sk.sh.: "then" crossed out; "in those times" added in lh. in the margin and included in a.o.d.
25. A.o.d.: "piano" instead of "pianos"
26. (Hq.tp.)Sk.cr.: "(?)" inserted above "ages" in ink; Sk.tp.: "(?)" typed after "ages"
27. Hq.tp.: "music" added after "Hindu"; changed to "Hindusmusic" by adding "s" in space between; Sk.tp.: "music" instead of "Hindu"; (Sk.tp.)Sk.cr.: "Hindus" added in margin in ink.; Sk.an.: "Hindu"
28. Sk.sh.: "reference" written above in lh., and included in a.o.d in place of "remembrance"
29. Sk.sh.: "strains" written in lh. and changed to read "streams"; a.o.d.: "streams" instead of "strains"
30. A.o.d.: "find and" omitted
31. Sk.sh.: "ages and" crossed off; included in a.o.d.
32. A.o.d.: "has influenced" instead of "influences"
33. Hq.tp.: "An" instead of "A"
34. A.o.d.: "was" instead of "is"
35. A.o.d.: "is" inserted after "today"
36. Sk.sh.: "or West" inserted, included in a.o.d.
37. Sk.tp.: "the" instead of "a"; (Sk.tp.)Sk.cr.: "the" changed to "a"; Sk.an.: "a" affirmed
38. Hq.tp.: "at" instead of "in"; (Hq.tp.)Sk.cr.: changed back to "in"
39. A.o.d.: "from the metaphysical point of view" instead of "from the point of view, metaphysic's point of view"
40. Sk.sh.: "from the point of view," in sh. crossed out;
41. A.o.d.: "science makes" instead of "sciences make"

make of knowing and realizing that the vibration is at the root at[42] the whole creation, that was a certainty to them, and at the basis of their whole science. They knew that was,[43] what has created, and what is holding, and in which is held the whole manifestation and here[44] the whole cosmos is one power, and that is vibration. And it was therefore that the astrolog.[45] science which had much to do about[46] with the influence upon human beings and upon different countries, that the same science came out of that science of vibration.

And so music as a science was known by them to have a great deal to do with the influence of the planets. And the continual moving and working of the planets and their action, upon which[47] earth was the basis of the foundation of their[48] *raga*s[49] on which was founded their music. In the Sanskrit tradition of ancient times there were verses to be found having relation of certain planets. Therefore according[50] the influence of the planets of the cosmos, they made their programme and that pr.[51] was carried out through the whole year.

One might think that it is too vague to perceive and that one could[52] make a programme upon the influences[53] of the planets. But at the same time the whole humanity in all periods have arranged their lives according to the planetary influences just the same. [54] In order to keep their music akin to know[55] nature, it was necessary for them to give the liberty to the singer and player to sing and play as he wished. Naturally uniformity lacked and it[56] could not be made as a standardized system. It therefore always remained not as an education, but all only as an individualistic art. And for this reason the music of the ancient people had to go through advantages and a great many disadv.[57] Which[58], the advantages were this, that a musician and a[59] singer or[60] a player was never bound to sing in a particular way in order to execute properly the music which he wanted to play[61] to the[62], before the people. But

42. Sk.sh.: "at" crossed out, changed to "of"; a.o.d.: "of"
43. Sk.sh.: "was," crossed off; omitted in a.o.d.
44. Sk.sh.: "here" crossed out; omitted in a.o.d.
45. Sk.sh.: "astrolog." in lh. abbr. for "astrological"; written out in a.o.d.
46. Sk.sh.: "about" in sh. crossed out but reinstated; omitted in a.o.d.
47. Hq.tp.: "the" added; (Hq.tp.)Sk.cr.: "which" crossed out; Sk.tp.: "the" instead of "which"
48. A.o.d.: "the foundation of their" omitted
49. Hq.tp.: "and" added after "*ragas*"; (Hq.tp.)Sk.cr.: "and" crossed off
50. A.o.d.: "to" added
51. Sk.sh.: "pr." underscored, probably referring to previous "programme"; a.o.d.: "programme"
52. A.o.d.: "not" inserted after "could"
53. Hq.tp.: "influence" instead of "influences"
54. Sk.sh.: a blank
55. Sk.sh.: "know" crossed out and omitted in a.o.d.
56. Hq.tp.: "they" instead of "it"; (Hq.tp.)Sk.cr.: "it" reinstated
57. Sk.sh.: "disadv." for "disadvantages"; a.o.d.: "disadvantages"
58. Sk.sh.: "which" in sh. crossed out, and omitted in a.o.d.
59. Hq.tp.: "and a" omitted; (Hq.tp.)Sk.cr.: "a" inserted; Sk.tp.: "a" instead of "and a"
60. Hq.tp.: "or" omitted; (Hq.tp.)Sk.cr.: "or" reinstated
61. Hq.tp.: "place" instead of "play"
62. Sk.sh.: "to the," crossed out and omitted in a.o.d.

he was always free there[63] to give his music to which he was inspired [64] for the time.

It gave him his full liberty to express his emotions, his passions without any outward restrictions[65] to which he should obey. No doubt when there came a number of singers and players it was then necessary to make a certain [66] standard, but yet that standard did not restrict[67] them very much. And it is this order which was called music. The word music or *sangith*[68] in Sanskrit language has three aspects. One aspect is singing[69]. The other aspect is playing and the third aspect is the movements. They have never left the science of movement or dance as a separate thing of music; they have always *compris*[70] the three aspects of what they called music.

Besides these three ideas, as the music of the Eastern people developed in[71] each aspect of these three aspects developed also. For instance, the way of the singing of the most refined people was quite different of the way how the peasants sang, the song of the temple altogether different from the song of the stage. And the difference was so great that it was not only that there were particular rules and regulations[72] to be followed, or there was more mechanical difference, but there was a natural difference.

The most important or valuable thing that the music of the ancient people produced and which gave a great benefit of it to humanity was one: They distinguished the different aspects of music and thereby they came to realize that there was a certain way of expressing the tone and rhythm which brought about a greater emotion or inclination towards action.

And they found out together with it that there is a certain kind of use of time and rhythm which brought about a greater equilibrium and a greater poise. This science, developing after their practice of many years, formed in itself a special psychological science or art and this science was called Yoga. The special name for this was *mantra* Y.[73], [74]M.Y.[75] means: which[74] meaning of the word Yoga is unity or connection; and *mantra* Yoga means the sacred union with the deeper life,[76] between the outer life and the deeper life. For

---

63. Sk.sh.: "there" crossed out and omitted in a.o.d.
64. Ibid.: a blank
65. A.o.d.: "restriction" instead of "restrictions"
66. Sk.sh.: illegible sh. symbol, possibly for "perform"; (nothing in other documents)
67. Sk.sh.: "restrict" first crossed off, then repeated afterwards
68. A variant of "*sangita*" meaning "symphony" in Sanskrit - see Glossary
69. A.o.d.: "language" instead of "singing"
70. Sk.sh.: "*compris*" in lh. underlined for emphasis; a rare instance where the P-o-M. apparently spoke a French word, "*compris*", meaning "understood" or "included" in English; Hq.tp.: a blank; (Hq.tp.)Sk.cr.: "combined" handwritten in blank; Sk.tp.: "combined"
71. A.o.d.: "in" omitted
72. Sk.tp.: "and regulations" omitted ; (Sk.tp.)Sk.cr., Sk.an.: "and regulations" reinstated
73. Sk.sh.: "Y." in lh. abbr. for "Yoga"; written out in a.o.d.
74. A.o.d.: "The" instead of "M.Y. means: which"
75. Sk.sh.: "M.Y." abbr. lh. for "*mantra* Yoga", then crossed out
76. Sk.sh.: "with the deeper life," crossed out, and omitted in a.o.d.

they found out that there are want[77] psychological inclinations [78] . One of the tendencies [79] of the breath is going outward and the other inclination is going inward. And these two tendencies are as[80] to be found in the nature also, in the ebb and flow, in the sunset and sunrise. One sees the difference in oneself. The vibrations of one's own body and action make a great difference in the morning and evening. Therefore, they regulate the rhythm of the circulation of the heart and of every action of the breath by the help and by the[81] vibration of music of tone and rhythm both.

This took them from the audible vibrations to the inward vibrations, which means from sound to breath, which in the language of the Hindus is one and the same. It is the *sura*[82], which is a name for the sound and breath, one thing blended in another because it is the same thing in the end. It is the breath of an object which may be called a sound and it is the audibility of the breath which may be called [83] voice. And therefore breath and voice are not two things. Even breath and sound are not two things, if one could understand that both have the same basis.

If there is an explanation can be given why man rejoices as[84] or is impressed by the music played before him, is it all[85] only a[86] pastime[87] or [88]? No, there is something else[89] besides it. The principal reason is that in man there is a perpetual rhythm going on which is the sign of life in him, a rhythm which is expressed in his pulsation and his heartbeats, even in his heart. And upon this rhythm depends his health. Not only his health but his moods. Therefore anywhere a rhythm[90] continued it must have an effect upon every person; and upon every person its influence[91] is distinct and different.

It is amusing and interesting to know that when this jazz band came into existence which[92], everyone said to his friend: "O![93] something very[94] crazy has come in society" and yet one has not resisted. It came[95] more and more into fashion. And however a person hates it and is prejudiced against its

---

77. Ibid.: "want" crossed out, and omitted in a.o.d.
78. Ibid.: a blank for an incomplete sentence, lost word(s); not included in a.o.d.
79. Sk.sh., Hq.tp.: a blank; Sk.tp.: omitted
80. Sk.sh.: "as" crossed out, and omitted in a.o.d.
81. Sk.sh.: "and by the" crossed off; a.o.d.: "of" instead of "and by the"
82. Sanskrit word for "tune" or "breath" - see Glossary
83. Sk.sh.: a sh. symbol, semi-legible "*sima*", changed to read "*sama*" which means "hearing of music", i.e. voice; other documents include no word here
84. Sk.sh.: "as" crossed out, omitted in a.o.d.
85. Ibid.: "all" in sh. crossed out, omitted in a.o.d.
86. Sk.sh.: "amusement or a" inserted in parentheses in the margin between "a" and "pastime"; a.o.d.: "an amusement or a" instead of "a"
87. A.o.d.: sentence ends with "pastime?"
88. Sk.sh.: a blank
89. Hq.tp.: "else" omitted; (Hq.tp.)Sk.cr.: "else" reinstated
90. Sk.tp.: "is" added, then crossed out in type
91. Sk.sh.: "influence" in sh. crossed out; "effect" added in lh. below, and included in a.o.d.
92. Sk.sh.: "which" crossed out; omitted in a.o.d.
93. Ibid.: "O!" in sh. crossed out; omitted in a.o.d. (Sk.tp. leaves an open space here)
94. A.o.d.: "very" omitted
95. A.o.d.: "has come" instead of "came"

name, he at least likes to stand and listen to it for five min.[96] What is which[97] reason? The reason is that in whatever form the rhythm is emphasized, upon the body and mind of man, it is[98] a [99] psychological effect.

Another interesting thing I know, that once it is said of a very great Persian poet[100], who was a mystic at the same time, that he used to go[101] in a certain mood, then he used to—[102]pillar [103]in the middle of his house[103]—make circles around it and [104]chants, he would[104] speak and people to[105] write down what he said and it would be perfect poetry. [106]What is more amusing that I have known of a lawyer when he would find[107] in his bar, when he was doing his work, when he could not find the argument [108] he would turn round himself [108] and after that he would find the right argument. But we do not have[109] need to find the mystery to go to these cases.

But a person he would[110], he cannot find[107] he beats his fingers on the table or taps his fingers [111]and what he wants, there an idea[111] comes. And many who cannot get their thought through, they begin to walk through the room. When they have taken two, three, circles, their thought becomes right. If that is true, we come to the realization that the human body is a kind of mechanism which must be going on regularly. If it is stopped in some way there is something stopped in the body or[112] the mind. This argument brings one to understand that upon the rhythm, the mood, health and condition of mind depend[113]. Not only the rhythm he gets from music but also the rhythm of his own breath. His walking[114] about, that[115] rhythm[116] has also a great deal to do with the rhythm of his life. It is very easy[117] that there are certain kinds of sound which irritate man, which have a bad effect upon the nerves. Then

96. Sk.sh.: "min." in lh. for "minutes"; written out in a.o.d.
97. A.o.d.: "the" instead of "which"
98. Sk.tp.: "has" instead of "is"
99. Sk.sh.: illegible cross out
100. This is apparently a reference to Rumi (see List)
101. A.o.d.: "get" instead of "go"
102. A.o.d.: "there was a" added (missing in the sh.)
103. Sk.sh.: "in the middle of his house" inserted after "pillar", partially in sh. and lh.; included in a.o.d.
104. Sk.sh.: although Sk. wrote "chants" in sh., she then crossed it out and wrote "began" in lh. above;
a.o.d.: "began to" instead of "chants, he would"
105. Sk.sh.: "to" changed to "would" in sh.; a.o.d.: "would"
106. A.o.d.: "But" inserted before "what"
107. A.o.d.: "that" added after "find"
108. Sk.sh.: a blank
109. A.o.d.: "have" omitted
110. A.o.d.: "he would" omitted
111. Sk.sh.: first "what he wants" crossed out and then "an" crossed out to read "and there idea"; a.o.d.: "and the idea" instead
112. A.o.d.: "in" added after "or"
113. (Hq.tp.)Sk.cr.: "depend" changed to "depends"
114. A.o.d.: a blank with "walking" inserted in lh.
115. Hq.tp.: "this" instead of "that"; (Hq.tp.)Sk.cr.: "this" changed back to "that"
116. A.o.d.: "which" added after "rhythm"
117. Sk.sh.: apparently Sk. missed a verb after "easy"; a.o.d.: a blank instead of "easy"

there are other kinds of rhythm which have a soothing or[118] healing, [119]comforting effect upon the mind.

Music is the sound and rhythm and when the sound and rhythm is understood in its nature and character, then music would not only be something for a pastime but then music would become a source of healing and upliftment. The Sufis of the ancient times, the great mystics, they used to develop this art to bring about this[120] poise in life after the[121] everyday activity. It is this art which they call *sama,* and S.[122] has been the most sacred thing for the [123] Sufi essence[124], a meditation for them. They meditated by the help of music, by having a certain music played which had a certain effect upon the development of an individual. The great poets such as Rumi of Persia used to [125]have music for their meditation and by the help of music they used to[125] repose and control the[126] activity of the[127] body and mind.

When we see today there is a greater and greater tendency to nervousness, it is caused by the too much activity in life. The life is becoming artificial more and more every day and therefore with every step advanced, a man is missing that repose which has been as a yeast of the human race. And therefore for the betterment and education of humanity[128], the art of repose, which seems to be lost, is greatly needed to be found. Many people in the Western world who at any time read the tradition of the ancient people often thought that there was an art that seemed was lost, and that they should go to the East to find it. In order to make it easy for those who have the search of that art and the science which is most necessary in the evolution of mankind, the Sufi Movement has made a facility that those who wish to study and practise it may do so here instead of going so far in the East.

---

118. A.o.d.: "and" instead of "or"
119. (Hq.tp.)Sk.cr.: "a" inserted before "comforting"; Sk.tp.: "a" added
120. A.o.d.: "that" instead of "this"
121. A.o.d.: "their" instead of "the"
122. Sk.sh.: "S." abbr. in lh. for "*sama*"; written out in a.o.d.
123. Sk.sh.: an illegible sh. symbol
124. A.o.d.: "as" instead of "essence"
125. Hq.tp.: "have music for their meditation and by the help of music they used to" omitted; (Hq.tp.)Sk.cr.: same words inserted in lh.
126. Hq.tp.: "their" instead of "the"; (Hq.tp.)Sk.cr.: "their" changed back to "the"
127. Sk.sh.: Sk.'s sh. for "the" may be confused for "their" at times; a.o.d.: "their" instead of "the"
128. Sk.sh.: "today" in sh. inserted after "humanity", and included in a.o.d.

1

Paris, Sorbonne, February 18th [2]

The Persian Poets[3]

The belief which[4] exists that [5]poet is a prophet has been certainly realized in the land of Persia. The Pns.[6] had in all times great poets in their land and it has been called a land of poetry. In the first place for the reason that Persian language is most adaptable[7] to poetry and for the other reason that all the poetry of the Persians has a mystical touch in it. The literary value of the poetry only, keeps it at a[8] poetry but a[9] mystical value attached to the poetry makes the poetry prophecy.

Documents:

Sk.sh. = Sakina Furnée's shorthand reporting of the lecture, newly transcribed by B.v.d.B.

Lf.hw. = a handwritten reporting of a simultaneous French translation while the lecture was being given, made by Mlle H. Lefèbvre, an early French mureed living in Paris. This source is not mentioned further as it is fragmentary and does not add any further evidence to the English text.

Hq.tp. = a typescript made at Headquarters in Geneva ("N.72"), from an unknown source. Sakina's corrections are indicated in the notes as ("Hq.tp.)Sk.cr."

Sk.tp. = a typescript prepared by Sakina or under her direction. It is very close to the "Hq.tp." which was most likely used by Sakina, along with an unknown source, perhaps her own shorthand transcription. A few corrections by Sakina are indicated in the notes as ("Sk.tp.)Sk.cr." A typed copy of "Sk.tp.", with only one difference, is mentioned only in footnote 92.

Sk.hw. = Sakina's handwritten copy made from an unknown source (showing many differences from other documents). Murshida Sherifa Goodenough later edited this document, indicated in the notes as "(Sk.hw.)Gd.ed.", for use in preparation of the Social Gatheka series; (however, it was never incorporated into that series).

Sk.an. = some corrections by Sakina to "Sk.tp." on a separate list.

Notes

1. Sk.hw.: "Public Lecture" added in upper left corner
2. Sk.sh.: the year, 1924, not indicated; although Sk. does not note the year with the date, it is contained chronologically in the 1924 section of the shorthand book; Hq.tp., Sk.tp.: "1924" included; Sk.hw.: "Paris" omitted; (Sk.hw.)Gd.ed.: "Sorbonne" and the date crossed out
3. (Sk.hw.)Gd.ed.: "No.72" and "Social Gatheka" added above the title in lh. by Gd.
4. Sk.hw.: "that" instead of "which"; (Sk.hw.)Gd.ed.: "which" reinstated
5. (Sk.hw.)Gd.ed.: "the" inserted
6. Sk.sh.: "Pns." abbr. in sh. for "Persians"; written out in a.o.d.
7. Hq.tp., Sk.tp., Sk.hw.: "adoptable" instead of "adaptable"; (Sk.hw.)Gd.ed.: "adoptable" changed back to "adaptable"
8. A.o.d.: "a" instead of "at a"; (Sk.hw.)Gd.ed.: "a" crossed out to read "keeps it poetry"
9. (Sk.tp.)Sk.cr.: "a" changed to "the"; Sk.an.: affirms this change

The climate and atmosphere of Persia also has[10] been most helpful to their[11] poetry. Besides the nature of the people, most imaginative, that has made their poetry rich. At all times and at[12] all countries when the imagination has no[13] scope or[14] expansion the poetry dies, and materialism increases. The poet is a creator[15] and he creates in spite of all that stands before him; he creates a world of his own and by being[16] so naturally he rises above that plane, which[17] plane only makes the reality[18] of things which are visible and touchable[19]. When he sings to the sun songs[20] and when he smiles to the moon and[21] when he prays to the sea and when he looks at the plants and the forest and[22] in the desert, [23] he communicates with the[24] nature. In the eyes of the ordinary person he is imaginative, he is dreamy, he is visionary. His thoughts seem to be in the air, but if one asked the poet what he thinks of the others, he thinks that those who cannot fly in the air, they are on the earth. And it is natural that the creatures who can walk on the earth are not always able to fly in the air. Those who fly in the air must have wings and that difference you will find in the[25] human beings. For in the[25] human beings they[26] are all.

There are souls like in the germs and the[27] worms, and souls like animals and birds and again souls like jinns[28] and angels. Among human beings there[29] are all those who are dwellers in the[30] earth,[31] those who dwell in heaven, and those who dwell in the highest[32] of the sky, and in the deepest depth of the earth. Those who are able to soar upwards by the power of their

10. (Sk.hw.)Gd.ed.: "has" changed to "have"
11. A.o.d.: "the" instead of "their"
12. (Sk.hw.)Gd.ed.: "at" changed to "in"
13. Sk.hw.: "more" instead of "no"; (Sk.hw.)Sk.cr.: "no" reinstated
14. A.o.d.: "of" instead of "or"
15. Sk.sh.: alternate reading of the sh. symbol would be "creature"
16. (Sk.hw.)Gd.ed.: "by being" changed to "doing"
17. Hq.tp.: "the" instead of "which", corrected in type to "which"
18. (Sk.hw.)Gd.ed.: "plane only makes the reality" changed to "makes a reality only"
19. (Sk.hw.)Gd.ed.: "touchable" changed to "tangible"
20. Sk.sh.: "songs" crossed out and omitted in a.o.d.
21. Sk.hw.: "and" omitted, then inserted above by Sk.
22. Hq.tp.: "in life" added, then "in" crossed out in type; Sk.tp.: "life" added; Sk.hw.: "life" omitted, then inserted by Sk.
23. Sk.sh.: a blank with one or more words missing
24. (Sk.hw.)Gd.ed.: "the" crossed out
25. (Sk.hw.)Gd.ed.: "the" crossed out
26. Hq.tp.: "they" changed to "there"; Sk.tp.: "there" instead of "they"; (Sk.hw.)Gd.ed.: "they" changed to "there" and then "they" reinstated
27. Hq.tp., Sk.tp.: "the germs and" instead of "in the germs and the"; Sk.hw.: "germs and" instead of "in the germs and the"
28. Sk.sh.: "jinns" is written in lh. over a previously illegible word
29. Sk.hw.: "they" instead of "there"; (Sk.hw.)Gd.ed.: "there" reinstated
30. Hq.tp., Sk.tp.: "are dwellers of the" instead of "are dwellers in the"; Sk.hw.: "dwell on" instead of "are dwellers in the"; (Sk.hw.)Gd.ed.: changed to "are dwellers on"
31. Sk.hw.: "and" added
32. Hq.tp., Sk.tp.: a blank after "highest" with dots typed in on Sk.tp., and dots in ink on Hq.tp.; (Sk.hw.)Gd.ed.: a blank with "heights" inserted

imagination, it is they who have been living persons,[33] poets. What they said was not only a statement, it was a music in[34] itself. [35]It did not have only a rhythm but it had a tone in it.[35] It made their soul[36] dance and it would make anyone dance who heard their poetry. As Hafiz[37] of Shiraz gives a challenge to[38] the dignified [39] men of his country. He says: "Pious friends, you would forget your dignity if you would hear the song which came[40] from my glowing heart". And it is such souls who have been able to touch the highest summits of life that they[41] have been able to bring some truth which helps[42] the interpretation of human nature and of the inner law of life.

Those poets who have made poetry for the sake of fame or name or popularity, or that it[43] may be appreciated by others, that is another thing. For it is business, it is not poetry. Poetry is an art, an art of the most high[44] aspect. The
communication that the poet forms with nature in the end brings him to make that communication with himself and by that[45] communication he goes deeper and deeper within and without, communicating with life everywhere. And this[46] communication brings to[47] him the music of a far distant land and this[48] music brings to him[49] an ecstasy. In this E.[50] his whole being is filled with joy, he forgets the worries and anxieties of life; he rises above the praises and blames[51] of this earth, and things of this world become of less importance for him. He stands on the earth, but gazes in[52] the heavens; his outlook on life becomes broadened, [53]sight becomes keen. He sees things that no one is interested in, that no one sees. And it is that[54] which teaches us that what may be called heaven or paradise is not very far from mankind. It is always

33. Sk.sh., (Hq.tp)Sk.cr.: "persons," crossed out; Sk.tp., Sk.hw.: "persons," omitted
34. Sk.tp.: "in" omitted; (Sk.tp.)Sk.cr.: "in" typed in the margin
35. (Sk.hw.)Gd.ed.: sentence changed to read "It had not only a rhythm; but a tone in it."
36. Hq.tp., Sk.tp.: "souls" instead of "soul"
37. Hafiz (see List)
38. (Sk.hw.)Gd.ed.: changed to read "challenges" instead of "gives a challenge to"
39. Sk.sh.: "pious" in lh. inserted after "dignified" and included in a.o.d.
40. (Sk.hw.)Gd.ed.: "came" changed into "comes"
41. Sk.hw.: "those that" instead of "that they"
42. Sk.hw.: "has been" instead of "helps"
43. Ibid.: "they" instead of "it"
44. (Sk.hw.)Gd.ed.: "most high" changed to "highest"
45. (Sk.hw.)Gd.ed.: "that" changed to "this"
46. Hq.tp., Sk.tp.: "that" instead of "this"
47. Hq.tp.: "to" omitted, added above in type; Sk.hw.: "him to" instead of "to him"; (Sk.hw.)Gd.ed.: "to" crossed out
48. Sk.hw.: "that" instead of "this"
49. Hq.tp.: "bring to him" instead of "brings to him"; Sk.hw.: "brings him to" instead of "brings to him"; (Sk.hw.)Sk.cr.: changed back to "brings to him"
50. Sk.sh.: "E." in lh. abbr. for "ecstasy" and written out in a.o.d.
51. A.o.d.: "praise and blame" instead of "praises and blames"
52. (Sk.hw.)Gd.ed.: "in" changed to "at"
53. A.o.d.: "and his" added
54. Hq.tp.: "that" omitted; (Hq.tp.)Sk.cr.: "this" inserted in lh. above; Sk.tp.: "this" instead of "that"

near him[55] if he only looked at it. Our life is what we look at. If we look at the right thing then it is right. If we look at the wrong thing then it is wrong[56]. What makes[57] life? According to our own attitude and therefore, the poet by nature is the creator of his own beauty; not[58] therefore his proof[59] to be self-sufficient, so[60] indifferent and independent, which becomes[61] as his[62] wings for him to fly upwards. The fears that the[63] life has, the worries that life can offer, the trouble and difficulties which everyone feels in life in the midst of the world, the poet also is in the same position and yet he rises above it, that these things may not touch him.

No doubt, the poet is much more sensitive to the troubles and difficulties of life than an ordinary person. If he would take all things as they come to him, all the jarring influences that disturb the peace of mind, and all the rough edges of life that every person has to rub against, he would not be able to maintain[64] it. If he would make his heart hardened, not so sensitive, then he would close also his heart from the inspiration which comes as poetry. Therefore, in order to lay the doors of his heart open, the sensitiveness is there, and the one who communicates with life within and without is open to all influences, whether agreeable or disagreeable, without any protection. [65] And only the[66] escape that he can make from all disturbances of life is only one[67], and that is by rising above it all.

The *Shah-nama*[68], an ancient poetic scripture of the Persians, shows the prophetic gift of the poet. No doubt even before the writer of the *Shah-nama*, the message of Zarathustra[69], the prophetic message, which was given to the people of Persia, was poetic from the beginning to the[70] end; and the most interesting thing was[71] that Z.'s[72] scripture and his life from the beginning to the end shows how a poet rises from earth to heaven. For it, from beginning to end, suggests[73] one a communication of Zarathustra with

---

55. (Sk.hw.)Gd.ed.: "him" changed to "man"
56. Sk.sh.: an illegible sign
57. Sk.hw.: "We make" instead of "What makes"
58. A.o.d.: "and" instead of "not"
59. A.o.d.: "he proves" instead of "his proof"
60. Ibid.: "also" instead of "so"
61. Sk.hw.: "become" instead of "becomes"; (Sk.hw.)Gd.ed.: changed to "to which becomes"
62. Sk.tp.: "his" omitted, but typed in the margin
63. (Sk.hw.)Gd.ed.: "the" crossed out
64. (Sk.hw.)Gd.ed.: "maintain" changed to "sustain"
65. Sk.sh.: a blank
66. (Sk.hw.)Gd.ed.: numbers 2 and 1 written under "only the", to read "the only"
67. (Sk.hw.)Gd.ed.: "only one" changed to "one alone"
68. Sk.sh.: actually "*Shanama*" varied with "*Shahenama*" in lh. (see Glossary)
69. Zarathustra (see List)
70. (Sk.hw.)Gd.ed.: "the" crossed out, then reinstated
71. A.o.d.: "is" instead of "was"
72. Sk.sh.: "Z." in lh. abbr. for "Zarathustra"; the "s" may indicate the possessive or may be an abbr. for "spoke"; a.o.d.: "Zarathustra's"
73. (Sk.hw.)Gd.ed.: "to" inserted

the[74] nature, with its beauty, and may show how[75] every step he took further and so touches[76] deeper and deeper the depth of life.

And it is by[77] the praise of the beauty in nature, and by finding the source of this art of creation in the artist which[78] is behind [79] Zarathustra forms[80] his religion. And what form of worship did he teach? He taught the same worship, the worship by which he began his poetry and in which he finished it. He said to his pupils: "Stand before the sea, look at the vastness of it, bow to[81] it, to the source and goal of this". He said to his disciples: "Look at the sun and see what joy it brings [82] . And what is it[83] at the back of it? Where does the[84] come from[85]? Think of its source and goal and bow your head to it". People then thought that it was a sun worship; it was not a sun-worship. It was a worship of life[86] light which is the source and goal of all. That communication within and without extended the range of a poet's sight sometimes so much that it was beyond the comprehension of the average man. When the Shah of Persia said that he would like to see a tradition of his country, a history which was not to be found at that time, that poet who was intuitive[87] and inspirational[87] said: "Yes, I will make it and bring it". He then began to practice throwing his searchlight as far back in the past as possible, and after the appointed time[88] he was able to prepare that book of tradition and he brought it to the court. It is said that the psychical power of that poet was so great that[89] there was someone at the court sneering at the idea that: How could it[90] be possible for a man to look back at the past

---

74. (Sk.hw.)Gd.ed.: "the" crossed out
75. Sk.sh.: "may" in sh. crossed out; Hq.tp., Sk.tp.: "shows us how" instead of "may show how"; Sk.hw.: "show how" instead of "may show how"; (Sk.hw.)Gd.ed.: "show how" changed to "shows us how at"
76. Hq.tp., Sk.tp.: "so touched" instead of "so touches"; (Sk.hw.)Gd.ed.: "and so touches" changed to "he touches"
77. Sk.hw.: "by" omitted; (Sk.hw.)Gd.ed.: "on" inserted after "is" to read "is on" instead of "is by"
78. (Sk.hw.)Gd.ed.: "which" changed to "who"
79. Sk.sh.: a blank; Sk.hw.: a blank; (Sk.hw.)Gd.ed.: "that" inserted, crossed out and then reinstated
80. Sk.hw.: "formed" instead of "forms"; (Sk.hw.)Gd.ed.: "s" written above the ending "ed", then crossed out, reinstating "formed"
81. A.o.d.: "before" instead of "to"
82. Sk.sh.: a blank
83. Sk.sh.: "it" crossed out and omitted in a.o.d.
84. Sk.sh.: "the" is actually written here in sh.; a.o.d.: "it" instead of "the"
85. (Sk.hw.)Gd.ed.: sentence changed to read "where it comes from"
86. Sk.sh.: "life" crossed out and omitted in a.o.d.
87. Sk.sh.: noted a "1" under "inspirational" and a "2" under "intuitive"; a.o.d.: "inspirational and intuitive"
88. (Sk.hw.)Gd.ed.: "had passed" added
89. (Sk.hw.)Gd.ed.: "when" inserted after "that"
90. Ibid.: "that: "How could it" changed to "how it could"

so far? He[91] brought him it[92] and put his hand on it[93] and said: "Now see;[94] there is all in it that I have seen in the past". It is human. It is not superhuman, though the examples of this kind are rarely to be found. For in the life of every person to a certain extent past, present and future is[95] manifest. How many examples we can recollect of this past war? When those who had their dear ones on the other side[96], were able to know the condition of their dear ones,[97] feel it. Any pure-hearted person, any loving person, a sympathetic good person will be able to perceive the past, present and future to some extent. If the same light as a searchlight was thrown back a little further, from another position it could go much further than a man can comprehend. Some have to develop this[98] gift but some are born with it. And those who are born with it, among them where[99] we find some[100] certain people who perhaps know a thing ten [101]twelve years before what will happen[102]. Therefore[103]poet is not only the one who writes flowery words[104]; poet is the one who throws his soul in the past, who can throw his light in the future, and make that clear which has not yet come but which is designed beforehand, which exists there in the abstract.

It is that poetry which becomes a[105] inspirational poetry. It is through that poetry that[106] the intricate aspects of metaphysics can be taught. All the *Upanishads* of the Vedanta[107] are in one[108] poetry. The *sura* of[109] *Qur'an*, [110] Zarathustra's scripture is[111] in all[112] poetry. All those prophets,

91. Ibid.: "he" changed to "the poet"
92. Sk.sh.: "it" crossed out; corrected to read "near"; "near" in a.o.d.
93. Hq.tp.: "him" instead of "it"; (Hq.tp.)Sk.cr.: "him" crossed out and "it (the book)" inserted above;
Sk.tp.: "(the book)" added; (Sk.tp.)Sk.cr.: "it (the book)" crossed out and "his back" inserted in the margin in ink; the re-typed version of Sk.tp. does not include this correction; (Sk.hw.)Gd.ed.: "it" changed to "him"
94. Hq.tp., Sk.tp.: "And the man saw with his own eyes that which was written in the book" added after "see"
95. (Sk.hw.)Gd.ed.: "is" changed to "are"
96. (Sk.hw.)Gd.ed.: "on the other side" changed to "at the front"
97. A.o.d.: "and" added
98. Sk.hw.: "that" instead of "this"
99. Sk.sh.: "where" crossed out and omitted in a.o.d.
100. (Sk.hw.)Gd.ed.: "some" crossed out
101. Sk.hw.: "or" added
102. (Sk.hw.)Gd.ed.: "what will happen" changed to "it happens"
103. (Sk.hw:)Gd.ed.: "the" inserted
104. Hq.tp., Sk.tp.: "works" instead of "words"; Sk.tp.(Sk.cr.): "(words?)" in ink in margin; (Sk.hw.)Gd.ed.: "the" inserted after "words"; Sk.an.: "words" affirmed
105. Sk.hw.: "a" omitted; a.o.d.: "an" instead of "a"
106. Sk.hw.: "true that in poetry" instead of "through that poetry that"
107. *Upanishads* of the Vedanta (see Glossary)
108. A.o.d.: "one" omitted
109. A.o.d.: "*Surahs*" instead of "*sura*"; "*sura*" means a chapter in the *Qur'an* (see Glossary); (Sk.hw.)Gd.ed.: "the" inserted after "of" to read "*Surahs* of the *Koran*"
110. Sk.sh.: a blank
111. (Sk.hw.)Gd.ed.: "is" changed to "are"
112. A. o. d.: "all in" instead of "in all"

at any[113] time they came, they[114] brought the message in poetry. It may not be a[115] poetry as we consider it, but if we study it, we shall find that it is all poetic. The development of poetry in Persia came at a time when there was a great conflict between the orthodox and between[116] the free-thinkers. The time was such that the law of the nation was a religious law[117], and no one was at liberty to express his free ideas [118] which might be in conflict with[119] religious ideas. And at such times there were great thinkers such as Firdousi[120] [121] Natar[122] [123] there were thinkers such as Jell.[124] Rumi, Sa'di[125], Hafiz, Nadan[126], who [127] not only poets, but who were poetry itself. They were living in another world. [128] Although they appeared to be on the earth. Their outlook on life, their keen light[129] was different to everyone[130]. The words which arose[131] from them were not brought up by an effort. They were natural flames rising up out of the heart. And these words remained[132] as flames enlightening souls in all times, whichever soul[133] these words have touched. The poetry of Jalal-ud-Din Rumi has made the greatest impression upon humanity. Although Jalal-ud-Din Rumi was inspired in the first place by Attar, Jalal-ud-Din Rumi was a most qualified man who had a gift of speech. And yet his soul was waiting for an [134], enlightenment which came in the later part of his life. It was a dervish[135] who came into his life, a man in rags showing no qualification that [136]may be recognized as[137]

---

113. (Sk.hw.)Gd.ed.: "any" changed to "whatever"
114. (Sk.hw.)Gd.ed.: "they" crossed out
115. Ibid.: "a" crossed out
116. (Sk.hw.)Gd.ed.: "between" crossed out
117. Sk.hw.: "also" instead of "law"; (Sk.hw.)Sk.cr.: "law" reinstated
118. Sk.sh.: an illegible cross out
119. A.o.d.: "the" added
120. Firdousi (see List)
121. Sk.sh.: a blank
122. Sk.sh.: "Natar" in lh., later corrected to read "Attar" (see List); included in a.o.d. as "Attar"
123. Ibid.: a blank
124. Ibid.: "Jell." abbr. for: "Jalal-ud-Din, and written out in a.o.d. (see List)
125. Sa'di (see List)
126. No reference to a poet of this name has been found; (Sk.hw.)Gd.ed.: "Nadan" changed to "Nizami" (see List)
127. Sk.sh.: an unreadable, improperly composed sh. symbol; a.o.d.: "were" added
128. Sk.sh.: a blank
129. Ibid.: although "light" in sh. is written here clearly, occasionally Sakina has been known to inadvertently write an "l" symbol for an "s" symbol; a.o.d.: "sight" instead of "light"
130. (Sk.hw.)Gd.ed.: "to everyone" changed to read "from everyone's"
131. (Sk.hw.)Gd.ed.: "arose" changed to "rose"
132. Hq.tp., Sk.tp.: "remain" instead of "remained"
133. Sk.hw.: "souls" instead of "soul"; (Sk.hw.)Gd.ed.: crossed out the plural "s" to reinstate "soul"
134. Sk.sh.: a blank, later "enlightenment" written above it, then crossed out, followed again by "enlightenment"
135. One of the words used to refer to Sufis in the East - see Glossary
136. (Sk.hw.)Gd.ed.: "may be recognized as a learned" changed to "he might be recognized as a learned man"
137. A.o.d.: "a" added after "as";

learned[136] by the world; and yet a man who was tuned[138] with the infinite. Who had in[139] so to speak, in religious terms, the kingdom of God. That man happened to come in the home of Jalal-ud-Din Rumi, and Jalal-ud-Din Rumi, as his habit, he[140] welcomed him in his home. And after having a conversation found out that it is not learning, it is living the[141] knowledge that counts. For he had read so much, and he had thought so much and had seen so many and that[142] he found that it is not that. It is living. It is not saying, it is being. When he realized [143]that, when ShamsTabriz[144] was leaving, that: "The king[143] of the earth and of heaven of whom the[145] people have spoken, I have today seen in the form of man". For he saw how wide[146] can be the heart of man and how deep can touch the soul of man, how high the spirit of man can reach. This[147] impression made Jalal-ud-Din Rumi[148] for a long period[149] of time in a sort of ecstasy. And during this ex.[150] what he wrote[150] was called the *Diwan*[151] of ShamsTabriz. For he began to see, owing to the oneness with the heart of his teacher, that all[152] his teacher had so[153] thought[154], had spoken[155] in words. And it is for that reason he did not call it his book, he called it his teacher's book. The book that [156]Rumi wrote afterwards was[157] *Masnavi-i-Manavi*[158], a book which is a living scripture in itself, which has enlightened numberless souls in the East. It has led the sincere seeker as far as he was able to go; and yet[159] so simple, no

138. Sk.sh.: "tuned" crossed out with "in tune" in lh. above, and included in a.o.d.
139. Sk.sh.: "in" crossed out, with "gained" in lh. added and included in a.o.d.; (Sk.hw.)Gd.ed.: "so" crossed out to read: "gained to speak"
140. (Sk.hw.)Gd.ed.: "he" changed to "was"
141. (Sk.hw.)Gd.ed.: "the" crossed out
142. Ibid.: "many and that" changed to "many people and then"
143. Hq.tp., Sk.tp.: "that, when Shamstabrez was leaving, he wrote one verse, that: the King" instead of "that, when Shamstabrez was leaving, that the king"; Sk.hw.: "that, he wrote his verse when Shamstabrez was leaving: that the God"; (Sk.hw.)Gd.ed.: "that" before "the God" crossed out
144. Sk.sh.: the name is usually written "Shams-i Tabriz", but the "i" would be difficult to hear for sh.
145. (Sk.hw.)Gd.ed.: "the" crossed out
146. Sk.sh.: "white" in lh. beneath, then crossed out and "wide" in lh. written above
147. Sk.hw.: "That" instead of "This"
148. (Sk.hw.)Gd.ed.: "be" inserted after "Rumi"
149. Sk.sh.: "period" crossed out, then re-written behind it and "period" in lh. written above
150. Sk.sh.: "ex." in lh. abbr. for "ecstasy", followed by a blank; "ecstasy" in a.o.d.; Sk.hw.: "this ecstasy" changed to "that ecstasy"; (Sk.hw.)Gd.ed.: "during that ecstasy what he wrote" changed to "what he wrote during that ecstasy"
151. *Diwan* (see List)
152. Sk.tp., Sk.an.: "all that" instead of "that all"
153. Sk.sh.: "so" crossed out and omitted in a.o.d.
154. (Sk.tp.)Sk.cr.: "(taught)" written in ink in the margin, after "thought"; Sk.an.: "had thought (taught?)"; apparently Sk. was not clear about this
155. Sk.hw.: "he spoke" instead of "had spoken"
156. Sk.hw.: "Jalal-ud-Din" added
157. Sk.hw.: "the" added
158. *Masnavi-i-Manavi*: the major poem of Rumi - see List
159. (Sk.hw.)Gd.ed.: "it is" inserted

complexity, no dogma[160], no principles, no great moral teaching, no expression of piety. What he has written is the law of life. And he has personified[161] that law in a kind of picture. Only the difference between Jalal-ud-Din Rumi's work and between[162] the work of the great Hafiz of Persia is that Hafiz has here[163] pictured the life without; Rumi has pictured the life within. But if I[164] were to compare the three great poets of Persia I would call Hafiz[165] the body of the poet, Hafiz the heart of the poet, and Rumi the soul of the poet.

Sufism has been the wisdom of the[166] poets. No poet in Persia there has[167] ever been who was not a Sufi. Every poet of note[168] in Persia has given a certain aspect of the Sufi idea; and great care has been taken that the mind of the orthodox people may not be hurt. And therefore in the Persian poetry they[169] had to make a new terminology, they had to use the[170] words such as wine and the bowl and the beloved and the rose, words which would not offend the orthodox mind, and at the same time would serve as symbolical of those[171] expressions to explain the divine law.

The work of the Sufi Movement is to give the interpretation of the ideas[172] of these poets; to give their ideas[173] in the[174] words that could be understood; understood[175] by the people in the[176] modern times. For the value of those ideas is as great just now as ever.

177

---

160. A. o. d.: "dogmas" instead of "dogma"
161. Sk.sh.: "person" in lh. written underneath "personified"
162. (Sk.hw.)Gd.ed.: "between" crossed out
163. A.o.d.: "here" omitted
164. Sk.hw.: "one" instead of "I" (original sh. shows the sh. symbol for the personal pronoun "I")
165. Sk.sh.: "Hafiz" in lh. crossed out, "Sadi" (for Sa'di) added in lh. and included in a.o.d.
166. A.o.d.: "these" instead of "the"
167. (Sk.hw.)Gd.ed.: "there has" changed to "has there" by writing "2" and "1" underneath
168. Sk.sh.: "*connu*" (French for "known") written in lh. above "note"; Hq.tp., Sk.tp.: "notice" instead of "note"; Sk.hw.: "known" instead of "of note"
169. Sk.hw.: "Persian poets" instead of "in the Persian poetry"; (Sk.hw.)Gd.ed.: "therefore Persian poets they" changed to "the Persian poet"
170. (Sk.hw.)Gd.ed.: "they had to use the" changed to "had to use"
171. Sk.sh.: "of those" crossed out; omitted in a.o.d.
172. Sk.hw.: "idea" instead of "ideas"; (Sk.hw.)Gd.ed.: "ideas" reinstated
173. Sk.hw.: "idea" instead of "ideas"; (Sk.hw.)Gd.ed.: "ideas" reinstated
174. (Sk.hw.)Gd.ed.: "the" crossed out
175. A.o.d.: the second "understood" omitted
176. Sk.hw.: "at the" instead of "in the"; (Sk.hw.)Gd.ed.: "at the" changed to "in"
177. Hq.tp., Sk.tp.: "May God bless you" added; Sk.an.: Sk. writes: "last words 'May God bless you' - let it stand"

Sakina's shorthand reporting

1 Paris, Baronne d'Eichthal,[2] February 20th 1924

Resist not Evil[3]

[4]Beloved ones of God, I should like to speak a few words today on

Documents:

Sk.sh. = Sakina Furnée's shorthand reporting of the lecture, newly transcribed by B.v.d.B.

Lf.hw. = a handwritten reporting of a simultaneous French translation while the lecture was being given, made by Mlle H. Lefèbvre, not mentioned further as it is fragmentary.

Hq.tp. = a typescript made at Headquarters, Geneva ("No.73"). A second tp. on a Hq. microfiche has only one difference mentioned in note 97 as "Hq.tp.2".

Sk.hw. = a manuscript in Sakina Furnée's handwriting made from an unknown source, perhaps her shorthand transcription. She made a few corrections, indicated in the notes as "(Sk.hw.)Sk.cr." Mda. Sherifa Goodenough added the location.

er.tp. = a typescript, without the q.a., made by Sakina or under her direction, probably typed by Kismet Stam. At the top Sakina wrote: "compared with steno - Sakina". Mda. Sherifa Goodenough edited this document in ink, indicated in the notes as "(er.tp.)Gd.ed." (Although it may be that some of the changes are corrections made by the typist, perhaps Kismet, as the handwriting is in some places difficult to decipher.)

Sk.tp. = a typescript prepared by Sakina or under her direction, made from "(er.tp.)Gd.ed." Later, this corrected Sk.tp. was retyped, and then corrected further by Sk. to include the introductory sentence ("Beloved ones of God....") and other changes using "Hq.tp." A copy of this tp. has a note at the top: "compared to Kismet's". Then this corrected document was retyped (see "Sk.an." below) and a few more corrections were added by Sk. For the sake of simplicity, any differences that appear in the final retype from the first are shown in the notes as "(Sk.tp.)Sk.cr."

Sk.an. = some corrections by Sakina to "Sk.tp.", on a separate list. One page is dated "July 1967".

A highly edited version of this lecture appeared in *The Sufi Message* series, vol. VIII (104-108; London, 1963), *Sufi Teachings*; it does not appear in the notes.

Notes:

1. Hq.tp.: "No. 73" typed at upper left; er.tp.: "Private Lecture" inserted in unknown hw.; Sk.tp.: "Private Lecture" typed upper left
2. Hq.tp.: "Paris" omitted; Sk.hw.: location omitted; er.tp.: date and location omitted, later added in unknown hw. (Sk.hw.)Gd.ed.: "Paris Baronne d'Eichthal" inserted under the date in unknown hw.
3. Hq.tp., Sk.hw.: title omitted (see next note)
4. Hq.tp., Sk.hw.: "Resist not evil" underlined at the end of this sentence, as the title; (Sk.hw.)Sk.cr.: introductory words crossed out ("Beloved... phrase") leaving "resist not evil" as the title; er.tp., Sk.tp.: sentence omitted; (Sk.tp.)Sk.cr.: reinstated

the subject of the[5] Christ[6] phrase "resist not evil"[7].[4]

Often one wonders at the[8] saying and it is not always to give it[9] the right interpretation. In order to give an interpretation to[10] this, the first thing is to explain what evil means. Is there any particular action, or is there any particular thing that[11] one will[12] point out as evil? No doubt man is always apt to point out to[13] a certain action as evil. But nothing can be evil as a fixed principle. Then what is it? It is something which is void of harmony. It is something which lacks beauty. It is something which is missing love in it. Beyond and above all it is [14] which is not fitting in the accommodation of life. What fits in[15] the accommodation that life offers cannot be an evil. It is the character of the[16] evil, [17]is significant by it[18] not being fitting in the accommodation. Evil is likened to a fire. The nature of the[19] fire is to destroy everything that comes in its fold[20]. But at the same time the power of evil is as great as the power of the fire, and yet evil is as fixed[21] as fire, for the fire does not endure, so evil does not last. As fire destroys it[22] itself, so evil is its own destruction. Why it is[23] said: "Do not resist evil"? Because resistance gives life to evil. Non-resistance[24] lets it burn itself. In the form of [25] anger, passion, greed, stubbornness one sees evil, in the form of deceit, treachery; but the root of evil is one and that is selfishness. In one[26] person's heart perhaps therefore[27] evil is manifest in[28] the surface; in another

5. (Sk.tp.)Sk.cr.: "the" crossed out
6. Hq.tp., Sk.hw., Sk.tp., Sk.an.: "Christ's" instead of "Christ"
7. See Matthew 5:39
8. Hq.tp., Sk.hw.: "this" instead of "the"; (Sk.tp.)Sk.cr., Sk.an.: "the" changed to "this"
9. Sk.hw., Er.tp., Sk.tp.: "given" instead of "to give it"
10. (Er.tp.)Gd.ed.: "to" changed to "of", then "to" reinstated
11. Hq.tp.: "which" instead of "that"; (Sk.tp.)Sk.cr.: "that" changed to "which"
12. A.o.d.: "can" instead of "will"
13. (Er.tp.)Gd.ed.: "to" crossed out, and omitted in Sk.tp., Sk.an.
14. Sk.sh.: a blank, "something" in sh. written above; a.o.d.: "something" included
15. Hq.tp., Sk.hw., Er.tp.: a second "in" added after "in"; (er.tp.)Gd.ed.: the second "in" crossed out; (Sk.tp.)Sk.cr.: the second "in" reinstated
16. (Sk.tp.)Sk.cr.: "the" crossed out; Sk.an.: "the" omitted
17. (Er.tp.)Gd.ed.: "that" inserted and included in Sk.tp.
18. (Er.tp.)Gd.ed.: "significant by it" changed to "signified by its"; (Sk.tp.)Sk.cr.: "signified by its" changed to "significant by its" then back to "signified by its"; Sk.an.: after several notes, Sk. agrees to "signified by its" and adds: "This is a correction by Ms. G. [probably Gd.]; this is grammatically probably better and does not change the meaning"
19. (Er.tp.)Gd.ed.: "the" crossed out, and omitted in Sk.tp.
20. Sk.sh.: actually "foold" written in lh., then the second "o" crossed out; "fuel" added above, then crossed out; Hq.tp.: "fuel" instead of "fold"; Sk.hw.: "fuel" added above "fold"; then "fuel" crossed out and "fold" reinstated
21. A.o.d.: "weak" instead of "fixed"
22. Sk.sh.: "it" in sh. crossed out, and omitted in a.o.d.
23. (Er.tp.)Gd.ed.: "it is" changed to "is it", followed by Sk.tp.
24. Er.tp.: "no resistance" instead of "non-resistance"; (er.tp.)Gd.ed.: "non-resistance" reinstated
25. Sk.sh.: a blank
26. Sk.hw.: "a" instead of "one"; (Sk.hw.)Sk.cr.: "one" reinstated
27. A.o.d.: "the" instead of "therefore"
28. Hq.tp., er.tp., Sk.tp.: "on" instead of "in"; (Sk.hw.)Sk.cr.: "in" changed to "on"

person it is in the depth and there is a saying in the East that[29]: Do not invoke the name of the[30] Satan or else[31] he[32] will rise from its[33] grave. An inconsiderate or tactless[34] person always falls in[35] the error on waking that[36] evil, even if it was[37] asleep. For he does not know the music of life. In order to live in the world one should become a musician of life. Every person therein is a note and when one feels this[38] way, then he has before him an instrument. The whole world is an instrument upon [39] which a symphony is to be played.

Even in small things one can observe the same law[40]. Very often the great trouble that one[41] has in his[42] life is not owing to the difficulty of [43]others, but owing to the[44] less comprehension of human nature. If one knew human nature this[45] would be the first and the last lesson to learn: not to resist evil. For resistance becomes a[46] fuel to the fire. If you tell someone: Do not do that[47], if you tell someone: Why did you do it?, if you say[48] someone: You have done such and such [49]thing, by all these things you only make the evil stronger. You make the person [50] firmer in his fault.

Everyone in this world can be a teacher, but not a real teacher. A real teacher is the one who always teaches himself, and as[51] more he teaches himself, the more he finds that[52] there is so much to be taught, that[53] this self has so many lacks that the whole lifetime[54] is not enough to teach it, and the

---

29. (Er.tp.)Gd.ed.: "that" crossed out, and omitted in Sk.tp.
30. (Er.tp.)Gd.ed.: "the" crossed out, and omitted in Sk.tp.
31. Ibid.: "else" crossed out and omitted in Sk.tp.
32. A.o.d.: "it" instead of "he"; (er.tp.)Gd.ed.: "it" changed to "he", followed by Sk.tp.
33. (Er.tp.)Gd.ed.: "its" changed to "his", followed by Sk.tp.
34. Hq.tp.: "thoughtless" instead of "tactless"; (Sk.tp.)Sk.cr.: parentheses inserted in lh. around "tact-" in "tactless", and "thought" written above; Sk.an.: "thoughtless" in place of "tactless"
35. (Er.tp.)Gd.ed.: "in" changed to "into", followed by Sk.tp.
36. Hq.tp.: "of wakening that" instead of "on waking that"; Sk.hw., er.tp., Sk.tp.: "of wakening this" instead of "on waking that"
37. A.o.d.: "were" instead of "was"
38. Hq.tp.: "that" instead of "this"
39. Sk.sh.: acutally "which" written in sh. twice, the first "which" crossed out later and omitted in a.o.d.
40. Sk.hw.: "this law" instead of "the same law"; (Sk.hw.)Sk.cr.: "the same law" reinstated
41. Sk.hw.: "one" omitted ; (Sk.hw.)Sk.cr.: reinstated; (er.tp.)Gd.ed.: "one" changed to "a person", followed by Sk.tp.; (Sk.tp.)Sk.cr.: "a person" in lh. parentheses, "one" written above; Sk.an.: "one" affirmed
42. (Sk.tp.)Sk.cr.: "his" in lh. parentheses and "one's" written above; Sk.an.: "one's" affirmed
43. A.o.d.: "the" added
44. (Hq.tp.)Gd.ed.: "the" crossed out, and omitted in Sk.tp.
45. A.o.d.: "that" instead of "this"
46. (Er.tp.)Gd.ed.: "a" crossed out, and omitted in Sk.tp.
47. Sk.hw., er.tp., Sk.tp.: "this" instead of "that"
48. Hq.tp.: "say to" instead of "say"; Sk.hw. er.tp., Sk.tp.: "tell" instead of "say"; (Sk.tp.)Sk.cr.: "tell" changed to "say to"
49. Hq.tp.: "a" added; (Sk.tp.)Sk.cr., Sk.an.: "a" inserted
50. Sk.sh.: an illegible cross out
51. (Er.tp.)Gd.ed.: "as" changed to "the", followed by Sk.tp.
52. Sk.hw.: "that" omitted; (Sk.hw.)Sk.cr.: reinstated
53. (Er.tp.)Gd.ed.: "that" crossed out, and omitted in Sk.tp.
54. Sk.hw.: "-time" of "lifetime" omitted; (Sk.hw.)Sk.cr:: reinstated

more [55]self learns, the more it overlooks the evil in the others. It does not mean that the evil is[56] in the others. It only means that one finds that the enemy [57]which one was seeing outwardly, [58]in oneself. And the [59] enemy[57] which[60] one was faced with in the outer life, one finds in one's own all[61] heart. It makes one feel humiliated but it teaches the true lesson to find one's self having the same element against[62] which one wishes to resist against[63] another.

Life is a place where a gentle movement is necessary. [64]Thought, speech or[65] action, in everything, a[66] rhythm must be controlled. A[67] law of harmony should be observed in all that one does. One must know that walking barefooted[68] upon the thorns even[69] will not allow one to be free from accusation. The thorns will accuse one of having trampled upon, down[70] them. If to that extent is[71] the delicacy of living in this[72] world[71], can anyone say that[73]: I have gained sufficient wisdom? Or can anyone say[74]: I like[75] [76] afford to live in this world without giving a[77] thought to this [78]problem?

The problem of evil is great and[79] many cannot tolerate to listen, to hear[80] its name. But they are faced to[81] it every moment of their life. And therefore not solving this problem cannot help. Besides this everyone is

---

55. (Er.tp.)Gd.ed.: "the" inserted, and included in Sk.tp.
56. Sk.hw.: a small blank after "is"; (er.tp.)Sk.cr.: "(not?)" inserted; (Sk.tp.)Sk.cr.: "not" included
57. Er.tp., Sk.tp.: "which one was...and the [blank] enemy" omitted; (Sk.tp.)Sk.cr.: these words reinstated; (Sk.tp.)Sk.cr.: "which" changed to "whom"; Sk.an.: "whom" affirmed
58. Sk.hw., Sk.tp.: "is" added
59. Sk.sh.: a word which starts with a "w" in sh.; however the remaining sh. symbols fail to form an actual word; Hq.tp., Sk.tp.: "worst" added; Sk.hw.: "words" added with dots underneath
60. (Er.tp.)Gd.ed.: "which" changed to "whom" followed by Sk.tp., Sk.an.
61. Sk.sh.: "all" in sh. crossed out and omitted in a.o.d.
62. (Er.tp.)Gd.ed.: "against" crossed out, and omitted in Sk.tp.,
63. (Er.tp.)Gd.ed.: "against" changed to "in", followed by Sk.tp.,
64. Ibid.: "In" inserted, and included in Sk.tp.
65. Sk.hw.: "and" instead of "or"; (Sk.hw.)Sk.cr.: "or" reinstated
66. (Er.tp.)Gd.ed.: "a" changed to "the", followed by Sk.tp.
67. (Er.tp.)Gd.ed.: "A" changed to "The", then back to "A"
68. Ibid.: "that walking barefooted" changed to "when walking barefoot", followed by Sk.tp.
69. Sk.hw.: "(they)" added; er.tp., Sk.tp.: "they" included; (er.tp.)Gd.ed.: parentheses around "they" added, then crossed out
70. Sk.sh.: "down" in sh. crossed out and omitted in a.o.d.
71. (Er.tp.)Gd.ed.: "to that extent is" changed to "is to that extent" and moved to after "world", followed by Sk.tp.
72. Hq.tp1.: "the" instead of "this"
73. (Er.tp.)Gd.ed.: "that" crossed out, and omitted in Sk.tp.
74. Sk.hw:, er.tp.: "ought anyone say" instead of "can anyone say"; (er.tp.)Gd.ed.: changed to "ought anyone to say", followed by Sk.tp.; (Sk.tp.)Sk.cr., Sk.an.: "can anyone say" reinstated
75. A.o.d.: "can" instead of "like"
76. Sk.sh.: a blank
77. (Er.tp.)Gd.ed.: "a" crossed out, and omitted in Sk.tp.
78. Sk.hw.: "trouble" written first, crossed out and followed by "problem"
79. A.o.d.: "and" omitted, then a new sentence starts here
80. (Er.tp.)Gd.ed.: "to listen, to hear" changed to "hearing", and so in Sk.tp.
81. (Er.tp.)Gd.ed.: "to" changed to "with", followed by Sk.tp.

ready to judge or to observe, take note[82] of the evil of another, not knowing that sometimes the surface of a thing is quite different from its depth. May be that what is seeming[83] evil has something good inside it. Or what is in appearance [84] it[85] may have a spark of evil inside. And from what standard we can[86] determine evil and good and who can judge the evil and good of [87] any mankind[88]? If one can judge, it is on[89] one's own evil and good that one can judge. No one except God has the power to judge another. Yes, the just[90] sense of justice that is given to man is to judge[91] his own actions and acts[92]; if one[93] judges himself he uses it the[94] best because for that purpose the sense of justice was given to him.

When we look at life with a telescope we shall find that it is nothing but a struggle of living, even[95] individuals or[96] collectively; and it appears that if there is anything worth-while in this life it is what is besides this struggle: the giving and taking of kindness and love and doing any actions[97] of selfishness[98]. However much[99] qualified a person[100] in the things of the world, his qualification reaches to[101] a certain length it does not go beyond. It is the qualification of life's understanding[102], the understanding of the law which is working behind it, [103]is the whole qualification required; and it is

---

82. Hq.tp.: "take notice" instead of "take note"; Sk.hw., er.tp., Sk.tp.: "to take notice" instead of "take note"
83. (Er.tp.)Gd.ed.: "that what is seeming" changed to "what seems", followed by Sk.tp.
84. Sk.sh.: "good" inserted lh. and included in a.o.d.
85. (Er.tp.)Gd.ed.: "it" crossed out, and omitted in Sk.tp.
86. (Er.tp.)Gd.ed.: "from what standard we can" changed to "by what standard can we", followed by Sk.tp.
87. Sk.sh.: an illegible word crossed out
88. (Er.tp.)Gd.ed.: "mankind" changed to "man" and "any" crossed out, then reinstated; Sk.tp.: "man" instead of "mankind"
89. Sk.sh.: "on" crossed off and parenthesized; omitted in a.o.d.
90. Sk.sh.: "just" crossed out and omitted in a.o.d.
91. (Er.tp.)Gd.ed.: "to judge" changed to "for judging", followed by Sk.tp.; Sk.an.: "to judge" reinstated
92. Sk.sh.: "acts" crossed out and omitted in a.o.d.
93. A.o.d.: "he" instead of "one"
94. (Er.tp.)Gd.ed.: "the" crossed out, and omitted in Sk.tp.
95. Sk.sh.: "even" crossed out, and omitted in a.o.d.
96. Hq.tp.: "individually and" instead of "individuals or"; Sk.hw.: "individuals and"; (Sk.hw.)Sk.cr.: "individuals or" reinstated; (er.tp.)Gd.ed.: "individuals or" changed to "individuals and"; Sk.tp.: "individually or" instead of "individuals or"
97. A.o.d.: "action" instead of "actions"
98. Sk.sh.: Sk. wrote out "fishness" in sh., then added an "s" symbol at the start of the "f" sound to compose "selfishness"; Hq.tp.2: "unselfishness" instead of "selfishness"; (er.tp.)Sk.cr.: "less" inserted in pencil over "selfishness"; (er.tp.)Gd.ed.: "less" crossed out and "un" inserted to read "unselfishness"; Sk.tp.: "unselfishness"; Sk.an.: Sk. supports "selflessness", then agrees to "unselfishness"
99. (Er.tp.)Gd.ed.: "much" crossed out, and omitted in Sk.tp.; Sk.an.: "much" reinstated
100. (Er.tp.)Gd.ed.: "is" inserted, and included in Sk.tp.
101. Ibid.: "to" crossed out, and omitted in Sk.tp.
102. (Er.tp.)Gd.ed.: "life's understanding" changed to "the understanding of life"; Sk.tp.: "the understanding of life"; Sk.an.: "life's understanding" reinstated
103. (Er.tp.)Gd.ed.: "that" inserted, and included in Sk.tp.

that[104] q.[105] only[106] which will diminish the continual struggle that one has in life. It will diminish[107] in that[108] way: It will give man less to resist. It will make a person more tolerant to[109] the natural condition of human beings. No sooner one imagines, thinks[110] that you cannot expect from a person what he is not capable of thinking or doing, he[111] becomes tolerant. The difficulty is that everyone demands of another person more in the way of thought and consideration, in the way of kindness and love. [112]One is more [113] justice and [113] wants,[112] he wants more justice and fairness on the part of another. And his standard may be so high that another person cannot keep[114] it. It is the high expectation from every side that[115] one has to receive from others. It is that which makes one disappointed. And generally what happened that one[116] does not only sit quiet after being disappointed, he resists and so the struggle of life continues. Compassion comes by this thought that[117]: I cannot expect [118]from a person who is unable of thinking or doing as I expect from him[118]. It is simply like this: [119]to feel that the tree of the pear[120] must give roses and the tree of the roses must give jasmines[121]. Every person is a certain plant. It is[122] not the same plant. Yes, we may be fond of roses, but every plant does not give roses. If we want roses we must only seek the plant

---

104. A.o.d.: "this" instead of "that"
105. Sk.sh.: "q." in sh. abbr. for "qualification"; written out in a.o.d.
106. Sk.sh.: "only" in sh. crossed out and "alone" in lh. added above, followed by a.o.d.
107. (Er.tp.)Gd.ed.: "it" inserted, and included in Sk.tp.
108. A.o.d.: "this" instead of "that"
109. (Er.tp.)Gd.ed.: "to" changed to "of", followed by Sk.tp.
110. Sk.sh.: "imagines" in sh. crossed out and omitted in a.o.d.; (er.tp.)Gd.ed.: "one thinks" changed to "does one think", followed by Sk.tp.
111. (Er.tp.)Gd.ed.: "he" changed to "than one", followed by Sk.tp.
112. Sk.sh.: Sk. first wrote "One is more [blank] justice and [blank] wants," in sh., then crossed out "one is more" and "wants,"; the sh. symbols for "is", "as" and "once" are similar - it isn't clear what was intended here); Hq.tp., Sk.hw.: "One is more [blank] justice and [blank] wants," omitted; (Sk.hw.)Sk.cr.: "justice and . . ." inserted above "love. He"; er.tp.: ", justice and . . . ." instead of". One is more [blank] justice and [blank] wants," ; (er.tp.)Gd.ed.: "fairness" inserted in the blank; Sk.tp.: ", justice and fairness." instead of ". One is more [blank] justice and [blank] wants,"; (Sk.tp.)Sk.cr.: ", justice and fairness" crossed out, to read the same as Hq.tp., Sk.hw.
113. Sk.sh.: a blank
114. (Er.tp.)Gd.ed.: "to" inserted, and included in Sk.tp.
115. (Er.tp.)Gd.ed.: "that" changed to "of what", followed by Sk.tp.
116. Hq.tp., Sk.hw.: "happens that one" instead of "happened that one"; (er.tp.)Gd.ed.: "happened that one" changed to "happens is that a person", followed by Sk.tp.
117. Er.tp.: "the thought that" instead of "this thought that"; (er.tp.)Gd.ed.: "that" crossed out, followed by Sk.tp.
118. (Er.tp.)Gd.ed.: "from a person who is unable of thinking or doing as I expect from him" changed to "of a person what he is unable to think or do as I expect it of him"; Sk.tp.: reads same as (er.tp.)Gd.ed.; Sk.an.: "it" after "expect" crossed out
119. Sk.hw., er.tp.: "that" added; (er.tp.)Gd.ed.: crossed out
120. (Er.tp.)Gd.ed.: "tree of the pear" changed to "peartree", followed by Sk.tp.
121. Hq.tp.: "rose must give jasmin" instead of "roses must give jasmines"; (er.tp.)Gd.ed.: "tree of the roses must give jasmines" changed to "rosetree must give jasmine", followed by Sk.tp.
122. (Er.tp.)Gd.ed.: "It is" crossed out, and omitted in Sk.tp.

of roses[123]. If it was not the rose plant, we must not be disappointed: [124]it is not the rose plant. It is not that. We should not be angry,[125] disappointed because[126] it[127] is not the rose plant that[128] does not give roses.[129] In this way we can correct ourself from[130] our own[131] deception[132] instead of demanding from[133] a tree which is not a rose tree, roses[133].

What education, what p.o.v.[134], what attitude in life would be most comfortable and will give happiness? It is this point of view of making an attitude [135]such as to overlook evil instead of resisting against[135] it. There are three ways of making life, struggling in the sea, the wave[136] of which, rising and falling at every[137] time. One[138] will struggle as long as the[139] life will permit, but the rising and the falling of the wave[136] in the sea will continue forever and ever. In the end he will be drowned and so is with man[140]. Man struggles[141] along being intoxicated in his struggle, but how long will it go[142]? As long as his energy will permit it. In the end he will be drowned. Yes, in this struggle he might seem powerful, he might seem to have won over others, [143]to have done things above[144] others. But what is it? In the end that person is drowned.

But there is another person who knows how to move harmoniously

---

123. (Er.tp.)Gd.ed.: "plant of roses" changed to "roseplant", followed by Sk.tp.
124. (Er.tp.)Gd.ed.: "that" inserted
125. Sk.sh.: "angry," in sh. crossed out, and omitted in a.o.d.
126. Hq.tp.: adds here: "the rose plant that does not give roses.", and then starts a new sentence
127. (Er.tp.)Gd.ed.: "it" changed to "that", followed by Sk.tp.; (Sk.tp.)Sk.cr., Sk.an.: "it" reinstated
128. (Er.tp.)Gd.ed.: "that" changed to "which", followed by Sk.tp.
129. Sk.hw., er.tp.: adds: "It is not the rose plant that does not give roses." again, a second time; (er.tp.)Gd.ed.: this additional sentence crossed out and replaced with "The plant that does not give roses is not the roseplant.", followed by Sk.tp. Then, in Sk.tp., Sk. adds parentheses around the preceding sentence: "(It is not...not give roses.)", apparently trying to work out the wording
130. Sk.hw., er.tp.: "ourselves from" instead of "ourself from"; (er.tp.)Gd.ed.: "ourselves from" changed to "ourselves of ", followed by Sk.tp., Sk.an.
131. Hq.tp.: "own" omitted
132. Sk.hw.: "disappointment" instead of "deception"; (Sk.hw.)Sk.cr.: changed to "deception"; (er.tp.)Gd.ed.: "deception" changed to "disappointment", followed by Sk.tp.; Sk.an.: after some debate, Sk. agrees to "disappointment"
133. (Er.tp.)Gd.ed.: "from" changed to "roses of " and "roses" omitted at end of sentence, followed by Sk.tp.
134. Sk.sh.: "p.o.v." abbr. for "point of view"; written out in a.o.d.
135. (Er.tp.)Gd.ed.: "such as to overlook evil instead of resisting against" changed to "of overlooking evil instead of resisting", followed by Sk.tp.
136. A.o.d.: "waves" instead of "wave"
137. (Er.tp.)Gd.ed.: "rising and falling at every" changed to "are rising and falling all the", followed by Sk.tp.
138. (Er.tp.)Gd.ed.: "One" changed to "A person", followed by Sk.tp.
139. (Sk.tp.)Sk.cr.: "the" crossed out, and omitted in Sk.an.
140. (Er.tp.)Gd.ed.: "and so is with man." changed to ". So it is with man in his life in the world", followed by Sk.tp., with parentheses added around "in his life in the world"
141. Hq.tp.: "struggling" instead of "struggles"
142. (Er.tp.)Gd.ed.: "on" inserted, followed by Sk.tp.
143. Sk.sh.: "he might seem" inserted in sh., and included in a.o.d.
144. Sk.hw.: "over" instead of "above"; (Sk.hw.)Sk.cr.: "above" reinstated

his hands[145] in the water and he has got the rhythm of moving his hands[146] and legs in the water; then he is swimming with the rising and falling of the waves. He is not struggling. This[147] man has a hope to arrive at[148] the port if only the port was[149] near. If the ideal of that man was[151] not too far when,[150] then he is the one to accomplish.

And the third person is the one who walks above, over the water. It is this[151] which is the meaning of Christ's walking over[152] the sea. The life[153] just like wave[154]. It is making its way continually. If one is disturbed by it he is disturbed[155]. He is[156] calm, [157] he will be calm. The one who will allow himself to be disturbed by it, he[158] will be disturbed more and more. Every day the one who will not take note[159] of it will keep his quiet which is his own within himself. The one who sees all things and yet rises above things is the one who will walk over[160] the sea.

No one can at once reach to[161] the highest summits[162] of life, of wisdom, in a moment's time. Even a lifetime is too short; yet hope is necessary. The one who hopes and sees the possibility, he walks to the summits[162]. The one who has no hope has no legs to mount on his[163] hill of wisdom, the summit of which is the desired goal.

164

---

145. (Er.tp.)Gd.ed.: "harmoniously his hands" changed to "his arms harmoniously", followed by Sk.tp.
146. (Er.tp.)Gd.ed.: "hands" changed to "arms", followed by Sk.tp.
147. Hq.tp.: "That" instead of "This"; Sk.hw.: "The" instead of "This"; (Sk.hw.)Sk.cr.: "This" reinstated
148. (Er.tp.)Gd.ed.: "to arrive at" changed to "of arriving in", followed by Sk.tp.
149. (Er.tp.)Gd.ed.: "was" changed to "is", followed by Sk.tp.
150. Sk.sh.: "when," crossed out and omitted in a.o.d.
151. Sk.hw.: "that" instead of "this"; (Sk.hw.)Sk.cr.: "this" reinstated
152. (Er.tp.)Gd.ed.: "over" changed to "on", followed by Sk.tp.
153. (Er.tp.)Gd.ed.: "The life" changed to "Life is", followed by Sk.tp.
154. A.o.d.: "waves" instead of "wave"
155. Sk.sh.: an illegible word is written underneath "he is" in sh.; Sk.hw.: "necessarily he will be disturbed" instead of "he is disturbed"; (Sk.hw.)Sk.cr.: "disturbance will..." written above "he will be disturbed"; er.tp.: "necessarily he will be disturbed" with "disturbance will" typed above; (er.tp.)Gd.ed.: changed to "necessarily he will be disturbed by its disturbance" followed by Sk.tp.
156. Hq.tp.: "If he is" instead of "He is"; Sk.hw., er.tp., Sk.tp.: "If he can keep" instead of "He is"
157. Sk.sh.: an illegible notation
158. (Er.tp.)Gd.ed.: "he" crossed out, and omitted in Sk.tp.
159. A.o.d.: "notice" instead of "note"
160. (Hq.tp.)Gd.ed.: "over" changed to "on", followed by Sk.tp.
161. (Er.tp.)Gd.ed.: "to" crossed out, and omitted in Sk.tp.
162. Er.tp., Sk.tp2: "summit" instead of "summits"
163. Hq.tp.: "the" instead of "his"; (er.tp.)Gd.ed.: "his" changed to "this", followed by Sk.tp.
164. Sk.hw.: "Questions and Answers after Lecture on Resist not Evil" written at top of page, followed by Sk.tp.; on a copy of Sk.tp., Sk. inserted "stencil 1968 till end of p5" in pencil above q.a., perhaps referring to the use of this tp. in the Pilgrimage series which she (continued...)

Question: *How is [165]a person who is the head of a small business or[165] institution to keep the position of not resisting[166] in the world?*

Answer: I have seen at the head of certain factories people who have won the heart[167] of everyone working[168] in the factory and another head of the[169] f.[170] against whom every worker in the factory is[171] speaking. May be that this next head[172] of the factory may make a greater profit than the other one. But at the same time in the end he will find that the first is more durable than the next. These manners[173] of wisdom and tenderness cannot be made as principles for people to be restricted to follow. The place of [174]knife a brush cannot take and therefore everyone has to use every manner and action according to the situation. Nevertheless that those[175] of not resisting evil[176] should be at the back of it.

Question: *How can you[177] manage with a person who is really bad?*

[178] Yes, it is this that if one[179] person is really bad that means that the whole surface is,[180] has become bad. But still the depth cannot be bad. For goodness is life itself and a person who is all bad cannot live. The very fact that he is living[181] shows

---

164. (...continued) worked with in the 1960s (no such stencil has been found)
165. Hq.tp.: "the person who is the head of some business or" instead of "a person who is the head of a small business or"; Sk.hw., Sk.tp.: "a person who is at the head of a business or some"; (Sk.tp.)Sk.cr.: changed to: "a person who is at the head of some business or"
166. Sk.sh.: "evil" in lh. inserted after "resisting"; Hq.tp.: "evil" added; (Sk.hw.)Sk.cr., (Sk.tp.)Sk.cr.: "evil" inserted
167. Hq.tp.: "hearts" instead of "heart"
168. Sk.hw., Sk.tp.,: "every worker" instead of "everyone working"; (Sk.tp.)Sk.cr.: "everyone working" reinstated
169. Sk.hw., Sk.tp.: "a" instead of "the"
170. Sk.sh.: "f." abbr. in sh. for "factory"; written out in a.o.d.
171. Sk.sh.: "was?" inserted in lh. above "is"; Hq.tp.: "was" instead of "is"; (Sk.tp.)Sk.cr.: "is" changed to "was"
172. Sk.hw.: "second head" instead of "next head"; (Sk.hw.)Sk.cr.: "(next)" inserted above "second"; Sk.tp., Sk.tp.: "second (next) head"; Sk.an.: "next head" agreed to
173. Sk.hw., Sk.tp.: "This manner" instead of "These manners"; (Sk.tp.)Sk.cr.: "These manners" reinstated
174. Sk.tp.: "a" added
175. A.o.d.: "thought" instead of "those"
176. Sk.hw.: "non-resisting" instead of "not resisting evil"; (Sk.hw.)Sk.cr.: "not resisting evil" reinstated
177. Sk.hw., Sk.tp.: "one" instead of "you"
178. A.o.d.: "Answer" indicated here (but not in Sk.sh.); in Sk.hw. "A" for "Answer" appears to have been added later in pencil
179. A.o.d.: "a" instead of "one"
180. Sk.sh.: "is," crossed out, and omitted in a.o.d.
181. Sk.hw., Sk.tp.: "alive" instead of "living"; (Sk.tp.)Sk.cr., Sk.an.: "living" reinstated

there,[182] there is a spark of goodness there. Besides as there are various objects, there are various persons; some show softness[183] outside, hardness inside. Some show hardness outside and softness inside. Some have[184] good in the depth and evil at[185] on the surface and some have[186] evil on the surface[187] and evil[188] in[189] the depth[190]. [191] because as many souls, so many different varieties there are.

Question: *Is there a system to take away the bad?*

Answer: The[192] system is the understanding of life more and more. [193] It is to keep the love element alive to try to keep a[194] harmonious attitude as much as possible and then to keep beauty before oneself [195]
[196]Humankind is always progressing and in that progress there [197]is, perhaps it is only a passing .[196, 197] [198]But I suppose that if it is[199] with grown up people it is much more difficult.[198] [200]But at the same time if the one has[201] the spirit that we are

182. A.o.d.: "that" instead of "there,"
183. Sk.hw.: "selfishness" instead of "softness"; (Sk.hw.)Sk.cr.: "softness" reinstated
184. Hq.tp.: "very" instead of "have"; (Sk.tp.)Sk.cr.: "have" changed to "very"; Sk.an.: "very" affirmed
185. Sk.sh.: "at" crossed out, and omitted in a.o.d.
186. (Sk.tp.)Sk.cr., Sk.an.: "have" crossed out;
187. Sk.hw.: "depth" instead of "surface"; Sk.tp.: "in the depth" instead of "on the surface"
188. Sk.sh.: "evil" crossed out, replaced with "good" in lh. above it, followed by a.o.d.
189. Sk.sh.: "in" changed in sh. to "on"
190. Sk.hw., Sk.tp.: "on the surface" instead of "in the depth"
191. Sk.sh.: a blank at the beginning of this sentence
192. Hq.tp.: "That" instead of "The"
193. Sk.sh.: a blank
194. Hq.tp.: "to" instead of "a"
195. Sk.sh.: half a line left open
196. Sk.hw., Sk.tp.: sentence omitted: "Humankind is always progressing and in that progress there is perhaps it is only a passing . . . ."; (Sk.tp.)Sk.cr.: "Human kind is always progressing; and in that progress there are passing phazes [sic]." inserted at bottom of page, crossed out and underneath it Sk. writes: "This sentence was not pronounced by Murshid. It must have been added later on." (It is, however, included in later copies of Sk.tp. without this note.)
197. Sk.sh.: "is" changed in sh. to "are", and "perhaps it is only a passing" crossed out; then a blank with "passing phases" inserted in lh. to read "are passing phases", followed by Hq.tp., Sk.tp., Sk.an.
198. (Sk.hw.)Sk.cr.: a "Q" is inserted in left margin next to this sentence, indicating a new "Question"; Sk.tp.: a new "Question" begins here (but not in the sh. or Hq.tp.)
199. Sk.tp.: "if it is" omitted; (Sk.tp.)Sk.cr.: reinstated
200. (Sk.hw.)Sk.cr.: "A." for "Answer" is inserted above the beginning of this sentence, and in the margin (neither the sh. nor Hq.tp. start an "Answer" here); and "It is," is inserted before "But"; Sk.tp.: follow (Sk.hw.)Sk.cr.
201. A.o.d.: "if one has" instead of "if the one has"; (Sk.tp.)Sk.cr.: "if one has" changed to "we should have"; Sk.an.: "we should have" in place of "if one has"; Sk. noted "how to change this - see it in the English stencil, will be the best solution"; the English stencil referred to is not in the archives

never grown up, that we have never closed[202] our heart from learning, that whatever the age we are always ready to accept what is harmonious[203] and beautiful. The idea is this, that when[204] one thinks that: What[205] I think is right, and one finds out arguments and reasons to make it [206]right over[207] what another person thinks is wrong and one finds out reasons to make it[206] wrong, that[208] person will always remain on the same place. But one who is ready to accept even from a child if there is anything that one says it[209] is wrong and one thinks: Yes, even [210]the child says it. It is a profit for me to accept it. For God has not only spoken through his prophets but he speaks through every person if we [211]open our heart to listen to it. The difficulty is that we become teachers. If we[211] kept ourselves a pupil [212] [213]through our whole life we can teach,[214] keep ourselves a pupil[213] and the teaching will come all the time from within and without. As soon as [215] we become teacher[216], we close our heart from him who alone is our teacher.

Question: *If one wants[217] to be kind to someone, how can one[218] prevent that?[219]*

Answer: Our part is to be kind. That person's part is to use [220] it

---

202. (Sk.tp.)Sk.cr.: "have never closed" changed to "should never close"; Sk.an.: reverses this change
203. Sk.sh.: "harmonious" crossed out; Sk.hw.: a blank; (Sk.hw.)Sk.cr.: "harmonious (?)" inserted in the blank; Sk.tp.: "(harmonious?)"; (Sk.tp.)Sk.cr.: parentheses and "?" crossed out, reinstating "harmonious"
204. Sk.sh.: "when" in sh. crossed out, and omitted in Sk.hw., Sk.tp.
205. Sk.hw.: "What" omitted; (Sk.hw.)Sk.cr.: reinstated
206. Sk.hw.: "right over what . . . reasons to make it" omitted; (Sk.hw.)Sk.cr.: reinstated at page bottom
207. A.o.d.: "and" instead of "over"
208. Sk.hw., Sk.tp.: ". This" instead of ", that"; (Sk.tp.)Sk.cr.: ", that" reinstated
209. (Sk.tp.)Sk.cr., Sk.an.: "that one says it" changed to "one says that";
210. Sk.tp.: "(so)" added; (Sk.tp.)Sk.cr.: crossed out
211. Sk.hw., Sk.tp.: words omitted : "open our heart . . . . teachers. If we"; (Sk.hw.)Sk.cr., (Sk.tp.)Sk.cr.: these words reinstated at bottom of page, beginning, however, with "opened" instead of "open"
212. Sk.sh.: a blank
213. Hq.tp.: "through our whole life we can keep ourselves a pupil" omitted but inserted in type at bottom of page (probably a typing error)
214. Sk.sh.: "teach," in sh. crossed out, and omitted in a.o.d.
215. Sk.sh.: actually "by" or "be", then "walk" in sh., then both crossed out
216. Sk.hw., Sk.tp.: "teachers" instead of "teacher"
217. Ibid.: "we want" instead of "one wants"
218. Ibid.: "we" instead of "one"
219. Sk.hw.: "person on making abuse of our kindness" added; (Sk.hw.)Sk.cr.: "making abuse" changed to "abusing"; Sk.tp.: "person abusing of our kindness" added
220. Sk.sh.: an illegible cross out

right[221]. It is not our part to see that the other person makes the right use [222]. If we shall think about it, we shall forget our business.

Question: *How can you[223] help at the same time if it is[224] that person who is doing harm? Who does not understand our kindness?*

Answer: Love is a conqueror and in the end he will conquer. It is not only the person outside that love will c.[225] [226]the conquering of which is the[227] conquering of God,[228] of the[229] kingdom of God. The power of love is penetrating. Nothing can resist it in the end. And by giving kindness we have not lost anything. It is an element which is never lessened. It is to[230] treasure which is divine. [231] when we see whether the person is worthy or unworthy, in that[232] case we limit our love in a channel. But when we allow that feeling of kindness to flow, then it will develop into a continual flowing condition and then kindness will work out its destiny, without any intention on our part.[233] [234]It is something that the whole life one must learn.[234]

[235]

---

221. Sk.hw., Sk.tp.: "rightly" instead of "right"
222. Ibid.: "of it" added
223. Ibid.: "one" instead of "you"
224. Sk.sh.: "if it is" crossed out, and omitted in a.o.d.
225. Sk.sh.: "c." in sh. for "conquer"; written out in a.o.d.
226. Hq.tp.: "It is" added and crossed out in type; (Sk.hw.)Sk.cr: "But it will conquer the self of the one who loves" inserted ("the self of the" is written over words no longer legible); Sk.tp.: follow (Sk.hw.)Sk.cr.
227. Sk.hw., Sk.tp.: "the" omitted; (Sk.hw.)Sk.cr., (Sk.tp.)Sk.cr.: reinstated
228. Sk.sh.: "of God," in sh. crossed out, and omitted in a.o.d.
229. Sk.hw.: "the" omitted, then inserted
230. A.o.d.: "a" instead of "to"
231. Sk.sh.: a blank at the beginning of this sentence
232. Sk.hw., Sk.tp.: "this" instead of "that"; (Sk.tp.)Sk.cr.: "that" reinstated
233. Sk.hw.: text ends here
234. Sk.sh.: parentheses later added around the last sentence; Sk.hw., Sk.tp.: sentence omitted;(Sk.tp.)Sk.cr.: sentence added in lh., crossed out and then Sk. wrote: "this last sentence was not pronounced by Murshid" (on the final retype of Sk.tp., the sentence is included without Sk.'s note)
235. Sk.hw.: in a different ink, Sk. adds: "Reported by Sakina.", then underneath she adds in pencil "but slightly different from Bio-type" (it is not clear what this refers to)

Sakina's shorthand reporting

[1]

[3,4] Rue du Dragon, Febr. 23rd, 1924[2]

[5]Beloved ones of God,

I would like to speak a few words to you on the subject of initiation.[3] The meaning of the word I.[6] is in the word itself. Initiation is the[7] initiative. In the first place every child that is born on earth is born with initiative. But then as he grows, more or less that spirit dies away, because the knowledge he gathers in his lifetime[8] gives together with courage[9] a doubt. This doubt increasing more and more, very often makes man lose that power of

---

Documents:

Sk.sh.	=	Sakina Furnée's shorthand reporting of the lecture, newly transcribed by B.v.d.B.
Hq.tp.	=	an early typescript made at Headquarters, Geneva, of unknown origin, possibly Sakina's shorthand transcription, no longer available. "N.74" and "Gatheka 26 for Cand." added later in unknown handwriting. A few corrections by Sakina are indicated in the notes as "(Hq.tp.)Sk.cr."
Sk.tp.1	=	a later typescript prepared by Sakina or under her direction, using "Hq.tp." and her shorthand. "Gatheka 26" later added in unknown handwriting. A few corrections by Sakina are indicated in the notes as "(Sk.tp.1)Sk.cr."
Gd.tp.	=	a typescript made by Murshida Sherifa Goodenough, without the q.a., and without reference to the Gathekas. It has numerous blanks, later filled in, and many differences from the other documents. Her corrections are indicated in the notes as "(Gd.tp.)Gd.cr."
Hq.st.	=	a stencil made at Headquarters, Geneva, for distribution of the Gatheka series to the Sufi Centres, without the q.a. It follows many of the changes in "(Gd.tp.)Gd.cr."
Sk.tp.2	=	a later Gatheka typescript, without the q.a., prepared by Sakina or under her direction. It is similar to "Gd.tp." and "Hq.st." Sakina's corrections are indicated in the notes as "(Sk.tp.2)Sk.cr.".

Notes:

1. Sk.tp.1: "Private Lecture" typed upper left
2. Hq.tp., Sk.tp.1: "Rue du Dragon" omitted; "for mureeds and friends in Paris" added; Hq.st., Sk.tp.2: date and location omitted (date inserted in lh. on a copy of Sk.tp.2)
3. Sk.sh.: The title "Initiation" written by Sk. in lh. in a different pencil, apparently added later; Hq.tp.: "initiation" underlined in lh. at end of first sentence as the title; Sk.tp.1, Gd.tp.: includes "Initiation" as the title; Sk.tp.2: Sufi Invocation added (see List), and the title "Initiation" also added
4. Sk.sh.: "Gatheka 26" written above the added title, and appears also to have been added later; Hq.tp., Sk.tp.1: "Gatheka 26" in unknown handwriting at top; Hq.st., Sk.tp.2: "Gatheka Number 26" and the Invocation added
5. Gd.tp., Hq.st., Sk.tp.2: "Beloved ones of God" and first sentence: "I would like...initiation." omitted
6. Sk.sh.: "I." in lh. abbr. for "Initiation"; written out in a.o.d.
7. Hq.st., Sk.tp.2: "the" omitted
8. Gd.tp.: "life" instead of "lifetime"
9. Gd.tp., Hq.st., Sk.tp.2: "together with the courage gives" instead of "gives together with courage"

initiation[10]. He then does not want to take a step before he sees whether it is the[11] land or[12] the[11] water. And very often water looks like land and land looks like water. Since according to the mystics the[11] life is an illusion, upon that illusion he bases his reason. Nevertheless this reasoning which he acquired[13], helps him in the life of[14] the world and yet very often it is this reasoning[15] which keeps him back from taking what is called the initiative. It is with this initiative spirit that anyone [16] who has accomplished something great in the world[17] has accomplished[18]. People call them mad[19] or fanatic[20] or crazy[21] in the beginning of their effort[22], but [23]after the result they thought that that person was the most wise[23]. Great prophets, the great makers of nations, the great inventors, the great discoverers, they all prove[24] this. And there is a question: Do they not see as a reasoning person sees, what is before him[25]? Yes, they see, but from[26] different eyes. Their p.o.v.[27] is different. It does not always agree with the point of view of an[28] average person. Therefore it is natural that people should call them fanatic[29]. People call that person fanatic[29], that person calls the people fanatic[29]. For that person sees perhaps more than the many around him. If anyone has helped himself to gain success after great failure or to get over an illness after a great suffering, that person has only come to this by this initiative spirit.

There are different kinds of initiation[30] that the souls experience. One kind of initiation is a natural initiation. A kind of natural unfoldment

---

10. (Sk.tp.1)Sk.cr.: "initiation" changed to "initiative";Gd.tp., Hq.st., Sk.tp.2: "the power of initiative" instead of "that power of initiation"
11. (Sk.tp.1)Sk.cr.: "the" crossed out; Gd.tp., Hq.st., Sk.tp.2: "the" omited
12. Hq.tp.: "of" instead of "or"
13. Hq.tp., Sk.tp.1: "requires" instead of "acquired"; (Sk.tp.1)Sk.cr.: "requires" changed to "acquires"; Gd.tp., Hq.st., Sk.tp.2: "reason which he acquires" instead of "reasoning which he acquired"
14. Gd.tp., Hq.st., Sk.tp.2: "his life in" instead of "the life of"
15. Gd.tp.: "reason" instead of "reasoning"
16. Sk.sh.: "in the world" inserted in sh. after "anyone", and included in a.o.d.
17. Gd.tp., Hq.st., Sk.tp.2: "in the world" omitted
18. Gd.tp.: "it" inserted in type then erased; Hq.st., Sk.tp.2: "it" added
19. Sk.tp.1: "mad" typed over, thus appearing crossed out on the carbon copy;Gd.tp.: a blank instead of "mad"
20. Gd.tp.: "fanatical" instead of "fanatic"
21. Gd.tp., Hq.st., Sk.tp.2: "or void of reason" added
22. Gd.tp., Hq.st., Sk.tp.2: "efforts" instead of "effort"
23. Gd.tp.: "in the end very often it is clear that that person was the wisest" instead of "after the result they thought that that person was the most wise"
24. Gd.tp., Hq.st., Sk.tp.2: "proved" instead of "prove"
25. Ibid: "them" instead of "him"
26. Ibid.: "with" instead of "from"
27. Sk.sh.: "p.o.v." abbr. for "point of view"; written out in a.o.d.
28. Gd.tp., Hq.st., Sk.tp.2: "the" instead of "an"
29. Gd.tp.: "fanatical" instead of "fanatic"
30. Gd.tp., Hq.st., Sk.tp.2: "initiations" instead of "initiation"

comes to the[31] soul for which the souls[32] cannot give any cause or reason; no effort or attempt has been made by a soul to experience it[33]. Sometimes the same initiation[34] comes after a great illness or pain or suffering[34]. It comes as an opening of the horizon. It comes as a flashlight[35] and in a moment the world becomes different. It is not that the world has changed. It is that[36] the person is tuned to a different pitch. He begins to think differently, feel differently, say[37] and act differently. The whole condition of the person[38] begins to change in connection with that person; one might[39] say that he begins to live from that moment. One might ask [40] in what way does it come? Does it come as a vision, as a dream, as a phenomena[41]? It might[42] come in any of the said[43] forms and yet one cannot fix the manner of its[44] manifestation manner[45].

And the other initiation which is known among[46] the mystics is the initiation that[47] one takes from a person living on the earth. Every mystical school therefore has[48] its own initiation. In the Orient, where mystical ideas are considered and regarded as most sacred, there any person who wishes to tread the spiritual path considers initiation as the most important[49] thing. When souls[50] like Jesus Christ had to be baptized by St. John[51], [52]no soul on the earth, can say that[53]: I have risen above the initiation. A person might ask me: Is it impossible? I will answer: There is nothing which is impossible[54] to attain the spiritual end[55] without initiation. I only can say that it is possible for a person to jump into the water and try to swim with an

---

31. A.o.d.: "a" instead of "the"
32. Ibid.: "soul" instead of "souls"
33. Gd.tp.: "it" omitted
34. Ibid.: "initiation" and "after a great illness or pain or suffering" omitted, then inserted in lh.
35. P-o-M. means by "flashlight" the sudden burst of light used by a photographer. See Oxford.
36. Gd.tp.: "It is that" omitted
37. (Sk.tp.1)Sk.cr.: "say" underlined and "see (?)" written above in lh.; Gd.tp., Sk.tp.2, Hq.st.: "see" instead of "say"
38. Gd.tp.: a blank instead of "person"
39. Ibid.: "light" instead of "might", probably a typing error
40. Sk.sh.: an inserted correction obliterated by one of two parentheses and "in" inserted in sh. instead
41. Hq.tp., Sk.tp.1, Gd.tp., Sk.tp.2: "phenomenon" instead of "phenomena"; P-o-M. characteristically used only the plural form, "phenomena"
42. Gd.tp.: "may" instead of "might"
43. Ibid.: "above" instead of "said"
44. Hq.tp.: "its" omitted; (Hq.tp.)Sk.cr.: "its" reinstated
45. Sk.sh.: "manner" crossed out, and omitted in a.o.d.
46. Gd.tp.: "to" instead of "among"; (Gd.tp.)Gd.cr.: "among" reinstated
47. Gd.tp.: "which" instead of "that"
48. Ibid.: "has had" instead of "therefore has"
49. Ibid.: "sacred" instead of "important"
50. Ibid.: "a soul" instead of "souls"
51. John the Baptist (see List)
52. Gd.tp.: "then" added
53. Gd.tp., Sk.tp.2: "that" omitted
54. Sk.tp.2: "even" added
55. Gd.tp.: "aim" instead of "end"

intention to arrive[56] at the port of New York. But it is,[57] his life is more secure if he will book his passage by the line where[58] the ships always pass. And[59] the same and even a[60] greater is the difference, is the difference between the[61] two souls, [62]one who wishes to journey in the spiritual path by taking initiation and the [63]other who refuses to do so[63]. The initiation that[64] a spiritual teacher gives means a trust given by the teacher to a[65] pupil, and a trust given by the pupil[66] to the teacher. And the progress of one initiative[67], depends upon how much of himself he gives to his teacher's guidance. One might give only a finger and the other[68] even a part of the finger; another[69] would give his whole hand. That makes a great difference. For if a pupil would ask to a[70] teacher: What do you ask of me?, the teacher will say: Your whole being. And as a[71] pupil will say[72]: Well, I will give a certain amount of my time and thought to your guidance, I will do a bit that comes in my way to do, will that be enough? The teacher will say: Yes, enough when[73] you think it is enough. But it is never enough in reality. One might think that[74]: It is[75] not giving away one's own point of view in order to follow another's[76] point of view? I will answer: No. If you have a point of view you never lose it. The point of view which you lose is not yours. And by looking at a thing from another's[77] point of view, you only enlarge your point of view. You have two points of view instead of one. If the thought of the pupil happens to be different than[78] of the teacher, by taking the teacher's thought it[79] is only doubled. [80]The pupil has his own point of

---

56. Ibid.: "of arriving" instead of "to arrive"
57. Sk.sh.: "it is," crossed out, and omitted in a.o.d.
58. Gd.tp.: "which" instead of "where"
59. Ibid.: "And" omitted
60. Sk.sh.: "a" crossed out, and omitted in a.o.d.
61. Sk.sh.: "is the difference between the" crossed out, and ", is the difference" omitted in a.o.d.
62. Gd.tp.: "the" added
63. Ibid.: "one who wishes to journey in the spiritual path without taking initiation" instead of "other who refuses to do so."
64. Ibid.: "which" instead of "that"
65. Ibid.: "the" instead of "a"
66. Ibid.: "which the pupil gives" instead of "given by the pupil"
67. A.o.d.: "the one initiated" instead of "one initiative"
68. Gd.tp.: "another" instead of "the other"
69. Ibid.: "the other" instead of "another"
70. Gd.tp.: "his" instead of "to a"; (Sk.tp.2)Sk.cr.: "to" crossed out
71. Gd.tp.: "if the" instead of "as a"; (Sk.tp.2)Sk.cr.: "as" changed to "if"
72. Sk.tp.2: "says" instead of "will say"
73. Gd.tp.: "as" instead of "enough when"
74. Ibid.: "that" omitted
75. A.o.d.: "is it" instead of "It is"
76. Gd.tp.: "another person's" instead of "another's"
77. Ibid.: "another person's" instead of "another's"
78. (Sk.tp.1)Sk.cr.: "than" changed to "from that"; Gd.tp., Sk.tp.2: "from that" instead of "than"; Hq.st.: "than that"
79. Gd.tp.: "point of view, the pupil's" instead of "thought it"
80. Ibid.: sentence omitted ("The pupil . . . just the same.")

view just the same.[80] He has something to make his choice[81] for his vision[82], the horizon of his thought is expanded. But a pupil[83] who will close himself and will[84] say: I will guard my point of view or[85] it will run away, he will never benefit by it[86].

The mystical part[87] is the most subtle[88] path to tread. The relation[89] between the teacher and pupil is too subtle for words to express. Besides the language of a mystical teacher is always illusive[90]. You cannot so to speak pin him, not[91] his words. You cannot ask of him to[92] clearly say that it is so and so, that it is[93] such and such; and if a mystic does it, he is not a mystic. If he is a mystic he cannot do it. For [94]mystic may seem standing on the earth, but he is flying in the air. Neither the air can[95] be made into a rock, nor a mystic can[96] be made into a gross entity. Neither his yes means[97] the same as the yes of the other[98]; nor his no means[99] the same as the no of the others[100]. Mystic language[101] is not the language of words. It is the language of meaning. It is to the greatest distress of the mystic that he has to use the words of everyday language which are not his words; he cannot [102]express himself in these words and the same[102] care[103], the same manner you will find in the action of the mystic. Every outward action of his will not express to ever be[104] the meaning which is behind it. Perhaps that[105] meaning is much more important[106] with the insignificant action outward[107]. The teacher therefore tests continually his pupil. He tells him and he does not tell him. For everything must come in its right time. Divine knowledge has never been

---

81. Gd.tp.: a long blank between "something" and "choice" filled in in lh. with "to make his"; Sk.tp.2: "from which" added between "something" and "to"
82. Gd.tp.: "his vision" omitted
83. Ibid.: "person" instead of "pupil"
84. Sk.tp.2: "will" omitted
85. Gd.tp.: "if not" instead of "or"
86. Ibid.: "is never" followed by a blank, instead of "will never benefit by it"
87. A.o.d.: "path" instead of "part"
88. Gd.tp.: "subtlest" instead of "most subtle"
89. Hq.tp.: "realisation" instead of "relation"; Sk.tp.1: "realisation (relation)"; (Sk.tp.1)Sk.cr.: changed back to "relation"
90. (Sk.tp.1)Sk.cr., (Gd.tp.)Gd.cr., (Sk.tp.2)Sk.cr.: "illusive" changed to "elusive"
91. Hq.tp., Sk.tp.1: "on" instead of ", not"; Gd.tp., Hq.st., Sk.tp.2: "to" instead of ", not"
92. Gd.tp., Hq.st., Sk.tp.2: "if he will" instead of "of him to"
93. Ibid.: "or" instead of "that it is"
94. Ibid.: "the" added
95. Ibid.: "can the air" instead of "the air can"
96. Ibid.: "can a mystic" instead of "a mystic can"
97. Ibid.: "does his yes mean" instead of "his yes means"
98. Gd.tp., Sk.tp.2: "another" instead of "the other"
99. Gd.tp., Hq.st., Sk.tp.2: "does his no mean" instead of "his no means"
100. Gd.tp.: "another" instead of "the others"; Hq.st., Sk.tp.2: "the" omitted
101. Gd.tp.: "Mystical language" instead of "Mystic language"; Hq.st., Sk.tp.2: "The language of the mystic" instead of "Mystic language"
102. Gd.tp.: passage mostly left blank; (Gd.tp.)Gd.cr.: filled in in lh. same as sh.
103. A.o.d.: "character" instead of "care"
104. Ibid.: "everybody" instead of "ever be"
105. Gd.tp.: "the" instead of "that"
106. Hq.tp., Sk.tp.1: "compared" added; Gd.tp., Hq.st., Sk.tp.2: "inwardly in comparison" added
107. Gd.tp., Hq.st., Sk.tp.2: "outwardly" instead of "outward"

taught in words, nor ever will it[108] be taught. The work of the[109], of a mystical[110] teacher is not to teach but to tune, to tune the pupil so that the pupil[111] may become the instrument of God. For the mystical teacher is not the player of the instrument, he is the tuner. When he has tuned the instrument, he gives it in the hand of the player[112] whose instrument[113] it is to play[114]. The beauty[115] of the mystical teacher is his service[116] in this direction as a tuner. Is dispute any good with a[117] spiritual teacher? Not at all, for the pupil may be speaking a different language. [118]The teacher speaks another[119] language. If there is no [120], how can the dispute be profitable? Therefore in the path of mysticism there is no dispute. Are there any rules in[121] this path to follow? No fixed rules. For every person there is a special rule. Yes, there is one law which applies to all things of[122] life. Sincerity is the only thing which is asked by a teacher, for truth is not the portion of the insincere. There may be several initiations he gives[123] to the pupil, that[124] the [125]teacher has taken in his[126] hand, but it depends upon the pupil to progress. [127]Teacher, as the parents are anxious[127], is naturally anxious to see the advancement of his pupil. There is no reason for the teacher to keep any[128] pupil backward[129], as there is no reason for any parents to keep their child back from success. For as in the happiness of the child[130] there is the happiness of the parents so in the advancement of the pupil there is the happiness[131] of the teacher.

But then there is another kind of initiation, which comes afterwards. And that initiation is an unfoldment of the soul. It comes as an after-effect

---

108. Ibid.: "will it ever" instead of "ever will it"
109. Sk.sh.: "of the" crossed out, and omitted in a.o.d.
110. Sk.tp.1: "mystic as" instead of "mystical"
111. Sk.tp.2: "pupil" omitted; (Sk.tp.2)Sk.cr.: reinstated
112. Sk.sh., Hq.tp.: "player" emphasized with hw. dots underneath; Gd.tp.: "Him" instead of "the player"
113. Gd.tp.: a blank; (Gd.tp.)Gd.cr.: "instrument" filled in in lh.
114. Gd.tp.: "it" added; (Gd.tp.)Gd.cr.: "it" crossed out
115. (Hq.tp.)Sk.cr.: "beauty" changed to "duty", and "duty" in a.o.d.
116. Gd.tp.: blank; (Gd.tp.)Gd.cr.: "service" filled in in lh.
117. Gd.tp.: "the" instead of "a"
118. Ibid.: "and" added
119. Ibid.: "in a different" instead of "another"
120. Sk.sh.: "common language" in sh. added above "no"; Hq.tp., Sk.tp.1, Hq.st., Sk.tp.2: "common language" included; Gd.tp.: "not one language" instead of "no common language"
121. Sk.tp.2: "on" instead of "in"
122. Gd.tp., Hq.st., Sk.tp.2: "in" instead of "of"
123. A.o.d.: "given" instead of "he gives"
124. Sk.tp.2: "whom" instead of "that"
125. Gd.tp.: "spiritual" added
126. A.o.d.: "his" omitted
127. Gd.tp., Hq.st., Sk.tp.2: "Just as the parents are anxious so the spiritual teacher" instead of "Teacher, as the parents are anxious"
128. Gd.tp.: "a" instead of "any"
129. Sk.tp.2: "back" instead of "backward"
130. Hq.tp.: Sk.tp.1: "children" instead of "child"
131. Sk.sh.: "happiness" in sh. crossed out, "satisfaction" added above in sh. and below in lh.; a.o.d.: "satisfaction"

of the[132] initiation that one had from the teacher. It comes as a kind of expansion and[133] consciousness; and the greatness of this initiation is depending[134] upon the length and width of the horizon of the consciousness. Many might[135] claim it, but few realize it. Those who realize, they do not[136] claim; as more fruitful a tree, the more it bends; so [137]more divine a spiritual realization[138], the more a person becomes humble. It is the less fruitful who becomes[139] more pretentious. Real initiate hardly speaks[140] of the word initiation; they do not[136] find profit in making others believe in[141] that they are initiate. They possess their gains[142] so they do not[136] want a gain outwardly. It is the one who has not got, who[143] wants from outside a recognition.
But one[144] might say, what is the profit of the[145] initiation? The answer is this[146]: True[147] religion, mysticism or philosophy, all[148] that we gain, it must result in one form, and that form is to be best fit[149] to serve our fellow-man[150].

151

Question: *When a pupil wants his master he,[152] he cannot see him. His master is not there. What must he do?*

Answer: He must try to learn to approach the master whom he has seen outwardly by closing his eyes in one moment's time.

Question: *How far can one leave on one side family duties, which so often prevent the pupil from giving his entire hand to his teacher?*

---

132. Gd.tp.: "this" instead of "the"
133. A.o.d.: "of" instead of "and"
134. Sk.sh.: "is" crossed out; a.o.d.: "depends" instead of "is depending"
135. Sk.sh.: "might" changed to read "may", and "may" in a.o.d.
136. Gd.tp.: "don't" instead of "do not"
137. Gd.tp., Hq.st., Sk.tp.2: "the" added
138. Gd.tp.: "spirit naturally" instead of "spiritual realization"
139. Hq.tp., Sk.tp.1, Gd.tp.: "become" instead of "becomes; (Hq.tp.)Sk.cr.: "becomes" reinstated
140. A.o.d.: "initiated ones hardly speak" instead of "initiate hardly speaks"
141. Gd.tp., Hq.st., Sk.tp.2: "in " omitted
142. Gd.tp. : "that gain" instead of "their gains"
143. Sk.sh.: "who" crossed out; Hq.tp., Sk.tp.1: "who" omitted
144. Gd.tp.: "you" instead of "one"
145. Sk.tp.2: "the" omitted
146. A.o.d.: "that" instead of "this"
147. Gd.tp., Hq.st., Sk.tp.2: "true" omitted
148. Hq.tp.: "is" instead of "all"; (Hq.tp.)Sk.cr.: "all" reinstated
149. Hq.tp., Sk.tp.1, Hq.st., Sk.tp.2: "fitted" instead of "fit"; Gd.tp.: "become better fitted" instead of "be best fit"
150. A.o.d.: "fellowmen" instead of "fellow-man"
151. Hq.st., Sk.tp.2: sentence added "To be read before Candidates for Initiation in the Sufi Order."
152. A.o.d.: "he," omitted

Answer: As far as he can.

Question: [153]*What must I do if I will become good but have obstacles, if I wish to become good, but there are so many obstacles for reaching the aim of being useful to humanity.*[153]

Answer: Obstacles naturally are many, for everyone who strives to be good; as,[154] as in accomplishing everything, there are obstacles. So in accomplishing this most important thing there are many more obstacles. And the best way is to be single-minded and the pursuit[155]: one's purpose, regardless of any obstacles that stand in the way.

Question: *Is the initiation, is*[156] *a reward* [157] *or an encouragement?*

Answer: It is neither of these. It is a step forward.

Question: *One must deserve that step forward?*

Answer: Well, the soul has automatically taken.

Question: *This step has been helped by the master?*

Answer: Yes, but the master's help is just like the ocean. The ocean has all the water. If you take a pitcher full, there is a pitcher full of water. If you take a glass, you have a glass full of water.

Question: *If we want to approach the master, are there moments more suitable then,*[158] *than others?*

Answer: Well, outwardly there are times which are more suitable than other times; but I should think whatever time the initiation is given that is the best time. [159]But when he is separate from his

153. Sk.sh.: "if I will become good but have obstacles" crossed out; then "I wish" in sh. added above "I will"; it is not clear what was intended here; a.o.d.: Question reads: "What must I do if I wish to become good but there are so many obstacles of reaching the aim of being useful to humanity?"
154. Sk.sh.: "as," in sh. crossed out, and omitted in a.o.d.
155. A.o.d.: "to pursue" instead of "the pursuit"
156. Sk.sh.: ", is" crossed out, and omitted in a.o.d.
157. Sk.sh.: a blank
158. A.o.d.: "then," omitted
159. Sk.sh.: this first part ("But . . . initiator") of the sentence is crossed out, and omitted in a.o.d.

initiator[159] [160], only it all depends upon the respondent attitude. The communication between two souls is not much different from the telephone or the wireless. And if one understands the construction of, of[161,162] and wireless it is much easier then to understand more of the communications between two souls. If I were to tell you my own experience, it has mostly[163] always happened that at the call of my murshid I was in his presence, I went[164], answered it. If there was a letter or a telegram it always reached me after I had seen my murshid when I returned home. But the fact of having had an initiation comes to the help of a person through the[165] whole life. Even if they leave or fall away, or think they become indifferent, I think[166] [167] it is just like this: There is one person going towards a place of pilgrimage and on the way he has become tired; instead[168] of walking, he sits and dozes and therefore what he has lost is the time. When he is awake he goes on in the same way to the pilgrimage. There is another one who has gone halfway and then he says: Well, I do not feel that there is anything to be had, and he turns back; so he has lost not only his time, but what he had to attain. So as he goes on, so he is far removed. I would rather a person [169] attempt to go to the shrine of pilgrimage, rather than turn his back to it. Besides, personally, if I found that instead of that shrine, it was a well, in which many who go are drowned, I, after having started to make a P.[170] to that shrine which was a well, I would prefer being drowned than turn back. But this principle I take personally for myself; I would not teach others to follow this.

Question: *In what moral condition comes one both to be,[171] become initiated [172] ?*

160. Sk.sh.: a blank
161. A.o.d.: the repeated ", of" omitted
162. Sk.sh.: actually "teleph." in lh. above "of" as an abbr. for "telephone", and "telephone" in a.o.d.
163. Sk.sh.: "mostly" in sh. crossed out, and omitted in a.o.d.
164. Ibid.: "went" in sh. crossed out, and omitted in a.o.d.
165. A.o.d.: "their" instead of "the"
166. Sk.sh.: "I think" in sh. crossed out, and omitted in a.o.d.
167. Sk.sh.: a blank
168. A.o.d.: "; instead" omitted
169. Sk.sh.: "didn't" inserted in sh. after "person"; a.o.d.: "did not" included
170. Sk.sh.: "P." abbr. for "pilgrimage" in lh. and written out in a.o.d.
171. Sk.sh.: "be" in sh. crossed out; a.o.d.: "must one be to" instead of "comes one both to be," (Sk.'s sh. symbols for "comes" and "both" are not clear)
172. Sk.sh.: a blank

Answer: Friendly attitude [173] and trust[174] confidence in one's,[175] oneself.

Question: Why,[176] what advantage is there to go on in something which is not as was expected[177] to be, instead of going back?

Answer: Spiritual objects is[178] not as tangible as the material objects and therefore the manner of obtaining it is also not the same. Once one has thought[179] in this way: I shall have the spiritual attainment, he certainly will have. A spiritual teacher apart, even if a person thought that in the stone there was something sacred and one attached oneself to the stone, there will come a day that he will get the spiritual realization from the stone. Though I shall repeat that a principle like this, I should never ask my pupils to follow. But to me, it is something religious that the [180] object that I considered sacred, if the whole world says: It is not, I shall still stick to it. If out of it a stream of water is rising over[181] flame of fire, I shall accept both. If in a battle one can give one's life in the spiritual strife, the life is too small a sacrifice to offer. Besides, I consider it is no life which is not sacrificed for something worthwhile; it is a death. By sacrifice I do not mean suicide; by sacrifice I mean rising above death. When a person no longer holds [182] his life from what he desires[183] and wishes to have, well, his life is blessed.

---

173. Sk.sh.: "towards all" inserted in sh., and included in a..o.d.
174. Ibid.: "trust" in sh. crossed out, and omitted in a.o.d.
175. Ibid.: "one's," in sh. crossed out, and omitted in a.o.d.
176. Ibid.: "Why," in sh. crossed out, and omitted in a.o.d.
177. A.o.d.: "one expected it" instead of "was expected"
178. (Sk.tp.1)Sk.cr.: "is" changed to "are"
179. A.o.d.: "that" added
180. Sk.sh.: illegible cross out
181. A.o.d.: "or" instead of "over"
182. Sk.sh.: "back" inserted in sh., and included in a.o.d.
183. Sk.sh.: "desires" crossed out and "considers spritual" inserted in sh.; followed by a.o.d.

Sakina's shorthand reporting

[1]Sorbonne, Feb 25th, 1924

2

[3]Beloved ones of God,

My subject of[4] this evening is the intellect and wisdom.[3] Often people confuse between these[5] two words I. and W.[6] Sometimes they use the word intellect for wisdom, sometimes wisdom for intellect. In the p.[7] of fact these are two different things altogether. The knowledge which is learned by knowing of[8] the names and forms in the outside world, it is that knowledge which[9] may be called intellect. There is another source of knowledge and that source of knowledge is within oneself. By[10] saying within oneself might confuse some people. One might think within oneself, might think[11] inside of one's body. But it is the ignorance of man of[12] himself. Man has a very

---

Documents:

Sk.sh.	=	Sakina Furnée's shorthand reporting, newly transcribed by B.v.d.B.
Lf.hw.	=	a handwritten reporting of a simultaneous French translation while the lecture was being given, made by Mlle H. Lefèbvre, not mentioned further as it is fragmentary and provides no further evidence for the English text.
Sk.tp.1	=	an early typescript, double spaced on long, fine paper, prepared by Sakina Furnée or under her supervision, from an unknown source. At the top, Sakina wrote "compared" in Dutch, indicating she had compared it to another document, perhaps her shorthand. She made a few corrections, indicated in the notes as "(Sk.tp.1)Sk.cr."
Sk.tp.2	=	a later typescript, prepared by Sakina Furnée or under her supervision, probably from Sk.tp.1 as they are nearly identical. Sakina made slightly different corrections to the typescript-original and a carbon copy of it also in the file; these are indicated in the notes as "(Sk.tp.2)Sk.cr."
Hq.st.	=	a stencilled copy made at Headquarters, Geneva, for distribution of the Social Gatheka series to the Sufi Centres. A typed copy, identical in wording, was later made by Sakina, which is not mentioned further.

Notes:

1. Sk.tp.1,2: "Paris" added before "Sorbonne"; Hq.st.: location and date omitted
2. Sk.sh., Sk.tp.1: title is missing; Sk.tp.2: "Public Lecture" added upper left, and below that the title: "INTELLECT AND WISDOM"; Hq.st.: "Social Gatheka" and "Number 53" added, followed by the Sufi Invocation (see List), and then the title: "INTELLECT AND WISDOM"
3. Sk.tp.1: "INTELLECT AND WISDOM" underlined in the first sentence as the title; Hq.st.: sentence omitted: "Beloved . . . wisdom."
4. Sk.tp.2: "of" omitted
5. Hq.st.: "the" instead of "between these"
6. Sk.sh.: "I.", "W." abbr. for "intellect", "wisdom"; written out in a.o.d.
7. Sk.sh.: "p." abbr. for "point"; written out in a.o.d.
8. Hq.st.: "of" omitted
9. Ibid.: ", it is that knowledge which" omitted
10. Ibid: "By" omitted
11. Ibid.: "means" instead of ", might think"
12. Ibid.: "of" omitted

poor idea of himself which keeps him in ignorance of [13]self. If man only knew how large[14], how wide, how deep, how high is his being, he would think, act and feel differently. But with all this length and width, depth[15] and height, when man is not conscious of it, he is as small as he thinks himself to be.

The essence of milk is butter, the essence of the flower is honey, the essence of the grapes is wine, and the essence of life is wisdom. Wisdom is not necessarily a knowledge of names and forms. Wisdom is the sum total of that knowledge which one gains from within and without. An intellectual, it is[16] person will argue, will dispute, but very often[17] a subject which he himself does not know fully and very often you see among those who dispute, dispute[18] and argue, [19]they dispute for the very reason that they do not know it[20] fully. Their argument on the outside makes one feel that they know it. But[21] the very reason that they argue, that shows[22] that they do not know it. The one who knows, he[23] does not need to argue, he knows it. [24]The very reason he knows it, he is so satisfied that that[25] satisfaction does not give him that hunger, that[26] that person who argues.

In the first place the trace of wisdom in the[27] nature can be found in studying the[27] instinct. The art of breathing[28] and making a nest among the birds, the art of swimming among the fishes, the art that exists in the[29] nature, besides that, the science that exists in the animals and birds who know their medicine when they are ill. In the ancient traditions of the Oriental people there exists a belief that first[30] medicine was [30]learned by the bear. The reason is[31] that the bear knew when he[32] was ill, where to go and what to find as an[33] herb or as a remedy to take, in order to bring about a

---

13. Ibid.: "his" added
14. Sk.sh.: inadvertently noted "lost" instead of "large"
15. Sk.tp.1: "depth" omitted; (Sk.tp.1)Sk.cr.: reinstated
16. A.o.d.: ", it is" omitted
17. Hq.st.: "upon" added
18. A.o.d.: the second ", dispute" omitted
19. Hq.st.: "that" added
20. Ibid.: "the subject" instead of "it"
21. Ibid.: "by" added
22. Ibid.: "it is evident" instead of "that shows"
23. Ibid.: ", he" omitted
24. Ibid.: "For" added
25. Ibid.: "this" instead of "that"
26. Sk.sh.: ", that" crossed out, then "as" inserted, followed by Sk.tp.1,2; Hq.st.: "as with" instead of ", that"
27. Hq.st.: "the" omitted
28. Sk.sh.: "breathing" crossed out; Sk. wrote and re-traced a word in lh. above "breathing" which is not legible; Sk.tp.1: "weaving" instead of "breathing"; (Sk.tp.1)Sk.cr.: "weaving" underscored, perhaps to indicate Sk. questioned it; Hq.st.: "breathing and" omitted
29. Hq.st.: "the" omitted
30. Ibid.: "first" moved to in front of "learned"
31. Ibid.: "was" instead of "is"
32. A.o.d.: "it" instead of "he"
33. Ibid.: "a" instead of "an"

cure. By[34] a deep study of this idea no scientist will deny the fact that among the[35] birds and animals there exists an instinct, that[36] in their illness and distress they[37] too[38] find the medicine[39].

Therefore, what we call intellectual study, it[40] is a collection of knowledge which has been given to man as a study to learn[41], and he understands it as an intellectual study, something to depend upon. But that is not all the knowledge, that is a limited part of the[42] knowledge. There is another fact[43] of knowledge which can be drawn of[44] the essence of life. That which is called instinct in the animals and birds in the lower creation, which[45] very i.[46] when developed a[47] man becomes intuition. It is not true when the psychologist[48], that all this[49] the child knows the child[50] has learned; whether a favorable attitude or an unfavorable attitude, whether a good manner or of[51] an ill manner. If two children were brought up[52] from[53] different parents and different races[52] without being trained in manner or wisdom, you will find that both will show their[54] manner and tendencies differently. If one were to think how much one learns from the outward[55] world, and how much one learns from within, it was not[56] an exaggeration if I were[57] to say that ninety nine percent one learns from within and one percent one learns from without, if one learned[58]. It is not true that[59] outwardly learned man becomes the great person or personality in the world. It is the inward learning that helps him[60] to become that. By this [61]I do not at all mean[61] that outward learning is not required. Outward learning is that[62] qualification of expressing that learning which one gets from within in a

34. Hq.st.: "After" instead of "By"
35. Ibid.: "the" omitted
36. Ibid.: "that" omitted
37. Sk.sh.: "they" crossed out, and omitted in a.o.d.
38. A.o.d.: "to" instead of "too"
39. Ibid.: "remedy" instead of "medicine"
40. Hq.st.: ", it" omitted
41. Ibid.: "for him to learn it" instead of "to learn"
42. Ibid.: "the" omitted
43. A.o.d.: "aspect" instead of "fact"
44. Hq.st.: "from" instead of "of"
45. Sk.tp.1,2: "the" instead of "which"; Hq.st.: "that" instead of "which"
46. Sk.sh.: "i." in sh. abbr. for "instinct", and written out in a.o.d.
47. Sk.sh.: "a", written over in sh. to read "in"
48. A.o.d.: "says" added
49. Ibid.: "that" instead of "this"
50. Hq.st.: "it" instead of "the child"
51. A.o.d.: "of" omitted
52. Hq.st.: "were brought up" moved to after "races"
53. Ibid.: "of" instead of "from"
54. Ibid.: "each will show its" instead of "both will show their"
55. A.o.d.: "outside" instead of "outward"
56. Sk.tp.1,2: "were" instead of "was not"; Hq.st.: "it would not be" instead of "was not"
57. Hq.st.: "if I were" omitted
58. Ibid.: "learns that" instead of "learned"
59. Ibid.: "the" added
60. Ibid.: "a man" instead of "him"
61. Ibid.: "it is not at all meant" instead of "I do not at all mean"
62. Ibid.: "as the" instead of "is that"

better form. But at the same time it is[63] the inner learning. If anyone has ever learned anything, he has learned from there[64].

[65]And now the subject comes how one has to pursue.[65] How does one pursue the wisdom which is within? By first realizing that intuition exists in him[66]. It is not every person who perhaps even believes in an[67] intuition. And among those who believe in the[68] intuition, they are not all who[69] trust in their intuition. No doubt, they have a reason not to trust because many times an intuition means,[70] seems to be a futile knowledge. But [71]if I were to say what reason it is[71] that intuition proves to be wrong, I will say[72] that it was not an intuition, but[73] thought that it was. Every person is not able to catch his first impulse, and the activity of mind always goes from one thing to another. Therefore as soon as from within there comes a thought [74] it goes to another and therefore [75]mind thinks it has thought[76]an idea[77]. And[78] therefore one thinks that[79]: I thought like this, but really speaking it was not an intuition; but after an intuition one goes a little further in thought and one thinks one has an intuition. In this way one begins to distrust intuition and when one distrusts his[80] own intuition one has no confidence in oneself. And to me[81] the meaning of faith is self-confidence. The one who has no c.[82] in oneself[83], whatever be his faith or belief, it is not substantial. If a person would come to me[84] and would say: I believe in you, I trust in[85] you, but only[86] I cannot trust in myself, I[87] would say: I appreciate very much your trust and belief, but I cannot depend upon you. But if another person comes and tells me[88]: I trust myself and do not know yet if

---

63. Ibid.: "from" added
64. Ibid.: "that he has learned" instead of "he has learned from there"
65. Ibid.: sentence omitted
66. Ibid.: "one" instead of "him"
67. Ibid.: "an" omitted
68. Ibid.: "the" omitted
69. Ibid.: "not all" instead of "they are not all who"
70. Sk.sh.: "means," crossed out, and omitted in a.o.d.
71. Hq.st.: "for what reason is it" instead of "if I were to say what reason it is"
72. Ibid.: "it is" instead of "I will say"
73. Sk.tp.1,2: "we" instead of "but"; Hq.st.: "they" instead of "but"
74. Sk.sh.: a blank; Hq.st.: "the activity of the mind" added, and the following "it" omitted
75. Hq.st.: "the" added
76. Ibid.: "of" added
77. Sk.tp.1,2: a blank; (Sk.tp.1)Sk.cr.: underscored "thought an idea" including the blank; Hq.st.: "but it has gone on to another idea" added
78. Hq.st.: "And" omitted
79. Ibid.: "that" omitted
80. Ibid.: "one's" instead of "his"
81. Ibid.: "to me" omitted
82. Sk.sh.: "c." in sh. abbr. for "confidence"; written out in a.o.d.
83. Hq.st.: "himself" instead of "oneself"
84. Ibid.: "a wise man" instead of "me"
85. Ibid.: "in" omitted
86. Ibid.: "only" omitted
87. Ibid.: "he" instead of "I"
88. Ibid.: "him" instead of "me"

I can trust you, I should[89] say: There is a hope for that man. For I[90] will know that he[91] has taken his first step already. He has to take his next step. The person[92] who cannot understand in, not[93] trust his own intuition, he[94] is perplexed, he does not know what of[95] wants. He will always[96] depend upon outer things which give him reasoning[97] and the things of[98] outer life which are subject to a continual change and [99] all[100] subject to death and destruction are not dependable. These things are called by the ancient Hindus an illusion; a person who thinks that[101]: I am a positivist because I depend upon outer reason [102] . He is dependable[103] of[104] something changeable and dependable[105] to death.

But now a question comes that[106]: How are we to know that it is an intuition? The thought-waves are just like voice-waves. It is quite easy and possible that a thought of another person helps[107] to float in that horizon[108] in which one is conscious and hears it and thinks[109]: It is my intuition. Very often what happens[110], a person feels a depression without any reason, a person feels humorous[111] without any particular reason. Very often it is a kind of floating thought or[112] feeling [113]of another person which passes through his[114] own mind and being, and he for that moment begins to feel[113] happy or unhappy, without any reason. And it happens very often to every person, during the day that there come thoughts and feelings and imaginations which he has never thought[115], or which he has no reason to

89. Ibid.: "he will" instead of "I should"
90. Ibid.: "he" instead of "I"
91. Ibid.: "person" instead of "he"
92. Hq.st.: "man" instead of "person"
93. Sk.sh.: "understand in," in sh. crossed out; a.o.d.: "understand in, not" omitted
94. Hq.st.: "he" omitted
95. Sk.sh.: "of" in sh. changed to "he" in sh.; and "he" in a.o.d.
96. Sk.tp.1: "always" omitted; (Sk.tp.1)Sk.cr.: reinstated
97. Hq.st.: "reasons" instead of "reasoning"
98. Hq.st.: "the" added
99. Sk.sh.: a blank
100. A.o.d.: "all" omitted
101. Hq.st.: "that" omitted
102. Sk.sh.: a blank; Sk.tp.1: "reasons" instead of "reason"; (Sk.tp.1)Sk.cr.: "reason" reinstated
103. Hq.st.: "is depending" instead of ". He is dependable"
104. Sk.sh.: "of" changed to "on" in sh., and "on" in a.o.d.
105. (Sk.tp.2)Sk.cr.: "(liable?)" inserted in margin of one copy in lh.; Hq.st.: "subject" instead of "dependable"
106. Hq.st.: "comes that" omitted
107. A.o.d.: "happens" instead of "helps"
108. Hq.st.: "scope" instead of "horizon"
109. Sk.tp.1,2: "that" added; Hq.st.: "one may hear it and think" instead of "hears it and thinks"
110. Hq.st.: "is that" added, and comma omitted
111. Hq.st.: "hilarious" instead of "humorous"
112. Sk.tp.1,2: "of" instead of "or"; (Sk.tp.2)Sk.cr.: "or" reinstated
113. Sk.tp.1: words omitted: "of another person . . . begins to feel"; (Sk.tp.1)Sk.cr.: reinstated
114. Hq.st.: "that person's" instead of "his"
115. Ibid.: "had" instead of "thought"

think[116]. It would not be then right[117] to call these things as[118] intuition. Water which is to be found in a little pit is not the water which is in the depth of the earth; and[119] therefore the thoughts which come and go floating on the surface are not to be depended upon. Real intuition is to be found in the depth of one's being. In the first place one must learn to believe in the existence of such a thing as intuition. The next thing is to be able to follow one's intuition, even at the cost of something valuable; even if one were deceived for some time after[120], one will not continually [121] deceive. Therefore a [122] one will find oneself on the right path. But the third thing is to make one's mind one-pointed, by the help of concentration which [123] would help[124] man to perceive the[125] intuition properly. Just like[126] hearing, the ears are so made that the voice-waves make a resonance[127] and become clear, so the mind must be made as[128] a[129] kind of accommodation[130] or mould in which the intuition may become clear. The difficulty is this:[131] that outwardly the work of the ear is different from the work of the eyes. [132] Mind does the both work[133], seeing and hearing at the same time. But besides this, mind is perceptive, also creative. But it cannot at the same time perceive and create both. For creating is expressing, and perceiving comes by receptivity. In the Sufi terms there are two temperaments among man[134]: l.[135] temperament and m.[136] temperament. The *jelal* temperament is expressive and the *jemal*[137] is receptive. And the temperament which [138]at the same time

---

116. Ibid.: "have" instead of "think"
117. Sk.tp.1: "right then" instead of "then right"; (Sk.tp.1)Sk.cr.: "then right" reinstated Hq.st.: "then, be right" instead of "be then right"
118. Hq.st.: "as" omitted
119. Ibid.: "and" omitted
120. Sk.sh.: "after" crossed out; omitted in a.o.d.; Sk.tp.1,2: "some times" instead of "some time"
121. Sk.sh.: a blank; Sk.tp.1,2: "continuably [sic] be deceived" instead of "continually deceive"; Hq.st.: "continually be deceived"
122. Sk.sh.: a blank; Sk.tp.1,2: "a" omitted, followed by a long blank; Hq.st.: "in the end" instead of "a [blank]"
123. Sk.sh.: an illegible cross out
124. Sk.sh.: "permit" in lh. above "help", and included in a.o.d. instead of "help"
125. Hq.st.: "the" omitted
126. Ibid.: "as for" instead of "like"
127. Ibid.: "in them" added
128. Ibid.: "as" omitted
129. Sk.tp.2: "a" omitted ; (Sk.tp.2)Sk.cr.: reinstated
130. Hq.st.: "capacity" instead of "accommodation"
131. Ibid.: "this:" omitted
132. Sk.sh.: a blank; Sk.tp.1,2: "But" added; Hq.st.: "But the" added
133. Sk.tp.1: "both the" instead of "the both"; (Sk.tp.1)Sk.cr.: "the both" reinstated; Sk.tp.2: first typed "the both the", then typed a cross out through the first "the" to read "both the"; Hq.st.: "both works" instead of "the both work"
134. A.o.d.: "men" instead of "man"
135. Sk.sh.: lower case "l." abbr. in lh. for "*jelal*" (see Glossary); written out in a.o.d.; Hq.st.: reads "the *jelal*"
136. Sk.sh.: "m." abbr. in lh. for "*jemal*" (see Glossary); written out in a.o.d.; Hq.st.: reads "the *jemal*"
137. Sk.tp.1,2: "temperament" added
138. Hq.st.: "is at the same time" instead of "at the same time when is"

when is[138] receptive and creative, that[139] temperament proves to be without result. It is this temperament which is called [140]*kemal* temperament [141] which has no result. It is,[142] that is why many people would like to hear and there are many other people who would like to speak. There are many people who would like [143]act and be active. There are others who would like to see others act, and [144]sit.

The one who works is pleased with working. The one who is sitting[145] is pleased to sit. Both enjoy what is akin to their temperament. Therefore one is creative [146]who acts; the other is receptive [147]who sits. But the[148] one can master one's life by taking these two different faculties in hand and both tried,[149] at times to be creative and at other times to be receptive. The one who is creative needs no doubt an action and a knowledge of action. But the one who is receptive, he[150] wants concentration and the attitude of mind which is receptive. The mind can become a receptacle of [151]knowledge which comes from within. If we find[152] among people, we shall find that among hundred persons[153] there are ninety-nine who are creative by nature, but one among them who is receptive enough to receive from his intuitive faculties.

The difficulty with the mind is[154] when one wishes to receive, the mind wishes to create. When one wishes to create, then the mind wishes to receive. By Hindus [155]mind is like[156] to a restive horse. A horse, unless you have put a rein upon it, will not be controlled and not take the direction which you want it to take. Therefore in order to attain the[157] wisdom which is as the essence of life and which is to be found within oneself, it[158] can only be attained by first making [159]mind obedient. And[160] the mind can be made

139. Ibid.: "this" instead of "that"
140. Ibid.: "the" added
141. Sk.sh.: a blank
142. Sk.sh.: "It is," crossed out, and omitted in a.o.d.
143. A.o.d.: "to" added
144. Hq.st.: "to" added
145. Sk.sh.: "is" crossed out; a.o.d.: "sits" instead of "is sitting"
146. Hq.st.: ", the one" added
147. Ibid.: ", he" added
148. A.o.d.: "the" omitted
149. Ibid.: "by trying" instead of "both tried,"
150. Hq.st.: ", he" omitted
151. A.o.d.: "the" added
152. Hq.st.: "look" instead of "find"
153. Sk.tp.1: "person" instead of "persons"; Hq.st.: "a hundred" instead of "hundred persons"
154. Hq.st.: "that" added
155. Ibid.: "the" added
156. A.o.d.: "likened" instead of "like"
157. Sk.tp.1,2: "that" instead of "the"; Hq.st.: "that" instead of "in order to attain the"
158. Hq.st.: ", it" omitted
159. Ibid.: "the" added
160. Ibid.: "And" omitted

obedient by the[161] concentration. People have easily understood[162] if you tell them about voice-culture that[163], how necessary it is, in order to sing well, to produce voice. Also one can easily understand what it is to learn the[164] physical culture in order to make the muscles strong. But when it comes to train[165] mind, in the first place a person asks: Is there a mind? [166] I thought that there was only a brain. And if it happens that the person believes in [167]mind, he does not know what can be done with it. Anything else he will find more valuable than the training of [168]mind. He might think that it is a work of the lazy people who have all sort[169] of luxury that[170] to give time to. It is the greatest mistake that man makes by keeping[171] away that culture which is the most necessary to begin from childhood as a training. And for[172] the question is[173] sometimes, a person asks[174]: Does a child not learn concentration when he goes to school? And my answer is[175]: Quite[176] the contrary; he mostly loses his concentration in the[177] school. When a little child begins to learn his mathematics and going from one to [178]hundred, he [179] his concentration[180]. The child has never an opportunity to sit quiet for one[181] moment. He has not often[182] opportunity to think of one thing for a moment. What therefore becomes[183]? Children become nervous. Today one sees that nervousness is to be found everywhere. If a person has equipped himself with a certain amount of education, he is found to be nervous[184]. Besides, after the education [185] the education is [186] . If [187]mind is not under his control, how can he use it? There is one thing to learn and there is

---

161. Ibid.: "the" omitted
162. Ibid.: "will easily understand" instead of "have easily understood"
163. Ibid.: "that" omitted
164. Ibid.: "the" omitted
165. Ibid.: "training the" instead of "train"
166. Sk.sh.: a blank
167. Hq.st.: "the" added
168. Ibid.: "the" added
169. Ibid.: "sorts" instead of "sort"
170. Sk.tp.1: "then" in lh. above "that"; Sk.tp.2: a blank instead of "that"; (Sk.tp.2)Sk.cr.: "that" reinstated; Hq.st.: "that" omitted
171. Hq.st.: "to keep" instead of "by keeping"
172. Sk.tp.1,2: "for" omitted
173. Hq.st.: "And for the question is" omitted
174. Ibid.: "says" instead of "asks"
175. Ibid.: "And my answer is" omitted
176. Ibid.: "on" added
177. Ibid.: "the" omitted
178. Ibid.: "a" added
179. Sk.sh.: a blank; Sk.tp.1,2: "loses" added
180. Hq.st.: "his concentration is lost" instead of "he [blank] his concentration"
181. Ibid.: "a" instead of "one"
182. Sk.tp.1,2: "often" omitted; (Sk.tp.1,2)Sk.cr: "not" changed to "no"; Hq.st.: "not an" instead of "not often"
183. Hq.st.: "comes about" instead of "becomes"
184. Sk.sh.: "to be nervous" in sh. added at bottom of the page, and included in a.o.d.
185. Sk.sh., Sk.tp.1,2: a blank
186. Sk.sh.: this sentence appears to be left unfinished; Sk.tp.1,2: a blank; Hq.st.: "is" omitted, and "has to be made use of" added
187. Hq.st.: "his" added

another thing: to make use of learning. It does not not[188] suffice the purpose to learn a song. By that he[189] cannot be a singer; he must learn to produce his voice also. And so it is with the intellectual[190] knowledge. A person has become a qualified person by studying for a long time and if he cannot use a[191] knowledge, what is the use?

There is a sufficient number of learned people; what today we want is people with master-minds, those who do not only see the life without, but within, who do not only draw [192]inspiration from the life without but also from the life within. Then they become the expression of this[193] perfect being, which is within, hidden behind this life of variety. I do not mean[194] by this that everyone learned becomes a mind[195] of super-being. I do not at all mean[196] that a person should be able to perform wonders or to perform miracles. I only by this mean[197] that a person may live a fuller life and may become a human being, in order to bring about better conditions in the world. What do we want? We want human beings. It is not necessary that all people must become most religious or most pious, or too good to live. We want wise men in business, in politics, in education, in all walks of life, those who do not only live on the surface and those who do not only show belief in the,[198] in matter, but those who believe[199] life within and without. It is such souls who will produce beauty. It is these souls which will harmonize the world, who will bring about the condition[200] which we need today. We want not only the knowledge of matter or spirit, but we want living in all walks of life. In one's business, in one's effort,[201] industry, in every art or science one is busy with, that[202] one might use that wisdom which is perfect in oneself. When the individual and [203]multitude will find beneath their feet a solid foundation on which they stand, from that day we will begin to say: Now we can hope for a better condition in the world. It is towards[204] this ideal that every effort of the Sufi Movement is directed. It is to attain to this mastery of mind that the[205] facilities have been given by the

---

188. A.o.d.: the second "not" omitted
189. Hq.st.: "a person" instead of "he"
190. Ibid.: "intuitive" instead of "intellectual"
191. Ibid.: "the" instead of "a"
192. Sk.tp.1: "their" added; (Sk.tp.1)Sk.cr.: crossed out
193. A.o.d.: "that" instead of "this"
194. Hq.st.: "It is not meant" instead of "I do not mean"
195. A.o.d.: "must become a kind" instead of "learned becomes a mind"
196. Hq.st.: "It is not at all meant" instead of "I do not at all mean"
197. Ibid.: "it is only meant by this" instead of "I only by this mean"
198. Sk.sh.: "show" and "in the" crossed out; a.o.d.: "believe" instead of "show belief in the,"
199. A.o.d.: "see" instead of "believe"
200. Hq.st.: "conditions" instead of "condition"
201. A.o.d.: "effort," omitted
202. Hq.st.: "that" omitted
203. Ibid.: "the" added
204. Ibid.: "toward" instead of "towards"
205. Ibid.: "the" omitted

Sufi Movement to those who wish to study and practise[206] in their lives.

207

---

206. Ibid.: "it" added
207. Sk.tp.1,2: "God bless you." added; Hq.st.: sentence added at the bottom: "To be read at the meetings of the Universal Brotherhood."

Sakina's shorthand reporting

[1]

Baronne d'Eichthal, 27th Febr. 1924[2]

[3,4]

[5]Beloved ones of God,

My subject this afternoon will be on faith[5], a word which[6] has been so little understood and I consider[7] to be a religious term. But really speaking, faith is not only something which is required in religion, but in all aspects of life that is the one thing that is required the most. It is the misinterpretation of faith that has taken away the value that could be attached to the word[8]. If not, if I were to say any word in the world, [9]in its sense is most valuable, it is faith. In the Orient they call faith: *yakin*[10] and there is another word used by the people of Arabia: *iman*[11]. There are many things

Documents:

Sk.sh.	=	Sakina Furnée's shorthand reporting, newly transcribed by B.v.d.B.
Lf.hw.	=	a handwritten reporting of a simultaneous French translation while the lecture was being given, made by Mlle H. Lefèbvre, not mentioned further as it is fragmentary and provides no further evidence for the English text.
Sk.tp.1	=	a typescript prepared by Sakina Furnée or under her supervision, from an unknown source. Her corrections are indicated in the notes as "(Sk.tp.1)Sk.cr."
Hq.st.	=	a stenciled copy, without the q.a., made at Headquarters, Geneva, for distribution of the Religious Gatheka series to the Sufi Centres.
er.tp.	=	a typescript of only the q.a., with numberous differences from the shorthand. Murshida Sherifa Goodenough edited this document, indicated in the notes as "(er.tp.)Gd.ed." A typed copy of this document in the file, marked "revised by Mda. Goodenough", is identical and therefore only mentioned in note 72.
Sk.tp.2	=	a typescript, without the q.a., prepared by Sakina Furnée or under her supervision; similar to Hq.st. One correction is indicated in the notes as "(Sk.tp.2)Sk.cr."
Sk.tp.3	=	a typescript, without the q.a., prepared by Sakina Furnée or under her supervision, from Hq.st. Sakina's corrections are indicated in the notes as "(Sk.tp.3)Sk.cr."

Notes:

1. Sk.tp.1: "Private Lecture" typed in upper left corner; Sk.tp.2: "Not in handwriting." typed in upper left corner
2. Sk.tp.1: "at Baronne d'Eichthal's." typed upper right; "Paris" added in lh.; Hq.st., Sk.tp.3: date and location omitted; date later added to Sk.tp.3 in unknown hw.; Sk.tp.2: location omitted
3. Hq.st., Sk.tp.3.: "Gatheka" and "Number 31" added, followed by the Sufi Invocation (see List)
4. Sk.sh.: the title "Faith" was later added by Sk., and is included in a.o.d.
5. Hq.st., Sk.tp.2,3: "Beloved ones . . . will be on faith" omitted
6. Hq.st., Sk.tp.2,3: "The word faith" instead of ", a word which"
7. A.o.d.: "often considered" instead of "I consider"
8. Sk.tp.1: "world" instead of "word"; (Sk.tp.1)Sk.cr.: "word" reinstated
9. (Sk.tp.2)Sk.cr.: "which" inserted
10. Sk.tp.1: "*Yaksen*" instead of "*yakin*" (see Glossary)
11. *Iman* (see Glossary)

sacred in the world, but faith the most. Not faith in what[12], but faith in itself. Faith comes from above. Doubt rises from below, from the earth. Therefore one thing is a[13] heavenly, the other earthly. When a person is more worldly, he is more doubting. The less worldly the more faith he has. You might find a person who had a great faith once, and then he has lost his faith, and at the same time you will study this,[14] his life has gone from a less worldly condition to a more worldly condition [15]. More absorbed in the life of this world makes one void of faith. This shows that faith is innate in human nature; doubt is which man partakes. As the sun is the light and the light which always is light, the clouds cover it. They do not cover the sun. They only cover the sun from our eyes.

When a person has no faith that does not mean that in the depth of his being there is no faith. There is a faith but that sun is covered by clouds. It is also just like the focusing of the camera, when the heart is exposed to the things of the world; then the[16] rising from the earth are always doubts[17] and they will cover. Doubt gives [18]pessimistic attitude. One questions: Will it be or will it not be? Do I think rightly or do I think wrongly? Am I on the right path or on the wrong path? Shall I succeed or shall I fail through life? Shall conditions be bad or worse, real[19]? And when there are two things, the earth inspires one[20]. The earth impresses one with doubts against the good thing; one likes[21] to conquer, to have it[22]. One desires that the thing should be better, and what one finds from the other[23] rising are the doubts. And therefore for his faith he does not get proper support from the earth and as man does not see God, he does not look above; he only looks on the earth, he wants a support from there. And the great lesson that the blessed ones have taught to humanity was raise,[24] to raise one's vision upwards and to find faith in something which is free from all doubt.

Therefore pessimism [25] and optimism both[26] are the different attitudes. One attitude looks downward. The other attitude looks upward. And very few of us really know what miracle is hidden in faith, what power

---

12. Sk.tp.3: "something" instead of "what"
13. Sk.sh.: "a" crossed out, and omitted in a.o.d.
14. A.o.d.: "that" instead of "this,"
15. Sk.sh.: a blank
16. (Sk.tp.1)Sk.cr.: "the" crossed out; Hq.st., Sk.tp.2,3: "the" omitted
17. Sk.tp.1: "doubt" instead of "doubts"; (Sk.tp.1)Sk.cr.: "doubts" reinstated
18. Hq.st., Sk.tp.2,3: "a" added
19. A.o.d.: "better or worse" instead of "bad or worse, real"
20. Sk.sh.: "the earth inspires one" crossed out, and omitted in a.o.d.
21. A.o.d.: "wants" instead of "likes"
22. Sk.tp.2,3: "it" omitted
23. A.o.d.: "earth" instead of "other"
24. Sk.sh.: "raise," crossed out, and omitted in a.o.d.
25. Sk.sh.: an illegible cross out
26. Hq.st., Sk.tp.2,3: "both" omitted

and inspiration is hidden in faith. We only[27] think that[28]: I can believe in some thing[29]. I cannot believe in some things. But what before[30] we believe, we want proof of it from the earth. In order to sustain our faith we want a sustenance from an unlimited source, but we look for sustenance to the earth, which is a limited source. When a person looks at the tank full of water and says: O! what a small supply, what shall I do for the next year? He is right, but at the same time he is looking at the tank. But when one looks above one will see that the source is there. From there[31] the rain falls and many such tanks can be filled, even rivers and[32] [33] full of water [34]. The blessing of all kind is there if we only prepare our heart to receive it. If the heart is small like a glass of water, even if it was taken to the sea, it can only fetch a glass of water. But if the heart is large [35] then it will bring that much water.

No doubt patience is the first lesson to learn in the path of faith, because it is the patience which gives one strength to the hope. My spiritual teacher used to say in his benediction that[36]: "May your faith be strengthened". As a youth I thought he would have said that[36]: May you live long, may you be happy, prosperous, or may you gain wisdom [37]. The meaning of which now I realize every moment of my life more and more, what he meant by it[38]. For in faith there is all. All that one wants, all that one needs, all that one wishes to attain through life, it is all hidden in one's faith.

It is most interesting and laughable sometimes that[39] how it is easy for man to fix his faith on small things, but on large things he cannot fix his faith. A man fixes his faith on an object not in man. For instance if you said to a person: Here is a medicine for you, a m.[40] which will cure you, it is very easy for him to have faith. [41] And when you say: Well, I will think for your cure, you will be cured[42], the first thing that will come to him will be the proof[43]. What is the reason? The reason is this, that he sees the object, he does not see the thought. I have met with a very great healer who had a great success and I asked him the secret of his working. He said: "The secret of

27. Sk.tp.1: "all" instead of "only"
28. Hq.st., Sk.tp.2,3: "that" omitted
29. A.o.d.: "things" instead of "thing"
30. Ibid.: "before" omitted
31. Hq.st., Sk.tp.2,3: "which" instead of "there"
32. Sk.sh.: "and" crossed out; Hq.st., Sk.tp.2,3: "and" omitted
33. Sk.sh., Sk.tp.2: a blank
34. Sk.sh.: a blank
35. Ibid.: a blank
36. Sk.tp.2, Hq.st., Sk.tp.3: "that" omitted
37. Sk.sh.: a blank
38. Hq.st., Sk.tp.2,3: "what he meant by it" omitted
39. Sk.tp.2, Hq.st., Sk.tp.3: "that" omitted
40. Sk.sh.: "m." abbr. for medicine; written out in a.o.d.
41. Sk.sh.: a blank
42. Sk.tp.1: "you will be cured," omitted
43. A.o.d.: "doubt" instead of "proof"

my working is that in the first place I have taken a religious shrine where people come and there they sit. They certainly come with faith in this[44] particular shrine. Well, then there is another thing that I give them, some kind of mixture of powder. Really speaking, they heal;[45] I heal them, but they have no[46] faith in that. I give them some powder or something to drink and then they feel better".

The whole effort that different religions have made has been to make man see what is hidden in a human being. Rituals and ceremonies and different forms all teach the same thing[47], that: find the secret and the mystery of life. Not only in the objects we[48], but when you have been[49] through it, in the human being. And the same thing one sees: that one can easily have faith in man, but it is difficult to have faith in God. For the reason that one can see a human being before him, but one cannot see the greatest power in[50] perfection, which is in [51]abstract. But faith is as a substance and if one does not possess that S.[52] then one cannot raise it to the highest ideal, which alone [53] faith.

Now the[54] medical science is coming to the realization of the importance of psychology. Although it is only considering the thought-waves and thought-power, but faith is something else to be considered and studied. My experience with numerous students on[55] that[56] line has shown me that there may be a person who would be able to concentrate and maintain a thought, but yet that person is not capable fully, because there is no faith at the back of it. Therefore faith is not something which may be called a thought. Faith is the ground itself. It is a ground. Thoughts spring up from that[57] ground as plants and if the land is not fertile then the plants cannot come up. And so if there is not faith for a thought then only[58] a thought is not beneficial. Besides this[59] there is another thing, that something, which can be accomplished by the power of thought in a year's time, is accomplished by the power of faith behind it in one day. Someone asked[60]

44. Ibid.: "that" instead of "this"
45. Sk.sh.: "they heal;" crossed out, and omitted in a.o.d.
46. Sk.tp.2, Hq.st., Sk.tp.3: "more" instead of "no"
47. Sk.tp.2: "things" instead of "thing"
48. Sk.sh.: "we" crossed out, and omitted in a.o.d.
49. A.o.d.: "passed" instead of "been"
50. Ibid.: "and" instead of "in"
51. Ibid.: "the" added
52. Sk.sh.: "S." in lh. abbr. for "substance"; written out in a.o.d.
53. Sk.sh.: a blank, with "merits" inserted in lh., and included in a.o.d.
54. Hq.st., Sk.tp.2,3: "the" omitted
55. Ibid.: "in" instead of "on"
56. Sk.tp.1: "this" instead of "that"
57. A.o.d.: "this" instead of "that"
58. Ibid.: "also" instead of "only"
59. Sk.tp.2, Hq.st., Sk.tp.3: "this" omitted
60. Hq.st., Sk.tp.2,3: "said to" instead of "asked"

a Brahman[61] who was worshipping an idol made of stone that: God is formless, he should not be worshipped in an idol of rock. The B.[62] answered that: It is a question of faith. If I have a[63] faith in this stone, God who is everywhere will speak through this stone, but if one has not the[64] faith, even the God of the abstract of heavens will not be able to s.[65] If that is so, is there anything that cannot be accomplished, that[66] cannot be raised by faith? When we look at it from a metaphysical p.o.v.[67] we shall find that the secret of the whole creation is faith. And the perfection of faith is, when the faith has risen to that ideal, that height where it can hold itself without any support. Faith, therefore, after[68] accomplishing all that is to accomplish[69] will be the one thing and that will prove to be all things.

[70]

----

[71]

Question: *How do I[72] gain that faith?*

Answer: By fighting with doubts. It is a continual fight because doubts are inheritance[73] of the earth. We are walking on the earth, just the same, [74]it is a continual fight.

Question: *But where the faith[75] can be this[76] master, after a certain time faith can be mastered[77]?*

Answer: Of course, faith can be mastered by this; as one will fight with doubts, so one will gain his victory over doubts.

---

61. Sk.sh.: Sk. wrote "Braham" in lh., which is close to the Sanskrit word "Brahman"; the more common English spelling is "Brahmin", see Ox. (also, see Glossary and note 62)
62. Sk.sh.: "B." in lh. for "Brahman"; written out in a.o.d.
63. Sk.tp.3: "a" omitted
64. Ibid.: "no" instead of "not the"
65. Sk.sh.: "s." written in lh. for "speak"; written out in a.o.d.
66. Ibid.: "that" crossed out
67. Ibid.: "p.o.v." in sh. abbr. for "point of view"; written out in a.o.d.
68. Hq.st., Sk.tp.2,3: "for" instead of "after"
69. (Sk.tp.3)Sk.cr.: "to accomplish" changed to "to be accomplished"
70. Hq.st., Sk.tp.3: "To be read before candidates for Initiation in the Sufi Order." added at end of text.
71. Er.tp.: "Q's & A's after lecture on Faith (Paris, Feb 27, '24) (Gatheka)" added in lh. at top; a typed copy of this document has the note, "revised by Mda. Goodenough", in an unknown hw.
72. Sk.tp.1: "you" instead of "I"; er.tp.: "does one" instead of "do I"
73. Sk.sh.: "inheritants" written in lh. above the sh. "inheritance", and "inheritants" in a.o.d.; (er.tp.)Gd.ed.: "inheritants" changed back to "inheritance"
74. A.o.d.: "so" added
75. (Er.tp.)Gd.ed.: "(doubt?)" inserted above "faith"
76. A.o.d.: "the" instead of "this"
77. Er.tp.: "master" instead of "mastered"

Question: *Does M.'s[78] teaching come from Arabia?*

Answer: Yes, these schools[79] were for a long time in A.[80] But now this particular school of the Sufi is a universal school. Truth is all[81] one and the same, only its different expressions are different. There existed a school in Arabia which was a school of Sufis.

Question: *Is there a possibility of there being a religious faith without being attached to any religion?*

Answer: Well, certainly the religion of every soul is his own. Outwardly, one may belong to one religion, but in[82] inwardly everyone has his own religion and that is his true religion. I do not at all mean by faith, as people say in a particular religion or gospel or idea. I say faith is in a person.

Question: *Can one obtain the spiritual plane, faith[83] by earthly fight?[84] [85] by someone who does not believe in spiritual [86].*

Answer: For that we say in the East, a teacher is most helpful. For instance, a person who has in his scientific attainment arrived to[87] a state[88] of Edison[89], he is there already; he only has to turn his face and he is there already. There are,[90] is perhaps a business man, all his life he has done nothing but gaining[91] wealth. A person religious or[92] orthodox, a pious person, who[93] will look upon him as a most material person. But one does not know in order to gain that much money, what fight

---

78. Sk.sh.: "M.'s" abbr. for "Murshid's"; written out in a.o.d.
79. A.o.d.: "this school" instead of "these schools"
80. Sk.sh.: "A." abbr. for "Arabia"; written out in a.o.d.
81. A.o.d.: "all" omitted
82. Ibid.: "in" omitted
83. Sk.sh.: "faith" crossed out, and omitted in a.o.d.
84. Er.tp.: question ends here
85. Sk.sh.: "by an inclusive material" added in sh. above a blank; Sk.tp.1: same words and blank included
86. Sk.sh., Sk.tp.1: a blank
87. (Er.tp.)Gd.ed.: "to" changed to "at"
88. Er.tp.: "stage" instead of "state"
89. Thomas Edison (see List)
90. Sk.sh.: "are," crossed out, and omitted in a.o.d.
91. (Er.tp.)Gd.ed.: "gaining" changed to "gain"
92. Er.tp.: "religions, an" instead of "religious or"; (er.tp.)Gd.ed.: "or" inserted above "an"
93. Sk.sh.: "who" crossed out, and omitted in a.o.d.

he had to go through in life and what sacrifices[94] and what struggles and consideration he had to give to it. It is not always easy to become a man of wealth and therefore if he had struggles[95] along and has arrived to[96] a point that he can be called, called[97] rich, he has just to change his attitude, he is there already.

Question: *Can faith have an effect on things which are[98] not religious?*

Answer: Oh yes, faith can be used in every direction. Just like the light. By the light you can study religion and fare forth in [99]heavens and do everything. For instance you [100] no one in the world has been able to accomplish a great thing without the power of faith, if he was a general, a businessman, an inventor, or if he was a religious man. And the power that the[101] faith gives is beyond words to explain. And the weakness and the poverty that exists[102] in the absence of faith is most deplorable. The person may have everything in life: youth, wealth, comfort[103], position and power, and if faith lacks he is poverty-struck[104].

Question: *The faith in the myth of Orpheus[105], how do you interpret it?*

Answer: There is no better picture for me to explain faith to me[106] than the picture of Orpheus. To put the story in a few lines, I will say that O.[107], the lover of Eurydice[108], after she had passed, sang to the gods of the cosmos. And by singing to the gods of the cosmos they granted that Eurydice will be given to him. But while passing through the lower planes of this earth, there is only one condition and that is, he must not look back.

---

94. Er.tp.: "experience" instead of "sacrifices"; (er.tp.)Gd.ed.: changed to "sacrifice"
95. A.o.d.: "has struggled" instead of "had struggles"
96. (Er.tp.)Gd.ed.: "to" changed to "at"
97. Sk.sh.: "called, called rich" verified in sh.; first "called" may pertain to receiving a call towards a spiritual direction; a.o.d.: the second ", called" omitted
98. Er.tp.: "which are" omitted; (er.tp.)Gd.ed.: reinstated
99. (Er.tp.)Gd.ed.: "the" inserted
100. Sk.sh.: "For instance you [blank]" crossed out, and omitted in a.o.d.
101. (Er.tp.)Gd.ed.: "the" crossed out
102. A.o.d.: "exist" instead of "exists"
103. Er.tp.: "comfort" omitted; (er.tp.)Gd.ed.: reinstated
104. (Er.tp.)Gd.ed.: "struck" changed to "stricken"
105. Orpheus (see List)
106. (Sk.tp.1)Sk.cr.: "me" changed to "you"
107. Sk.sh.: "O." abbr. for "Orpheus", and written out in a.o.d.
108. Eurydice (see List)

The[109] Mercury[110] was the[111] watch it, and as Orpheus went on[112] playing his instrument onward, so Eurydice followed him. And there came an inclination in the heart of Orpheus: I wonder whether Eurydice is following me?; and he looked back and as he looked back, Mercury took her away. There is no better picture than the Greeks have made for[113] faith, that as long as his faith was strong he could even bring the soul who was [114] was difficult to be brought and there the soul was; but even before accomplishing the object he had a slight doubt and that doubt took away. Are there not many people who say: In the beginning of my work or undertaking I had such a great faith and afterwards it went badly. But they do not know, it is [115]like the picture of Orpheus. The doubt sprang[116] up, that is why it went wrong. It is a[117] superstition of the black cat crossing a person; then they say if you are[118] thinking of something and the black cat has crossed then it cannot be[119]. It is symbolical. The black cat is the doubt.

Question: *If the object is right one[120] should first satisfy[121] if the object is worthy. Then we are bound to get it, unless your faith fails?*

Answer: Yes, that is true. [122]

That depends upon our attitude, if our heart is just like [123]compass, always seeking the right thing and therefore it is just like [124]compass, but[125] you can take it to any direction, it always points to the same side. So the heart, even if it was turned to any side, it will always turn to the right side. In

---

109. A.o.d.: "The" omitted
110. Mercury (see List)
111. Sk.sh.: "the" in sh. although "to" may have been intended; "to" in a.o.d.
112. Sk.tp.1, er.tp.: "and" instead of "on"; (er.tp.)Gd.ed.: "on" reinstated
113. A.o.d.: "of " instead of "for"
114. Sk.sh.: "was" crossed out, followed by another illegible cross out
115. Er.tp.: "just" added
116. Sk.tp.1: "springs" instead of "sprang"
117. Sk.tp.1: "There is a" instead of "It is a"; er.tp.: "There is" instead of "It is a"; (er.tp.)Gd.ed.: changed to "There is a"
118. Sk.sh.: "you are" in sh. crossed out; er.tp.: "were" instead of "are"; (er.tp.)Gd.ed.: "are" reinstated
119. A.o.d.: "done" added
120. Er.tp.: "we" instead of "one"
121. Sk.tp.1: "examine" instead of "satisfy"; er.tp.: "consider" instead of "first satisfy"; (er.tp.)Gd.ed.: changed to "first consider"
122. Sk.sh.: a line and a half left blank
123. Er.tp.: "a" added
124. Ibid.: "the" added
125. Ibid.: "but" omitted

other words: for the right doer it is most difficult to do wrong and for the wrong[126] person it is most difficult to do right.

Question: *The wrongdoer can come to the right one day?*

Answer: Right is the might and right is the depth and right is the ideal of every soul. For the idea is this,[127] a person who tells a lie, a person who deceives people, who is treacherous, [128] he will do it to the others, but he does not want his friend[129] to do the same to him; that same, that one[130] prefers differently.

---

126. Sk.tp.1: "doing" added
127. A.o.d.: "that" instead of "this,"
128. Sk.sh.: a blank
129. A.o.d.: "friends" instead of "friend"
130. Ibid.: "shows that he" instead of "same, that one"

Paris, le 4 Mars[1] 1924
chez Mme d'Eichthal

L'Homme Normal

Bien aimés de Dieu,

Selon les médecins, il y a une condition du corps et de l'esprit qu'on appelle normale. Selon un mystique, la personne nommée ainsi normale, n'est pas encore normale. L'épreuve du mystique est plus grande que celle du médecin ou du psychologue. Car le mystique voit dans chaque être un instrument, et il est normal quand il est bien accordé: ceci peut être vrai physiquement, moralement ~~intellectuellement~~[2] et spirituellement, et il faut passer par ces 4[3] épreuves pour pouvoir se trouver normal.

L'épreuve physique est la suivante: que la circulation du sang, les battements du coeur doivent être égaux, réguliers. Si ces deux battements, pouls et coeur, sont réguliers, ceci prouve que la respiration de la personne est rythmique[4] et harmonieuse. Toutes les douleurs, malaises, viennent de ceci: circulation du sang fonctionnant mal.

Ensuite, aspect mental: personne qui change souvent, qui pense une chose[5] aujourd'hui, une chose différent demain[6], cette personne n'est pas normale. Personne dont les sentiments sont tellement excités qu'ils perdent l'équilibre, cette personne non plus, pas normale; une personne[7] qui change, pendant une[8] journée, de[9] pensées et d'intentions, n'est pas normale. Qui ne sait pas tenir[10] parole, promesse, n'est pas normale. Pour un mystique celui

---

Document:

Lf.hw. = Mlle H. Lefèbvre's handwritten reporting of the simultaneous French translation of the lecture, given sentence by sentence as P-o-M. was speaking. No English version of the lecture has been found.

Notes:

1. The French date, "le 4 Mars", the the 4th of March
2. The word "intellectuellement" is crossed out in the manuscript; it is not possible to determine whether this was done at the time of the reporting or at a later time
3. The writing is unclear, but it seems the number "4" was altered to "3" or "2"
4. Another word was written first, then the word "rhythmique" was written over it; the original work is not decipherable
5. The words "qui" and "une chose" appear above the line
6. The words "une chose différente" appear below the line, followed by an indecipherable word, and then, perhaps, "demain"
7. The words "une personne" appear in the margin
8. The word "une" is written above the line
9. The word "de" appears in the margin
10. The word "tenir" (?) is hard to make out

qu'on nomme un "pécheur" [11]est seulement un être pas normal. Tout péché, tout mal est anormal.

Au point de vue spirituel, il se trouve caché dans l'être un régulateur de la vie, le coeur. On peut le mettre à l'épreuve, et si le coeur est dans sa condition normale, la personne est normale. Le coeur physique est normal quand le coeur fait son travail régulièrement. Le coeur mental est normal quand pensée et imagination sont solides et portent des fruits. Le coeur spirituel est normal quand il montre sa qualité, qui est l'amour. Le signe est le suivant: si le coeur . . . . . . est vivant, il est ouvert à la beauté sous toutes ses formes, matérielles et immatérielles, à la[12] finesse de la pensée, du sentiment, des manières. Quand il y a manque de manières, c'est que le coeur est anormal.

Les personnes qui blâment, ne savent pas ce qui est derrière. Qui ne ressent pas sympathie, pas émotion, montre que le coeur ne travaille pas bien, n'est pas en ordre.

En Orient, il y a des sages, et ceux qui font semblant d'être sages. On les découvre vite, car la personne qui n'est pas accordée ne peut pas faire semblant. Si on a l'air d'être accordé, on l'est. Plus on étudie ce sujet, plus on arrive à comprendre sa propre vie.

Il y a des moments où le pécheur le plus grand pourrait être un saint, et de même, il y a des moments où un saint pourrait être en désaccord. Une personne ne peut pas être toujours, toujours accordée. Instruments restent[13] accordés plus ou moins longtemps. Le but de la vie, c'est d'arriver à être accordé au diapason voulu. Santé, pouvoir, joie, paix, tout dépend de la façon dont on est accordé.

L'effet de la personne qui est en désaccord, c'est comme un piano non accordé; quand on joue, il trouble l'atmosphère. Celui qui est accordé est comme un piano bien accordé: un seul accord peut produire presque l'extase.

Qu'est-ce qui aide une personne à rester accordée? et qu'est-ce-qui fait qu'elle ne l'est pas? C'est de nouveau comme l'instrument: si on le déplace, secousse et mouvements le dérangent. De même pour les personnes qui doivent remuer, travailler toute[14] la journée; il leur faut le temps de se recueillir, c'est le temps d'accorder l'instrument. D'autres ont besoin[15] toujours, d'écouter et de[16] parler. Même ceux qui donnent et qui[17] reçoivent l'amour, ils ne savent pas ce qu'est ce pouvoir du coeur; que le vrai amour

---

11. The words "un être" are written above the line
12. The words "a la" appear above the line
13. The word "restent" is inserted in the text
14. The word "toute" is written over another word, now indecipherable
15. The words "ont besoin" were inserted here
16. The word "de" appears above the line
17. The word "qui" is written in the margin

est celui qui est ouvert à la beauté sous toutes ses formes; plus grand il devient, sans parole, sans voix, car alors pas besoin de dire j'existe; il est là; il est la vie même.

Quand ce coeur spirituel est occupé à donner et à recevoir l'amour, il est comme le corps physique qui bouge. Le vrai amour est la concentration dans[18] l'amour divin, qui s'exprime dans la sincérité, dans la fidélité, dans la reconnaissance, nécessairement, personne normale est vertueuse, la non-normale manque de vertu.

Comment réaliser ceci de plus en plus? En élargissant son point de vue; plus il est grande[19], plus grande est l'âme. Le point de vue n'est pas toujours large; l'influence de . . . ne . . . .

Dieu, qui est à la fois au ciel et sur la terre, ne demande pas que l'attention de l'homme soit toujours portée vers le ciel, puisqu'il est partout. Mais les mystiques conseillent de lever toujours les regards vers le ciel, pour qu'ils y trouvent la perfection qui leur est nécessaire. Ainsi, le point de vue est élargi[20]. Beaucoup de choses sont difficiles, mais rien n'est[21] impossible. C'est l'attachement aux choses de cette terre qui rend le point de vue limité et étroit, et toutes les misères viennent de là. Plus on élargit son point de vue, plus on est heureux. Le Sufi[22] enseigne à élargir son point de vue.

---

18. The word "dans" is written over another word, now indecipherable
19. First "grande" was written, then altered to "large"
20. The word "élargi" is written in the margin over another word, now indecipherable
21. The word "n'est" is written above the line
22. Lf. spelled the word "Sufi", as in English, rather than "Soufi", the French spelling

Murshida Sherifa Goodenough's typescript

1

Paris. Rue du Dragon.
March 7th, 1924

The Power Of The Word

There is nothing more important as a means to raise one's consciousness than the repetition of the right word. It is therefore that we read in the Bible[2] the[3] first was the word and the word was God. There is nothing that can be of a greater use and importance in the path of spiritual attainment than the repetition of the word. When we look in the traditions we find that from the time of the ancient great Hindu teachers, who lived many thousand years before Christ, the sacred word was in practice. And so you will find in all the great periods when a religious reform came to different countries, that the power of the word was considered to be of immense importance: during the Jewish religion at the time when it was given, and also in the Christian religion when it began.

It is the misunderstanding of certain words of Christ which has confused many followers of the Christian religion from[4] understanding the importance of the word. For instance, when it is said to keep from vain repetitions[5], a person in the Western World, when he[6] repetitions, he[7] just makes a literal translation; he does not know what is meant by it. The

Documents:

Gd.tp. = Murshida Sherifa Goodenough's typescript on her large-lettered typewriter. On this typescript, Gd. made editorial alterations, indicated by "(Gd.tp.)Gd.ed." in the notes.

Sk.tp. = A typescript prepared by Sakina Furnée or under her supervision, mainly following the editorial changes in (Gd.tp.)Gd.ed.

A highly edited version of this lecture appeared in *The Sufi Message* series, vol. 2 (London, 1960), *The Mysticism of Sound and Music*, "The Power of the Word", section 4, not included in the notes.

Notes:

1. (Gd.tp.)Gd.ed.: "Private Lecture" handwritten at top; Sk.tp.: "Private Lecture." typed at top (later crossed out), then "FOR MUREEDS."
2. John 1:1
3. (Gd.tp.)Gd.ed.: "the" crossed out, "that" substituted; (Sk.tp.)Sk.cr.: "the" altered to "that" in ink
4. (Gd.tp.)Gd.ed.: in margin, "and prevented them" added, then crossed out; then "from" crossed out, "in" substituted; Sk.tp.: "in"
5. See Matthew 6:7
6. (Gd.tp.)Gd.ed.: "reads" added in ink; Sk.tp.: "reads"
7. (Gd.tp.)Gd.ed.: "he" crossed out; Sk.tp.: "he" omitted

condition was this, that the word God had become so much used in common[8] that in everything that one wanted to convince another person[9]—whether true or a lie—he used the word God in it[10]. If one wanted to buy or sell to anybody, in order to convince of his own idea, he used to attach the name of God to the object he wanted to sell. And when anyone did not believe, the custom was to tell him: By the name of God it is true. It is therefore that this sentence was told[11]: Do not make vain repetitions of the sacred name; it is too sacred to be used in trade or business. But then those who could not understand the idea behind it, they said that it was the repetition that Christ did not want. If they would only think that even at the last moment the master has used the repetition of the sacred name![12] And it is the same sacred words which have[13] from the ancient times till now are given from one teacher to his pupils.

Mystical words may be used in different languages, but they do not belong to any language. Now, for instance, some of you have been given the practice of *zikar*[14]. It is to be found today used in the Arabic language; one might think that it is from Arabia. But then it is used in the Persian language also; one who does not know its existence in Arabia might think that it comes from Persia. It exists in the Hindu[15] language; one who does not know its existence in two languages might think that it is Hindu. It also exists in the Hebrew language. It is the same word which has been repeated by Christ himself as the last word. But also those before Christ, mystics whose origin was the ancient school of Egypt, they also repeated the same. There are sufficient proofs to prove this fact, that during the time of Abraham, who was initiated in the school of Egypt, this word was used.

Now coming to the Buddhistic and Vedantist[16] religions and philosophical schools, we find the words that have been used for many thousands of years, the same words even today are used. For the Hindus it has been a kind of science, the
science which they called Mantra Yoga[17], the science of the word, the dynamic power, the vital power that lies in the repetition of certain words.

---

8. (Gd.tp.)Gd.ed., Sk.tp.: "affairs" added
9. (Gd.tp.)Gd.ed., Sk.tp.: "of" added
10. (Gd.tp.)Gd.ed.: "in it" crossed out; Sk.tp.: "in it" omitted
11. (Gd.tp.)Gd.ed.: "sentence was told" crossed out, "phrase was said" substituted; Sk.tp.: "phrase was said"
12. P-o-M. refers to the last words of Christ as recorded in the gospels of Mark and Matthew, "*Eli, Eli, lama sabachthani*" (Aramaic for "My God, my God, why hast Thou abandoned me?", translated from the Hebrew opening of Psalm 22); see Matthew 27:46 and Mark 15:34
13. (Gd.tp.)Gd.ed.: "have" crossed out; Sk.tp.: "have" omitted
14. See *dhikr* in Glossary
15. Hindi, or Hindustani, especially literary Urdu, strongly influenced by Persian and Arabic and written in their alphabet
16. See Vedanta in Glossary
17. See Mantra and Yoga in Glossary

I have spoken about it in *The Mysticism of Sound*[18], yet it is never sufficient; there is so much that can be spoken on the subject.

And now the modern psychology is beginning to waken to the same idea, although it is searching for something in darkness and it has not yet found the secret of it. Nevertheless, what little it now perceives, when it believes in the power of word and its repetition, that gives a hope that sometime it will come to the realization that the ancient people have realized.

Now the work of the Sufi Order, therefore, is to give the combined theory of the Hebrew line of mystics and of the Hindu line of mystics joined together. By Hebrew I mean not only the mine[19] of Moses, but also Christ included. But there are two distinct mystical[20] lines, and both those distinct lines are joined in what is called the Sufi message. Besides this, to interpret in the modern form—that is the meaning of the message.

Now one might want to know: What is it in the word that helps, and why does it help? In answer to that I should say that there is no expression of life more vital than words, because the voice is an expressive manifestation of breath, and breath is the very life. Therefore, the effect of the word that one says does not only make an effect on another person, but it also makes an effect upon oneself. Every word that one says has its effect not only upon one's body but upon one's mind and one's spirit. A tactless word does not only offend another, but a foolish word uttered can prove to be of a great disadvantage to oneself.

Many times a person in a pessimistic mood may, in a kind of disturbed condition, wish for death, wish for failure, wish for anything ?(to happen)[21]. If they only knew what an effect it has, they would be frightened. I would advise a person that, even in pain, if he can refrain from saying: I am in pain, he would do a great good to himself. If a person who has met with a misfortune, if he[22] would even[23] saying: I am experiencing a misfortune, it would be the greatest thing. For when a person acknowledges the existence of something he does not want he only gives it a greater life. In the same way, when a person acknowledges something that he wants, he gives that also life. But when a person says: Oh, I have waited and waited and waited, my ship will never come, he is keeping his ship back in the sea, his ship will never arrive in the port. But the one who does not even see it, but says: It is coming, it is coming, he is calling it, it will come.

---

18. A book made from lectures of P-o-M., published in England in 1923
19. (Gd.tp.)Gd.ed.: "mine" corrected to "line"; Sk.tp.: "line"
20. Sk.tp.: "mystic" instead of "mystical"
21. (Gd.tp.)Gd.ed.: "?(to happen)" crossed out [the ? and parentheses indicate some question as to what P-o-M. said, perhaps in the unknown reporting from which the typescript was made]; Sk.tp.: "?(to happen)" omitted
22. (Gd.tp.)Gd.ed.: ", if he" crossed out; Sk.tp.: ", if he" omitted
23. (Gd.tp.)Gd.ed.: "avoid" inserted here; Sk.tp.: "avoid" added

Now, that is the part of the meaning of the word ~~that~~[24] I have said. But then the mystical word has a greater value than the word that one uses in one's everyday language. For mystical words have come from three distinct sources: scientific, astronomical, and intuitive. Intuitive words have come as sudden expressions from God-realized souls. Souls that have become tuned to the whole universe, whatever comes from their mouth, that word or that phrase is something which has a much greater power than the words that everybody says. But, a spiritual person apart, even in your everyday life, do you not see that one person perhaps among your friends, among your acquaintances there is, his one word has a weight, has a[25] power? Another person says a thousand words that go in at one ear and out at the other. Because in one person his mouth speaks, in another person his heart speaks, in another his soul speaks. There is a great difference. One might say: How can a spiritual person intuitively bring out a word which has a power? And the answer is that there is a possibility of a soul's becoming so much in tune with the whole universe that he hears, so to speak, the voice of the spheres. Therefore, what he says, it comes like the re-echo of the whole universe. For instance, why should this[26] little thing here[27] not serve as a wireless machine; why has one to have a wireless machine? In the same way the person who is in tune with the universe becomes like a wireless instrument; what comes from him is the voice of the universe.

Now,[28] leaving the personal aspect aside, coming to the scientific and astronomical aspects, I should like to say that a deep study of human anatomy will explain to a person that there are delicate nervous centres that can only be affected by certain vibrations, upon which centres the equilibrium and the health of mind and body depend. Very often by such scientific words used by people they have been cured even of illnesses, because it has given that vibration to that certain centre which was wanted to bring about that life which was necessary. If one goes deeper in the science of the word one will find that every vowel and every consonant has its certain effect upon one's mind and body. Very often you will find that, before seeing a person, by knowing his name you get a kind of impression what that person is like. It all shows that the name makes such a great difference upon[29] a person's character.

Besides, when we come to the astronomical subject it is a very vast subject and it has a connexion with every existing art and science, and

---

24. Gd.tp: the word "that" is crossed out in type; Sk.tp.: "that" omitted
25. Sk.tp.: "a" omitted
26. (Gd.tp.)Gd.ed.: "this" crossed out, replaced with "any"; Sk.tp.: "any"
27. (Gd.tp.)Gd.ed.: "here" crossed out [apparently, P-o-M. must have been referring to some small object].; Sk.tp.: "here" omitted
28. (Gd.tp.)Gd.ed.: "Now," crossed out; Sk.tp.: "Now," omitted
29. (Gd.tp.)Gd.ed.: "upon" altered to "in"; Sk.tp.: "in"

vowels and words have their connexion with the astronomical science. By invoking a certain word one invokes a certain planet, either in order to diminish its influence if it is unfavourable, or to increase its power if it is favourable. Therefore, in the astronomical science of the Hindus, whenever the name is given to a person (or every [30] is given to a person)[31], it is given according to the astronomical science.

Now only a few words of advice that I would like to give to my mureeds: (It is)[32] that it is most essential that initiation in the Order be not mentioned before others. Besides, all the exercises given to them, they are given individually and must not be told to another. Its action upon you, upon your life, upon your character, even, must not be spoken before the others. For others cannot understand it, and it would be of no advantage in any way. The mystical path is a secret path, and a mureed is more and more trusted on his proving to be worthy of the trust, which he can prove by developing the power of keeping secret. Because with every desire of the teacher to help a mureed, he cannot do much if the pupil does not show depth in himself. Therefore, the two great qualifications necessary to be developed are to keep in secret all the teachings that are given, and to be sincere in the path every day more and more. For as I have always said, the truth is the portion of the sincere ones.

---

30. (Gd.tp.)Gd.ed.: a blank in the typescript has "name" written in ink; Sk.tp.: "name" in type
31. The parentheses indicate some question as to what P-o-M. said, perhaps in the unknown reporting from which the typescript was made
32. (Gd.tp.)Gd.ed.: "(It is)" crossed out; Sk.tp.: "(It is)" omitted

III.5[1] March 12th, 1924[2]

Gatha

[3]

[4]

The[5] breath is a light in itself, and it becomes projected [6]as a light from a search-lantern[6] thrown upon an object. When the breath is coarse, undeveloped, it is full of material atoms which make its light dim[7], but a developed breath [8]sometimes is not different but even brighter than the light of the sun[8]. Breath, being a light from another dimension which is unknown to science today, it cannot be visible to the ordinary physical eyes. The glands of the physical eyes must be cleansed and purified first by *pasi anfas*[9] before the eyes can see the light of breath.

What people call [10]aura is the light of breath, but it is not everyone who sees it! A radiant countenance is a proof of an aura which lightens it, and the lack of it is the lack of light in the breath. A seer sees the sign of ~~a~~[11]

Documents:

Gd.hw. = Murshida Sherifa Goodenough's handwritten text, probably taken from dictation of P-o-M. As it cannot be determined whether the revisions were made during the dictation or later, they are included in the text. The crossed-out words are omitted in the subsequent documents except where noted.

Gd.tp. = Murshida Sherifa Goodenough's typescript on her large-lettered typewriter, showing several editorial changes from Gd.hw.

Hq.st. = a stencilled copy prepared at Headquarters, Geneva, for distribution to Sufi Centres, following the text in Gd.tp.

Sk.tp. = a typescript prepared by Sakina Furnée or under her supervision, following the text of Gd.tp.

Notes:

1. Gd.tp., Hq.st., Sk.tp.: "Series III." instead of "III.5"
2. Ibid.: "Number 5." instead of date.
3. Hq.st., Sk.tp.: the Sufi Invocation (see List) added here
4. Gd.tp., Hq.st.: "PASI ANFAS." added, then "BREATH."; Sk.tp.: "BREATH." first, then "PASI ANFAS."
5. Sk.tp.: later Sk. crossed out "The" in ink and began the sentence with "Breath"
6. Gd.tp., Hq.st., Sk.tp.: "like the beam from a searchlight" instead of "as a light from a search-lantern"
7. Ibid.: "dim its light" instead of "make its light dim"
8. Ibid.: reordered and reworded to read: "is sometimes not different from the light of the sun, but even brighter than that"
9. A category in P-o-M.'s teaching, meaning "watching the breath" (see Glossary)
10. Gd.tp., Hq.st., Sk.tp.: "the" added
11. Ibid.: the crossed-out "a" restored

death more clearly and ~~much~~ long before[12] than a physician can. The reason is that the seer sees in the aura of a person, whereas the physician sees only the condition of the body.

There is a ~~legend~~ belief in India that there are some cobras that have light in their head, the light by which they find their way through the dark. They make [13]hole in the earth miles long, and illuminate the hole by their own light which is centred in their head. As two positive and negative wires[14] ~~help~~ cause the electric light to manifest, so the two[15], *jelal* and *jemal*[16], ~~aspects~~ currents of breath[15] when connected in a head in the way they ought to[17], it causes[18] the light to manifest.

Many experience the phenomenon[19] of the light of breath, and yet doubt if it can be true, for they think it is perhaps an imagination. Others, who are incapable of seeing that light, confirm their doubt ~~to be real~~. [20]Sufi by the development of breath experiences this light, which becomes for him a proof of the existence of that dimension which is unknown to the ordinary world.

[21]

---

12. Ibid.: "longer beforehand" in place of "long before"
13. Ibid.: "a" added
14. Ibid.: reordered to read: "as two wires, positive and negative,"
15. Ibid.: "currents of breath" moved to after "so the two"
16. *Jelal* and *jemal* are words used in the teachings of P-o-M. to mean, roughly, "forceful" and "receptive" (see Glossary)
17. Gd.tp., Hq.st., Sk.tp.: "be" added
18. Ibid.: "cause" instead of "it causes"
19. Gd.hw.: "phenomenon" changed to "phenomena" (P-o-M. characteristically used the singular form "phenomenon" for both singular and plural); Gd.tp., Hq.st., Sk.tp.: "phenomena"
20. Gd.tp., Hq.st., Sk.tp.: "The" added
21. Hq.st.: adds "A skeleton outline of thought to be circulated among the members of the E. S. C. [Elementary Study Circle] only." (apparently an error, since this was included in series III);Sk.tp.: adds "A skeleton outline of thought for circulation among the members of the Senior Study Circle only."

Sherifa Goodenough's handwritten text

III.4 March 15th, '24

Takua Taharat[1]

Innocence is the real purity according to the mystic, for innocence is the sign of purity of heart. The intuitive faculties play a greater part in the life of the innocent. People call them simple ones, nevertheless ~~simplicity~~ innocence[2] proves often more beneficial in life than worldly cleverness. The innocent are most often[3] blessed by providence than those worldly-wise, always trying to get the best of everyone and [4]seize every opportunity that may seem~~s~~[5] to be advantageous in any way.

It is not easy for a clever person to try and become innocent; it is something natural and manifests with the blooming of the heart. Innocence is the sign of the thriving of a spiritual personality. If one can develop anything it is only this, that one may abstain from trying to be clever, and know that a selfish and clever person with all his qualification of getting the best of another, comes across, sooner or later, a person more clever[6] than

---

Documents:

Gd.hw. = a document in the handwriting of Murshida Sherifa Goodenough, who prepared the series of *Gatha*s (see Glossary) of which this is one, probably taken from the dictation of P-o-M. As several corrections occur in the text, and it is impossible to determine whether they were made at the time of the dictation or later, they have been incorporated into the text itself and footnoted.

Gd.tp. = a typed version of the text made on Sherifa Goodenough's large-lettered typewriter, showing a few editorial changes.

Hq.st. = a stencilled (cyclostyled) version made at Headquarters, Geneva, for distribution to Sufi Centres.

Hq.tp. = a typewritten copy prepared at Headquarters, Geneva, for distribution to Sufi Centres.

Notes:

1. A category in the teaching of P-o-M., translated as "Everyday Life" (see Glossary); a.o.d.: "GATHA" at the top, with "Series III" below on the left, and "Number 4" below on the right, followed in Hq.st. and Hq.tp. by the Sufi Invocation (see Glossary); Gd.tp. and Hq.st. add after "Takua Taharat" the translation "Everyday Life", which Hq.tp. places before "Takua Taharat"
2. Gd.hw.: originally "simplicity" was written, but then it was crossed out and "innocence" was written above; a.o.d. have just "innocence"
3. A.o.d.: "oftener" instead of "most often"
4. Ibid.: "to" added before "seize"
5. Gd.hw.: originally "seems" was written, but then the final "s" on "seems" was crossed out, and "may" was added above; a.o.d.: "may seem"
6. A.o.d.: "cleverer" instead of "more clever"

him[7]. Often a clever person finds his own chain tied around his legs.

No one has arrived at a higher degree of spirituality without innocence. Innocence does not mean not knowing; it only means knowing and yet not knowing. A stupid person must not be confused with an innocent person, for the ~~stupid~~[8] former is blind, whereas the latter only closes his eyes when he wants to. It is the wise, really, who becomes innocent on arriving at a stage of perfection in wisdom. It is two kinds of persons who show childlike simplicity in their lives: the silly one who shows childish traits, and the wise one who shows innocence.

[9]

---

7. Ibid.: "he" instead of "him"
8. Gd.hw.: "stupid" crossed out, and not included in any other documents
9. Hq.st.: "A skeleton outline of thought for circulation among the members of the E. S. C. [Elementary Study Circle] only."; Hq.tp.: the same, except "Senior Study Circle" instead of "E. S. C."

III.6[1] March 17th, '24

Gatha
Pasi Anfas [2]

Why is breath called *prana* by the Hindus? It is because it brings on the surface the essence from within. It is a current which is running from the outer spheres to the inner spirit. What it brings from the outer spheres to the inner spirit is not nearly so great as ~~what~~ that which[3] it brings from the inner spheres of life.

This being the condition, breath is vitalizing. Naturally, therefore, the breath of a man ~~of~~ in[4] sound health must give [5]another in his presence health[5]. The breath of a master-mind must vitalize the thought of another; and the breath of a spiritual person must illuminate those in his presence. By breath ~~gives life~~[6] a spiritually developed person can impart his physical energy, his thought power, and his ~~ligh~~[7] spiritual influence to the others with whom he may come in contact. It is natural, no doubt, [8]if the one who wishes

---

Documents:

Gd.hw. = a document handwritten by Murshida Sherifa Goodenough (on the backside of a printed announcement), evidently from dictation of P-o-M. As it is not possible to determine whether the cross outs and changes were made during the dictation or later, they are all included in the text.

Gd.tp. = a typed version of the text made on Murshida Sherifa Goodenough's large-lettered typewriter, showing a few editorial changes.

Hq.st. = a stencilled (cyclostyled) copy made at Headquarters, Geneva, for distribution to Sufi Centres.

Hq.tp. = a typed copy made at Headquarters, Geneva, for distribution to a limited number of Sufi Centres.

Notes:

1. A.o.d.: "Series III." to the left of "Gatha" and "Number 6." to the right, followed in Hq.st. and Hq.tp. by the Sufi Invocation (see Glossary)
2. Gd.hw., Hq.st.: "BREATH." added after "PASI ANFAS."; Hq.tp.: "BREATH." before "PASI ANFAS."
3. Gd.hw.: originally "what" was written, then corrected to "that which", as in all other documents
4. Ibid.: originally "of" was written, then crossed out and replaced with "in", as in all other documents
5. A.o.d.: reordered to read "health to another in his presence"
6. Gd.hw.: originally "Breath gives life" was written, then "gives life" crossed out and "By" added before "breath" to read "By breath", as in all other documents
7. Ibid.: "ligh" [light?] was written and crossed out
8. A.o.d.: "that" added

to impart has not ~~the~~ power[9] sufficient power to impart [10]becomes broken if there is a greater demand on his power and if there is little left with him. Sufis therefore consider [11]~~the meditation connected with breath even more~~ breathing connected with meditation[11] much more important than anything [12]in the world, their food, sleep, or comfort.

[13]

---

9. Gd.hw.: "the power" written, then "the" crossed out, with the number "2" added under "power" and the number "1" added under "sufficient", indicating a reversal; a.o.d.: "the power" omitted
10. A.o.d.: "he" added
11. Gd.hw.: originally "the meditations connected with breath even more" written, then crossed out and "breathing connected with meditation" written instead, as in all other documents
12. A.o.d.: "else" added
13. Hq.st.: "A skeleton outline of thought to be circulated among the members of the E. S. C. [Elementary Study Circle] only."; Hq.tp.: "A skeleton outline of thought for circulation among the members of the Senior Study Circle only."

Sherifa Goodenough's handwritten text

March 18th, '24

III.6.

Takua Taharat [1]

He alone is capable of removing from the heart of another doubt, deceit[2], fear, or malice whose heart is already pure from these things or who, at least, can empty his heart of these things. There is a weakness of the heart and there is a strength of the heart. The heart's weakness is caused by things it contains which ~~cause it~~ enfeeble~~ness~~ it[3], such as doubt, deceit[2], fear, and malice. The absence of these things produces that purity of heart[4] which in itself is a power. This power could be increased by faith, hope, and righteousness.

Purity of the heart causes its expansion, and the lack of purity makes it narrow. The mystic poet of Hyderabad, ~~Nizam~~[5] Asef, says, "If the heart is large, it can be largest of all things." Besides it is purity alone which opens the doors of the heart. All that ~~takes away~~[6] hinders that purity stands

---

Documents:

Gd.hw. = a document in the handwriting of Murshida Sherifa Goodenough, who prepared the series of Gathas (see Glossary) of which this is one, probably taken from the dictation of P-o-M. As several corrections occur in the text, and it is impossible to determine if they were made at the time of the dictation or later, they have been incorporated into the text itself and footnoted.

Gd.tp. = a typed version of the text made on Sherifa Goodenough's large-lettered typewriter, showing a few editorial changes.

Hq.st. = a stencilled (cyclostyled) version made at Headquarters, Geneva, for distribution to Sufi Centres.

Hq.tp. = a typewritten copy prepared at Headquarters, Geneva, for distribution to Sufi Centres.

Notes:

1. A category in the teaching of Pir-o-Murshid Inayat Khan, translated as "Everyday Life" (see Glossary); a.o.d.: "GATHA" at the top, with "Series III" below on the left, and "Number 6" below on the right, followed in Hq.st. and Hq.tp. by the Sufi Invocation (see Glossary). Gd.tp. and Hq.st. add after "Takua Taharat" the translation "Everyday Life", which Hq.tp. places before "Takua Taharat"
2. Gd.hw.: "deceit" added above line; included in all other documents
3. Ibid.: originally "cause it feebleness" was written, then "cause" and "-ness" were crossed out, "en-" added, and numbers written underneath to indicate moving "it"
4. Ibid.: "of heart" written above the line, and included in a.o.d
5. Ibid.: originally "Nizam" was written with a space after it, then crossed out; it is not included in any other documents
6. Ibid.: originally "takes away" was written, then crossed out, and not included in any other document

as a door closed[7] of the heart.

The pure-hearted may seem to be thinking, saying, or doing simple things, and yet there is a beauty and charm in all they do, for there is nothing more attractive than light itself. All that is besides light depends upon the light to show out its beauty; light is beauty in itself. Purity of the heart is the only condition that allows the inner stream to rise. The pure-hearted see deeper, though they say little. There is no pretence about them. What they know, they know; what they don't know, they don't know. The pure ones make all pure, for to them all is pure. Their presence makes everyone pure. As the pure water is the best tonic, so is the contact of the pure-hearted person. In the spiritual path, when one is able to accomplish this thing, ~~nothi~~[8] there is not much then [9] remains to be accomplished.

[10]

---

7. Ibid.: "door closed" was written, then numbers added underneath to indicate a reversal to "closed door", and so in a.o.d
8. Ibid.: "nothi" [nothing?] written and then crossed out
9. A.o.d: "that" added
10. Hq.st.: "A skeleton outline of thought to be circulated among the members of the E. S. C. [Elementary Study Circle] only."; Hq.tp.: the same, except "Senior Study Circle" instead of "E. S. C."

[1]Paris.
(Mme d'Eichthal)
March 22nd, 1924

Free Will

Life can be divided into two principal spheres, namely the sphere of abstraction[2] and the sphere of action. These two spheres have as their nature to create[3] action and to produce[4] abstraction[2]. In the one sphere, where there is abstraction[2], not only[5] the action of body but also the action of mind becomes[6] paralysed[7]. [8]And [9]when one is conscious in the other sphere[9], when one is conscious of [10]that sphere of action, one is far removed from

Documents:

Gd.hw. = Murshida Sherifa Goodenough's handwritten reporting of the first paragraph (the last sentence missing) of this lecture, used as the text for this paragraph.

Gd.tp. = Murshida Sherifa Goodenough's typescript (made on her large-lettered typewriter) made from an unknown reporting, used as the text for the lecture after the first paragraph. Gd. later used another copy of this tp. for further editing, indicated by "(Gd.tp.)Gd.ed." in the notes.

Sk.tp. = Sakina Furnée's later typescript of the lecture, based on Gd.tp. and incorporating some of the corrections there, sometimes changed back by Sk. in ink indicated by "(Sk.tp.)Sk.cr." in the notes.

Notes:

1. Gd. wrote at the top of her typescript, "Imperfect report."; it is not known what report may have been used to make this typescript, and it may well have been the differences from her own reporting of the first paragraph which led her to this conclusion. "(Mme d'Eichthal)" refers to the home in Paris of the national representative for France, where the lecture was given
2. Gd.tp.: "absorption" instead of "abstraction", changed back to "abstraction" in ink; (Sk.tp.)Sk.cr.: "abstraction" changed to "absorption" in ink
3. Gd.tp.: "absorb" instead of "create", changed back to "create" in ink
4. (Gd.tp.)Gd.ed.: "produce" changed to "absorb"
5. Gd.tp.: "even" instead of "only", changed in ink back to "only"; Sk.tp.: "only" changed to "even" in ink
6. Gd.hw.: originally "becomes" was written, then "is" written over it
7. Gd.tp.: "paralyses" instead of "becomes paralysed", changed in ink to "is paralysed"; Sk.tp.: "is paralysed"; (Sk.tp.)Sk.cr.: changed to "paralyses" in ink
8. Gd. tp.: this sentence reads: "In the other sphere, of action, when one is conscious of that sphere, then one is far removed from absorption.", but then (Gd.tp.)Gd.ed.: "In the other sphere, of action" crossed out and "that sphere, then" altered to "the other sphere, that of action," in ink, to read: "When one is conscious of the other sphere, that of action, then one is far removed from absorption"; Sk.tp.: "And when one is conscious of the other sphere, that sphere of action, one is far removed from abstraction.", then altered in ink to "In the other sphere, of action, when one is conscious of that sphere, then one is far removed from absorption"
9. Gd.hw..: "when one is conscious in the other sphere" crossed out
10. Ibid.: "the other sphere" added above the line

abstraction[8]. [11]By absorption I mean the absorbed[12] condition[11].

By this I mean that there are two kinds of people. One is most active, but cannot go into abstraction[13]. His every sense is responsive to all that strikes it. His eyes are attracted by all, his ears are ready to respond to all. And in order to see this difference [14]we do not need these two persons, but[14] we can take any two persons as an example. For two persons are not equal in their response to all that strikes their sense. If you are saying something, one person hears more than another. If you are showing something, one person sees more than another. [15]That only means that one is more wide awake than another.[15] There are different degrees of this wakefulness in the sphere of action.

But as there is this phenomenon to be noticed, so also there is another phenomenon to be noticed[16], but it is only to be noticed among very few—a thinker, a philosopher, a poet, a mystic—a phenomenon which will prove that a person living in the world is to a lesser or greater degree absent from the world. People call it [17]dreamy, being lazy, being drowsy[17], etc., but it is not so in all cases. Sometimes those who experience abstraction are experiencing in another sphere.

But now one might[18]: What do they see?[19] What is it they see? One might say a thousand things, yet one can never say entirely what they see, what they experience in this sphere.

There is a story told in Persia which gives an idea of this: There has been a belief, a belief coming from old legends, that there is a wall, a wall of laughter. And the legend is that where this wall is[20], the people thought they must see what was behind this wall. But whenever anyone climbed to the top of the wall, he laughed, jumped off, and never came back again. The people of the town began to think it was a wall of magic, and [21]it created a great curiosity to know[21] what was behind this wall. They thought of a certain method, of tying[22] the person's legs with iron chains and when he was on the top of the wall to pull[23] the chains so that he could not jump off on the other side. One courageous person undertook to climb this wall while the people

11. This sentence not in Gd.hw. and typed but crossed out in ink in Gd..tp.; (Sk.tp.)Sk.cr.: this sentence added in ink
12. Gd.tp.: changed to "abstracted" in ink
13. Ibid.: "abstraction" is typed over another, erased word ["absorption"?]
14. (Gd.tp.)Gd.ed.: "we do not need two persons, but" crossed out
15. Sk.tp.: this sentence omitted; (Sk.tp.)Sk.cr.: written in ink at the bottom of the page with a sign to insert it after the previous sentence
16. (Gd.tp.)Gd.ed.: "to be noticed," crossed out
17. Ibid.: "being" inserted here, and crossed out before the two following words: "being dreamy, lazy, drowsy"
18. Sk.tp.: "(say)" added, though "ask" seems more likely
19. (Gd.tp.)Gd.ed.: "What do they see?" crossed out
20. Ibid.: "is" changed to "was"
21. Gd.tp.: "it created a great curiosity to know" typed over erased type, now indecipherable
22. (Gd.tp.)Gd.ed.: "binding" instead of "tying"
23. Ibid.: "pulling" instead of "to pull"

held the other end of the chain. When this person came to the top of the wall he did as had done all the others—he looked, he laughed, and then tried to jump. And when he did that, the people pulled at the chain so that they dragged him back and he fell on their side of the wall. And when they surrounded him, full of curiosity to know what he would say, to their great disappointment he was dumb; he had lost the use of his[24] speech. This symbolical legend expresses that these two spheres, the sphere of action and the sphere of absorption[25], are divided by a wall [26]between them.

I was once very much struck by seeing a mystic who used to disguise himself, as many mystics do, as a man who was a little off. The great amusement was that the person was laughing with a[27] great joy, looking at the people passing in the street. No one could have thought him to be anything except what I have said. It was my patience which made me wait and watch. After a pause of a few moments and some thought given to the man's behaviour, my spirit, as it were, touched his spirit and I felt what he felt. A person with his calm, his serenity, on looking at this world, if he did not laugh, what would he do? It was more amusing for him than for a grown-up person the play of children, their little world, their limited imagination which they call sense, common sense, their limited vision, that dim light shed on all . . .[28]

By this I do not mean to say it is a good principle to live as that mystic, but I must say if there is another sphere, why should a man not experience it and live a more complete life instead of living a half life and depriving himself of the experience of the other half?

And now as to the other question, what does one see there, what is to be seen? These are two worlds, and the experience of that sphere has no words, because our words come from the experiences of this sphere. People may call it a joy, a sorrow, a sentiment, felicity, ecstasy, trance, but no word explains it. If it is sadness, it cannot be compared with the sadness of this world of action; if it is joy, it cannot be compared with the joy of this world. There is no comparison between that sphere and this sphere of action.

But what I want to say is that there is something to know besides this world which we love so and which we call free will. As far as this sphere of action, when a desire takes place in our mind, if it has free expression, we call it free will. If it is stopped by people or conditions we say that prevented

24. Ibid.: "his" crossed out
25. (Gd.tp.)Gd.ed.: "absorption" changed to "abstraction"; Sk.tp.: "(abstraction)" added after "absorption"
26. (Gd.tp.)Gd.ed.: "standing" added
27. Ibid.: "a" crossed out
28. Gd.tp, Sk.tp.: this ellipsis appears in the typescripts, apparently not, however, indicating any missing text; (Gd.tp.)Gd.ed.: ellipsis removed, and paragraph joined to the following paragraph

us from having free will. But what we learn from sphere there[29], whether one has the possibility of one's desire or whether it is hindered, there is a certain justice behind it. In every agreeable or disagreeable experience there is something which links it with that other sphere. The Sufis of other ages have called *Mukadar*[30], a power hidden behind this sphere of action, not devoid of wisdom but with perfect wisdom behind it.

Only when one reasons it out it is difficult to find a justification, because man looks at it from his point of view, according to this world of action, not[31] to the sphere of the abstract. Sometimes one says, I was late, but it was better that I was late. Sometimes one thinks a thing was not in his favour and afterwards he realizes it has been in his favour. Man is not capable always of knowing what is for his good, and often [32]what he thinks is not for his good, in that[33] there is something which is for his betterment.

But besides this, there is a word which we always use, accident. What we learn from that sphere is that there is no such thing as accident. For the effect of this sphere of action is that everything that was done with intention we say was done with intention, and a thing done without intention we call accident. This is not so. But then one may say, What about things brought about by conditions? But there are no conditions which have not been willed by a soul or souls. It is this that makes one think that behind the outer laws there is the inner law. And one begins to understand that law much better by getting into touch with that sphere, that sphere of abstraction.

The picture of these two spheres is this, that to him who belongs to the other sphere the people of this sphere seem like a drunken man, and they prove to be drunken. But also he who is in the abstract is apparently drunken, for he sees, speaks, and feels differently. And if a balance and a harmony can be brought about in this life it is by the experience of both spheres. The Sufi teaching is to experience both spheres and yet keep the equilibrium. For it is not only a religious necessity but a necessity in all walks of life. To a musician, a poet, a business man, a commercial man, a politician, it is inspiring. By this he is better fitted to fight his battle in this sphere of activity.

---

29. Gd.tp.: "there" added in margin; (Gd.tp.)Gd.ed.: "there" crossed out, and "is that" substituted;
(Sk.tp.)Sk.cr.: "there" crossed out in ink, "that" inserted before "sphere"
30. Gd.tp.,Sk.tp.: so typed, but probably it should be *al-Muqtadir*, name of God (no. 70 in some traditional lists of the 99 names of God), meaning "Power" (see Glossary)
31. (Gd.tp.)Gd.ed.: "according" added
32. Ibid.: "in" added here
33. Ibid.: "in that" crossed out

Sherifa Goodenough's handwritten text

Gatha III.7.[1] March 24, '24

Pasi Anfas.

Breath is likened to water. The flowing of the breath is like the flowing of a stream. Inhalation and exhalation show ebb and flow. [2]There are parts of the earth which water does not touch. They remain unfertile, barren.[2] So are[3] the centres in the body which,[3] with all their ~~capacity~~ intuitive innate capacities, remain unproductive[4]. Besides various diseases, in spite of all their apparent causes, often have one principal cause, and that is the lack of free flowing[5] of [6]breath. Many operations could be avoided and several illnesses[7] could be cured as knowing[8] the phenomena of breath.

The Hindu sacred rivers, Ganga and Jumna[9], are outward symbols of *jelal* and *jemal*[10], the two directions of the flow of the breath. And the

---

Documents:

Gd.hw. = Murshida Sherifa Goodenough's handwritten text, probably made from the dictation of P-o-M., with a few corrections apparently made during the dictation (and therefore included in the text) and some made later (which therefore appear in the notes).

Gd.tp. = a text typed on Murshida Sherifa Goodenough's large-lettered typewriter, an edited version from which the other documents were made.

Hq.tp. = a typescript made at Headquarters, Geneva, for distribution to a limited number of Sufi Centres.

Hq.st. = a stencilled text made at Headquarters, Geneva, for distribution to Sufi Centres.

Notes:

1. Gd.hw.: exceptionally, the series and number of this paper are indicated on the hw. text; Gd.tp.: "Series III." on the top left, "Gatha." in the centre, and "Number 7." on the top right, with "PASI ANFAS" and its translation "BREATH." below; Hq.tp.: as in Hq.st., except "BREATH." before "PASI ANFAS."; Hq.st.: as in Gd.tp., but with the Sufi Invocation (see List) added between the series and the title
2. Gd.hw.: "There are", "They" and "unfertile," later crossed out, making one sentence: "Parts of the earth which water does not touch remain barren", and so in a.o.d.
3. A.o.d.: "are" and "which," omitted
4. Ibid.: "if the breath does not reach them" added
5. Gd.hw.: later the "-ing" on the end of "flowing" was crossed out; a.o.d.: "flow"
6. Hq.tp., Hq.st.: "the" added
7. A.o.d.: "diseases" instead of "illnesses"
8. Ibid.: "by the knowledge of" instead of "as knowing"
9. Ganga and Jumna are Hindi forms of the names of the rivers known in English as the Ganges and the Yamuna
10. *Jelal* and *jemal* are words used by the P-o-M. to mean, roughly, "forceful" and "receptive" (see Glossary)

place where they meet is called *sangam*[11], the meeting or unity, which is considered most sacred by the Hindus. That *sangam* is the meeting of these two opposite flows. It is like the meeting of the two directions in the centre, which is named *kemal*[12] by the Sufis.

The water rises, passes[13], falls, and runs zigzag, and stands if held. So is breath. Every abovesaid action of breath has a meaning and has a peculiar effect, as even water ~~changes its magnetism~~[14] varies in its power and magnetism while going through the abovesaid directions. Water is a tonic, and breath is life itself. No tonic can be greater and better than breath. A spiritually[15] evolved person's presence, therefore, brings about a cure in cases where all remedies fail. Water is the necessity of life, and breath the only condition to live[16]. Without it life is impossible. Water falls as a rain from above; so breath [17]from above also, though from another dimension. Water rises as vapours; so breath rises with gasses, also with joys or depressions. Pure water is health-giving; pure breath gives life. Water partakes of all things mixing with it; so does breath.

[18]

---

11. *Sangam* is a Sanskrit word meaning "union", here referring to the confluence of the rivers at Allahabad (see Glossary)
12. *Kemal* is a word used by the P-o-M. to mean "perfection" (see Glossary)
13. Gd.hw.: originally "passes" was written, then crossed out and "runs" written above, then that too crossed out, and "passes" restored; "passes" in a.o.d.
14. Ibid.: originally "changes its magnetism" was written, then crossed out, and "varies in its power and magnetism" was written, apparently during the dictation, and so in a.o.d.
15. Hq.tp., Hq.st.: "spiritual", later corrected in ink in Hq.tp. to "spiritually"
16. A.o.d.: "for living" instead of "to live"
17. Ibid.: "is" added
18. Hq.tp.: "A skeleton outline of thought for circulation among the members of the Senior Study Circle only."; Hq.st.: "A skeleton outline of thought to be circulated among the members of the S. S. C. only."

III.7[1] [2] March 26th, '24

Takua Taharat[3]

Exaltation depends upon purity. The body cleansed gives an exaltation which is experienced by all living beings on the physical plane. The heart cleansed from[4] all impurities gives a much greater exaltation, which is experienced in the inner plane and ~~which~~ is reflected on the outer plane.

~~There are~~ Most of the[5] people little realize the meaning of exaltation. In point of fact all things that[6] man ~~seeks for prepares himself with~~[7] ~~are the causes~~[8] ~~most often~~ seeks for and becomes occupied with are most often methods adopted to obtain an exaltation, through food, perfume, music[9], or through the beauty of colour and line. No method, however, succeeds in experiencing[10] a ~~the longed for~~ fuller exaltation in the absence of the[11] purity of the[11] heart. In plain words, it is the pure-hearted who enjoy the beauty of[12] music, colour, or perfume more fully than those without purity of heart,

---

Documents:

Gd.hw. = Murshida Sherifa Goodenough's handwritten text, probably taken down from dictation of P-o-M. As the corrections may have been made at the time of the dictation, they have been left in the text. The crossed-out words were not included in subsequent documents.

Gd.tp. = Murshida Sherifa Goodenough 's typescript on her large-lettered typewriter, showing editorial changes from the Gd.hw.

Hq.st. = a stencilled copy prepared at Headquarters, Geneva, for distribution to Sufi Centres. The text is identical in wording to Gd.tp.

Sk.tp. = a typed copy prepared by Sakina Furnée or under her supervision, identical in wording to Gd.tp. and Hq.st.

Notes:

1. Gd.tp., Hq.st., Sk.tp.: "Series III" in place of "III.7", then, in the centre, "Gatha" and on the right, instead of the date, "Number 7"
2. Hq.st., Sk.tp.: the Sufi Invocation (see List) added here
3. *Takua Taharat* is a category in the teaching of P-o-M. (see List); Gd.tp., Hq.st.: as a title, "TAKUA TAHARAT" and "EVERYDAY LIFE"; Sk.tp.: "EVERYDAY LIFE" followed by "TAKUA TAHARAT"
4. Gd.tp., Hq.st., Sk.tp.: "from" changed to "of"
5. Ibid.: "of the" omitted
6. Gd.hw.: the word "that" is written over another, now indecipherable word
7. Ibid.: "prepares [?] himself with" is written above the line and crossed out
8. Ibid.: the word is difficult to read; "causes" is a possible reading
9. Ibid.: the word "music" is written above the line
10. Gd.tp., Hq.st., Sk.tp.: "giving the experience of" instead of "experiencing"
11. Ibid.: "the" omitted
12. Gd.hw.: the words "the beauty of" are written above the line

although the pure-hearted seem to need these things which bring about exaltation less, sometimes, for the very reason that the very purity of the heart gives them that exaltation which others strive to achieve by different methods.

Amir[13], the mystic poet, says, "Their eyes refused [14] wine, her ~~its~~ generous[15] offer, saying, 'We do not need thee, we are ~~already~~ intoxicated perpetually[16].'" The reason behind the pious refusing[17], at times, [18] music, art[19], gaiety, or merriment was that they already had the exaltation which others try to[20] gain by these things. It does not at all mean that the pious are always against things ~~which~~ belonging to[21] beauty and pleasure. It only means that they are rich by the feeling of exaltation which comes from within, without adopting for it any other methods. Nevertheless the pious are the ones who are capable of enjoying the[22] beauty in all its aspects fully. As Hafiz[23] says, "If the pious ~~of the world~~ ones would hear the[24] ~~my~~ song I sing they would get up and dance unrestrainedly."

[25] [26]

---

13. Amir Khusrau (see List)
14. Gd.tp., Hq.st., Sk.tp.: "the" added
15. Gd.hw.: the word "generous" is written above the line
16. Ibid.: the word "perpetually" appears above the line
17. Gd.tp., Hq.st., Sk.tp.: "refusal of the pious" instead of "pious refusing"
18. Ibid.: "of" added
19. Gd.hw.: the word "art" is written above the line
20. Ibid.: the words "try to" are written above the line
21. Gd.tp., Hq.st., Sk.tp.: "of" instead of "belonging to"
22. Ibid.: "the" omitted
23. Hafiz (see List)
24. Gd.hw.: the word "the" appears to be written over another, now indecipherable word
25. Hq.st.: adds "A skeleton outline of thought to be circulated among the members of the S. S. C. [Senior Study Circle] only" added; Sk.tp.: adds "A skeleton outline of thought for circulation among the members of the Senior Study Circle only."
26. A note at the bottom in Gd.'s hw. reads: "III Ta Ta 8", indicating Takua Taharat, series III, number 8; the 8 was then crossed out and "7" written in what appears to be another hand

Sherifa Goodenough's typewritten copy

[1]

Rue du Dragon, Paris
March 28th, 1924

The Law of Life

All that comes to a person, in reality one[2] arrives at it. By this I do not mean to say that a person[3] [4]makes it, creates it, earns it, deserves it, or that it comes[4] to him by chance. All that comes may come to a person in the abovesaid[5] five ways, but at the same time in reality a person[6] arrives at it. The aforesaid things are realms through which a certain thing comes. But what brings about a thing[7], that is the person himself. This subtle idea remains hidden until a person had[8] an insight into the law of life and that he[9] notices clearly its inner working. For instance if one said that a person came to a certain position, rank, or in[10] possession of a certain[11] wealth or fame by working for it—yes, outwardly it is true. But many work and don't[12] arrive

---

Documents:

Gd.tp. = Murshida Sherifa Goodenough's typescript on her large-lettered typewriter, with the place and date at top right, made from an unknown reporting.

Hq.st. = a stencilled version prepared at Headquarters, Geneva, for circulation to Sufi Centres before 1927, probably edited by Murshida Sherifa Goodenough.

Sk.tp. = a typed copy of Hq.st., prepared by Sakina Furnée or under her supervision, with two minor corrections, and therefore mentioned only in notes 13 and 43.

SR. = a version published in *The Sufi Record*, Vol. IV, No. 3 (April-June 1932), based on Hq.st., with further editorial changes, probably by Mrs. Khushi Marya Cushing, who edited that privately circulated journal.

Notes:

1. Gd.tp.: "N. 97" (evidently an archive number) written by hand upper left, and under the title in Gd.hw. "Gatheka No. 10 for cand[idates]"; Hq.st.: "GATHEKA." in the middle on top, then on the right "Number 10.", followed by the Sufi Invocation (see Glossary); location and date omitted, as in SR.
2. Hq.st., SR.: "he" instead of "one"
3. SR.: "he" instead of "a person"
4. Hq.st., SR.: passage rewritten to read: "does not make it, create it, earn it, deserve it, or that it does not come"
5. Ibid.: "above" instead of "abovesaid"
6. SR.: "he" instead of "a person"
7. Hq.st., SR.: "a thing about" instead of "about a thing"
8. Ibid.: "has" instead of "had"
9. Ibid.: "that he" omitted
10. Ibid.: "into" instead of "in"
11. Ibid.: "a certain" omitted
12. Ibid.: "do not" instead of "don't"

at it. Besides one might say that all blessings[13] of providence come to one if one deserves them. But one can see so much in life which is contrary to this principle. For there are many in the world who don't[12] deserve and yet they attain to them[14].

With every appearance of free will there seems to be a[15] helplessness in every direction of life. Besides,[16] what man calls chance, there is so much against it too. For a deep insight into life will prove that what seems to be a[15] chance is not in reality a[15] chance. It seems to be a[15] chance, as illusion is the nature of life.

But now I should like[17] to explain more briefly[18] what I mean by the arriving at a certain thing. Every soul is, so to speak, continually making its way toward something, sometimes consciously and sometimes unconsciously. What outwardly[19] a person does[19] is an appearance of an[20] action, an action which may have no connection with his inner working, which[21] is like a journey. Everyone does not know[22] toward[23] what he is making a[24] way, and yet everyone is making a[24] way. Whether one is making a[25] way toward the goal one has desired or whether one is making a[25] way toward quite the contrary goal [26]he has never desired, one does not know. But when the goal is realized on the physical plane, at that time[27] a person becomes conscious: I have not worked for it, I have not created it, I have not deserved it, I have not earned it; how is it possible that it has come? If it is a desired object[28] then perhaps he gives the credit of it to himself, he tries to believe: I have in some way made it. And if it is not desirable then one wants to attribute it to someone else, or [29]for some or[30] other reason[29] it has happened like this[31]. But in reality it is a destination at which one has arrived at the end of his[32] journey. You cannot definitely say that [33]one has made it,

---

13. Hq.st.: "blessing" instead of "blessings" (probably a typographical error); Sk.tp. "blessings"
14. Hq.st., SR.: "to them" omitted
15. Ibid.: "a" omitted
16. Ibid.: "And as to" instead of "Besides,"
17. Ibid.: "I should like" omitted
18. Ibid.: "fully" instead of "briefly"
19. Ibid.: "outwardly" moved to after "a person does"
20. Ibid.: "an" omitted
21. SR.: "It" instead of "which"
22. Hq.st., SR.: "Not everyone knows" instead of "Everyone does not know"
23. SR.: "towards" instead of toward"
24. Hq.st., SR.: "his" instead of "a"
25. Ibid.: "one's" instead of "a"
26. Ibid.: "which" added before "he"
27. Ibid.: "then" instead of "at that time"
28. Ibid.: "an object desired by him" instead of "a desired object"
29. Ibid.: "to suppose that for some reason or other" instead of "for some or other reason"
30. Gd.tp.: "or" typed in margin with a sign to insert it here
31. Hq.st., SR.: "that" instead of "this"
32. Ibid.: "one's" instead of "his"
33. Gd.tp.: a "(2)" inserted before "made", indicating it should be second in the series, and a "(1)" inserted before "created", indicating it should be first in the series; Hq.st.: "one has created it, one has made it,"; SR.: "one has created it, or has made it,"

one has created it,[33] that one has deserved it, or it has come by accident. What can be said is that one has journeyed toward it, either consciously or unconsciously, and has arrived at it. Therefore, in point of fact no one in his desirable experience[34] or undesirable experience[35] has gone away[36] from his[37] destination at which he was meant to arrive.

Nevertheless what is most necessary is to connect the outward action with the inward journey, the harmony of which certainly will prove to be a cause of ease and comfort. It is by[38] this that it is meant [39]that one must have harmony within oneself. And once this harmony is established one begins to see the cause of all things more than one sees[40] in its absence. One might ask in what way a[41] harmony could be established between the inner journey and outward action. What generally happens is this, that one[42] is so much absorbed in his outward action that his inner attitude become[43] obscured to his view. And the first necessary thing[44] is to remove that[45] screen that hides from one's sight the inner attitude. Everyone is conscious of what he does, but he is[46] not conscious of his inner attitude. In other words, everyone knows what he is doing, but everyone does not necessarily know towards what he is going.

No doubt the more one is conscious ~~the~~[47] of it, the less becomes one's action, for thought controls action, but it only gives a rhythm, a balance to life. [48]A person who is capable of running and not knowing where he is going, compared with that person, another person is better who is walking slowly but who knows toward what he is going.[48]

There are two distinct parts of one action: There is an action of our inner life and there is an action of our outer life, the inner being and the outer being. The outer being is a physical action and the inner action is our attitude. Both may be actions of free will, but in a certain way they[49] both prove to be mechanical or automatic actions. No doubt the inner action has a great power and influence upon the outer action. A person may be busy all

---

34. Hq.st., SR.: "experience" omitted
35. Ibid.: "experiences" instead of "experience"
36. Ibid.: "departed" instead of "gone away"
37. SR.: "the" instead of "his"
38. Hq.st., SR.: "by" omitted
39. Ibid.: "by saying" inserted before "that"
40. SR.: "it" inserted
41. Hq.st., SR.: "a" omitted
42. Ibid.: "a person" instead of "one"
43. Sk.tp., SR.: "becomes" instead of "become"
44. SR.: "thing" moved to before "necessary"
45. Ibid.: "the" instead of "that"
46. Hq.st., SR.: "he is" omitted
47. Gd.tp.: "the" typed, but crossed out in type
48. Hq.st., SR.: sentence rewritten to read: "Compared with a person who is capable of running, not knowing where he is going, another is better off who is walking slowly, but knows toward what he is going."
49. Gd.tp.: "they" typed in margin with a sign to insert it here

day doing something,[50] but at the same time if the attitude is working against him he can never have a[51] success in his work. A person by his outward action may deserve a great prize, but for his inner action he may not be deserving it. And therefore if these two actions are contrary to one another there is no construction and there is no [52] of the desired results. The true result, the result that is desirable, comes by the harmony of these two activities.

[53]

---

50. Hq.st., SR.: "in doing a thing;" instead of "doing something,"
51. Ibid.: "a" omitted
52. Gd.tp.: a blank; Hq.st., SR.: "attainment" instead of blank
53. Hq.st.: "To be circulated among the Candidates for Initiation in the Sufi Order." added

[1]

Le Mot Croyance

[2] Le mot croyance a variété de significations. Quatre aspects différents:
1○ Croyance ordinaire, l'un dit une chose, l'autre la croit et parmi cent personnes, une peut-être croira autrement. Non seulement les simples, mais très intelligents. Ils ont des croyances sans fondement. Par exemple, la multitude se meut aujourd'hui par cette même croyance, c'est pourquoi il est malaisé de définir une similitude d'une croyance sans fondement. Ce n'est pas toujours la pensée du plus grand nombre qui est bonne, mais quelquefois une seule. Ce n'est pas beaucoup ainsi maintenant. On arrive à réaliser que la pensée d'un seul peut être la meilleure, mais quelquefois une seule. Ce n'est pas beaucoup ainsi maintenant. On arrive à réaliser que la pensée d'un seul peut être meilleure que celle de la multitude. Ce qui dans le monde a été accompli de grand, par la pensée d'une seule personne.
2○ Il y a croyance dans une personne en qui on a confiance, semble [3] de la première, mais différente. Généralement une personne est portée à croire tout ce qu'elle entend. On croit plus facilement quand les gens sont pessimistes, et croient dans le mal. Parlez contre quelqu'un, même bon, et tout le monde sera prêt à croire.
3○ Sorte; croyance dans un poète, un prophète, un [4] . La nature de cette croyance diffère des autres, il a une nature sacrée.
4○ Sorte de croyance qui est un phénomène en elle-même, et celle-là seulement peut s'appeler foi. Celui qui croit ne donne pas de raison. Je crois parce que je crois. Je ne puis vous exprimer, vous ne savez pas mon langage. Cette croyance peut être en toutes choses, c'est la capacité d'avoir cette croyance qui est le plus grand bonheur. Dans cette signification, du mot foi,

---

Documents:

Lf.hw. = in Mlle H. Lefèbvre's handwriting, a reporting of the simultaneous French translation given, sentence by sentence, as P-o-M. was speaking. No English version of the lecture has been found in the archives to date. In several places, the hw. is very difficult or impossible to decipher.

Notes:

1. There is no date in Mlle Lefèbvre's notebook for this lecture; however, the previous lecture is date 4 March and the following lecture is dated 3 May, so the lecture is tentatively dated March, 1924.
2. Mlle Lefèbvre wrote "Murshid", indicating that P-o-M. began to speak
3. An indecipherable word
4. A blank

c'est [5] . La foi est une conviction qu'aucun raisonnement, rien, ne peut changer. Quand une personne dit: Je crois, elle ne voit pas; ensuite, cette foi est un si grande [6] Si vous avez la foi, l'idole même vous parlera. Il y a beaucoup de croyances, mais il n'y a qu'une seule foi; la bigoterie, c'est de s'arrêter sur une marche. Celui qui suit aveuglément, et ne voit rien au-dessus de cela. Celui-là atteint à la fin le fruit de l'initiation. Rien d'autre: que votre foi soit assurée. Dans l'affermissement de la foi, il y a tout le bonheur possible. Ce qui nous empêche d'arriver, dans la vie, c'est le manque de foi [7]

Il n'y a qu'un seul secret: c'est le pouvoir de la foi, [8] la foi y introduit la paix.

Dans [9] sculpteur en train de faire statue, plus [10]
commençant à devenir comme un être vivant
[11]

Tout que l'homme à devenir [12]
La perfection de toute [13] et de cette croyance n'est pas suffisante; il faut [14] c'est la foi. Dieu est rendu vivant pour chacun par le développement de la foi.

---

5. An indecipherable word
6. An indecipherable word, crossed out
7. An indecipherable word or two, crossed out
8. Two or three short, indecipherable words
9. An indecipherable word, perhaps the title of P-o-M.'s play "Una"
10. Four indecipherable words
11. There are four lines, written very rapidly, all indecipherable
12. An indecipherable word
13. An indecipherable word
14. A long, indecipherable word

Printed in the magazine *Sufism*

1

The Mystery of Breath

A Report of an Address by Inayat Khan.

Beloved ones of God, my subject this evening is "The Mystery of Breath."

Breath seems to be the sign of the beginning and of the end of life. With the first breath that is drawn the body is said to be alive, and when the breath departs, then the body is spoken of as dead. It is for this reason that the Yogis have called the breath *prana*[2], meaning the very life. But besides this, all the slight changes that take place in man's body come from an alteration in the mechanism of the breath; therefore in all ages physicians have observed the signs of a person's condition in different illnesses from the beat of the pulse, which is caused by the breath. Mental changes are also caused by breath; for instance, there are people with whom it is better not to talk when they first rise from sleep—they are excitable and irritable at that time; again, there are others who listen better then than at any other time. Some people come home from their work, or their office in the evening, and at that hour they are irritable and difficult; if you let them rest for an[3] hour or so they gradually change. All this shows that the condition of the breath changes the mental condition at that moment. The rhythm of the breath is very rapid immediately after concentration on work, and has an influence on the mind; after awhile this rhythm changes and becomes normal, and so the condition of mind changes also. In sleep, some people work up the rhythm

---

Document:

SF. = an article in the magazine *Sufism*, the edition of March, 1924, where it appeared as pages 9-11. No original for the text is known; it was probably edited for publication by Murshida Sophia Saintsbury-Green, the editor of *Sufism*. The words which appear in italics are so in the article.

Sk.tp. = a typed copy made by Sakina Furnée or under her supervision, which is an exact copy of the article, and is therefore not mentioned in the notes.

Notes:

1. It is not known where or when the P-o-M. gave the talk on which this article was based; however, it is likely it was given in England (possibly between Jan. 26 and Feb. 6), as most of his lectures published as articles in *Sufism* were, and its publication date is March, 1924
2. In the magazine, "Prama" is written, but this is undoubtedly an error for *prana* (see Glossary)
3. The magazine has "a" by mistake

of breath and the condition of the mind becomes unsettled and disturbed, but as a rule sleep helps the breath to be normal, and its influence produces tranquillity of mind.

It can be seen how various emotions, passions and sentiments change the rhythm of the breath Sometimes the breath goes out of man's control in emotions, such as anger, passion or fear; man has then no control over his words or actions.

When man loses control over himself, the first thing he loses is control of breath; this is the basis of the philosophy that by gaining control over the breath man can gain control over himself. The one who controls the breath is the ruler over his mind and body. How few really know how to breathe aright and what are the methods of keeping the channels of breath clear and in order, for breath uncontrolled is dangerous.

In mystical terms they have called the two different directions of the breath by different terms, and have considered them to be like the sun and the moon, representing the positive and negative aspects of the power and influence of breath. How few really know how many times in the day and night the breath changes its direction, and how through different parts of mind and body it works and produces different effects and results. How often the ignorance of man in the science of breath makes him act or think or speak against its influence, which is like swimming against the tide. We often notice in life that at one time success is achieved by the least little effort and at another the greatest effort produces nothing but failure. Shiva, the great lord of the Yogis, has said, "He who has knowledge of breath, knows the secret of the whole universe."[4]

What we generally know as breath is that little inhaling and exhaling which we feel through the nostrils; we think that is breath and give little importance to it, while in reality breath is a life-current running through the innermost part of man's being to the surface, and it would be no exaggeration, according to the mystical point of view, to say that the breath connects heaven and earth. It is the mystery of breath which shows the mystic that life is not the material part of man's being, but consists of the part of his being which is unseen. Breath is the bridge between the soul and body, keeping the two connected, and is the medium of action and reaction upon each other.

In the *Koran*[5] it is said, "We have made man to be the king of our creation", which in other words means that man himself is the dominion, as well as the king of that dominion, that dominion being his body and mind,

4. The source of this quotation has not been found to date
5. In the article it is written "Koran", the most common spelling in 1924, although *Qur'an* has since become the standard spelling in English; the source of the exact quotation which follows has not been found to date (however, see ii.30)

and the king his spirit, his soul. As a horse can be controlled and directed by getting the rein in hand, so life can be controlled and directed by getting control of breath.

Every school of mystics has as its most important and sacred teaching in the way of attainment the control and understanding of the mystery of breath. Modern science has discovered the importance of physical culture and breathing correctly, and that for all diseases of the lungs there is no greater or more beneficial remedy than sending the patient to a place suitable for breathing freely, and the psychologist will some day come to realize that for all illnesses and disorders of the mind, the way of breathing also is the best remedy.

With the mystic, breath is not only a science, but the knowledge of breath is mysticism; and mysticism to the thinker is both science and religion. The mystery of breath is not a thing that can be comprehended by the brain only. The principles of mysticism rise from the heart of man; they are learnt by intuition and proved by reason. It is not only a faith, though it is born of faith, it is faith with proof. Therefore its study and practice has been kept a mystery, not that it may be monopolized for a certain school, for no true mystic can be without generosity! The first sign of a mystic is that he is ready to give to everyone. The first and last lesson is to give, to give to the end, to give everything you possess; there is no end to the giving of the mystic, as there is no end to the inspiration he receives. If it has been made a mystery it is only as one would keep an object of glass from a little child, fearing that he might break it and hurt himself and others.

Think what an intoxication is the life of the world! Realize what are man's needs, temptations and desires—*what* would he not do to attain them? Man is so absorbed in striving after all these things that he does not know what he really wants or how rightly to obtain it; he does not know what harm he may cause to himself or others, and he uses power not knowing what will be the result. Therefore, to give mysticism to all is like giving a sword unsheathed to a drunken man—you do not know whom he will kill, or how he may wound himself. But, mysticism apart, it is necessary that everyone should know how to live a balanced life, a life of power and tranquillity, and how therefore to use and control the power of breath that he may be better fitted to manage his life.

If we consider the conditions of life today, we see that, however much man thinks he has progressed, certain aspects of life are neglected in the way of health, repose, balanced thinking, and in the way of kindness and love to one another; all these things are lacking, and the spirit of the present time seems to be going in quite the opposite direction. Selfishness seems to be so much on the increase; real religion, the spirit of forgiveness, generous giving, a regard for old age, refinement, culture, all seem to be disappearing.

Man in general does not know even if there is a God or truth; and if this is the spirit, how can we expect to find that harmony, peace and love which make heaven upon earth? It is useless to discuss the peace of the world; what is just now necessary is to create peace in ourselves, that we ourselves become examples of love, harmony and peace; this is the only way of saving ourselves *and* the world. Let man try to become more considerate of others, let him ask himself, "Of what use am I in the world? Am I born for any purpose?" and then try to train himself to self-control by the mystery of breath, the best means for accomplishing that purpose.

Sherifa Goodenough's handwritten (pencil) text

1 2

The Problem of the Day

Beloved ones of God, friends to whom I speak, but see only with my soul, not with the physical eyes, you who listen to what I say by the medium of this new invention, radio. I speak to you heart to heart on the most important[3] subject, on the problem of the day,[4] the question[5] that stands before us to solve. We don't[6] need to expect that it is the nations or[7] the great temporal powers who can [8]only solve the problem. No, you and I, however limited and humble in our lives, can think[9] over this problem, can think of its solution, and can do in our small way what we can in order to bring about better times.

In spite of all the progress that in the modern civilization has been made in all departments of life, such as commerce, industry, [10]economics, the

Documents:

Gd.hw.1	=	a document handwritten in pencil by Murshida Sherifa Goodenough, possibly from the radio address or in preparation for it. Later, editorial changes were made in this document as indicated in the footnotes by "(Gd.hw.1)Gd.ed."
Gd.hw.2	=	a document handwritten in ink by Gd., with editorial changes from Gd.hw.1, apparently as a preparation for the Hq.st., which follows it closely.
er.tp.	=	an early typewritten copy, rather poorly typed, of unknown origin, mostly following Gd.hw.1 and reflecting much of the editing on that document.
Hq.st.	=	a stencilled copy made at Headquarters, Geneva, for distribution to Sufi Centres as part of the Gatheka (see List and Glossary) series, closely following Gd.hw.2.

Notes:

1. Gd.hw.2: "Gatheka." in the upper left-hand corner
2. Gd.hw.2: "Paris" and then below "(given from the Tour Eiffel)" (see List); later, after the parentheses, "1922" written, apparently in error; er.tp.: "March 1924 (?)" written in pencil at top in an unknown hw., and the note at the end of Gd.hw.1 (see footnote 41) typed at the top; Hq.st.: "GATHEKA." at the center on top, then below to the right "Number 35.", followed by the Sufi Invocation (see Glossary); "(given from the Tour Eiffel.)" under title
3. Gd.hw.1: originally another word, now indecipherable, written, with "important" written over it
4. Gd.hw.1: a gap of a full line indicates that perhaps Gd. thought a new paragraph would begin here
5. (Gd.hw.1)Gd.ed.: "question" later crossed out, "problem" written above; a.o.d.: "problem"
6. Gd.hw.2, Hq.st.: "do not" instead of "don't"
7. (Gd.hw.1)Gd.ed.: "the nations or" later crossed out; a.o.d.: omitted
8. Hq.st.: "only" moved to before "can"
9. (Gd.hw.1)Gd.ed.: "think" later crossed out and "ponder" written above; Gd.hw.2, Hq.st.: "wonder" instead of "think"; er.tp.: "ponder"
10. (Gd.hw.1)Gd.ed.: "politics and" inserted later above line; a.o.d.: "politics and" included

question remains if we have really progressed. If one can[11] observes the superficiality of life which man lives today in so-called civilized parts of the world, one shall certainly find that man today is far removed from nature, [12]from the nature within and without, and has become an exile, [13]as his father Adam, from the Garden of Eden,[13] the ideal state of life. The more laws are being made, the more crimes are committed; the more mechanism is prepared, [14]the work has increased and little is[15] done; the more [16]courts are made, the more cases occur; the more physicians, the more diseases. The avariciousness[17] has come to the fore, so that [18]either aristocratic or democratic system justice seems to be absent. Education is becoming burdensome every day of the[19] life upon the new generation, which is the hope of the world. In order to accomplish something in the line of education a youth, who has sacrificed the kingly life[20] of childhood and the blossom of youth, has already aged. But even after that sacrifice he has little help[21] for his future life. There are[22] a thousand things to discourage him in every walk of life where he finds competition. With every regard [23]to the right of the woman[23] that has been given in this age, woman's responsibility of life is much more increased. She has to fight her battle in the open field, which naturally exhausts her energy and courage, causing her to lose her inherent fine nature rubbing[24] against the rough edges of life constantly.

The prejudice and the hatred and the distrust that exists between nations, whether friends or foes, every nation being absorbed in its own interest, regardless of the people in general, all this reflected on the mentality of individuals, [25]made life difficult for rich and poor both. One sees everywhere one turns his head material strife. Every ideal, every principle has to be sacrificed for it.

---

11. (Gd.hw.1)Gd.ed.: "can" crossed out; a.o.d.: "can" omitted
12. Gd.hw.2: "within and" written, then crossed out, probably a copying error
13. (Gd.hw.1)Gd.ed.: "as his father Adam, from the Garden of Eden," later crossed out; a.o.d.: "from" instead of "as his father Adam, from the Garden of Eden,"
14. Gd.hw.2, Hq.st.: "the more" added
15. Ibid.: "being" added
16. Gd.hw.1: originally another now indecipherable word [possibly "suits"] written, with "court" written over it, and then "law" added above to make "lawcourts"; Gd.hw.2: "lawsuits" written, then later changed to "lawcourts"; er.tp.: "lawcourts"; Hq.st.: "lawsuits"
17. (Gd.hw.1)Gd.ed.: "The avariciousness" later crossed out, and "Cupidity" substituted; a.o.d.: "Cupidity"
18. (Gd.hw.1)Gd.ed.: "under" added above the line; Gd.hw.2: "under either an", then altered to "whether with an"; er.tp.: "under either"; Hq.st.: "whether with an"
19. Gd.hw.2, Hq.st.: "the" omitted
20. Ibid.: "time" instead of "life"
21. (Gd.hw.1)Gd.ed.: "help" altered to "hope"; a.o.d.: "hope"
22. (Gd.hw.1)Gd.ed.: "are" appears to have been written first, later written over by "come"; a.o.d.: "come"
23. Gd.hw.2, Hq.st.: "for the rights of woman" instead of "to the right of the woman"
24. (Gd.hw.1)Gd.ed.: "rubbing" altered later to "having to rub"; Gd.hw.2, er.tp, Hq.st.: "having to rub"
25. Gd.hw.1: "has" added above; a.o.d.: "has"

There are movements[26] working to make conditions better and yet among such movements[26] one finds the whole effort being direction[27] to make their own condition better. If A has got a loaf of bread, B wants to snatch it away from him. [28]And for this robbery he justifies himself saying that: He has no right to have that loaf, I must have it, since I fight for my right.[28] People with ideal, manner, or culture find life difficult to live. Those without these get along better, for they are more capable of battling in the present struggle of life. During these past [29]years man has proved to be his own enemy, and if it continued in the same way he will prove to be his worst enemy.

The question arises, what may be done if conditions are such as they are? The answer is that everything that can be done to widen the outlook of man, to make man understand life better, to raise man to a greater ideal,[30] to a higher ideal, to show man the practicality of an unselfish life is worth-while. There may be many movements working along this line, but there can never be enough workers. [31]For it is a world-felt need[31] and every man[32] must consider it his sacred duty to contribute his services[33] in any or every eff[34] way he can. The Sufi Movement ~~is devoted~~[35] which is composed of [36]the workers for God and humanity[36] from all[37] different sections[38] of humanity, is endeavouring to bring about better conditions without interfering with anyone's religion, custom, or[39]. For devotion to God and humanity is the only object it has placed before itself. May this message[40] reach far and

26. (Gd.hw.1)Gd.ed.: "movements" crossed out, and "institutions" substituted; a.o.d.: "institutions"
27. A.o.d.: "direction" corrected to "directed"
28. (Gd.hw.1)Gd.ed.: later altered to read: "And to do this robbery, he justifies himself saying, 'He has to have that loaf, I am entitled to have it, as I stand for my right.'"; Gd.hw.2, Hq.st.: "And for this robbery he justifies himself" omitted, and the rest of the sentence reads: "saying that, 'I am entitled to have it, as I stand for my right.'"; er.tp.: "And to do this robbing, he justifies himself, saying, 'He has no right to have that loaf, I am entitled to have it, as I stand for my right.'"
29. Gd.hw.1: "few" added above; a.o.d.: "few"
30. (Gd.hw.1)Gd.ed.: "to a greater ideal," crossed out; er.tp.: "to a greater ideal," omitted, but then added in ink in an unknown hw.
31. Gd.hw.2: "For it is a world-felt need" written above line, having apparently been inadvertently omitted in copying
32. (Gd.hw.1)Gd.ed.: "man" crossed out, with a gap following, and "conscientious" and "thoughtful" written above, also crossed out; a.o.d.: "conscientious man"
33. Gd.hw.2, Hq.st.: "his services" omitted
34. (Gd.hw.1)Gd.ed.:"in any or" and "eff" [effective?] crossed out; Gd.hw.2, Hq.st.: "in any and every" instead of "in any or every eff"; er.tp.: "in every" instead of "in any or every eff"
35. Gd.hw.1: "is devoted" crossed out, apparently while composing document, and omitted in a.o.d.
36. (Gd.hw.1)Gd.ed.: "the workers for God and humanity" crossed out, "members" written above; a.o.d.: "members"
37. Gd.hw.1: "from all" crossed out
38. Gd.hw.2: "nations", then altered to "sections"
39. Gd.hw.1: "or" crossed out here, and inserted between "religion" and "custom"; a.o.d.: "religion or custom"
40. Gd.hw.2, Hq.st.: "Movement" instead of "message"

wide, illuminating and making the whole humanity one brotherhood. God bless you.

[41]

---

41. Gd.hw.1: at the end is a note, apparently a reminder to say this on the radio: "Mention address - in introducing: c/o Madame Lafitte, 26 rue du Dragon, Paris, Sufi Movement France"; Hq.st.: "To be read before Candidates for Initiation in the Sufi Order." added

[1]

Murshida Sherifa Goodenough's handwritten reporting

Takua Taharat [2]

There is generally a tendency seen in those treading the spiritual path to feel discouraged on[3] having bad impressions upon their heart of their own faults and shortcomings, who[4] begin to feel they are too unworthy for [5] have anything to do with ~~spiri~~ things of a sacred nature. But it is a great error, in spite of all the virtue that[6] humility has in it. When one acknowledges something wrong or impure[7] in oneself, one gives that wrong a soul out of one's own spirit, and by abstaining[8] from all that is good and beautiful, spiritual and sacred, one[9], instead of developing the spirit of rejecting all errors, in time[9] becomes a receptacle of what is wrongs[10]. He goes on disapproving [11]yet collecting errors, so producing within himself an

Documents:

Gd.hw. = a document handwritten by Murshida Sherifa Goodenough (on the backside of a printed announcement), evidently from dictation of P-o-M. One cross out appears to have been made during the dictation and so is included in the text. The other cross outs and changes appear to have been made after the dictation, and are therefore indicated in the notes rather than in the text itself. There is no indication of a date, so this text has been tentatively dated in March because several other such dictations occurred in that month (March 12, 15, 17, 18, 24, and 26).

Gd.tp. = a typed version of the text made on Murshida Sherifa Goodenough's large-lettered typewriter, showing a few editorial changes.

Hq.st. = a stencilled (cyclostyled) copy made at Headquarters, Geneva, for distribution to Sufi Centres.

Hq.tp. = a typed copy made at Headquarters, Geneva, for distribution to a limited number of Sufi Centres.

Notes:

1. Gd.hw.: later "III.5" written upper left, indicating the series and number in the Gathas (see List)
2. *Takua Taharat* is a category in the teachings of P-o-M. (see List); Gd.tp.: on the top, "Series III. GATHA. Number 5." and then lower, "TAKUA TAHARAT. EVERYDAY LIFE."; Hq.st., Hq.tp.: the same on the top, but with the Sufi Invocation (see List) inserted between the two lines, and the Hq.tp. has "EVERYDAY LIFE." before "TAKUA TAHARAT."
3. A.o.d.: "at" instead of "on"
4. Ibid.: end of sentence at "shortcomings" and "And they" instead of "who"
5. Gd.hw.: originally "for" was written followed by a now indecipherable word (perhaps "one"), as "for" was crossed out and "to" was written right over the other word
6. A.o.d.: "that" omitted
7. Gd.hw.: later the words "or impure" were crossed out, and are omitted in a.o.d.
8. Gd.hw.: "abstaining" crossed out, and "withdrawing" written above; a.o.d.: "withdrawing"
9. A.o.d.: "one" moved to after "in time"
10. Gd.hw.: "wrongs" is clearly written, corrected to "wrong" in a.o.d.
11. Ibid.: "and" added above line, and included in a.o.d.

ever-growing[12] conflict which some[13] never ends. When a man becomes[14] helpless before his infirmities, he becomes a slave to his errors; he feels within himself an obedient servant to his adversary.

The greater the purity is[15] developed in the heart, the greater becomes the power of man. As great is[15] the power of man within himself, so great becomes his power on others. A hair's breadth can divide power from weakness, which appear to have as large[16] a gulf[17] as between land and the sky.

[18]

---

12. Ibid.: "an ever-growing" crossed out and "a perpetual" substituted, and so in a.o.d.
13. Ibid.: "which some" crossed out, and "that" substituted, and so in a.o.d.
14. A.o.d.: "become" instead of "becomes" (but in Hq.tp. the "s" is added in ink)
15. Ibid.: "is" omitted
16. Ibid.: "wide" instead of "large"
17. Ibid.: "between them" added
18. Hq.st.: "A skeleton outline of thought to be circulated among the members of the E. S. C. [Elementary Study Circle] only."; Hq.tp.: "A skeleton outline of thought for circulation among the members of the Senior Study Circle only."

A Headquarters typescript from an unknown reporting

1 Headquarters, April 2, '24

Beloved ones of God,

I would like to speak this day[2] on the subject of spiritual attainment. The way how spiritual attainment is made must be seen from quite another point of view. It cannot be attained at the same manner as in the material way. And what discourages [3] is that after striving for a year, one does not seem to have arrived at anything. The person who strives to attain things of this world finds the proof of having attained by holding them. A person says, this is mine, because he possesses it. The spiritual attainment, on the contrary, wants to take the possessions away. It does not even allow you to possess yourself. This becomes a great disappointment for a person whose only realization of having attained is in possession. This attainment comes by not attaining.

Then there is the question, what is the difference between the spiritual person and the person who possesses nothing? The difference is great, the difference is indeed great, for the spiritual person in the absence of any possessions is still rich. What is the reason? The reason is this: The one who does not possess anything is conscious of limitation; the spiritual person, in the absence of even possessing himself, is conscious of perfection. Then one asks: How can a limited man be conscious of perfection? The answer is: The limited man has limited himself, he is limited because he is conscious to be[4] limited. It is not his true self which is limited. That which is limited is what he holds, not man himself. That is the possibility that made

Documents:

Hq.tp. = A Headquarters typescript made from an unknown reporting. On this typescript, Murshida Sherifa Goodenough did slight editing, indicated by "(Hq.tp.)Gd.ed" in the notes.

Sk.tp. = A typescript prepared under Sakina Furnée's supervision, which is identical in wording to (Hq.tp.)Gd.ed., and is therefore mentioned only in notes 1 and 8.

Notes:

1. Sk.tp.: "Public Lecture." typed in upper lefthand corner; later "Public" crossed out, and "Private" substituted in ink; on another copy, both crossed out and "For Mureeds" added in ink
2. (Hq.tp.)Gd.ed.: "this day" changed to "today"
3. Hq.tp.: a small blank
4. (Hq.tp.)Gd.ed.: "to be" changed to "of being"

Christ say: "Be ye perfect as[5] your Father is perfect"[6].

Spiritual knowledge is not in learning something, it is in discovering something, so to speak, to break the fetters of the false consciousness and allow the soul to unfold itself with light and power. What does the word spiritual mean really? Spiritual is spirit-consciousness. When a person is conscious of his body he cannot be spiritual. It is like a king who does not know his kingdom. The moment he is conscious of being a king, he is a king. Every soul is born a king; afterwards he becomes a slave. Every soul is born with kingly possibility; by this wicked world it is taken away. This is said in symbolical stories, in the story of Rama, from whom his beloved Sita was taken away. Every soul has to conquer this, to fight for this kingdom. In that fight the spiritual kingdom is attained. No one will fight for you, nor teacher, nor anybody else. Yes, those who are more evolved than you can help you, but you have to fight your battle, your way to that spiritual goal. An intellectual[7] thinks that by adding to knowledge he may attain spiritual knowledge. This is not so. The secret of life is boundless. Knowledge is limited. Eyes see very little distance. So limited is the human mind, how far can it see? And those who see can see by not seeing, learn by not learning. The way of spiritual attainment is contrary to the way of all attainment concerning matter. In material attainment you must take, for spiritual attainment you must give. In material attainment you must learn, in spiritual attainment you must unlearn. Material attainment is one side, spiritual attainment the other side, the opposite direction.

The word spiritual simply means spirit-consciousness; if a person is conscious of his body and thinks this is all that can be known of himself, the spirit is covered. It is not that he has not got a soul, but his soul is obscured. In English they say: He has lost his soul. No, it is only covered. Can anything possessed be lost? If man thinks this, he is limited. Neither objects nor beings are lost. They are covered for a moment, yet they are all there. No one[8] made can ever be destroyed It is only covering and uncovering. All relations and connections—nothing is separable. The separation is outward; inwardly they are never separated. They are separated from one's consciousness, but when the consciousness is [9]commodated, then nothing in the world can separate them. What does one learn by this? Spiritual attainment is to be reached by the raising of the consciousness from limitation to perfection.

There is another side of the question: there is no one, wise or

---

5. In Hq.tp. originally "as" was typed twice, and then the second one was crossed out
6. Matthew 5:48: "Be ye perfect as your Father in heaven is perfect"
7. (Hq.tp.)Gd.ed.: "person" inserted
8. (Hq.tp.)Gd.ed.: "nothing?" in the margin suggested in place of "No one", and in Sk.tp. "Nothing" is substituted
9. (Hq.tp.)Gd.ed.: "commodated" (not a recognized usage) changed to "accommodated"

foolish, there is no one who is not progressing slowly or quickly toward the spiritual goal. The only difference is that one is attracted to it, facing his goal, making his way toward it, while the other one has his back turned to it. And he is held and is drawn, without him[10] being conscious of it. Poor man does not know where he is taken, but goes just the same. His punishment is that he does not see the glory he is approaching, and his torture that he has been drawn in the opposite pole he desires. His punishment is not different from the infant going into the water of the lake and whose mother pulls him back by his shirt, but he is looking at the lake. From a religious point of view it is very unjust toward the perfect Judge to be deprived of that perfect bliss which is spiritual attainment. But from the point of view of metaphysics, no soul will be deprived of this knowledge some time or other through eternity.

Now coming to the question, what Sufism teaches on the subject. Sufism avoids words, words from which differences and distinctions arrive[11]. Words can never express fully truth. Words promote argument. All these differences of religions are differences of words; in sense they do not differ, only in words. For in sense they all have come from one source, and to the same source they return. And this very source is the store, is life, light, and power for them. Then how can differences be made by man's limitations? This is the way of the Sufi: if he does not meet somebody in one particular idea, he takes a step higher instead of differing in the lower plane. Therefore for the wise person there is no difficulty. The main thing that Sufism teaches is to dive deep within oneself, and to prepare mind and body by contemplation to make the being a shrine of God, the purpose for which it was created.

----

[12]

Question: *Murshid, may I ask the explanation of three sayings from* Gayan*? They are: "All longing in the heart deprives it of freedom,"*[13] *"'To suppress desire is to suppress divine impulse,"*[14] *"Ideal is the means and its breaking is the goal."*[15]

---

10. (Hq.tp.)Gd.ed.: "him" changed to "his"
11. (Hq.tp.)Gd.ed.: "arrive" changed to "come"
12. In all versions, the q.a. are on a separate page titled "QUESTIONS AND ANSWERS AFTER THE LECTURE ON 'SPIRITUAL ATTAINMENT'" (though, in fact, there is only one question and answer). This page may not have been originally a part of Hq.tp., as it uses different spacing and shows no editing by Gd. Its origin is unknown.
13. The *Gayan*, a book of sayings of Pir-o-Murshid Inayat Khan, had recently been published at the time this lecture was given. For the complete history of each saying see *The Complete Works of Pir-o-Murshid Hazrat Inayat Khan*, Sayings I (London/The Hague 1989). The first saying is Bola 180, pp.82-3, and the precise text is: "All that produces longing in the heart deprives it of its freedom."
14. Chala 99, p. 152, which reads: "To repress desire is to suppress a divine impulse."
15. Bola 52, p. 36: "The ideal is the means; but its breaking is the goal."

Answer: "All longing in the heart deprives it of freedom." The truth is, as soon as there is a longing, one is tied by an iron chain, but a stronger chain than an iron chain. Desire is the condition to be bound. It is not a moral, but a statement, a philosophy. If one followed it,...[16] one cannot live without desire. One might just as well be a rock. No doubt one should have the same freedom as the rock, be quite free if one were free from desire. But even the rock is longing for the day to come when desire is coming. The desire of fulfilment will come in the development in the human form.

The second question is, "To suppress desire is to suppress divine impulse." Everybody is not able to understand this and to have a proper judgement to this idea. Those who divide "divine" and "not divine" certainly make the greatest error; either all is divine or nothing is divine. The only division is the division of machine and engineer. The mind of God is working and the instrument of God is working. The one is God who is working, the other the machine of God which is working. What comes as a desire has God...[15] a divine impulse. And the pious man, ignoring this he makes a false conception, he makes of God a captive in heaven.

And the third question is about "Ideal is the means but its breaking is the goal." The picture of the ideal is like the egg. Its breaking is the fulfilment, when the children come[17] forth. Breaking is like blooming of flowers. Even so it is necessary for the ideal to break. If it is not broken, then the ideal is not used.

---

16. Hq.tp.: Nearly half a line is left blank in the typescript
17. Hq.tp.: Originally "comes" was typed, but the "s" was crossed out, probably correcting a typing error

A Headquarters typescript, possibly transcribed from the reporting

Bvd. des Tranchées, 44[1]
April 3, 1924

Beloved ones of God,

I would like to speak this day[2] on the subject of dreams and inspiration[3]. When considering the idea of dream[4] one finds that although it is something which is known to everybody, this subject leads to deeper side of life, because it is from the meaning of[5] dream[4] that one begins to realize two things: [6]something is active when the body is asleep, and to the deep thinker this gives him[7] faith in the life hereafter. For this gives the proof that when the body is not active, then even[8] the person is active, and it[9] seems to be no[10] less[11] than in the physical body. And if he finds a difference, it is a difference of time. For here he may pass from one land[12] to another in two hours instead of doing it in a month. In no way he is hindered; the hindrance of[13] the physical plane is far greater. From England to America he jumps in one moment. There he flies[14]. The facility of that plane is much greater. There is no difficulty of changing the condition, from illness to health, from

Documents:

Hq.tp. = a typescript from Headquarters, Geneva, with several errors in the English. It is on long paper, double spaced, and may represent a transcription from an unknown shorthand reporting by a professional stenographer (as such were easily available in Geneva, seat of the League of Nations).

Hq.st. = another typescript from Headquarters, Geneva, on a stencil (but not in the usual series for distribution to Sufi Centres). Some of the English has been corrected. Later, on a copy of this stencil, Murshida Sherifa Goodenough did extensive editing, indicated in the notes by "(Hq.st.)Gd.ed."

er. tp. = an early typescript following exactly the editing in "(Hq.st.)Gd.ed." and therefore not mentioned in the notes, except in three places where Sakina Furnée inked in suggestions for the text indicated by "(er.tp.)Sk.cr."

Notes:

1. A location in Geneva where the lecture was given
2. (Hq.st.)Gd.ed.: "this day" changed to "today"
3. The words "dreams and inspiration" are underlined in Hq.tp., but not in Hq.st.
4. Hq.st.: "dreams" instead of "dream"
5. (Hq.st.)Gd.ed.: "the meaning of" crossed out
6. Ibid.: "one is that" inserted
7. Ibid.: "him" crossed out
8. Ibid.: numbers indicate reversal to "even then"
9. Ibid.: "it" changed to "he"
10. Hq.tp.: either "no" was typed over "so", or "so" was typed over "no"; "no" seems to make more sense here
11. (Hq.st.)Gd.ed.: "so" inserted
12. Ibid.: "land" changed to "country"
13. Ibid.: "of" changed to "on"
14. Ibid.: "There he flies" changed to "He flies there"

failure to success in one moment. People say yes, yes,[15] but it is imagination, a working of the mind. But what is mind? Mind is that in which the world is reflected. Heaven and earth are accommodated in it. Is that a small thing? What is the physical body compared to the mind? It is a world in itself. The physical body is like a drop in the ocean. It is nothing[16] than ignorance that man does not know the[17] kingdom in himself, if only he were conscious of it. Why is he not? Because he wishes to hold; only then something exists[18]. He does not wish to confess to himself[19] the existence of sentiment. For then they say[20]: it has[21] no account, there[22] is nothing. So about thought, [23]it is only imagination, it is nothing. But science and art come from imagination, from the mind, not from a rock, not from the physical body. The source from[24] all knowledge is the mind, not an object. Mind means "I". It is the mind which identifies; the body is an illusion. When the mind is depressed, we say: I am sad. Not the body, but the mind was depressed. So the real identification is the mind, not the body.

If in a dream man is able to see himself, what does that show? That after what is called death, yet[25] man is not formless; that nothing is lost; that only the freedom is gained which was lost. The absence of this knowledge makes man afraid of[26] this physical body, makes him have a horror of death. But what is death? Nothing but a sleep. A sleep of the body which was a cloak. One can take it away and yet be living. Man will realize after all [27]talk about death that he is alive, that he has not lost but gained. Man is in the physical world to learn. Besides this the dream teaches that law is working, that all that seems[28] surprising, accidental, a sudden happening, was not sudden, no accident. It seemed accidentent[29] because it was not connected with the conditions. There happens nothing which does not go through the mind. Man has turned his back to[30] it, he is open only to [31]manifestation. It was no surprise, it was only preparing. Did they not say in all the countries when the war came: we did not know. Yes, it was so to

---

15. Hq.st.: the second "yes," crossed out
16. (Hq.st.)Gd.ed.: "nothing" changed to "for no other reason"
17. Ibid.: "the" changed to "that there is a"
18. Ibid.: "for him" inserted
19. Ibid.: "confess to himself" changed to "admit"
20. Ibid.: "then they say" changed to "he says"
21. Ibid.: "has" changed to "is of"
22. Ibid.: "there" changed to "it"
23. Ibid.: "they say" inserted
24. Ibid.: "from" changed to "of"
25. Ibid.: "yet" crossed out
26. Ibid.: "of" changed to "for"
27. Ibid.: "the" inserted
28. Hq.st.: "seemed" instead of "seems"
29. In the typescript "accidentent" is written; it cannot be determined whether P-o-M. said this, or if it was mistakenly heard and transcribed this way by the unknown person taking down the lecture; Hq.st.: "accidental"
30. (Hq.st.)Gd.ed.: "to" changed to "on"
31. Ibid.: "the" inserted

those who slept, but the awakened had seen the preparation. In all things we see this.

Every accident, pleasant or unpleasant, has a long preparation before it. First it exists in the mind, then in the physical[32]. A dream shows the depth of life; through a dream we see things. One may ask: What is the meaning? Has every dream a meaning? [33] The only[34] thing is this: There are those in the[35] country who do not know its language. So it is with minds. Some minds are not yet capable of expressing themselves, so the dreams are upset[36] down, a chaos. They see a goat with the ears of an elephant. The mind wanted to express itself[37]. There is a meaning in what the child says, but it has not yet learned, it has no words; it can only cry or make a sound, yet this has a meaning. So it is with dreams which are not expressed correctly. But you may say: How can the mind learn to express itself? It has to become itself. Often [38]mind is disturbed, inharmonious, restless. When a person is drunk, he wants to say yes, and he says no. So is the expression of the mind in a dream. It is a marvellous thing to study the science of dreams. How wonderful that a dream of the poet is poetical, of the musician harmonious. Why is this? Because their mind is trained, their mind has become individual[39]. Their mind expresses itself in the realm of that[40]. Sometimes one marvels at the dreams one hears[41] experienced by poetic souls. You will see the sequence from the first act till the last. You will see that every little action has a certain meaning. More interesting still is the symbolical dream, to see the meaning behind it. It is a wonderful thing that to the simple person comes a simple dream; when a person is confused then the dream is confused. So you see the person in the straight[42] dream, in the dream with fear, with joy, with grief. Then the dream shows the sadness. But this is not small[43], this is not past[44], it was not a dream, it is as real as life on the physical plane. Is this life not a dream? Are the eyes not closed? The king has forgotten his palace. Man says: Oh, it is a dream, it is nothing. But this dream can be the whole life of the past. This dream can be tomorrow. It is

32. Ibid.: "in the physical" changed to "on the physical plane"
33. Ibid.: "Every dream has a meaning," inserted
34. Ibid.: "The" moved to after "only" to read: "only the thing"
35. Ibid.: "the" changed to "a"
36. Hq.tp., Hq.st.: "upset" is typed, but the usual expression is "upside down"; (Hq.st.)Gd.ed.: "upside"
37. (Hq.st.)Gd.ed.: "but was not able to" inserted
38. Ibid.: "the" inserted
39. (Hq.st.)Gd.ed.: the word "individual" is crossed out, but no other word is substituted; (er.tp.)Sk.cr.: later, Sk. inked in the word "focused" in the blank in the typescript
40. (Hq.st.)Gd.ed.: "that" changed to "art"
41. Ibid.: "of" inserted
42. (Hq.st.)Gd.ed.: "straight" crossed out; (er.tp.)Sk.cr.: Sk. added "straight" back in ink, then crossed that out and wrote "simple"
43. (Hq.st.)Gd.ed.: "small" changed to "a small thing"
44. Ibid.: "past" changed to "a pastime"

only on the physical plane that it was a dream. The condition in[45] which the mind has passed[46] makes it only a dream. But man says: Yes, but when we awake we find a house, therefore this is reality. If we dream of a palace, we find no palace. This is true and not true. The palaces which are built in that world are as much our own, are much more our own. As soon as the body dies, this is left that is always there. If it is a dream of pleasure, the pleasure will come. If it is a dream of light of love, then all is there. It is a treasure you can depend upon; death cannot take it away. It is a glimpse of that idea which[47] the Bible says : "Where your treasure is, there is your heart"[48]. We can find glimpses of that [49]comparing dreams with the wakeful state. Whatever we hold, the longer we have held it, the more firmly it is established, [50]than what we hold in [51]hand. Then we create a world for us to live[52]. This is the secret of the whole life. How must[53] words explain[54]?

Now a question arises: Where does inspiration come from? Is it the work of the mind? Is it produced as [55]a factory? No. There is a store-house of all knowledge that has ever been or ever will be. What is it? That[56] is the divine mind. Where is the divine mind? It is in the depth of your being, far and yet so near. If a person is before you, you might see it[57], even at a distance of hundred miles. But if you are just close to that person, and your back is turned to it, you cannot see[58]. If you look at that person, there is communication. If only there is want[59] of reaching, then the reaching is at hand[60]. What is it that gives inspiration to the musician? What is it?[61] It is the fairy ghost pictured[62] in thousand forms. And yet it is a voice from the depth of one's own heart. The mind begins to call out. When the heart-ears[63] are open, then comes perfection. Then the composer conceives in one moment what will be perfect [64]hundred years later, what will be perfect at[65] any age. After the death of the heart of the composer, this will be living.

45. Ibid.: "in" changed to "into"
46. Hq.tp., Hq.st.: "past" is typed, but the context seems to call for "passed" (pronounced the same)
47. (Hq.st.)Gd.ed.: "which" changed to "when"
48. Matthew 6:21: "For where your treasure is, there your heart will be also"
49. (Hq.st.)Gd.ed.: "by" inserted
50. Ibid.: "and it can be more firmly established" inserted
51. Ibid.: "our" inserted
52. Ibid.: "in" inserted
53. Ibid.: "must" changed to "can"
54. Ibid.: "it" inserted
55. Ibid.: "in" inserted
56. Ibid.: "That" changed to "It"
57. Ibid.: "it" changed to "him"
58. Ibid.: "him" inserted
59. Ibid.: "want" changed to "the desire"
60. Ibid.: "the reaching is at hand" changed to "it is possible to reach"
61. Ibid.: "What is it?" crossed out
62. Ibid.: "the fairy ghost pictured" changed to "a fairy, a ghost; it can be pictured"
63. Ibid.: "heart-ears" changed to "heart's ears"
64. Ibid.: "a" inserted
65. Ibid.: "at" changed to "in"

This comes not of the brain, it comes from the fountain from the bottom of the heart, from the divine mind. One may study counterpoints[66] and notes and be puzzling for a whole year, and never come to the right point. Poets may be working for years, only that moment[67] reach the divine mind. They digged[68] till[69] the depth, till they reached the living water. In some parts[70] you have to dig a little, in some parts[70] much, but in the bottom of the heart is inspiration. What [71]brain makes is mortal. One can easily see this by an example. There are two ways: the way of heritage, the other way of making. Mostly man depends on heritage, some few make. Medicine when it is inspiration is a divine heritage. But where does the divine mind collect the knowledge of all minds? This knowledge is in the divine mind as[72] all the heat is in the sun. Its origin is in the sun. So one can never say: I have invented, I have discovered. It all comes from one source.

There are different forms of inspiration. The beginning is impression. When[73] a person sees, he is impressed. He can be impressed by kindness, by goodness, that is the beginning. For this no clairvoyance is necessary; everyone has that gift to a certain extent. For people who have experience of life it is more difficult than for children, who really get an impression of people. Some make them afraid, some annoyed, others pleased, or joyous. This is the way of children. Grown up[74] often cannot partake that impression, the direct and natural impression of children. Besides, there is the link of love and sympathy. Words do not need[75] to express it, only a little light or shade. You do not need to say or to do to express the increase of[76] love. By impression one feels. What does this show? That the world of the body is dead, that the world of the heart is living. Who is conscious of the body is dead. But alas, how many dead persons live, and their number is increasing, the number of those who do not believe in the existence of the mind. Then there is intuition, a further step. This step is like a voice who[77] tells one, who[77] warns, the voice of the heart who[78] says: No, do it not[79], or: Do it. That decides.[80] Many say: But

66. Ibid.: "counterpoints" changed to "counterpoint"
67. Ibid.: first "only that moment" changed to "at that moment they", but then again altered to "and at one moment"
68. Hq.tp., Hq.st.: "digged", now an obsolete form, may have been heard by P-o-M. in his youth in India
69. (Hq.st.)Gd.ed.: "digged till" changed to "dig to"
70. Ibid.: "parts" changed to "hearts"
71. (Hq.st.)Gd.ed.: "the" inserted
72. Hq.tp.: "als" is typed, Dutch for "as" (a linguistic slip?); Hq.st.: "as"
73. (Hq.st.)Gd.ed.: "When" changed to "By what"
74. All the typescripts have "Grown up", but the context calls for "Grownups", meaning adults
75. (Hq.st.)Gd.ed.: "do not need" changed to "are not needed"
76. Ibid.: "increase of" crossed out
77. Ibid.: "who" changed to "that"
78. Ibid.: "who" changed to "which"
79. Ibid.: "do it not" changed to "do not do it"
80. Ibid.: "That decides." crossed out

very often it was not the right intuition. But if they study they will find out it was right, but you must hear it at once. It rings once, not twice. Besides, the doubting person says: which was the right? The first or the second voice? They mix them up. The more they are doubting, the more become confused. A person may blame intuition, but he fools himself, not intuition. In the form of warning, in the form suggestion, comes the decision[81].

Then there is a further manifestation, that is inspiration. The heart becomes absorbed in art, in poetry, in beauty. As a stream comes the whole phrase; in one stream it comes. What was not possible to be made in six months, comes in one moment's time. You have only to take it down. There is a great delight after this having[82] come. The one to whom this comes does not give the credit to himself; he gives the credit to the king of all beauty.

And another step further is the inspiration in the form of a dream, the vision. What[83] the person sees clearly will happen perhaps after twelve years, that[84] is vision or knowledge of the past. It is like a flash[85]. One sees the whole series like a moving picture. Where does one get this? When the heart is focussed on the divine mind because all is there as a moving picture. There was a poet of Persia, Firdausi[86]; he was asked by the king to write the history of the land. He was promised by this king to receive[87] a gold coin for every verse. After this promise Firdausi went into the solitude and wrote the tradition of centuries. Characters, lives, deeds, he saw it all as a play, and he wrote of it in verse. When he returned in[88] the court, the king was so much impressed, he thought it wonderful. But many in the world will always repulse[89]. The truth is only recepted[90] by the few. Many made a bad expression[91], many showed scepticism. It went so far that they told the king that it was all Firdausi's imagination. It hurt him terribly. He took this person and held his hand upon his head, and said to him: "Now, close your eyes and look." This person saw like a moving picture and exclaimed: "I have seen." The poet 's heart was struck and he would not accept the gold coins. The message given by the great ones, by the prophets and masters, by Rama, by Krishna, what was it? Not imagination. It was that record which can be found by diving deep, that prophecy given to the world as a lesson,

81. Ibid.: "comes the decision" changed to "intuition comes"
82. Ibid.: "having" changed to "has"
83. Ibid.: "What" changed to "When"
84. Ibid.: "that" changed to "then there"
85. Although "flesh" is typed, it seems clearly a typographical error for "flash'
86. In the typescript the name is written "Firdosi (?)"; the standard spelling in English is Firdausi (ee List), and the work P-o-M. refers to is the *Shah Nameh*; Hq.st.: blanks where the name appears; (Hq.st.)Gd.ed.: "Firdausi" written in the blanks
87. (Hq.st.)Gd.ed.: "to receive" crossed out
88. Ibid.: "in" changed to "to"
89. (Er.tp.)Sk.cr.: Sk. wrote "refute" in ink over "repulse"
90. Hq.tp., Hq.st.: "recepted" (see note 29 above); (Hq.st.)Gd.ed.: "recepted" changed to "accepted"
91. (Hq.st.)Gd.ed.: "made a bad expression" changed to "spoke ill of it"

living in the world, like a scripture. It is [92]direct communion given by all masters.

Then there is another thing, one step forward, that is revelation. When one has come to this degree of revelation, then every thing and being is living; a rock, a tree, is living; the air, the sky, the stars, all are living. One communicates to[93] everything . Nature, characters, one reads their history. Wherever the glance falls, on nature, on characters, one sees the future. That is revelation, that is the magic lantern of Aladdin. Once discovered, it throws its light to the right or to the left, and all things will become clear.

God bless you.

---

92. Ibid.: "a" inserted
93. Ibid.: "to" changed to "with"

A stencil made at Headquarters, Geneva, from an unknown reporting

Headquarters
April 4, '24

Beloved Ones of God,

I would like to speak on the subject of the different paths through which one attains the spiritual goal. There are two distinct paths, and both[1] are quite contrary one from another[2]. The one is the path of resignation, the other is the path of struggle. No doubt in the path of struggle there is also resignation, and in the path of resignation there is also struggle. The only thing is, that the one who is treading the path of resignation has only one thought: to be resigned. And for the one who strikes the path of struggle, the main object is to struggle. Christ has taught these two paths in a symbolical way when he says to Thomas[3]: "Take your sword and sheathe it"[4]. The taking of the sword means struggle, to cover it is resignation. The necessity of these two paths is so great; it is not possible that the one is ignored, and that only one is accepted.

Often people make the meaning of Sufism as passivism. But it is not passivism, it is activism and passivism both. It is the knowing of the secret of life of man on earth, of what he needs, for his character, for his condition. When we reflect upon these principles, we find that in life there are things to which we can only be resigned. It is easy to be resigned to things that one cannot help, but if one has the power to struggle it is difficult to be resigned. But a person who is resigned in easy conditions and does not find it difficult, that person does not know resignation. For instance, there is a person whose poor relations wanted a part of his capital because they were in great need, and in spite of all needs, this person could not be resigned to let them have that part of it. Then in the night came the robbers. They broke in the house

---

Documents:

Hq.st. = A stencil (but not one of the series) made at Headquarters, Geneva. Later, Murshida Sherifa Goodenough made some editorial changes on a copy of this stencil, indicated by "(Hq.st.)Gd.ed." Three changes (one made twice) were not made by Gd.; they are indicated by (Hq.st.)cr.

Sk.tp. = A typescript made by Sakina Furnée or under her supervision. This typescript follows exactly "Hq.st." with the editorial changes in "(Hq.st.)Gd.ed." and is therefore mentioned only in notes 3 and 10.

Notes:

1. (Hq.st.)Gd.ed.: "both" changed to "they"
2. (Hq.st.)Gd.ed.: "one from another" changed to "to one another"
3. (Hq.st.)cr.: In an unidentifiable hw. (possibly Sk., not Gd.), "Thomas" crossed out and "Peter" substituted, and the same change made in ink in Sk.tp.
4. P-o-M. refers to the story in John 18 where Peter cuts off the ear of the high priest's slave, after which Jesus says, "Put your sword back into its sheath" (John 18:11)

and went away with the fortune. The next day this person resigned with it[5]. This resignation is no virtue. To resign is when one has the power to manage, and then resigns[6].

All the great ones have seen the value of resignation and have taught it. Christ has said: If someone wants you to walk a distance with him, walk with him a longer distance[7]. What does that teach? Resignation. One might think that resignation is impractical[8]. This selfish world will take the best of one. Yes, it is true, but the loss is much less, compared to the gain. If only the heart can sustain the loss. If one is not contented with what has been done it is better not to resign. For an instance: if an acquaintance comes to your house and asks to take your umbrella, and you say yes. Now comes the time that you want to go out; it is raining and your umbrella is taken. Now you grumble about that acquaintance: how stupid of him, how could he have the boldness to ask my only umbrella? That resignation is of no good, it bears no fruit. This resignation would only be a virtue when going in the rain yet you were satisfied because the other person was safe from it; that only is virtue of resignation. One who is really resigned does not show it; it is not an easy thing. How many people in this world try to learn wonderful spiritual things. But the simple thing of resignation is miraculous. For this virtue is not only beautiful, it is a miracle. And there are little things in which there is resignation, in which we do not see resignation, and where yet it is. Those around us might ask us to do something to which we feel not pleased. Those around us perhaps say something that we do not wish to take silently, we wish to talk back. Then there are the little pin-pricks from those around us in everyday life. If we are not resigned we feel excited every moment. Therefore to be resigned is not weakness, it is a great strength.

When one goes further one finds that one can be resigned even to cold and heat, with places congenial and uncongenial; that all has a meaning, a benefit. And if we do not form a habit of being resigned, we just as well could have resigned. Not having resigned to an experience is a loss of occasion. Besides this there are two forces working: the individual power and the collective power. In Sufi terms the one is *qadr*[9], the other *qaza*[9]. Very often the individual power will not surrender. If this is not so, it is crushed. For an instance, in a country someone is called to the arms, but he says he will not join. In spite of all the beauty of his ideal he is helpless before the might of the whole nation. Here one must resign under the

---

5. (Hq.st.)Gd.ed.: "with it" changed to "himself to that"
6. (Hq.st.)Gd.ed.: "and then resigns" changed to "then to resign"
7. Matthew 5:41: "If anyone forces you to go one mile, go also the second mile"
8. (Hq.st)cr.: "impractical" was typed first, then changed in ink (it cannot be determined by whom) to "unpractical" (a rare but attested word), even though "impractical" is the much more common usage
9. Hq.st.: typed "Kadar" and "Kaza", the transcriptions of the Arabic words used in P-o-M.'s day (see Glossary)

condition where there is a conflict between a less and a greater power; here resignation is the only solution.

No doubt everything must be understood rightly. Resignation preached foolishly is not a benefit. There was a *mureed*[10] learning from a *murshid*[10] the lesson of resignation, and the simple mureed, thinking of this subject, was walking when a mad elephant was coming from the other side. As this mureed was going in the thought of resignation, he stayed in the midst of the road. There was a wise man who told him to go away, but he would not because he was resigning to the elephant, until he was pushed away by the strength of the elephant. They brought him to his murshid who asked him: "How are you hurt so much?" He answered that he [11]practising resignation. The murshid said: "But was not there anybody who told you to go away?" "Yes", he answered, "but I would not listen". "But", said the murshid, "why did not you resign to that person?" Therefore often beautiful principles can be practised to the greatest disadvantage.

Nevertheless resignation has proved to be the path of saints, because it develops patience in man. And what is patience? It is all treasure there is. Nothing is more valuable, nothing a greater bliss than patience. There is a story of a prophet who was very ill, and who suffered many years. But through his suffering his insight became more clear. His suffering was so great that those around him became tired of it, and so he had to seek the refuge of God in the forest, to relieve[12] them of his pain. As his sight was keen and the ears of his heart were open, he heard from trees: "I am the medicine of your disease". The prophet asked: "Has the time of my cure come?" There came a voice: "No". Then he said: "Why shall I take you then?" Another time he had another experience. He heard: "I am the medicine of your disease". He asked: "Has the time of my cure come?" The answer came: "Yes". The prophet said: "Why shall I take you?" For he could still not resign.

When we think of this extreme ideal we might ask: "But is this not unpractical[13]?" Specially in this time, where there are so many treatments, so many mechanical things. But a thoughtful person will find how many people have ruined their lives by going from one treatment to another, lacking patience and resignation in which reside their absolute cure. The remedy is not always the answer of the difficulty; often patience is the answer. It seems as if man becomes more and more impatient every day owing to his superfluous life. There is hardly any resignation to little things. But it is better to resign than to struggle.

---

10. Sufis use the word *mureed* for an initiate, *murshid* for a spiritual teacher (see Glossary)
11. (Hq.st.)cr.: "was" added in ink (by Sk.?); the "was" is typed in Sk.tp.
12. Hq.st.: "relief" is typed, but this seems clearly a mistake for "relieve"
13. (Hq.st.)cr.: "impractical" later changed in ink to "unpractical" (see note 8 above)

When we put the mystic light upon this subject, we find that we form a harmonious connection with the infinite by being resigned. How to learn it? Must we do it by being resigned to God? No, that is a greater lesson to learn. The first thing to learn is to resign to the little difficulties in life. And what is that? Not to be as something that strikes against everything coming against it. When one were able to manage this, one would not need to cultivate a great power. Then the presence of that person is a healing. Such a person is in the world more than every branch of the rose: they have many thorns, and there is hardly one flower.

14

Question: *Some people say, "I cannot rise above my faults". What could they do to overcome them?*

Answer: As I have said: struggle in the spiritual path, struggle is the only thing. I shall give an example of a person facing a struggle: a person who has a disagreeable conversation, who has an inclination to retort. At the same time this person has no battle with this, of giving back. By letting his force go out, by insulting back, he has lost his power. By controlling this inclination, one has a thousandfold greater power. For the moment that it happens, to humiliate oneself, to crush one's pride, to crush oneself, one feels crushed both sides, by not answering and then by crushing oneself. "I have given back too" gives a little pride, a satisfaction.

Question: *What is the way the dance of the soul expresses itself?*

Answer: The difference is of the water in the tank and the running water of a stream. In the tank, it is still, lying dead. So a person can be dull, heavy, depressed. The water of the running stream is dancing at every step. So the dancing soul is ready to see the beauty of music, truth, colour, line. The dancing soul it is which attracts to itself as the little stream of water, and will bring pleasure and satisfaction to all who see.

---

14. Hq.st.: Typed on a separate piece of paper with the date and place indicated on top and the heading "Questions and answers after the lecture on the subject of 'The different paths through which one reaches the spiritual goal'"

A stencil prepared at Headquarters, Geneva

Headquarters[1], April 5th, 1924

Brotherhood Meeting

Beloved Ones of God,

I would like to speak on the subject of the work of the Sufi Brotherhood. When one does at this time see so many different movements working for brotherhood, one might[2] ask, what is the Sufi Brotherhood doing among all those[3] movements of brotherhood? And in answer to this question I say: If there were twenty thousand more movements of brotherhood[4], it would not be enough for the need of today. Besides, to[5] the point of view of the Sufi Brotherhood [6]whatever is the form, whatever the society, this form, this society are[7] our ideal[6]. [8]We think it a privilege to give our[8] humble service in the great cause of the[9] world brotherhood. [10]We do not think our Brotherhood superior to others; there is only one brotherhood.[10] No doubt

---

Documents:

Hq.st.. = a stencil prepared at Headquarters, Geneva, for distribution to Sufi Centres.

er.tp. = an early typescript, double-spaced on fine paper. Typescripts of this type are usually identified as "Sk.tp.", as they were prepared under Sk.'s supervision; however, in this case, there are very many differences between this text and the Hq.st. which Sk. copied for her set, and in some places this text is fuller. It must have been copied from some version no longer in the archives.

Sk.tp. = a typescript prepared by Sakina Furnée or under her supervision, closely following Hq.st. Sakina made one correction in type and suggested several others in ink, indicated by "(Sk.tp.)Sk.cr." in the notes.

Notes:

1. Er.tp.: "Sufi International Headquarters" instead of "Headquarters", and typed under the date.
2. Ibid.: "may" instead of "might"
3. Ibid.: "these" instead of "those"
4. Ibid.: "brotherhoods" instead of "movements of brotherhood"
5. Ibid.: "to" omitted
6. Ibid.: "is that whatever form, whatever society it may be, it is our ideal, our wish" instead of "whatever is the form, whatever the society, this form, this society are our ideal"
7. (Sk.tp.)Sk.cr.: "are" altered to "is" in ink
8. Er.tp.: "Our privilege is a" instead of "We think it a privilege to give our"
9. Ibid.: "the" omitted
10. Ibid.: "We do not claim the superiority of our Brotherhood; we do not say it is the only one brotherhood." instead of "We do not think our Brotherhood superior to others; there is only one brotherhood."

one service will be done by different souls; we work[11] according to our[12] own individual method, so we[13] are best able to serve humanity. We consider[14] absurd to say: Your method is wrong, ours[15] is right. As long as we are doing our best, that is all we want and[16] all we do.

And now I should like to speak a few words on the work and the ideal we have before us. There is no doubt that everywhere in the world [17]seems to be wakened[18] a desire[18] toward spirituality, and [19]there is no doubt that[19] all over [20]the world lives[21] a desire for brotherhood, for cooperation. That being the case, every effort is made [22]to answer the call of humanity, every effort is made by right and by wrong[22]. And as there is no apparent proof, as the proof is in the result, the[23] right and the wrong naturally are confused. For an instance, [24]instead of brotherhood-communities have come[25] trade- and business-communities[24] and thereby[26] fight and [27]opposition, because of their thinking differently[27]. They say, we are against war, [28]making a financial war. Besides they have only the name of the thought or the ideal; [29]mostly they fight each one another [30]. They have a[31] disposition to fight.

This has occupied our thought for a long time. [32]What is the way to avoid it?[32] We have tried our best till now and will try always[33] to avoid forming [34]a community. Yes, we could not help forming a nucleus, as it is

---

11. Ibid.: "; we work" omitted
12. Ibid.: "our" changed to "their"
13. Ibid.: "we" changed to "they"
14. Ibid.: "it" added
15. Er.tp.: "our method" instead of "our"; (Sk.tp.)Sk.cr.: "our" changed to "ours"
16. Er.tp.: a comma instead of "and"
17. Ibid.: "there" added
18. Ibid.: "wakened" moved to after "a desire"
19. Ibid.: "there is no doubt that" changed to "no doubt"
20. Ibid.: "in" added
21. Ibid.: "there is" instead of "lives"
22. Ibid.: "by right and wrong thinking to answer the call of humanity" instead of "to answer the call of humanity, every effort is made by right and by wrong"
23. Ibid.: "the" omitted
24. This part of the sentence has been left as punctuated in the documents; however, since P-o-M. shortly speaks of the undesirability of forming communities in brotherhood work, is seems possible he may have said: "instead of brotherhood, communities have come, trade- and business-communities. . ."
25. Er.tp.: "there are" instead of "have come"
26. Ibid.: "which" instead of "and thereby"
27. Ibid.: "oppose each other, the one thinking different from the other" instead of "opposition, because of their thinking differently"
28. Ibid.: "but they are" added
29. Ibid.: "but" added
30. Ibid.: "are fighting each one with the other" instead of "fight each one another"
31. Ibid.: "Because, it is their" instead of "They have a"
32. Ibid.: ", and" instead of ". What is the way to avoid it?"
33. Ibid.: "always try" instead of "try always"
34. Ibid.: "into" added

necessary to sail in the sea to have[35] a ship, [36]it is necessary to have a form by which you are best able to serve humanity. We tried to do our best to remain without a name, but even cats and dogs have names[37]. People called it old, higher, new thought, and that became[38] their name. But[39] is there any new thought? Can there be an[40] old thought? Every old thought is new. Besides [41]it is difficult to discriminate between the higher and the lower thought[41]. We have tried to do[42] our best not to give an[43] importance to [44]name. [45]As long as one has sentiment for humanity we stand by his side[45].

But [46]the question comes: How must[47] brotherhood be taught, [48]what can help to become brothers[48]? In every house the[49] parents teach their children[50] to be brothers, and[51] it is not even in their power to produce brotherhood in their own house[52]. And preachers go out and say[53]: become brothers. But [54]it is not only by preaching that you become a brother, because you have[54] thousand arguments against it, [55]even poetical ones, and grudges and prejudices[55]. [56]When each one will remember what has been done, how can they become brothers?[56] It is useless to preach even [57]for years and years, it cannot[58]. [59]Only one thing is necessary: to produce understanding[59].

---

35. Ibid.: "with" instead of "to have"
36. Ibid.: "so" added
37. Ibid.: "a name" instead of "names"
38. Ibid.: "because" instead of "became" (probably a typographical error)
39. Ibid.: "At the same time how many thousands of 'thoughts' there may be," instead of "But"
40. Ibid.: "an" omitted
41. Ibid.: "higher and lower, it is difficult to discriminate" instead of "it is difficult to discriminate between the higher and the lower thought"
42. Ibid.: "to do" omitted
43. Ibid.: "an" omitted
44. Ibid.: "the" added
45. Ibid.: ", only knowing we stand by the side of humanity" instead of "As long as one has sentiment for humanity we stand by his side"
46. Ibid.: "now" added
47. Ibid.: "can" instead of "must"
48. Ibid.: "how can we help that people may become brothers" instead of "what can help to become brothers"
49. Ibid.: "any" instead of "the"
50. Ibid.: "their children" omitted
51. Ibid.: ". But" instead of ", and"
52. Ibid.: "houses" instead of "house"
53. Ibid.: "preach" instead of "say"
54. Ibid.: "there are" instead of "it is not only by preaching that you become a brother, because you have"
55. Ibid.: ": poetical arguments, grudges, prejudices" instead of "even poetical ones, and grudges and prejudices"
56. Ibid.: "After one remembers what one has done to make them become brothers, one says:" instead of "When each one will remember what has been done, how can they become brothers?"
57. Ibid.: "if it were" added
58. Er.tp.: "it cannot" omitted; (Sk.tp.)Sk.cr.: "suffice" added in ink; on a different copy of Sk.tp., first "help" written in ink, then crossed out and "suffice" written instead
59. Er.tp.: "Then [sic] only thing which can produce brotherhood is understanding" (the "n" of the opening "Then" is lightly typed, by mistake) instead of "Only one thing is necessary: to produce understanding"

And what does give understanding? Not the knowledge of [60]a fact, but eternal truth, through it we unite[60]. So we come to [61]the essence of religion, to the thought of uniting in truth[61]. The central thing is that truth. In order to make one tolerant to another[62], we must not say, but waken[63], that he may understand.

This remembers me[64] an amusing incident. Once I had a new pupil to whom I was giving instructions, and [65]the last thing was that before retiring every night he had to send thoughts[66] of love and compassion to all living beings. This pupil [67]instantly horrified at the idea and[68] said: yes, all, but not my[69] neighbouring country. I did not resist, [70]took it tolerantly, understanding his[71] sour[72] heart. [73]Would arguing have helped? No. So[73] I said: "You are quite right. Forget the neighbour[74] while thinking of humanity". The [75] pupil smiled; he had expected an argument. [76]Yet he felt not satisfied and after six months he was able to think of [77]whole humanity[76]. [78]It is not preaching that is needed, but the hammering on the hearts, so that they naturally will understand[78].

Another abuse of this ideal is the desire to be spiritually awakened. But how do they want to be awakened[79]? [80]Do they want to see psychic phenomena, to have occult powers?[80] But[81] have we not seen great countries,

---

60. Ibid.: "facts, but the knowledge of the eternal truth; we unite through that" instead of "a fact, but eternal Truth, through it we unite"
61. Ibid.: "the thought: the essence of religion is uniting in truth;" instead of "the essence of religion, to the thought of uniting in Truth"
62. Ibid.: "the one tolerant to the other" instead of "one tolerant to another"
63. (Sk.tp.)Sk.cr.: "the other" added in ink, then crossed out
64. Er.tp.: "I remember" instead of "This remembers me"; (Sk.tp.)Sk.cr.: "(reminds me of)" added in type, then "remembers me" crossed out in ink, and parentheses around "(reminds me of)" removed
65. Er.tp.: "while giving them" added
66. Ibid.: "should send a thought" instead of "had to send thoughts"
67. Er.tp.: "was"; (Sk.tp.)Sk.cr.: "was" added in ink
68. Er.tp.: ". He" instead of "and"
69. Ibid.: "the" instead of "my"
70. Ibid.: "and" added
71. Ibid.: "that it came from a" instead of "his"
72. (Sk.tp.)Sk.cr.: "sour" changed to "sore" in ink
73. Er.tp.: "Instead of arguing" in place of "Would arguing have helped? No. So"
74. Ibid.: "neighbouring country" instead of "neighbour"
75. Sk.tp.: a short, indecipherable word crossed out in type
76. Er.tp.: "But after six months he felt not satisfied. So gradually he was brought to the understanding of this idea" instead of "Yet he felt not satisfied and after six months he was able to think of whole humanity"
77. (Sk.tp.)Sk.cr.: "the" added in ink
78. Er.tp.: "Hammering brotherhood on the hearts is of no use. It is not preaching that is needed. Tuning is needed, that they may naturally understand" instead of "It is not preaching that is needed, but the hammering on the hearts, so that they naturally will understand"
79. Ibid.: "wakened" instead of "awakened"
80. Ibid.: "By psychic phenomena, powers, by occultism." instead of "Do they want to see psychic phenomena, to have occult powers?"
81. Ibid.: "And" instead of "But"

ancient countries as Egypt, North India[82], possess[83] magic, occult and[84] mystical conceptions? What did that do? The same in their way as the scientific inventions during the war, as they used the[85] magic powers for the benefit of the[86] own ego. Therefore being absorbed in the attainment of the material world, [87]trying to do things with magic [88]to one another has been [89]cause of[88] ruined nations, of [90] great distress to humanity in all ages. [91]Prophets and saints of[92] all ages have warned against it[93]; in their words one finds simple things[94] as could be taught to children. Therefore today to the intellectual seeker of complexities the ancient scriptures mean nothing. [95]The accustomed thought of today is the thought of the purse of gold, and if the cabinet is enfavoured[96] with one[95]. Imagine what a[97] great scope to evil[98], to lead astray[99]. It hinders[100] true service, respect, love, consideration for one another. But in spite of the[101] difficulties, are we not trying to do our best? I am[102] thankful to say that in different countries we have joined together in this humble activity, an activity [103]nearer to our heart as nothing[104] else[103].

Now the question is: What is the way of attaining to that truth which teaches by itself brotherhood? That truth is pictured in the symbol of the cross. The perpendicular line suggests diving deep in[105] oneself, from the outer in[105] the innermost consciousness, [106]man reaching from the point of human to that point of the divine[106]. And what does the horizontal line

---

82. Ibid.: "Egypt, and the North of India" instead of "as Egypt, North India"
83. Ibid.: "having" instead of "possess"
84. Ibid.: a comma instead of "and"
85. Er.tp.: ". They were using their" instead of ", as they used the"
86. Er.tp.: "their" instead of "the"
87. Ibid.: "they were" added
88. Ibid.: ". It" instead of "to one another has been cause of"
89. (Sk.tp.)Sk.cr.: "the" added in ink
90. Er.tp.: "and brought" instead of ", of"
91. Ibid.: "The" added
92. Ibid.: "in" instead of "of"
93. Ibid.: "this" instead of "it"
94. Ibid.: "they said simple" instead of "one finds simple things"
95. Ibid.: "They say: 'What I want to know is how to influence the customer's thought, how to get the purse of gold out of his pocket'. If there is any kind of thought, it is the thought of power: 'that the Cabinet may fall', or 'that the Cabinet may be enfavoured with me'" instead of "The accustomed thought of today is the thought of the purse of gold and if the cabinet is enfavoured with one"
96. This unattested form may have been coined by P-o-M.; it appears in all documents.
97. Er.tp.: "a" omitted
98. Ibid.: "for evil attainment" instead of "to evil"
99. Ibid.: "from kindness" added
100. Ibid.: "It hinders" omitted
101. Ibid.: "all" instead of "the"
102. Ibid.: "We are" instead of "I am"
103. Ibid.: "which is so near to our heart that [blank] nothing we shall not give as a sacrifice to make it flourish" instead of "nearer to our heart as nothing else"
104. (Sk.tp.)Sk.cr.: "than anything" substituted for "as nothing" in ink
105. Er.tp.: "into" instead of "in"
106. Ibid.: "that man may reach from that point where he is human to that point where he is divine" instead of "man reaching from the point of human to that point of the divine"

suggest[107]? Expansion. That is the thought:[108] [109]I and my neighbour are not only friends, we are only one[109]. Then there is no doubt that [110]the same interest exists[111] for the neighbour[112] as for oneself. No doubt, without rising to that conception, it is very difficult to understand this. Man must [113]realize it by meditation. When he[114] touches the innermost self of his being, then he[115] sees in another person himself. And it is only then that real sympathy comes. [116]It is as the love from a mother for her child[116]. The mother naturally rises to [117]that conception. She does not only know the child as her own[117], but sees in him[118] her own being. And she lives[119] in the pleasure and the happiness of the child; in the absence of [120]happiness of the child there is no pleasure and happiness for her[120]. What is it[121] after all, the love of the mother, developed without consciousness[122]: It is the realized[123] oneness with the[124] child. [125]From love and continual devotion is born unity, is born oneness[125].

Now there is another question: A person [126]may say, must we teach that, must we lecture about that which is difficult to learn?[126] The answer is: [127]The interior[128] knowledge is not enough. It is not sufficient to say: My neighbour and I are one[127]; that is only imagination. There are two things:

---

107. Ibid.: "the horizontal line suggests" instead of "does the horizontal line suggest"
108. Ibid.: "That is the thought:" omitted
109. Ibid.: "I and my neighbours, not only my friends, are one" instead of "I and my neighbour are not only friends, we are only one"
110. Ibid.: "there will be" inserted
111. Ibid.: "exists" omitted
112. Ibid.: "one's neighbours" instead of "the neighbour"
113. Ibid.: "actually" added
114. Ibid.: "man" instead of "he"
115. Ibid.: "man" instead of "then he"
116. Ibid.: "For an instance, this can be seen in the love of the mother for the child" instead of "It is as the love from a mother for her child"
117. Ibid.· "the conception that she does not know intellectually" instead of "that conception. She does not only know the child as her own"
118. Ibid.: "the child" instead of "him"
119. Ibid.: "is happy" instead of "lives"
120. Ibid.: "his pleasure and happiness she cannot be happy" instead of "happiness of the child there is no pleasure and happiness for her"
121. Ibid.: "it" omitted
122. Ibid.: "which has developed without her being conscious of it" instead of "developed without consciousness"
123. Ibid.: "she has realized the" instead of "it is the realized"
124. Ibid.: "her" instead of "the"
125. Ibid.: "But this realization does not belong only to the relation between mother and child. Love and devotion and unity, they are born of the feeling of oneness" instead of "From love and continual devotion is born unity, is born oneness"
126. Ibid.: "says: 'Is it difficult to learn this, difficult to teach this.'" instead of "may say, must we teach that, must we lecture about that which is difficult to learn?"
127. Ibid.: "'knowledge is not sufficient'. To know 'I and my neighbour is one' is not enough" instead of "the interior knowledge is not enough. It is not sufficient to say: my neighbour and I are one"
128. (Sk.tp.)Sk.cr.: "interior" changed to "outer" in ink; on another copy of Sk.tp., first "interior" crossed out and "inner" written in ink, then "inner" crossed out and "outer" written instead

conception and conviction. Conception is [129]the crescent, conviction is [129]the full moon. What is learned by study is conception, but that is not sufficient. [130]The conception must be deepened, as the moon rises. As conception is deepened, it results into conviction[130]. The working of the Sufi Movement with students and workers is[131] the idea of deepening the conception till[132] conviction results.
[133]

---

129. Er.tp.: "like" added
130. Ibid.: "Conception must be deepened. As the crescent rises to the full moon, so the conception must be deepened until it results in conviction" instead of "The conception must be deepened, as the moon rises. As conception is deepened it results into conviction"
131. Ibid.: "has at its background" instead of "is"
132. Ibid.: "until" in place of "till"
133. Ibid.: "God bless you." added

A typescript prepared under Sakina Furnée's supervision

1

Geneva, Sunday April 6th, 1924
Atelier Hugly[2]

Friends,[3]

I should like to say that the performances have made me feel at home. Although East and West are two opposite poles, one thing makes them[4] meet: love, harmony and beauty. But all these three are to be found in one and that is[5] the[6] art. Many say that art is only an imitation of nature[7], but I should say that[8] art is the[9] finishing of nature. Therefore [10]art is the accomplishing of the purpose of creation. And no sooner [11]the artist [12]realizes this than[13] art becomes his religion. Today in the world there are many creeds, one opposed to the other. And there is the greatest necessity of[14] bringing about a better understanding among[15] the[16] sections of humanity. Many methods the wise have applied[17] for this accomplishment[18]. But art is

---

Documents:

Sk.tp.1 = A typescript prepared under Sakina Furnée's supervision, containing the most complete text of the remarks.

Hq.st. = A stecilled copy prepared at Headquarters, Geneva, with a partial, already edited text. Murshida Sherifa Goodenough did further editing on a copy of this stencil, indicated in the notes by "(Hq.st.)Gd.ed."

Sk.tp.2 = Another typescript prepared by Sakina Furnée or under her supervision, incorporating a few of the changes in "Hq.st." and "(Hq.st.)Gd.ed." There is one correction indicated by "(Sk.tp.2)Sk.cr."

Notes:

1. Sk.tp.2: "Expression of thanks after performance." typed at top of document
2. A performance space in Geneva where the performance took place
3. Hq.st., Sk.tp.2: "Friends," omitted
4. Ibid.: "us" instead of "them"
5. Ibid.: ", in" instead of "and that is"
6. (Hq.st.)Gd.ed.: "the" crossed out; Sk.tp.2: "in" instead of "the"
7. Hq.st.: "of nature" omitted; (Hq.st.)Gd.ed.: "of nature" added
8. Ibid.: "that" omitted
9. Ibid.: "a" instead of "the"
10. Hq.st., Sk.tp.2: "in" added
11. (Hq.st.)Gd.ed.: "does" inserted; Sk.tp.2: "does" added
12. Sk.tp.2: "realize" instead of "realizes"
13. Hq.st.: "than" omitted; (Hq.st.)Gd.ed.: "than" added
14. (Hq.st.)Gd.ed.: "of" changed to "for"; Sk.tp.2: "for"
15. Hq.st.: "amongst" instead of "among"; (Hq.st.)Gd.ed.: changed back to "among"
16. Ibid.: "all" instead of "the"
17. Ibid.: "of this world apply" instead of "have applied"
18. Hq.st., Sk.tp.2: "the accomplishment of this purpose" instead of "this accomplishment"

the most desirable method to bring[19] about[20] this[21] better understanding.

Here, on this program[22], artists from different nationalities have played, sung and danced [23]and accomplished it all into one single beauty[22]. [24] I ask you therefore to accept my heartful thanks for the beautiful performance of today. I had a great pleasure of coming here. I am sure I shall remember it long.[23]

---

19. (Hq.st.)Gd.ed., Sk.tp.2: "to bring" changed to "of bringing"
20. Sk.tp.2: "about" omitted; (Sk.tp.2)Sk.cr.: "about" added in ink by Sk.
21. Hq.st.: "a" instead of "this"
22. (Hq.st.)Gd.ed.: "program" changed to "programme" (the more usual British spelling); Sk.tp.2: "programme"
23. Hq.st., Sk.tp.2: "; it was all accomplished in one single beauty" instead of "and accomplished it all into one single beauty"
24. Hq.st.: the last three sentences omitted: "I ask you . . . . remember it long."

A stencil made at Headquarters, Geneva

Headquarters. April 6, '24

Devotional Service

Beloved Ones of God,

After this service I want to say a few words on the idea of this form of worship. No one with some thought will ever deny that there is one God, one truth, one goal, one source, and one longing in the human heart: to arrive to spiritual realization. That is the yearning of every soul, in every race and faith. But why are there so many creeds, castes[1], and religions? One might say, it comes from human nature. Every person has his own way of worshipping, his own ideas, his religion. It is nothing to be surprised[2] that there is such a variety of churches and beliefs. What can surprise is that they do not tolerate, that they think their own way the best way, and the other way wrong.

The Sufi Movement, therefore, in its form of this blessed worship is endeavouring to bring union between the followers of the different religions, so that no one of whatever faith may be able to say: My Great One, my Lord has not an altar, is not mentioned in its prayers. When God is one, wisdom is one. We respect and tolerate and learn just to lay our hearts open to wisdom. Wisdom is not belonging to the East or to the West, it is a divine heritage, it is for us all. We bow to wisdom, we try to be the propounders of that wisdom. Whatever creed, we respect it.

Yes, there are people who say: Why is there any necessity of form? Allow me to say that the soul first was without form, before it was manifested in the body. The body has become so near and dear to us that we forget our soul; it has become foreigned[3] of this form, so that all that is form only seems real; from all other things, we do not know if they exist. About the soul we say: It may be; or still more: It does not exist. But what is mind? A moving picture in the brain. We do not touch it, and feel that it exists.

Documents:

Hq.st. = a stencil prepared at Headquarters, Geneva.

Sk.tp. = a typed copy, probably made from Hq.st., by Sakina Furnée or under her supervision. One editorial change is indicated by "(Sk.tp.)Sk.ed." in a note.

Notes:

1. Hq.st., Sk.tp.: the manuscripts read "casts", but "castes" seems clearly correct here
2. (Sk.tp.)Sk.ed.: "at" added in ink
3. Hq.st., Sk.tp.: this unattested form may have been coined by P-o-M.

Many go to church to worship [4]church, not God. It is difficult for man to have his ideal in the abstract alone. That is the last stage. What is the use of art and beauty? It is a medium of spiritual realization. If we see beauty of form, we wish to experience abstract wisdom. Matter and spirit are one. Within and without, above and below, everywhere is the glory of God.

Now coming to the question: How must this form of worship be spread through the world? For we have to introduce an ideal. Those who look with eyes of faith see all the ones behind us, those who have come from time to time, their ambitions, their prayers. One who worships feels the power around us. Working in the abstract we shall manifest it before the world. It is our happy privilege to work for this great ideal among those who from time to time have come to humanity and are blessed by God.

4. Hq.st.: "the" added in hw. before "church"; Sk.tp.: "the" included in type

A stencil from Headquarters, Geneva

---

[1] Headquarters, April 7th, 1924

Beloved ones of God,

I would like to speak this afternoon on the subject of the spiritual attainment, and that life proves to be a continual struggle. The only difference with the worldly life lies in the other direction. In worldly life [2]can be business, of[3] politics or industry, or whatever be your life's path; if you prove to be lacking that power that enables you to struggle along, you will not meet anything but failure. You may be a very good person, a saintly person, a spiritual person, that does not count. For this reason many in the world lose[4] their faith in goodness, in spirituality, because they see this does not mean anything in worldly life. It is absurd for a spiritual person to say: By your goodness, spirituality and piety your worldly struggle will be helped. No, it cannot be helped. You must have inspiration and power to answer life's demand in life's struggle. By this I want to say to my friends seeking the spiritual path that they must not forget that floating on air is of no good, that standing on earth is the first thing necessary. There are many who dream, who live in the air, but that does not answer our purpose. They may say: We are doing spiritual work, yet we are in bad circumstances. But the language of this path is different, the law of this path is different. It is for this reason that I make these two paths separate: to realize that the one thing has little to do with the other. This does not mean that the wicked person

---

Documents:

Hq.st. = a stencil (but not one of the series) prepared at Headquarters, Geneva, from an unknown reporting.

Sk.tp. = a typescript prepared by Sakina Furnée or under her supervision. On a copy of this document, Sk. made some apparent corrections, indicated by "(Sk.tp.)Sk.cr." in the notes.

A highly edited version of this lecture was printed in *The Sufi Message* series, volume VI, *The Alchemy of Happiness* (London, 1962, pp. 93-7), as "The Struggle of Life (2)". It is not included in the notes.

Notes:

1. Sk.tp.: "Public Lecture." typed in upper left-hand corner; (Sk.tp.)Sk.cr.: "Public" crossed out, and "Private" written above, then "Private Lecture" crossed out and "for Mureeds." written above
2. (Sk.tp.)Sk.cr.: "it" inserted in ink
3. Ibid.: "of" changed to "or"
4. Hq.st., Sk.tp.: "loose" is typed, but the context calls for "lose"; (Sk.tp.)Sk.cr.: "loose" changed to "lose"

succeeds, that success is gained by evil or by an evil character. Nevertheless[5] we must not blame spirituality for failure in worldly things. For worldly things are[6] another inspiration. If that was not so, all great sages would have been millionaires.

Now coming to the question of the spiritual path. The worldly struggle is an outward struggle; the spiritual struggle is an inward struggle. No sooner one takes the spiritual direction, the first enemy is one's little self. What does the little self do? It is the most mischievous self. When you say: I want to fight, it says: I am yourself, you want to fight me? And when it brings failure, it is wise enough and says: It was someone else. All those who failed in life, do they accuse themselves? No. It has always been the next person. And when they have gained, then they say: I have done it. If they love something and have not got it, they say: This person has come between. In little and big things it is all the same. The little self does not admit a fault, but always finds it in another. Besides, its vanity, its pride, its smallness, its egoistical tendency, its contentment keeps one blind. The little self does not hinder the worldly path as it hinders the spiritual path. I remember a Persian verse made by my *murshid*[7], which relates to the little self. I shall translate it: "When I feel that now I must make peace with my little self, it finds time to prepare another attack." That is our condition. In the little faults it is of little consequences, we do not even think of it. But every little fault is a flag for the little self, for its own dominion. In this way of battling it is depriving man, who is the sovereign of the kingdom of God. Very few can realize the great power that lies in battling with and conquering the little self. But what generally man does? He says: My self is already in such a conflict with this world, must I also battle with this self? So he gives the kingdom of this little self to this little self, depriving himself of the divine power that is hidden in the heart of man.

There is in man the false self and the real self. The real self has eternal life in it; the false self has mortal life in it. The real self is wisdom; the false self is ignorance. The real self can rise to perfection; the false self is limitation. The real self has all good; the false self is productive of all evil. One can see in oneself both: God and the other person. By conquering the other one, one realizes God. This power has been called Satan. But is it a power? In reality it is not. It is and it is not. It is a shadow and yet it is nothing. If we realize this we see that the false self has no existence of its own. As soon as the soul has risen above the false self it begins to realize its nobility.

---

5. (Sk.tp.)Sk.cr.: "Nevertheless" crossed out, and "On the other hand" inserted instead
6. Ibid.: "are" crossed out, and "have" inserted instead
7. Sufis use the word *murshid* to refer to a spiritual teacher (see Glossary); here P-o-M. refers to his own teacher, Abu Hashim Madani (see List)

But how can we come to a practical aspect of it? How does it show itself? In which form? It rises up in support to its own interest. It defends itself from the attack of others. It feels exclusive to everyone. It knows itself as a separate entity of friend and of foe. It concerns itself to all that is just now, blind to the future and ignorant of the past. It manifests in the form of self-pity. It expresses in the form of vengeance. It lives feeding upon bitterness, and its life is always in obscurity. Its condition is restlessness and discontentment. It has a continual appetite to have all that is there, it is never content, it has no trust in anyone, no thought for anyone, no consideration for anyone. It has [8]lack of consciousness[9] and therefore of manner. The little self only considers one's[10] own benefit, one's[10] own comfort; giving to others, to those around it, is something dreadful for the little self, for it knows no sacrifice. Renunciation for it is dreadful, worse than death. That is the little self.

When we see it in somebody, we blame that person, we dislike that person, but we overlook the same element in ourselves. No soul in the world can say: I have it not in me. If only the soul was just, it would see. For often it is the unjust person who blames another. The more just you become, the more quiet you will be in all circumstances. Outwardly you will see faults in others; inwardly you will see the sum total within yourself. For an instance, a little child cannot help loving. Here is a thief, a robber; the child wants to love him, because the child is sinless. Why is it? Because the thief is not wakened in the child. The child comes from heaven, the thief from earth, no accommodation is there; therefore there is no thief to the child. We accept things because they are in us. If we consider our knowledge, perhaps among thousand things we have experienced, most of them are told us by others and we have believed them at once. As soon as a person tells us something about a wicked one, we say: Now we know, we were quite sure of it. The most wonderful thing is, that when a person says: This person is good, then everyone thinks: Is it really true? If one knew all about him? Is it possible to be good? Good seems to be something unnatural.

Now coming to the question: Is it necessary that one struggles? Why should one take the spiritual path? Is that tyranny of oneself? It is that by doing this one moulds one's character, one makes one's personality. It is that in this resides all religion. When a person begins to think: I must not bring harm to, or hurt anyone I meet, worthy or unworthy, friend or foe, then only he begins his work in the spiritual direction. Spirituality is not in wonderworking. Spirituality is attained by good manner, by right manner.

---

8. (Sk.tp.)Sk.cr.: "a" inserted
9. Ibid.: "consciousness" altered in ink to read "conscientiousness"
10. Ibid.: "one's" changed to "its" in ink

Where is the shrine of God? In the heart of man. As soon as he begins to consider the feeling of another, he begins to worship God. That feeling is not what gives profit, but what other way is there of worship to God? One might say: It is difficult to please everyone. No doubt, it is difficult. It becomes more difficult if one has in oneself the inclination to please everyone. There is a story of a murshid, who was going with his *mureed*s[11] to some village. He was making a fast; the mureeds also had taken the vow of fasting. They arrived in a peasant's house, who with enthusiasm and happiness had arranged a dinner. Of course, when it was brought to table, the murshid went and sat down, but the pupils did not dare because of their vow of fasting. Yet they would not mention, as spiritual persons never mention such things. As to the murshid, they thought, "Murshid will have forgotten the vow." (Murshids are forgetful.) After the dinner was finished they went out, and the pupils said: "Did you not forget your vow of fasting?" "No", said the murshid, "I had not forgotten, but I preferred breaking my fast to breaking the heart of that man, who with all that enthusiasm prepared that food."

If only we think of everyday life, of all little things which by ~~overlooking make~~ being overlooked make us lose[12] an opportunity of doing some good. Every moment of life is an opportunity of being conscious of human feeling. In prosperity, in adversity, in all conditions, it costs little; only the thought is necessary. A person may be good within, but he may not be conscious of little things. There is no greater religion than love. And the best form of love is to be conscientious of the feelings of those with whom we are in contact in everyday life. As further one goes there come more difficulties, one finds greater faults as one advances in the spiritual path. It is not the number of faults that increases, but the sense that becomes so keen, otherwise one would not have found them. It is like a musician: the more he knows, the better he plays, the more faults he hears. The one who does not find faults is becoming worse in reality. There is no end of faults. If one thinks of this, it makes one humble. Before realizing this aspect of truth, there is an aspect of metaphysics, which does not make one humble: the profane thought, God is in me. Yes, God is in the depth of the heart. But the intellect is of no use if the doors of the heart are not open. It is the realization of our numberless faults which makes one humble, the effacement of the little self from the consciousness. It is by the effacement of the little self that lies real spiritual attainment.

Now coming to the question: What is real spiritual consciousness?

---

11. The word *mureed* is used by Sufis to refer to an initiate (see Glossary)
12. Hq.st., Sk.tp.: "loose" is typed, but the context calls for "lose"; (Sk.tp.)Sk.cr.: "loose" changed to "lose" in ink

Spiritual consciousness is consciousness of the spirit. Before [13]that consciousness the little self was[14] covering it. When this is moved aside, then what is there? Then there is spirit. Call it whatever you may, it is what it is.

---

13. (Sk.tp.)Sk.cr.: "one is aware of" inserted
14. Ibid.: "was" changed to "is"

1° CONFERENZA[1]
Roma, 23 aprile 1924

La Voce Interna

L'intuizione mondiale che sfugge alla nostra visione materiale è una cosa molto importante che noi dovremmo sforzarci di raggiungere. Essa non è una mera fantasia, ma qualche cosa di reale. La logica può essere seguita in ciò che noi chiamiamo istinto. Molti credono che il torto e il giusto si siano imparati dopo esser venuti in questo mondo e non già prima. Questo è un errore che può essere scoperto quando andiamo alle radici del giusto e dell'ingiusto. Spesso, pure, l'uomo crede giuste o ingiuste le cose secondo il loro risultato; ma ciò non è filosofico. La visione delle cose consiste nel penetrarle all'origine di esse . . . . C'è in altri termini, tra la causa e l'effetto una ragione che è un'armonia preesistente. Così pure ci sono vari colori; ma non c'è la figura: questa bisogna crearla, intuirla. Perciò l'ispirazione è nell'essere umano. E quel che c'è da indagare è quell'amore alla legge dell'armonia. Per quanto un essere sia corrotto e malvagio, egli sente avversione per la malvagità di un altro e questo dimostra che il bene esiste nell'uomo. L'uomo che è agitato con sé stesso e col mondo esterno non può avere armonia. L'armonia non dipende dall'uomo esterno, ma dall'intimo dell'anima. L'uomo che ha scoperto questa legge ha scoperto l'intuizione. L'intuizione è anche nelle bestie, in generale, e negli uccelli. L'animale, vivendo una vita naturale, non è sviato da quel senso profondo e innato che è l'intuizione per mezzo della quale percepisce spesso il pericolo o la disgrazia che sta per sopraggiungere. L'uomo da ciò può dedurre che più egli si unifica con la vita profonda più il suo senso di intuizione si svilupperà, venendo così in possesso della sua naturale ricchezza. Quando si guarda dietro alle scienze e alle arti si vede che esse vengono dall'intuizione. Ed è questa intuizione del linguaggio che ha indotto gl'indù a chiamare (Mantra?)

Document:

MD.hw. = a handwritten reporting of the simultaneous Italian translation, given by Prof. Carlo Formichi, a prominent Indian scholar of that day, sentence by sentence while P-o-M. was speaking, by Dott. Prof. Antonio Mendicini, a Roman psychiatrist.

Notes:

1. This was the first of three lectures given by P-o-M. at the University of Rome

. . . . Oggi giorno, abituati a studiare le cose esterne, l'intuizione è venuta quasi a sparire e ciò è male. L'uomo è dotato d'intuizione quando è in armonia; e venendo alla questione, bisogna riconoscere e dire che fra l'uomo e la donna chi è più dotato di questo senso è la donna, la quale, in ciò lo batte sempre. Del resto, sia l'uomo che la donna, quando lavorano col cervello, sono meno dotati d'intuizione di coloro che lavorano col cuore. Oggi noi sogliamo bollare col titolo di superstizione tutte queste cose, ma è certo che anche le bestie hanno l'intuizione. L'anima dell'uomo è come un'acqua agitata nella quale egli non può veder nulla dei suoi sentimenti, mentre la bestia lo può. La bestia non ha nessuna credenza, mentre l'uomo non vuol credere neppure a sé stesso. La voce interna si chiama impressione. Una persona dotata d'intuizione capisce senza nessun segno ciò che pensa un altro. Non di rado quando s'incontra una persona si ha una impressione piacevole o spiacevole di essa. Talvolta, avvicinandola, ci si sente attratti o respinti; la mente non sa chi sia, ma l'anima lo sa. Si tratta di vibrazioni che fanno sentire all'uomo lo stato d'animo d'un altro. Ciò può accadere anche a distanza, sempre che la persona sia dotata di squisita intuizione. Dall'impressione si passa all'intuizione. Prima d'intraprendere qualche opera abbiamo l'impressione che avremo degli impedimenti o che tutto andrà liscio. E qui entra di mezzo la sfera della coscienza. Quando l'uomo comincia a dubitare della propria intuizione, egli non sa più che fin dove possono portare i suoi piedi; egli conosce solo i limiti del suo essere e non ha idea di che cosa può essere capace la sua coscienza. Ciò nonostante vi sono casi in cui la coscienza si vendica e l'uomo deve riconoscerlo. Vi sono pure i sogni. Ogni sogno deve avere un significato, perché ogni movenza, ogni atto, ne ha uno. Ma vi sono sogni che non hanno né capo né coda, e ciò viene dalla confusione della mente. La cosa più interessante è che i sogni degli artisti, dei poeti, dei pensatori, sono elaborati, non sono come quelli di un uomo comune. Nell'intuizione c'è sempre ispirazione. Ecco perché c'è sempre ispirazione nei sogni di tutti questi artisti, poeti e pensatori. Un poeta può stare anche sei mesi senza la sua matita senza perciò essere poi impedito di andare poi direttamente a quella sfera che gli darà la immortalità. Noi possiamo per anni e anni rivedere le cose dei grandi artisti senza sentircene mai stanchi perché vediamo in essi l'ispirazione che le ha create. Vi sono prodotti che vengono da sorgenti inaspettate ed altri che derivano da sorgenti perfette. Quello che . . . al babbo : oh! Io ne so più di te! E quest'idea di valere più di un altro è l'idea dominante di . . . . E appena l'uomo crede di saperne più di un altro, egli chiude il proprio cuore. Non solo non sappiamo tutto, ma quello che sappiamo deve essere esperimentato. Occorre una ferma pazienza. Quanto più un uomo diventa dotto, tanto più egli sente essere difficile esprimere quello che ha imparato . . . . Altri parlano per il gusto di parlare. La cultura del cuore consiste nel sentire, nel pensare ciò che sente il cuore. Con ciò non voglio dire che si debba escludere la cultura del pensiero; ma ci deve essere un'armonia tra cuore e pensiero. In generale quando si vede una persona si crede che sia in buona salute, ma in realtà la salute non c'è se il cuore non c'è. E qual è il segno che il cuore è desto? E' che questa persona ha i sensi aperti a tutto ciò che è bello e buono. Cinque sono le tappe da percorrere.

1° Quando l'uomo si trova in conflitto con l'umanità; questo trasforma l'uomo in un uomo ricco.

2° Quando l'uomo in conflitto coll'Umanità sente pure di poter resistere ad essa. 3° Egli sente che sugli ostacoli può esercitare un certo influsso su gli altri e allora il suo cammino è più facile.

4° Come l'acqua; voi potete colpirla, ma va sempre avanti.

5° stadio, quello della luce assomiglia al sole: tutti i vapori, tutte le nuvole non possono arrivare al sole.

Amici, quando si è raggiunto un certo grado nella cultura del cuore. Si somiglia ad un nuotatore che è portato su dai flutti e che continua . . . .

2° CONFERENZA[1]
Roma, 24 Aprile 1924

La Cultura del Cuore

Amici, vi chiedo . . . Non è facile parlare del cuore, nel mondo; è più facile parlare della mente nel mondo, ed è appunto del cuore che intendo parlare. Noi parliamo del cuore come di qualche cosa di fantastico, d'immaginativo, ma in realtà non sappiamo cosa è il cuore. Ciò che richiede l'uomo ai nostri giorni è una spiegazione scientifica . . . . Molti confondono l'idea della mente con quella del cuore; altri separano la mente dal cuore. Ma in realtà è la superficie della mente che è mente, ed il fondo della mente che costituisce il cuore. In sanscrito la mente si chiama *manas* ed in inglese *mens*[2]. Questo suggerisce che la mente è l'uomo, la mente è ciò che fa l'uomo. E nasce ora la questione: la mente deve confondersi con quello che si chiama cervello? E il cuore deve confondersi con quel muscolo di carne che è il cuore? La spiegazione è che il corpo umano è un riflesso di tutto ciò che si trova nell'Universo e ciò che è nell'Universo si trova nel nostro piccolo io. Non è proprio una necessità che si debba mettere il . . . . Quindi abbiamo la stessa relazione che passa fra il flauto e la musica. In realtà il cuore è qualche cosa di troppo vasto, di troppo ampio perché possa essere limitato in questa angusta sfera del corpo. È molto difficile valendoci soltanto del linguaggio umano esprimere cos'è il cuore. Il cuore non va misurato con le dimensioni familiari all'uomo. Il cuore può intuirsi quando si pensa l'occhio. Pensate alla piccolezza di questo organo e alla capacità che ha di riflettere l'immenso orizzonte. Il cuore riflette in se stesso tutto quanto I'Universo. Non tutti si rendono conto di ciò; bisogna pensare . . . . L'uomo è talmente convinto della sua piccolezza che non può concepire la grandezza che è in lui. Venendo ora al punto metafisico della questione . . . . Vi sono 5 aspetti del cuore: 1° Il creatore del pensiero; 2° Il ricettacolo del sentimento . . . . La mente è il creatore del pensiero; è quella che lo rende sempre migliore. C'è poi colui che conserva l'elemento conservatore del pensiero. Questo conservatore è la memoria, la quale non deve confondersi

---

Document:

MD.hw. = a handwritten reporting of the simultaneous Italian translation, given by Prof. Carlo Formichi, a prominent Indian scholar of that day, sentence by sentence while P-o-M. was speaking, by Dott. Prof. Antonio Mendicini, a Roman psychiatrist.

Notes:

1. This was the second of three lectures given by P-o-M. at the University of Rome
2. Apparently an error for "mind"

con un grammofono . . . . e così pure quello che chiamasi il giudice del pensiero non è un giudice . . . . E così pure la mente è ricettiva di sentimento ma non è passiva; essa produce il pensiero. C'è il quinto aspetto, il più interessante in quanto l'uomo l'ha prodotto lui stesso. E questa concezione che l'uomo ha fatto gli permette di dire: io. Però questo concetto dell'io, rimane, si ma a misura che l'uomo si evolve, anche l'io si evolve. Così un bambino chiama se stesso bambino, ma quando è adulto, si chiama adulto e l'idea dell'infanzia è cancellata.

Ecco come si vede che l'io in sostanza rimane sempre lo stesso, ma la concezione cambia. Ecco come in noi ci sono due io; uno che permane e l'altro che si evolve continuamente. In realtà un uomo nelle varie sue evoluzioni non sa . . . . E nell'Oriente e nell'Occidente ci possono essere molti credi, ma in realtà non ci può essere che una sola verità. La verità è il retaggio dell'Umanità; non appartiene né all'Oriente né all'Occidente. Ci sono i gradi per i quali l'uomo deve passare sono l'osservazione, l'esplorazione e l'espressione . . . . La vita moderna ha provato grandi ostacoli per la ricerca della verità. I nostri bambini, appena possono parlare dicono . . . . L'artista tocca nella sua ispirazione è qualche cosa che non è assolutamente lui; è qualche cosa di perfetto che viene dalla ispirazione. È la pietra filosofale che qualunque cosa tocca, muta in oro. Un uomo dal cuore aperto viene in comunicazione con tutto quello che è fuori di lui e che è dentro di lui.

3° CONFERENZA[1]
Roma, 25 aprile 1924

La Libertà dell'Anima

Amici per la terza conferenza delle serie che tratta delta libertà dell'Anima io invoco la vostra indulgenza.

Ci sono due parole che formano questa frase: libertà dell'anima, ma la libertà. . . Tutto è di vedere che cosa s'intenda. . . . Libertà vuol dire la libertà dalla prigionia. La prigionia è una condizione che segue la liberazione. Se non ci fosse prigionia non vi sarebbe nessuna libertà. Ed ora nasce la questione: in che cosa consiste questa prigionia dalla quale l'anima deve emanciparsi? Senza parlare dell'umanità, anche la creazione più bassa, le piante, le bestie, le rocce, le acque aspirano a questa libertà . Che cos'è che commuove il vostro cuore quando vi trovate in seno alla madre natura? È la libertà. Le montagne e le rocce pare stiano ad aspettare questo momento in cui possono raggiungere la liberazione. Ed è questo sentimento che solleva il cuore dell'uomo quando si trova sulle montagne ed aspira a questa liberazione. E così pure gli alberi, sebbene. . . . I pensatori di tutte le età: saggi, poeti, pensatori cercano la solitudine non più per evitare la folla, ma per mettersi in comunicazione con la natura e raggiungere la liberazione. Chi soffre e chi ha sofferto dove troverà la consolazione? E molte volte le rocce che aspettano pazientemente, perdono questa pazienza ed abbiamo un'eruzione vulcanica nella quale si manifesta questo desiderio della liberazione. I piccoli rivoli, quando non possono ottenere questa liberazione, ecco che straripano. Ed è la stessa aspirazione che si manifesta nell'uomo. La differenza è che l'uomo, affaccendato nelle cure del mondo, perde il tempo per meditare su queste cose e comprenderne la ragione profonda. Così, nelle famiglie, vediamo talvolta la moglie contro il marito, il fratello contro il fratello, l'amico contro l'amico. Tutto ciò è motivato da quel desiderio, da quella aspirazione incosciente di liberazione ch'essi sentono nella forma di un impulso. Sotto qualunque forma questa agitazione si manifesti, essa è un

---

Document:

MD.hw. = a handwritten reporting of the simultaneous Italian translation, given by Prof. Carlo Formichi, a prominent Indian scholar of that day, sentence by sentence while P-o-M. was speaking, by Dott. Prof. Antonio Mendicini, a Roman psychiatrist.

Notes:

1. This was the third of three lectures given by P-o-M. at the University of Rome

indice che l'uomo va cercando questa libertà. E c'è oltre a questa un'altra aspirazione: la silenziosa speranza che l'umanità nutrisce nel suo cuore . . . . Ed è questa speranza quella che rende bella la vita. Voi potrete trovare un uomo che non abbia neppure un soldo ed egli sarà felice perché spera nel domani. Tutte le pene, tutte le afflizioni si superano perché si spera che un giorno si sarà da esse liberati. Anche se chiedete all'uomo che cosa desidera, ben ve lo saprà dire, ma pure c'è qualche cosa . . . . Ci sono tante pene e dolori nella vita, ma la somma di tutte le pene e di tutte le tragedie è una sola: questa tragedia è la limitazione ed essa non è che cattività, prigionia. (Qui?)[2] un famoso poeta persiano, dice: Perché la musica del flauto parla tanto al vostro cuore? Perché essa vi narra il suo dolore . . . e lo stesso avviene nell'uomo; come questa canna è stata staccata dal suo tronco, così l'uomo che soffre vi racconta la storia del suo dolore. Ed accade che se l'uomo non dice il suo dolore è perché i fori del suo flauto non sono stati ancora praticati. Ma un giorno questi buchi vi saranno ed allora egli darà la sua musica. E lo stesso poeta dice che colui il quale si separa dalla sua patria dopo poco egli aspira a ritornarvi e a cibarsi di quei cibi. Così l'uomo desidera ritornare alla sua vera patria, alla patria celeste. Fra cento uomini si troverà tuttavia quell'uno che ricorda il sogno della vita celeste; gli altri novantanove non se lo ricordano. Quell'uno che ricorda il sogno desidera quel ritorno. Ecco perché vi sono alcuni che vogliono mettersi sul sentiero ed altri no—quelli, cioè, che non ricordano. E nasce ora la questione: L'uomo è stato trasportato realmente da un posto all'altro oppure è stato sempre allo stesso posto e pensa egli al posto d'origine? La leggenda biblica spiega. L'uomo da un paese è stato trasportato in un altro ma se vogliamo dare a quel mito una interpretazione filosofica, dobbiamo credere che l'uomo . . . ed egli non riconosce più la sua patria di origine . . . E che cos'è questo fiato che esce dalla bocca dell'uomo ed offusca la vista sua come nebbia ? Questo fiato è l'illusione. Ma perché la crea, questa nebbia, questa illusione? Egli la crea perché è la sua natura che lo induce a ciò. Ma che cosa mai lo incoraggia a creare questa illusione? Il piacere. E allora si potrebbe chiedere: giacchè l'uomo prova piacere a creare quest'illusione, perché mai dovrebbe essere una cosa cattiva? L'illusione dà, si, un piacere, ma questo piacere preclude la sua felicità.. E l'uomo confonde il piacere con la felicità . . . Da un certo punto di vista sarebbe ingiusto rinunciare alia felicità ma si deve rinunciare a certi piaceri . . . Ma se l'anima deve essere infelice, sarebbe stato meglio che non vi fosse stata l'anima. No, la sua aspirazione è e deve essere la felicità. Nasce un'altra questione: se, come abbiamo detto . . . C'è poi nella natura dell'uomo qualche altra cosa che può compensare questo aspetto? C'è. È, soltanto questione di metodo per vedere come deve lavorare l'uomo. Io mi

2. Pir-o-Murshid Inayat Khan must have said "Jelal-ud-Din Rumi", the poet he was about to quote

sono valso di questa immagine della nebbia; solo come ci si può servire di una immagine, come di una similitudine. Ci sono quattro cose che al tempo stesso—virtù o errori—superatele l'uomo può dirsi giunto nella sfera della libertà . Quello che lega l'uomo sono i piaceri mondani. E se l'uomo riesce con tutta la forza della sua anima a superarli egli può dire di aver varcato il primo gradino. Ma perché rinunciare a questi piaceri della terra che sono un diritto? Deve rinunciarvi perché questi piaceri lo rendono schiavo—Ora ci sono due modi di comprendere il modo di liberarsi—Io vedo una prigione; io ho paura e non ci voglio entrare. Oppure: no, ci voglio entrare ed avrò la forza di sbarrarne le porte onde uscirne. Ora, chi ha cercato di evitare la prigione vi cadrà e solo colui che vi sarà entrato e ne avrà spezzato le sbarre ne sarà liberato. C'è un'altra cosa: le ricchezze della terra. Le ricchezze in sé e per sé non sono felicità; è il piacere di possederle ciò che vincola l'uomo alle ricchezze. Ora un uomo che le ha acquistate e le ha conservate, può dire di non averle avute; mentre chi ne ha usato bene può dire di averle possedute. Ora fra l'uomo che si contenta di poco e guadagna poco e quello che guadagna molto e spende bene, il secondo è il più perfetto. Le ricchezze della terra sono fatte per l'uomo ed egli deve acquistarle per usarne bene. C'è un terzo vincolo che lega l'uomo: il dovere sia verso la famiglia sia verso la patria, sia verso la razza. Così un uomo che è tutto preso dalle cure domestiche e dimentica ciò che succede nella città non è certo da ammirare. Ma per poco che dopo aver assolto ai doveri della famiglia, si occupi delta sua razza, quegli ha imbroccata la via giusta. Bisogna cercare di espandersi e di compiere altri doveri anche più alti. Negli antichi tempi c'erano le famiglie. Così ristrette; oggi si cono le nazioni. Così l'uomo che permane nella sua virtù e non cerca di andare avanti, quest'uomo non progredisce, va indietro. C'è il quarto vincolo: la speranza in una vita futura. Egli aderisce intimamente. Questa speranza che si è formata . . . Anche se un uomo non è schiavo della terra, può esserlo di quest'idea . . . Perché (la felicità, forse) della vita deve trovarsi solo nella libertà.

Murshida Sherifa Goodenough's typescript

Paris (Mme d'Eichthal)
May 3rd, 1924

The Power of Spirit over Matter

If a person were to say, "Spirit and matter are two things", I would say, "Yes", but if a person said that spirit and matter are one, I would say yes also. The one who sees them as two sees the two ends of one line, and the one who sees them as one sees the centre of that one line. Whether one calls it matter or spirit, it is the same. I would prefer to call it spirit, for spirit is the origin from which the matter has come.

Matter is a condition of spirit, a condition which changes the original aspect of spirit just as ice is a condition of water. You cannot call water ice, but ice is from water and it returns to water. And so the spirit in a certain condition become[1] matter. Therefore matter is spirit in another aspect of its being.

Once I was travelling with a young man, who said to me, "I don't believe in anything." I said, "Perhaps there is something in which you believe." He said, I believe in the eternity of matter." I said to him, "Your belief is not very different from mine." He was very astonished to hear these words from me. And, giving him the further explanation of the same thing, I said, "What you call eternal matter I call eternal spirit." When people don't want to agree the words help them, but if you drop down the difference of the word often you can come to an agreement.

Another question is,"What is what we call spirit, is it a part of what exists?" The spirit is the all-pervading life from which all has come
[2] and this cannot be limited by giving it a name[3]

Document:

Gd.tp. = a typescript made on Murshida Sherifa Goodenough's large-lettered typewriter of a part of the lecture, possibly taken down by Murshida Goodenough herself. Comparison with the French reporting (which follows) indicates that for this portion of the lecture, the English text is fuller.

Notes:

1. The typescript has "become" although it should say "becomes"
2. A blank in the typescript of half a line
3. The typescript ends abruptly, without punctuation

3 mai
Chez d'Eichtal

Le pouvoir de l'esprit sur la matière

Bien-aimés de Dieu,

Bien souvent on fait une telle séparation entre l'esprit et la matière c'est comme un abîme qu'on creuse entre eux, et il devient difficile de trouver le lien entre les deux. Il n'y a qu'une seule chose: qu'on l'appelle esprit ou matière. Je préfère l'appeler esprit. Je l'appelle esprit parce que dans chaque chose il y a la vie, soit apparente, soit à l'état latent. Celui qui les voit comme deux choses différentes les voit comme les deux bouts d'une ligne.

Celui qui les voit comme une rencontre le centre. La matière est un état de l'esprit, qui en change l'aspect originel: comme la glace est un effet de l'eau, ainsi l'esprit dans un certain état devient matière.

hist[4]. Jeune homme qui dit je ne crois à rien. Peut-être croyez-vous à quelque chose? Je crois à l'éternité de la matière. Peu différence: étonnement du jeune homme. C'est ce que vous nommez matière que nous nommons esprit. Les mots créent le désaccord[5]; sans les mots on arrive à se mettre d'accord.

Jusqu'à quel point l'esprit a-t-il dominé la matière? Comme la glace est de l'eau, et qu'elle y retourne, ainsi en est-il de l'esprit. Seulement l'esprit en soi-même contient tous les éléments, connus à la science, et ceux qui forment l'intelligence. On pourrait appeler l'esprit le tout[5]; et le nom que la religion lui donne est encore plus grand. Le monde arrive graduellement à comprendre le pouvoir de l'esprit sur la matière. Fakir, légendes: beaucoup sont vraies, d'autres ne sont que des imaginations. Chaque phénomène qui contient la vérité est imité par celui qui ne connaît que ce qui est faux.

Document:

Lf.hw. = a reporting in the handwriting of Mlle H. Lefèbvre of the simultaneous French translation of the lecture, given sentence by sentence as P-o-M. was speaking. Comparison with the preceding English text of a small portion of the lecture indicates the fragmentary, incomplete nature of this reporting.

Notes:

4. "hist." is an abbreviation for the French word "histoire", indicating that what follows is a story
5. This part of the sentence is underlined in the hw., perhaps indicating that P-o-M. emphasized these words while speaking

Quelquefois, par le pouvoir de l'esprit, des maladies causées par l'esprit mauvais sont guéries. Quand personnes mordues par scorpion ou serpent, il y a poison dans le corps. Une maladie mentale peut être guérie par la suggestion, mais quand il y a poison, il faut autre chose que suggestion ou hypnotisme. La procédure de guérison a été suivie par les âmes pieuses. Dans les temps anciens même peuples qui se trouvaient encore à l'état primitif. . . .

La civilisation a ôté la croyance à ceux qui ne croient que la raison; mais elle reste dans les peuples primitifs. Ces peuples primitifs ont la santé meilleure que les civilisés.

Races de Indes; le guérisseur est assis, ayant devant lui un petit tambour. Quand le malade entre, le guérisseur commence à jouer sur ce tambour, et à chanter. Pendant ce temps les pensées et sentiments du malade sont absorbés. Ce bruit est désagréable aux oreilles d'un musicien, mais il agit sur les malades, et quand il a établi un certain rythme, il commence à parler à la maladie. Et dès ce moment le malade comprend que la maladie ne fait plus partie de lui-même. La conclusion est de séparer le malade de la personne. Ce guérisseur primitif continue à parler aux malades.

Les fleurs reçoivent l'influence des individus: dans certaines mains, conservent leur fraîcheur; dans d'autres, se fanent. Plantes arrosées par personnes différentes, effets différents. Les fleurs sentent quelquefois plus que les personnes. Cela dépend de l'état chimique de la personne ou de sa respiration.
Même s'il s'agit d'une réaction chimique, il y a, dessous, quelque chose qui vient de l'esprit.

Aux Indes, légende: jeune homme avait passé sa jeunesse. . . et partout où il passait jardin fleurissait; c'est une légende, mais remarquons que certaines personnes apportent avec elles la [6] et la joie, et d'autres, le contraire.

hist.[7]: Un homme, dans sa jeunesse alla chercher du travail; on le chargea de vendre des bouteilles vides, et le maître commençait à s'enrichir; il ne croyait plus pouvoir devenir riche et remarqua coïncidence avec l'entrée de l'autre. Il l'associa, et ils devinrent les plus gros marchands de Bombay.

Raison pour laquelle chez une personne tout va bien, et chez une autre, toujours mal. La cause originelle se trouve dans l'esprit.

Dans les écritures arabes, on dit que quand un pays doit être détruit etc[8] Quelquefois un seul homme change la direction d'un pays. On peut

6. One indecipherable word, which could be the English word "party"
7. Once again, the word "hist." (histoire) indicates the beginning of a story
8. Mlle Lefèbvre wrote "etc.", probably indicating some words she was not able to write down (although P-o-M. sometimes said "et cetera")

donner raison qu'il avait une éducation parfaite, très capable, seul celui-là peut l'accomplir qui est né pour ce but. Rumi[9] dit: la terre, l'eau, le feu, l'air, sont pour Dieu des choses qui attendent son commandement. La conclusion: conflit entre la personne et les conditions qui l'entourent. Ou bien sera enseveli sous la glace ou bien glace fondue par. . . La condition ne doit pas accabler l'homme. Si l'homme connaît la manière de faire la guerre il en triomphera; sinon il sera victime.

[10]Quand on fait la paix avec le moi, le moi s'occupe pendant ce temps à préparer une nouvelle guerre. Se tenir au-dessus de la partie inférieure du moi.[10]

9. Normally the name of Jalal-ud-Din Rumi (see List) is spelled "Roumi" in French
10. These last two sentences are written after the lecture, separated by a line; they may have been part of an answer to a question, or they may have been added on another occasion (see lecture of April 7 for a similar verse from Abu Hashim Madani)

[1]

Spring, 1924[2]
(Mme d'Eichthal)[3]

The Being of Man

Beloved Ones of God,

I should like to speak a few words on the subject of the being of man. Man is made of two qualities: the receiving quality and the repelling quality, and this he shows in all aspects of his life. For instance physically he receives and at the same time becomes a kind of subject to the influences, to illnesses, all that his body ~~admits~~ accepts or admits in itself. For an instance if there were two or three persons in the same atmosphere they are not affected in the same way. One receives even physical illnesses, one repels the same. Besides that there is one person who will take physical magnetism at once like a sponge, and another will reject it.

And when we come to the question of mind, we find the same tendencies working continuously[4]. A person who is subject to receive worries and pains and sorrows and troubles and so[5] will attract these things to himself, while another person, wherever he goes, he attracts all joy and pleasure, even a little possibility of pleasure he will attract at once. One might ask what makes this[6] so; what is it? And the answer is that what one collects in oneself he becomes that same thing. For instance in the form of food, way of living, in the way of sound, physical atoms that help him to live

---

Documents:

Sz.hw. = a reporting handwritten by Shabaz Mitchell, who took down some of the lectures in the series "The Problem of the Day" in the autumn of 1922 (see *Complete Works* 1922 II). He must have been visiting Paris, and none of P-o-M.'s regular secretaries happened to be present at this lecture, so he took it down.

Sk.tp. = a typescript prepared by Sakina Furnée or under her supervision, apparently made from the Sz.hw. and corrected in ink to be closer to that document.

Lf.hw. = a reporting in the handwriting of Mlle H. Lefèbvre of the simultaneous French translation given as P-o-M. was speaking. For the most part, the text resembles the English and provides no further evidence as to what P-o-M. said. However, at the end it includes several sentences which do not appear in the English, which are therefore written out in the last note.

Notes:

1. Sz.hw.: Murshida Sherifa Goodenough later wrote "This report is very incomplete and very imperfect" on the top of this document
2. The precise date, 10 May 1924, is from Lf.hw.
3. Indicates the lecture was given in the Paris home of the National Representative for France, Mme d'Eichthal
4. Sz.hw.: the "-ously" on the end of "continuously" crossed out, and "-ally" substituted to read "continually"; Sk.tp.: "continually"
5. Sk.tp.: "and so" omitted, but later added in ink
6. Ibid.: "them" typed, later corrected in ink to "this"

a life physically healthy. And so it is with the mind; if one is accustomed to absorb sorrow, then naturally he attracts the atoms of sadness which become his being. If a person is always accustomed to collect good impressions, joy, etc., he naturally becomes a happy person, he rejects what makes him unhappy.

It is therefore you find two opinions. If you asked one person: What is your opinion about the world, they will reply: The world is terribly gloomy, there is everywhere sorrow and distress, nothing to make it worth living—think to what extent sorrow exists, falsehood exists—it is not worthwhile living. And you will ask another person who will say: Everything is to be found here, it is a privilege to live in this world; no promise of paradise will give him the desire to leave this. Does not this show that it is not the world but the person himself? It is that if there is a ~~personality~~ possibility of sorrow there will be every possibility here, and if there is a possibility of joy there is every opportunity. It depends entirely on what one is seeking for.

But one would say: no one would seek for sorrow, but although (. . . one does not know it?)[7] there are persons who go automatically towards it. Myself I have seen people who after a malady of twenty years, part from it as if leaving an old friend. Only what happens is this, that one calls pain, sorrow an enemy, but it is a dear enemy. One who becomes accustomed to suffer the pain it becomes unconsciously his friend. As very often a person complains all the time of his friend, yet loves him well. It is not everyone's work to decide definitely (for himself)[8] what he is seeking[9].

The first step that a person makes in ~~himself~~ knowing what his soul seeks, that soul is blessed. What happens is that days pass and a man knows not ~~verba~~ veritably what he is seeking. Only after meeting the thing he knows what he seeks. If he practises even for a whole life in knowing he wanted, he would make a great progress.

A great yearning for happiness that gives happiness. It is ~~so~~ useless to say there so much good in suffering.

Besides that happiness is the nature of man and this being the[10] original nature, man continues to desire ~~happiness~~ it. No doubt if we look at life philosophically, nothing is wasted, suffering has its reward also. Nevertheless it is not a method through which to pass. Those who consider suffering a virtue, and desire pain, make a great error. If one could only pass through the suffering that life throws upon one, one has already done a great deal. In [11] ancient times people, in order to arrive at spirituality, tortured

7. Ibid.: ellipses placed before and after the parentheses
8. Ibid.: "(or himself)" typed, and later in ink "or" corrected to "for" and parentheses crossed out
9. Sz.hw.: "seeking" is written right over another word, crossed out and indecipherable
10. Sk.tp.: "and this being the" mistyped as "abd tgus beubg tge" (through misplacement of fingers on the keyboard), later corrected in ink
11. Sz.hw.: a short word, two letters, indecipherable, crossed out between "In" and "ancient"

themselves. It is not really meant, one should not imitate. Of course those who in order to make an experiment brought . . . [12] upon themselves that[13] is an experiment. For an instance if a person, in order to . . . and went to the North Pole or venture in an aeroplane, and to a very far distant place—that is another thing. But suffering in itself is not really a virtue. The virtue is to fight it bravely and courageously, and with a hope that you will one day break the cloud, and come out of it.[14] But one holds it,—it is my friend—, —I wish to have it, hold it—, I happen to see a great many cases of this sort.

---

12. Sz.hw.: above the ellipsis, the words "pain-torture?" are written; Sk.tp.: only the ellipsis
13. Sz.hw.: the word "that" underlined, probably indicating that P-o-M. emphasized the word while speaking
14. The French text (Lf.hw.) continues from this point: "Exemple exagéré: un jour, une personne avait très grand souffrance. Cette personne commença par dire: la vie ne contient rien pour moi, rien dans la vie à quoi je puisse m'intéresser. Je lui dis: Regardez le soleil, la lumière du soleil; lui vaut que nous nous intéressions. Les jours que vous devez passer vous les passerez soit heureuse soit malheureuse, en donnant aux autres ou bonheur ou malheur. Elle dit: je suis malheureuse moi-même; je n'y puis rien. Si vous réussissez. . . . Dans le cas contraire, vous rendez malheureux et vous serez malheureuse vous-même. En résumé, l'homme amasse en ce monde la gaieté ou la tristesse, et devient son être entier." The French ends here, with no indication of the material in the fragmentary sentence which follows in Sz.hw.

Murshida Sherifa Goodenough's typescript

1

Paris
Rue du Dragon
2 May 16th, 1924

The Doctrine of Karma

In Hindu theology the doctrine of *karma*[3] is much more emphasized than in the religions of the Beni Israel. By Hindu theology I do not mean only the Vedantic or Brahmanic, but I also mean[4] the Buddhistic. By the religion of Beni Israel I do not mean to say the Judaic only, but also Christian and Moslem. The whole theory of the Hindu philosophy is based upon the doctrine of karma. The moral of the Beni Israel is also based upon karma. Only the[5] difference is that on one side the moral is made on karma, on the other side the philosophy is based on karma.

And now, what is the meaning of the word karma? The meaning of the word karma is action. It is quite evident that what one sows one reaps. The present is the echo of the past, the future is the reflection of the present, and therefore it is logical that the past makes the present and the present makes the future. Nevertheless, in the Sufi school there is little spoken on this subject. And very often people interested in the doctrine of karma begin to wonder, "Why is Sufism not speaking on the subject? Is it opposed to it?" And the answer is that it is not at all opposed to it. But [6]the way it looks at it, the way[6] a Sufi looks at it, he cannot help but close his lips.

Documents:

Gd.tp. = a typescript made on Murshida Sherifa Goodenough's large-lettered typewriter, presumably from her own reporting, but probably already edited. Later, Mda. Goodenough made two corrections by hand, indicated by "(Gd.tp.)Gd.cr." in the notes.

Hq.st. = a stencilled copy prepared at Headquarters, Geneva, for distribution to Sufi Centres as part of the Gatheka series (see Glossary). It shows considerable further editing from Gd.tp.

Sk.tp. = a typescript prepared by Sakina Furnée or under her supervision, copied from Hq.st. and showing one difference in wording and a slightly different sentence added at the end. It is therefore mentioned only in notes 36 and 44.

Notes:

1. Gd.tp.: Gd. later wrote "Gatheka" above the title, and "Reported by: Sherifa Goodenough" under the date
2. Hq.st.: "Gatheka" and "No. 9" added at top, followed by the Sufi Invocation (see List)
3. For the word *karma*, see Glossary
4. Hq.st.: "I" and "mean" omitted, to read "but also"
5. Ibid.: "The only" instead of "Only the"
6. Ibid.: "in the way" instead of "the way it looks at it, the way"

In the first place what one[7] calls right or wrong, it[8] is according to his own knowledge. He calls something right which he knows to be[9], which he has learned to call right. He calls something wrong which he has learned to call wrong. And in this way there may be different[10] nations, communities, races, [11]their conceptions of right and wrong may differ[11]. A person accuses another of wrong[12] only on the grounds that he knows it to be[13] wrong. And how does he know it to be wrong? It is because he has learned it, he has read it in a book, or he has been told[14]. People have looked with horror, with hatred, with prejudice at the doings of one another, individuals, communities, nations and races. And yet there is no label, there is no stamp, there is no seal upon the actions which point them out to be[15] right or wrong. This is one aspect of the thing.

Now the other way of looking at it: At every step of evolution man's conception of good and bad, of right and wrong changes. And you might ask me, "How does it change? Does he sees many wrongs[16], or does he see less wrongs[17] as he evolves?" One might naturally think that by the virtue of one's evolution one might see more wrongs. But that is not the case. The more one evolves the less wrong he sees. Then it is not always the action, it is the motive behind it. Sometimes a wrong action[18], apparently[18], may be right on account of the motive at the back. Therefore the ignorant is ready to form an opinion of another person's action, but for the wise it is most difficult to form an opinion of the action of another.

Now coming to the religious idea. If a man spiritually evolves[19], he sees less wrong and less[20] at every time of his evolution. How can God be counting the little faults of human beings, who know so little about life? We read in the Bible, "God is love."[21] What does love mean? Love means forgiveness, love does not mean judging. When people make God as[22] a cruel judge, sitting in the seat of justice[23], getting hold of every person and asking him of his faults, judging him for his actions, giving him the

---

7. Ibid.: "a person" instead of "one"
8. Ibid.: ", it" omitted
9. Ibid.: "as right" instead of "to be"
10. Ibid.: "various" instead of "different"
11. Ibid.: "differing" [sic] inserted before "their conceptions", and "may differ" at the end of the sentence omitted.
12. Ibid.: "doing" added (as a separate word) after "wrong"
13. Ibid.: "as" instead of "to be"
14. Ibid.: "so" added after "told"
15. Ibid.: "as being" instead of "to be"
16. Ibid.: "more wrong" instead of "many wrongs"
17. Ibid.: "wrong" in place of "wrongs"
18. Ibid.: "an action" instead of "a wrong action", and "wrong" after "apparently"
19. Ibid.: "spiritually evolves" reversed to read "evolves spiritually"
20. Ibid.: "less and less wrong" instead of "less wrong and less"
21. I John 4:8
22. Hq.st.: "of God" in place of "God as"
23. Ibid.: "judgment" instead of "justice"

sentence[24], then to be cast away from the heavens, then where is the God of love?

Now leaving the religious idea aside and coming to philosophy: Is man a machine or is man an engineer? If he is a machine then he must go on for years and years and years under a kind of mechanical action of his evil actions, and if he is a machine then he is not responsible for his actions. If he is an engineer, then he is responsible for his actions. But if he is responsible for his actions, then he is the master of his actions, the master of his destiny. If he is an engineer, then he is the master of his destiny; he makes his destiny as he wishes.

Taking this point of view, the Sufi says, "It is true that if things are wrong with me, it is the effect of my actions. But that does not mean that I should submit to it, I should be resigned to it because it is from my past actions. But I must make my destiny, because I am the engineer." The difference is: I have seen [25] a person say, "Well[26], I have been ill for so many years, but I have been resigned to it. I took it easily because it is my karma, I am paying back." By that he can[27] prolong the paying, which was perhaps for ten years, he may prolong it[28] for the whole life. The Sufi in this case acts not only as a patient but as a doctor at the same time of[29] himself. He says, "Is my condition bad? Is it the effect of the past? I am going to cure it. The past has brought the present, but this my present I will make the future." It only means that he does not allow the past influences to overpower his life; he wants to produce just now the influence to make his life better.

But besides that there is a still more essential subject attached to it. Before a person takes upon himself his responsibility of paying back the past, does he ask himself, "What was I in the past?" If he does not know of it, why must he hold himself responsible for it? You can only be responsible for something with which your conscience is tinted. And that is quite sufficient[30] to carry in life its load. Why add to it a load of the unknown past?

But besides, when you look at yourself philosophically, what do you find? The keener your sight becomes, the less[31] you can find fragments[31] of yourself. The more conscious of reality you become, the less conscious you

---

24. Ibid.: "sentencing" instead of "giving him the sentence"
25. Gd.tp.: a blank; (Gd.tp.)Gd.cr.: later inserted by hand, "myself"
26. Hq.st.: "Well," omitted
27. Ibid.: "may" instead of "can"
28. Ibid.: "he may prolong it" omitted
29. Ibid.: "to" instead of "of"
30. Ibid.: "a quite sufficient load" instead of "quite sufficient" and "its load" and the end of the sentence omitted
31. Ibid.: "fragments" moved to after "less"

are of your small self. And all this burden of the past action[32], it is taken by man without [33]being invited to take it up. He could just as well have ignored it. It gives him no benefit, it only gives him a moment's satisfaction, [34]that, "It is just that I am in this trouble", and this just[35] fortifies his trouble. The pain that could have been finished, that continues because he has fortified the pain.

The main object of the septeric[36] work is to put away that thought of oneself—What I was? What I am? And what I shall be?—to put away[37] for a moment. He[38] can be very well occupied if he[39] thought about life as a whole, what it is, what it must have been, what it will be. It is this idea which produces a kind of synthetic point of view and united[40] instead of dispersing. It is constructive, and the secret of spiritual liberation is to be found in this. The Brahmins, the Vedantists, the Buddhists, who hold the idea of karma as the foremost doctrine, no sooner do[41] they touch the idea of the goal that is to be attained by spirituality, which they call *mukti* or *nirvana*[42] than they[43] rise above the idea of karma. For it is the condition that unless a person has risen above that idea he does not touch nirvana. The verbal meaning of nirvana is—[44]*-vana* is the colour, *nir-* means no[44]—no label, no colour, no division. It is seeing the whole life as one, realizing it. It is in this that there is the secret of nirvana.

[45]

---

32. Ibid.: "actions" in place of "action"
33. Ibid.: "his" added before "being"
34. Ibid.: "to think" added before "that"
35. Ibid.: "justice" instead of "just"
36. (Gd.tp.)Gd.cr.: later, Gd. crossed out the "sep" of "septeric" (an unknown word) and wrote "eso" instead, to make "esoteric"; Hq.tp.: "esoteric"
37. Hq.st.: "it" added after "away"; Sk.tp.: "it" before "away" (perhaps a copying error, or unconscious correction of the English)
38. Ibid.: "One" instead of "He"
39. Ibid.: "one" instead of "he"
40. Ibid.: "unites" instead of "united"
41. Ibid.: "as soon as" in place of "no sooner do"
42. For the words *mukti* and *nirvana*, as well as Vedanta and Brahmin, see Glossary
43. Hq.st.: "than they" omitted
44. Ibid.: "(Vana = colour Nir = meaning no)" instead of "*-vana* is the colour, *nir-* means no"
45. Hq.st.: "To be circulated among the Candidates for Initiation th the Sufi Order." added; Sk.tp.: "To be read before Candidates for Initiation in the Sufi Order"

17 mai
B[nne] d'Eichthal

Les manières d'arriver à la vie [1]

Il n'y a pas des voies différentes mais des manières; il y a une seule voie: n'importe de quel nom on l'appelle, pourvu qu'on soit dans la bonne voie, c'est l'essentiel - travailleurs différents pour atteindre le but élevé; 4 classes: par la connaissance, par le mot sacré, par la piété, et par la dévotion. Ces différentes manières sont adaptées à des tempéraments différents. II y a tempérament que l'on peut nommer analytique, celui-là ne peut pas croire qu'il n'existe qu'un seul; si on lui dit que 2 moitiés font un, que 4 quarts font un, alors, il comprend. Ce tempérament analytique arrive à la voie supérieure par l'analyse intellectuel. Il fera d'abord son étude par l'étude des philosophies, mais il n'arrivera pas à une compréhension parfaite tant qu'elle analysera la vie extérieure, mais c'est soi-même qu'il faut analyser. Il verra que tout ce qui existe sur terre est représenté dans son être propre: végétal, animal, minéral, tout en lui. Tout ce qu'elle peut imaginer dans les cieux et sur la terre, elle le trouvera en elle-même, et elle comprend que [2]

L'homme est alors plus capable de comprendre la nature de toutes choses: philosophie, religion, page ouverte qu'il peut lire. Sans doute il lui faut passer par un procédé et il faut, pour analyser, ôter de sa pensée sa propre construction, c'est- à-dire le corps physique, formé d'atomes physiques, et l'intellect, formé de pensée. Pour connaître une chose, il faut pouvoir voir en elle, la pénétrer.

Les mystiques, comment s'y prennent-ils? Ils voient cette construction comme quatre enveloppes différentes; 1° enveloppe physique; 2° construction de la respiration 3° construction de l'esprit, imagination, pensées 4° construction du sentiment. Et derrière ces 4 constructions il y a un être caché; à ce moment l'homme devient capable de séparer ces 4 choses et de réaliser son être originel. En d'autres termes, l'homme peut se réaliser lui-même par l'étude de la construction de son être.

Document:

Lf.hw. = Mlle H. Lefèbvre's handwritten reporting of the simultaneous French translation of the lecture, given sentence by sentence as P-o-M. was speaking. No English version of the lecture has been found.

Notes:

1. The last word is written in a very small space, and is very hard to read; it may say "spirituelle"
2. This sentence was left unfinished

Autre manière: elle consiste dans l'accomplissement des bonnes actions. Un homme conscient de ses obligations envers ses semblables, qui considère son devoir comme une chose sacrée, sans le savoir, s'harmonise avec l'harmonie de l'univers et sa vie même le prépare à la voie élevée; faisant équilibre entre le travail et le repos, beaucoup d'êtres sont bons et ne sont pas spirituels; mais facile [3]

La bonté, c'est l'harmonie; personne harmonieuse est une personne bonne. Et sans le savoir, elle devient[4] spirituelle.

3e. manière: c'est celle de la méditation. Sans la méditation la vie de l'homme manque d'équilibre. C'est un art par lequel on acquiert cette puissance et cette inspiration qui sont latents dans l'homme. La béatitude dont l'homme jouit par la méditation pas refusé aux autres. Les créatures naturelles n'ont pas besoin de cet art; ils reçoivent déjà cette bénédiction. Par la méditation il découvre une chose qui était cachée au-dedans de lui-même. Par exemple, personne seule qui désire lui au [5] avec une autre personne, cela vient de vie artificielle, n'a pas fait connaissance avec lui-même.

Souvent, pendant voyage, pensée: chacun avait devant lui un journal, tandis qu'on avait devant soi matériel suffisant, soit qu'on regarde physionomie des personnes, soit nature si l'on avait pénétration chaque être deviendrait un livre plus intéressant que tout. Intéressant observer comment différentes personnes se donnent des occasions de faire du bien, réagissent les uns sur les autres.

Pour cette personne, la vie entière est un livre sacré qu'elle lit continuellement.

Mille choses font la vie artificielle, cette vie qui prive l'homme de la joie intérieure. Par la méditation on établit un équilibre entre le travail et le repos. Je ne conseille pas quitter monde, et s'en aller dans les forêts - celui qui donne toute sa journée aux affaires pourrait bien dormir une heure.

Même, mettant de côté la spiritualité, l'être entier est affecté, les nerfs malades en ce moment, l'éducation, l'action, pas de repos.

Pour entrer plus profondément dans le sujet de la méditation. Pas seulement s'asseoir immobile, et fermer les yeux. Par la méditation l'être peut se détourner de tout aspect de la vie, ou s'appliquer à tout aspect de la vie.

Pour qui possède l'art de la méditation sujet difficile à mettre dans des mots.

Le champ de vision de l'homme: longueur, largeur, profondeur, et en plus de ceci capacité de l'intelligence capable de contenir tout ce qui est

3. This phrase was left incomplete
4. This word is very difficult to make out
5. An indecipherable word

devant lui. Il n'y a plus de mots pour exprimer cette dimension si l'on étudiait mieux cette capacité.

L'intelligence qui conçoit [6] qui assimile.

C'est pour sonder les profondeurs de [7]

C'est [8] garder [9]

Malgré la connaissance que l'homme préserve de ses connaissances.

Plus on observe au-dedans de soi-même.

Comme la vision par un oeil seulement est [10] , c'est quand on réunit les deux que l'homme commence à voir. La raison est que tandis que [11]

La 4e manière pour atteindre la connaissance supérieure est la dévotion.

Celui qui est dévotionneux a déjà nature méditative. L'amour est l'origine et la fin de l'être entier.

C'est cette substance qu'on peut appeler esprit.

Dieu est amour.

Dans le saint comme dans le pécheur, s'il y a une étincelle d'amour; et s'il y a [12]

Si on a confiance dans l'amour on voit qu'il n'y a rien d'autre qui mène vers le but [13]

Qu'est-ce que l'amour? Si c'est un échange, c'est un commerce.

L'amour, c'est le sacrifice. Philosophiquement, l'amour est la vie; le manque d'amour est le manque de vie. Comment apprendre à aimer si l'on a pas en soi de l'amour?

Comment le développer; question absurde: l'amour est, l'homme en est fait. Le manque d'amour est le manque de conscience de [14]

Le sentier de la dévotion est le plus facile; on acquiert tous les pouvoirs, l'inspiration. Grandes personnalités venues sur la terre, qu'est-ce qu'ils apportaient; ce qui fait qu'on les a adorés, aimés, c'est l'amour. La manière de l'amour , la plus facile comme la plus difficile.

[15]Roumi: beau vers:

Que vous aimiez un être humain ou que vous aimiez Dieu, vous êtes conduits devant le Dieu de l'amour;

---

6. One or two words erased and crossed out
7. The rest of this line left blank
8. A short, indecipherable crossed out word
9. About eight words written very hastily and indecipherable
10. A word very difficult to read, which might be "incomplète"
11. The rest of this line left incomplete
12. The rest of this line left incomplete
13. After "but" three or four letters, not apparently making a word
14. The rest of this line left blank
15. This passage is separated by a line from the lecture. It may have been recited by P-o-M. on this or another occasion, or may have come from another source

Tant qu'on dit: Moi—l'amour n'a pas accompli son oeuvre.
L'amour est comme un océan, il peut n'y en avoir qu'une goutte mais il peut devenir océan.
Quand un être a formé en elle cette goutte, par amour parent, compatriotes, humain, peut devenir océan.
Il y a mille vertus; mais elles sont toutes comme des branches, et la racine est l'amour.[15]

Mme de Stürler, 22 May 1924[1]

2

My *Mureeds*[3],

[4]It is not necessary to explain in words the joy that I feel in coming and seeing you again, for in the initiation we are so linked together that distance in reality is not a[5] distance; nevertheless in this physical plane to meet together is also necessary.[4] And now I wish to explain how many things are necessary for a mureed.

The first thing most necessary for a mureed is to try to keep up the spiritual exercises which are given without any break. If you are tired ever[6], if you were occupied too much, if conditions were not favorable, I do not mean that it is urged upon you, but I mean that it is for your betterment to keep those exercises without a gap between them. Would you believe, if I may say so, that the effect of certain practices comes even[7] after ten years or twelve years? A person without patience might think that[8]: I did not have

Documents:

Sk.sh.	=	Sakina Furnée's shorthand reporting of the lecture, newly transcribed by B.v.d.B.
Hq.tp.	=	a typescript prepared at Headquarters, Geneva, "No. 79" from an unknown source.
Sk.tp.1	=	a typescript prepared by Sakina or under her direction, from "Hq.tp." A few corrections by Sakina are indicated in the notes as "(Sk.tp.1)Sk.cr."
Hq.st.	=	a stencilled copy made at Headquarters, Geneva, for distribution of the Gatheka series to the Sufi Centres.
Sk.tp.2	=	a typed copy of Hq.st., prepared by Sakina or under her direction, identical in wording, and therefore not mentioned after note 2 except in the corrections by Sakina, indicated in the notes as "(Sk.tp.2)Sk.cr."

Notes:

1. Hq.tp., Sk.tp.1: "for mureeds in Brussels" added and "Mme de Stürler" omitted; Hq.st.: date and location omitted
2. Hq.tp.: "To keep up the Spiritual Exercises" added as the title; Sk.tp.1: "FOR MUREEDS." added upper left; Hq.st., Sk.tp.2: "Gatheka Number 34" added followed by the Sufi Invocation (see List); below this is: "How many things are necessary for a mureed." as a title; it is partly crossed through on Sk.tp.2 to read: "THINGS NECESSARY FOR A MUREED."
3. The word *mureed* is used by Sufis for an initiate (see Glossary); Hq.st.: "My *Mureeds*," omitted
4. Hq.st.: sentence omitted: "It is not . . . is also necessary."
5. Hq.tp.: "no" instead of "not a"; then "not a" reinstated partially in type and partially in lh.
6. Hq.tp., Sk.tp.1: "ever" omitted
7. Hq.st.: "come" instead of "comes even", and "even" typed above the space after "come"; (Sk.tp.2)Sk.cr.: "comes even" reinstated
8. Hq.st.: "that" omitted

immediate results after two, three months. But he may not think so. If they[9] are seeds which you sow in the ground which[10] take root and a plant comes. But in order for the plant to be fruitful it takes ten years. This is the spiritual sowing. It might take much longer time in some cases. In some cases the next day the result might[11] show. There are some plants which come quicker, others which take time to take fruit[12]. But still the spiritual sowing has its result and a sure result. [13] therefore to[14] doubt, nor discourage[15], to[16] give up hope, but to[17] continue persevering in this path.

Now the second necessity for the mureed is the study part. It must not be a study only as the reading of a book. It must be a study of engraving upon one's heart. The Gathas[18], [19]Gathekas[18], all the literature it[20] is given, however simple it might seem to grasp it, because you will find that it is creative in itself. It is a phrase just now. After six months the same phrase will flourish; there will come branches, flowers and fruits in this[21] phrase. It is a simple phrase but it is a for[22] living phrase; the more you will study and grasp it, the more your heart will be creative. There[23] not consider it a study only, but a meditation, even in your studies.

The third important thing in the life of a mureed is to live a life of balance, of regularity. Not too much work nor[24] too much of the[25] rest; a balance between activity and repose. Because when we put the idea before the world, we shall be responsible to show it in our lives. Therefore our lives must be as balanced as possible.

Besides that, in eating, in[26] drinking there must be a kind of necessary[27] moderation which I am sure many of us have, and a kind of

---

9. Hq.st.: "there" instead of "they"
10. A.o.d.: "they" instead of "which"
11. Hq.tp.: "will" instead of "might", changed in type to reinstate "might"
12. Hq.st.: "root" instead of "fruit"
13. Sk.sh.: a correction in sh. to read "never"; a.o.d. read "Never"
14. Hq.st.: "to" omitted
15. Sk.sh.: "to" in sh. added below "discourage"; Hq.tp., Sk.tp.1: "to be discouraged" instead of "nor discourage"; Hq.st.: "never be discouraged"
16. Hq.st.: "never" instead of "to"
17. Hq.st.: "to" omitted
18. Gathas, Gathekas: a category of the teachings of P-o-M. (see List)
19. Hq.st.: "the" added
20. A.o.d.: "that" instead of "it"
21. Ibid.: "that" instead of "this"
22. Ibid.: "for" omitted
23. Ibid.: "Therefore" instead of "There"; Hq.st.: "do" added after "Therefore"
24. Hq.tp.: "not" instead of "nor"
25. Sk.sh.: "of the" crossed out, and omitted in a.o.d.
26. Sk.sh.: "in" crossed out, but included in a.o.d.
27. A.o.d.: "necessary" omitted

concentration[28] from the meditative p.o.v.[29] Because for the spirit-growth[30] a certain [31] is more recommended than another. Therefore we in the spiritual path cannot always be neglectful of that question.

And now there comes the fourth question: How must our attitude be towards the others? Towards the mureeds our attitude must be affectionate, sympathetic[32]. Towards non-mureeds, our attitude must be tolerant[33]. The best thing in the world is not to force upon others what we understand and what we believe. By forcing upon others we only spoil them. By discussing, arguing with them we do not accomplish anything. Besides, for a mureed it is most advisable that he must keep his conversation limited as not to[34] say things which might seem to the others too occult, too mystical, too spiritual. Our conversation must be like an ordinary conversation. Things about spirits and ghosts and elementals, apparitions and all sorts of things; people like to talk about their past and present and next incarnation, what they were and what they will be, we must not [35] commit ourself in talking about these things. These things are for every individual to find out for himself. By talking neither we do good to outside[36] nor good to ourself[37]. If we can only talk about simple things of everyday life that[38] are so many things that we shall have enough subjects to speak when[39] with others.

Ideas of the air must be left in the air. Standing on the earth we must talk [40] leaving every individual to live[41] free for himself as we like to be left for[42] ourselves. Besides, the Sufi does not give a distinct[43] idea of these things, because Sufism is freedom, freedom of conception of belief. It does not give people any dogmas, that you must believe those,[44] this or that. It does not present before humanity particular dogmas and very often for the same reason, Sufism is accused of being against certain dogmas. But it is not so. If we do not speak about them it is not that we are against, but because

---

28. A.o.d.: "consideration" instead of "concentration"
29. Sk.sh.: "p.o.v." abbr. for "point of view", and written out in a.o.d.
30. A.o.d.: "spiritual growth" instead of "spirit-growth"
31. Sk.sh.: a blank; a.o.d.: "food" in place of the blank
32. Hq.tp., Sk.tp.1: "sympathy" instead of ", sympathetic"
33. Hq.tp., Sk.tp.1: "sympathy" added
34. Hq.st.: "to" omitted; (Sk.tp.2)Sk.cr.: changed to read "so as not to"
35. Sk.sh.: a blank
36. A.o.d.: "ourself" instead of "outside"; (Sk.tp.2)Sk.cr.: "ourself" changed to "ourselves"
37. Sk.sh.: "ourself" crossed out "the others" in sh. inserted; a.o.d.: "others"
38. A.o.d.: "there" instead of "that"
39. Sk.sh.: "when" changed to "to"; Hq.tp., Sk.tp.1: "over" instead of "when"; Hq.st.: "about" instead of "when"
40. Sk.sh., Hq.tp., Sk.tp.1: a blank
41. Sk.sh.: "to" is written across an illegible symbol and "live" is crossed out; "to live" omitted in a.o.d.
42. Sk.sh.: "for" changed to "free", and "free" in a.o.d.
43. Hq.tp., Sk.tp.1: "definite" instead of "distinct"
44. A.o.d.: "those," omitted

we do not like to speak about them. We prefer being silent [45]than talking too much about them. There[46] are things of intimate conversation. When a mureed is conversing with his *murshid*[47], with his fellow-mureed, perhaps one talks about it. These are not the things to talk at the tea-table. It means to make the inner laws of life and nature ridiculous. When nature, when life itself covers its laws, then it means that they are[48] best be covered. When we uncover them we certainly commit a fault against the hidden nature of things.

It is therefore it is called mysticism[49]. By word:[50] mysticism[49] is[51] keeping the cover over the hidden laws of nature which are meant to be covered. As soon as one uncovers them, in nature[52] in the first place one does not know their value. Then he goes no further, he cannot go any[53] further. It is the one who knows their value who will go further. [54]Who has no respect for them, who brings them to the market, cannot go any further; he has a set-back. As further we go we shall have to face a great trial. As soon as people know that we are interested in these things, they will ask a lot of questions. You,[55] they will want us to make a prophecy, want us to say uncommon things that will interest them. We shall be put to test in things[56].

So you can quite see that it is the path of silence. The more we keep our lips closed, the more the way is open, the more doors are open for us. The attitude itself opens them. We do not need to open them. We only need to expect them. What is not common is not common. When you want to make them common that means putting down the[57] heaven on the earth, instead of rising[58] the earth towards heaven. Our attitude therefore with the others must be humble, unpretentious and ordinary.

Now the fifth thing. We must not leave our meditations[59] and prayers just to those fixed times, when we do[60]. Because that is only the winding of the thing. But in our everyday life we ought to bring the sense of it into our action, in every thing we do, at home or outside. We must use that latent power and inspiration aroused by our meditations; we should make use of it. By practising to make use of it we shall benefit ourselves and others by

---

45. Hq.st.: "rather" added
46. A.o.d.: "These" instead of "There"
47. The word *murshid* is used by Sufis for a spiritual guide (see Glossary)
48. Hq.st.: "had" instead of "are"
49. Hq.tp., Sk.tp.1: "Sufism" instead of "mysticism"
50. Hq.st.: "By word:" omitted
51. (Sk.tp.1)Sk.cr.: "meant" inserted
52. Sk.sh.: "in nature" changed in sh. to "it means"; a.o.d.: "it means" in place of "in nature"
53. Hq.tp.: "any" omitted ; (Hq.tp.)Sk.cr.: reinstated
54. Hq.tp.: "It is" added, and crossed out (in type)
55. Sk.sh.: "You," in sh. crossed out, and omitted in a.o.d.
56. Sk.sh.: "in things" crossed out, and omitted in a.o.d.
57. (Sk.tp.2)Sk.cr.: parentheses added around "the"
58. A.o.d.: "raising" instead of "rising"
59. Ibid.: "meditation" instead of "meditations"
60. Hq.st.: "them" added

all we are doing.

[61]Now with these words I close my conversation and would like you now to ask me, to ask[62] any questions that you may desire in connection with your work.[61]

Question: *In religion one is taught generally of the God outside, not quite outside, but outside of us, and still we have God inside too. Now perhaps one persons[63] who does not believe of[64] the God outside and only of[64] the God inside, will show perhaps[65] more[66] confidence and more character[67] because he develops everything of himself. Now the attitude that one has been taught in religion is to be dependent and that does not give real confidence.*

Answer: Those who think that God is not outside but inside, they are as wrong as those who believe that God is not inside but outside. Really speaking, God is inside and outside both. But in the beginning it is most necessary to begin in[68] believing in the God outside because from our childhood we have learned everything from outside. By looking at the eyes from[69] others we say that is the eye, also[70]. Everything that we learn from outside we see in our self[71], but we have always learned outside. But[72] so even to learn to see God, we must begin to believe[73] God outside. The Creator, the Judge, the Knower of all things, the Forgiver; and when we have understood him better, then the next stage is to believe[73] the God within. This[74] complete,[75] then that God

61. Ibid.: sentence omitted: "Now with these . . . with your work."
62. Sk.sh.: ", to ask" crossed out, and omitted in a.o.d.
63. A.o.d.: "a person" instead of "one persons'"
64. A.o.d.: "in" instead of "of"
65. Hq.tp., Sk.tp.1: "perhaps" omitted
66. Hq.st.: "no" instead of "more"
67. Hq.st.: "no care" instead of "more character"
68. Sk.sh.: "in" in sh. changed to "by", and "by" in a.o.d.; Hq.tp.: first typed "that by", then typed cross out through "that"
69. Hq.tp., Sk.tp.1: "the" added; Hq.st.: "of" instead of "from"
70. Hq.tp., Sk.tp.1: "also" omitted; Hq.st.: "; so" instead of ", also."
71. A.o.d.: "ourselves" instead of "our self"
72. Sk.sh.: "But" crossed out, and omitted in a.o.d.
73. A.o.d.: "see" instead of "believe"
74. Hq.tp., Sk.tp.1: "that" instead of "This"
75. A.o.d.: "completes." instead of "complete,"

which[76] we have seen outside, we find inside, which[77] completes the worshipping. But if we have only found him outside then we are the worshippers, but we have separated[78] from him and there is no communion and the purpose is the communion.

Question: *"In the Rosegar."[79,80] the will of God[81] is the will of God ? [82]Our will is not always pure?*

Answer: When we go deeper in the search of the hidden law of life we shall find that there is only one will which is acting behind it all. There are not many wills. We cannot call God all-powerful if there was another one, also, who is powerful even to a small degree besides God. There is one power that[83] life, will, existence: that is God . . . . When we come to[84] that deeper idea we will find that there is one will that is the will of God. That is a[85] metaphysical, a philosophical idea; not for the common person; [86]ordinary person will not understand that. How can it be?, he will doubt. It is not good for him to know it. But for us it is right to know that there is one life that is the life of God. There is one being that is the Being[87] . . . . As the prophets of old have said that: not one atom moves by[88] the power[89] and will of God. Rumi, in *Masnavi*[90]: "Even[91] the earth and water and fire, which seem to us as dead things, before God they are living beings, obedient to his will[92] and therefore behind it all there is only one will". But in order to realize it we must first be

---

76. Sk.sh.: "which" crossed out, but included in a.o.d.
77. A.o.d.: "that" instead of "which"
78. Sk.sh.: "have" crossed out; Hq.tp., Sk.tp.1: "are separate" instead of "have separated"; Hq.st.: "separate us" instead of "have separated"
79. Sk.sh.: "Rosegar." abbr. in lh. for "Rosegarden", and written out in a.o.d., *In an Eastern Rose Garden* (see List)
80. Hq.tp., Sk.tp.1: "it says" added; Hq.st.: "we read" added
81. Sk.sh.: "God" crossed out, "man" in sh. above, and "man" in a.o.d.
82. A.o.d.: "but" added
83. Sk.sh.: "that" crossed out, and omitted in a.o.d.
84. Hq.st.: "go over" instead of "come to"
85. Hq.tp.: "a" omitted ; then reinstated lh.
86. Hq.tp., Sk.tp.1: "an" added; Hq.st.: "the" added
87. A.o.d.: "of God" added
88. Sk.sh.: "by" in sh., then corr. to read "without", and "without" in a.o.d.
89. Sk.sh.: "power" crossed out; a.o.d.: "power and" omitted
90. *Masnavi* (see List); Hq.tp., Sk.tp.1: "his" added before "*Masnavi*" and "says" after; Hq.st.: "the *Masnavi* says"
91. Hq.st.: "even" omitted
92. Sk.sh.: it is possible that this quotation ended here, however there is no attempt made by Sakina to show this as such

responsible for our own action, and[93] the action of another we must forgive, [94]. In this way we progress. If [95] . Very often we are too[96] ready to form an oppose[97] about other persons' actions and forget our own errors. Therefore the best things[98] is to take ourselves[99] to task, in that[100] way we are improving[101].

Question: *But there are things which are really wrong, which one cannot be tolerant to[102]?*

Answer: The wrong-doer has his own wrong as his worst enemy. Besides us[103] being hard on him, his own wrong is his enemy, he is himself in a trouble. He is his own enemy, the conditions, the circumstance[104], the people he will meet; from every side he will receive a hate sooner or later. We may be making a mistake, we do not know behind a person's action what is hidden. Therefore be tolerant, forgiving[105]. Very often a seeming[106] wrong has a hidden right and very often a hidden[107] seeming[106] right has a hidden wrong. Besides, we cannot always judge very well. In order for us to judge, in the first place we have no right to judge, unless we have become spectators. Then only we begin to learn how to judge. But when we are in the middle of the struggle we cannot judge.

Question: *There is really no fault[108], guilt[109] but simply a responsibility? Whenever an individual has acted he was compelled by circumstances. Or[110] these circumstances have compelled that individual to act as he did. I thought an individual really can be*

---

93. Hq.tp., Sk.tp.1: "or" instead of "and"; Hq.st.: "for" instead of "and"
94. Sk.sh.: "tolerate" in sh. inserted above a blank, and included in a.o.d.
95. Ibid.: "If" crossed out, followed by a blank, and omitted in a.o.d.
96. Ibid.: "too" crossed out, but included in a.o.d.
97. Ibid.: "oppose" re-traced to read "opinion", and "opinion" in a.o.d.
98. Ibid.: wrote plural "s" symbol after the sound "ing"; "thing" in a.o.d.
99. Hq.st.: "ourself" instead of "ourselves"
100. Hq.st.: "this" instead of "that"
101. A.o.d.: "improve" instead of "are improving"
102. Hq.st.: "of" instead of "to"
103. Hq.st.: "our" instead of "us"
104. A.o.d.: "circumstances" instead of "circumstance"
105. Hq.st.: "forgive" instead of "forgiving"
106. Hq.tp., Sk.tp.1: "simple" instead of "seeming"
107. Sk.sh.: "hidden" crossed out, and omitted in a.o.d.
108. Sk.sh.: "fault" crossed out, and omitted in a.o.d.
109. Hq.tp., Sk.tp.1: "guilty" instead of "guilt"; (Sk.tp.1)Sk.cr.: "guilt" reinstated
110. Hq.tp., Sk.tp.1: "All" instead of "Or"

	guilty. [111] *only shows that he was not so wise as he has*[112]*, we have expected him to be* [113] *according to the spiritual evolutions*[114] [115] *responsibility* [116] *no real guilt, but simple*[117] *responsibility?*
Answer:	Your explanation is very good of it. Quite right.
Question:	*What should be the attitude of a Sufi towards Catholics in general. A question which I first*[118]*. There are a lot of*[119] *C.*[120] *very pious, mystical, a high degree of*[121]*; would*[122] *they sympathize with Sufism? It would benefit them to hear over*[123] *Sufism in general.*
Answer:	Sufism is for human beings, if they are Catholic[124] or Prot.[125] Because it brings to humanity the culture of a,[126] a church. It brings to humanity the culture[127] of humanity, the culture of mankind. It then does not keep them back. The Sufi says you are free to do your Catholic practices or to[128] [129]Protestant, as the Hindu, Jew, Buddhist[129] . If the Catholic says: You must not[130] go to the Sufi, then the Sufi is not responsible for that. Only this is again[131] a culture for humanity. It only gives you a stimulance[132], which is the spirit of all religion[133], which is the essence of all religion[133]. It is truth itself. My experiences in

---

111. Sk.sh.: a blank; Hq.tp., Sk.tp.1: "He" added; Hq.st.: "Or does it only show" instead of "only shows"
112. Ibid.: "he has" crossed out, and omitted in a.o.d.
113. Ibid.: a blank;
114. A.o.d.: "evolution" instead of "evolutions"
115. Sk.sh., Hq.tp., Sk.tp.1: a blank; Hq.st.: sentence ends with "evolution?"
116. Sk.sh.: a blank
117. Hq.tp., Sk.tp.1: "Not really guilty, but simply" instead of "no real guilt, but simple"
118. Sk.sh.: "question which I first" crossed out, and omitted in a.o.d.
119. Hq.tp., Sk.tp.1: "many" instead of "a lot of"
120. Sk.sh.: "C." in lh. abbr. for "Catholics", and written out in a.o.d.
121. A.o.d.: "to a high degree" instead of "a high degree of"
122. Hq.st.: "do" instead of "would"
123. A.o.d.: "of" instead of "over"
124. Hq.tp., Hq.st.: "Catholics" instead of "Catholic"
125. Sk.sh.: "Prot." in lh. abbr. for "Protestant" and written out in a.o.d.; Hq.st.: "Protestants"
126. Sk.sh.: the first "a" crossed out; a.o.d.: "no cult of a" instead of "the culture of a, a"
127. Hq.st.: "cult" instead of "culture"
128. Hq.st.: "your" instead of "to"
129. Hq.tp., Sk.tp.1: "Protestants as to Hindus, Jews, Buddhists."; Hq.st.: "Protestant practices, as to the Hindu, the Jew, the Buddhist."
130. Hq.st.: "not" omitted; (Hq.st.)Sk.cr.: reinstated
131. A.o.d.: "again" omitted
132. Hq.st.: "stimulus" instead of "stimulance"
133. Hq.tp., Sk.tp.1: "religions" instead of "religion"

Italy have[134] been of a great value to me. I have been now visiting Italy two times[135], Florence and Rome. One might think that Rome is a place where there is a great Catholic influence and that it might be very difficult to make that mind understand, but it is not so. I have found there some souls who are most interested in the deeper ideas[136] [137], most open to it. Yes, there are[138], they are[138] outward difficulties, but there are no inward difficulties. But that is a great encouragement to me. If there were inward difficulties that takes any [139] away of me. That gives me no scope. Outward difficulties are difficulties for me, but still they give[140] me a courage. There I can,[141] I can at least talk to souls who understand. I am very pleased, they at least understood it. The one who understands, he values it; then you have found something very satisfactorily[142]. The one who does not understand may be very [143] to follow you, but that is a difficulty for more[144]. I had three open meetings at the University of Rome; crowded audiences, the rector presided me. There was another open meeting for all[145], at a Countess' house, where the cultured classes were and the response was wonderful. Our strength is in the truth; that is our strength. We shall bring truth before humanity. We shall lay it in their presence. Those[146] who neglect it, that is their responsibility. We have done our work.
[147]

---

134. A.o.d.: "experience in Italy has" instead of "experiences in Italy have"
135. A.o.d.: "twice" instead of "two times"
136. Hq.st.: "ideals" instead of "ideas"
137. Sk.sh.: a blank
138. Sk.sh.: "there are" crossed out; a.o.d.: "There are" included and "they are" omitted
139. Sk.sh.: the sh. symbolism is unclear; actually Sk. wrote "leant" in sh. for "life"; a.o.d.; "my life" instead of "any [blank]"
140. Hq.tp., Sk.tp.1: "it gives" instead of "they give"
141. Sk.sh.: "There I" crossed out; "There I can," omitted in a.o.d.
142. Hq.tp., Sk.tp.1: "satisfactory" instead of "satisfactorily"
143. Sk.sh.: a blank, with an upstroke in sh. indiscernible; blank also included in Hq.tp. and Sk.tp.1.; Hq.st.: "willing" added in place of the blank
144. A.o.d.: "me" instead of "more"
145. Sk.sh.: "for all" crossed out, and omitted in a.o.d.
146. Hq.st.: "Then" instead of "Those"
147. Hq.st.: sentence added: "To be read before Candidates for Initiation in the Sufi Order."

Sakina's shorthand reporting

[1]

Rue de Loxum, 22 Mai 1924[2]

The Aim of Life[3]

[4]Beloved ones of God,

I ask your indulgence to my subject of this evening which is the Aim of Life[3,4]. As to the main object of life there cannot be but one object; and as to the external object of life, there are as many objects as many beings. There is one object of life for the reason that there is one life. In spite of many apparently appearing, in spite of many lives outwardly appearing, there exists one and only life. It is in this thought that we can combine and it is from this thought that true wisdom is learned. No doubt that main object of life cannot be at once understood and therefore the best thing for every person is to pursue his object in life first, and in the accomplishment of his

---

Documents:

Sk.sh. = Sakina Furnée's shorthand reporting of the lecture, newly transcribed by B.v.d.B.

Hq.tp. = a typescript made at Headquarter's, Geneva, "N.78", from an unknown source. Sakina later made corrections to this document while preparing "Sk.tp.", indicated in the notes as "(Hq.tp.)Sk.cr."

er.tp. = an early typescript made from an unknown source, perhaps Sakina's shorthand, as at the top she added a note: "compared with steno - Sakina". She made corrections to it while later preparing "Sk.tp.", indicated in the notes as "(er.tp.)Sk.cr."

Fm.hw. = a handwritten ink copy made by Murshida Fazal Mai Egeling (see List) from an unknown source, perhaps "er.tp." as it follows this closely. Fazal Mai also edited while copying. Many words are underscored in pencil, but this is not mentioned in the notes.

Sk.tp. = a later typescript prepared by Sakina or under her direction, using "Hq.tp." and "er.tp." Apparently Sakina corrected "Hq.tp." and "er.tp." in the process also. Her corrections are indicated in the notes as "(Sk.tp.)Sk.cr."

Sr.Sk. = a separate list of corrections prepared by Sakina while working with Sirdar van Tuyll on "Sk.tp."

Notes:

1. Hq.tp.: "N.78" inserted in lh. at upper left; (er.tp.)Sk.cr.: Sakina added "compared with steno - Sakina" in lh. at the top; Sk.tp.: "Public Lecture" inserted in lh. upper left
2. Sk.sh.: date added with different pencil, in lh.; "Mai" is French for "May"; a.o.d.: "May" instead of "Mai"; Hq.tp.: "Bruxelles" added; er.tp., Sk.tp.: "Brussels" instead of "Rue de Loxum"; (er.tp.)Sk.cr.: "For Mureeds and Friends" in lh.; Fm.hw.: date and location omitted; "May 22, 1924" added iin pencil
3. Sk.sh.: the title "The Aim of Life" added later with a different pencil in lh.; Sk. also left four lines open above her sh. text; Hq.tp.: title omitted; a.o.d.: "The Aim of Life"
4. Er.tp., Fm.hw., Sk.tp.: sentence omitted, "Beloved ones . . . Aim of Life."

personal object some day he will arrive to accomplish[5] that inner object. When man does not understand this he thinks there is something else to accomplish and[6] all this[7] is before him that is not accomplished and therefore he remains at a failure. The person who is not definite about his object has not yet begun his journey [8]in the path of life. The first thing therefore is for a person[8] to definitely determine his object before[9] himself. However small that object is, when he has determined it he has begun his life.

We find in the lives of many people sometimes all through their life, they do not happen to find their[10] vocation of their life and what happens? In the end they consider their life a failure. All through their life they go in one thing or another[11]; yet not knowing their life's object they can[12] accomplish [13] so little.

When people say: Why I do not succeed? In answer to that I always say: Because you have not yet found your object. As soon as a person has found his life's object he begins to feel in this world at home. Before that[14] he feels in a strange world. No sooner a person has found his way, he proves to be fortunate, because all things he shall want[15] to accomplish, they come to him by themselves. If the whole world was against him, he gets,[16] got such a power that he can stand on his object against the whole world. He gets such a patience then, when he has,[17] he is on the way to his object that whatever unfortunate[18] happens, it does not discourage him. No doubt as long as one has not found it, then one goes in one thing and then in a second[19] and he thinks that life is against him[20]. Then he begins to find faults[21] with individuals, conditions, planets[22], climate; with all things. Therefore what is called fortunate, what is called successful, that[23] is to have the right object. When a person is not wearing the clothes made for himself,

---

5. Er.tp., Fm.hw., Sk.tp.: "at accomplishing" instead of "to accomplish"
6. Hq.tp.: "and" omitted
7. A.o.d.: "that" instead of "this"
8. Fm.hw.: The following words omitted: "in the path of life. The first thing therefore is for a person"
9. Hq.tp.: "before" omitted; (Hq.tp.)Sk.cr.: reinstated
10. Hq.tp.: "their" changed to "the" in type; a.o.d.: "the" instead of "their"
11. Hq.tp.: "things" added and crossed out in type
12. Er.tp.: "can" omitted, then inserted above in type
13. Sk.sh.: a blank
14. Fm.hw.: "that" omitted, then inserted above
15. Sk.sh.: "shall" crossed out; a.o.d.: "he wants" instead of "he shall want"
16. Ibid.: "gets," crossed out; included in a.o.d. in place of the next word, "got"
17. Ibid.: "he has," crossed out and omitted in a.o.d.
18. Er.tp., Fm.hw., Sk.tp.: "misfortune" instead of "unfortunate"
19. Sk.sh.: "second" in sh. corrected to read "another"; Hq.tp.: "another and in another" instead of "a second"; a.o.d.: "another and again in another"
20. Hq.tp.: first typed "him", then corrected in type to "me"
21. A.o.d.: "fault" instead of "faults"
22. Er.tp., Fm.hw., Sk.tp.: "plans" instead of "planets"; (er.tp., Sk.tp.)Sk.cr.: "planets" reinstated
23. Er.tp., Sk.tp.: "that" omitted

then he says it is loose or too short. When it[24] are[25] his clothes he feels comfortable, they are his. [26]Real thing therefore is to give freedom to every soul, to choose his object in life and if he finds in his object at home, to[27] know that he is on the right path.

When a person is on the path, then also there are certain things to be considered. When a person has a [28] to unravel, to loosen, in the meantime a person gives him a knife to cut it, [29] he has lost a great deal in his[30] life. It is a small thing, but by not accomplishing it a person has gone back. It is a kind of taking a back step. This is a little example I have given, but in everything one does, if one has not that patience and confidence to go forward, then one loses a great deal. However small a work a person has undertaken, if he accomplishes it, he has accomplished something great. It is not what work a person has accomplished, it is the very fact of accomplishing which gives him the power and [31] .

And now[32] coming to the question of this[33] object, which is the object of every soul; that object may be called the[34] spiritual attainment. A person may go all his life without it, but there will come a time in his life when he may not admit, but he will begin to look for it. Because [35] spiritual attainment is not only an acquired knowledge, it is the soul's appetite. And there will come some day in life that a person will feel the soul's appetite more than any appetite. No doubt every soul has an unconscious yearning to satisfy this[36] soul's appetite, but at the same time one's absorption in everyday life that[37] keeps one so occupied that one has no[38] time to this[39], pay attention to the[40] soul's appetite.

Now,[41] the definition[42] of spiritual attainment can be found in studying human nature, for the nature of man is one and the same, might[43] he be spiritual or material. There are five things that man yearns for: life,

---

24. Hq.tp.: first typed "they", then changed to "it" in type; a.o.d.: "they"
25. Apparently P-o-M. thought the verb should agree with "clothes" , and therefore said "are"
26. A.o.d.: "The" added
27. Sk.sh.: illegible marks above "to"; er.tp., Sk.tp.: "then" added before "to"
28. Ibid.: an illegible crossed out word, "knot" in lh. above, and "knot" included in a.o.d.
29. Sk.sh.: a blank space in the sh. may indicate that P-o-M. paused before completing the sentence.
30. Fm.hw.: "his" omitted
31. Ibid.: "and" crossed out, followed by a blank; a.o.d. end with "power."
32. Fm.hw.: "And now" omitted
33. A.o.d.: "that" instead of "this"
34. Er.tp., Fm.hw., Sk.tp.: "the" omitted
35. Sk.sh.: "yearns" written in lh. above a blank, but not included in a.o.d.
36. Fm.hw.: "that" instead of "this"
37. Sk.sh.: "that" crossed out, and omitted in a.o.d.
38. Sk.tp.: first typed "not", then typed through "t" to read "no"
39. Sk.sh.: "this" crossed out , and omitted in a.o.d.
40. Sk.sh.: "to the" inserted in sh. above, and included in a.o.d.
41. Fm.hw.: "Now," omitted
42. Hq.tp.: "destination" instead of "definition"
43. A.o.d.: "may" instead of "might"

knowledge, power, happiness, and peace. Now[44] the continual appetite which is felt[45] in the deepest self yearns for either[46] of these five things [47] . Now[48] in order to answer his appetite what does man do? In order to answer the desire to live, one eats and drinks and protects one's self from all dangers of life. And yet the appetite is not fully satisfied because all danger he may escape, but the last danger he cannot escape, which man calls death. In order to answer the next thing which is called power, a man does[49] everything in order to gain the[50] physical strength; power by influence; rank; every kind of power he seeks in order to be powerful. And he always knocks against disappointments, because he always sees that if there is a power of ten degrees, reality[51] is another power of twenty degrees to knock against it. Just think of the great nations, ones[52] whose military powers[53] so great, one could not have thought that in one[54] moment they will fall down. One could have thought that if they will fall down it will take thousands of years for them to fall down, so great was their power. We do not need to look for it in their[55] history, we have just seen enter[56] in these[57] past few, two[58] years; we have but to look at the map.

Then the third kind of appetite is the[59] happiness. Man tries to answer it by pleasures[60], not knowing that pleasures of this world do not answer for that happiness which his soul really seeks after. Man's[61] attempts are in vain. He finds in the end that every effort he made for pleasure, he made with a greater loss than gain. Beside[62] that which is not enduring, that which is not real in its nature is not satisfactory.

Then that desire for[63] knowledge. This[64] knowledge gives a tendency to study. And man might study and study[65] all through his life. If he read all the great libraries, all the books, there will still remain that question, "why?"

---

44. Fm.hw.: "Now" omitted
45. Hq.tp.: "formed" instead of "felt"
46. Er.tp., Fm.hw., Sk.tp.: "one or the other" instead of "either"
47. Sk.sh.: a blank
48. Er.tp., Fm.hw., Sk.tp.: "Now" omitted
49. Sk.sh.: this sh. symbol may also be read: "does not" (due to a slight curve at the end of the sh. symbol)
50. Er.tp., Fm.hw., Sk.tp.: "the" omitted
51. A.o.d.: "there" instead of "reality"
52. A.o.d.: "once" instead of "ones"
53. Fm.hw.: "were" added
54. Er.tp., Fm.hw., Sk.tp.: "a" instead of "one"
55. Hq.tp.: "the" instead of "their"; a.o.d.: "their" omitted
56. Sk.sh.: "enter" in sh. crossed out, and omitted in a.o.d.
57. Hq.tp.: corrected while typing from "this" to "these"; er.tp., Fm.hw., Sk.tp.: "this" instead of "these"; (er.tp., Sk.tp.)Sk.cr., Sr.Sk.: "these" reinstated
58. A.o.d.: ", two" omitted
59. Er.tp., Fm.hw., Sk.tp.: "the" omitted
60. Er.tp., Fm.hw.: "pleasure" instead of "pleasures"
61. Hq.tp.: first typed "Man" then squeezed in "'s" in type; Fm.hw.: "Man" instead of "Man's"
62. A.o.d.: "Besides" instead of "Beside"
63. Hq.tp.: "of" instead of "for"
64. Ibid.: "That" instead of "This"
65. Ibid.: "mankind studies and studies" instead of "man might study and study"

That "why" will not be answered by the books he will study, by exploring the facts which are outside the life. In the first place the depth of nature is so profound that man's limited life is not long enough to probe the depths of life. Yes, comparatively or relatively you might say one is more studied[66] than another, but no one by the outer study of life comes to the satisfaction of life.

And then there is the appetite for peace. In order to find peace one leaves one's environments which trouble him. One wants to go away from people. One wants to sit quiet and rest. But even a person not ready for this[67] peace, even if he went in the caves of Himalay.[68], away from the whole[69] world, even there he would not find peace.

By the explanation of these five aspects of appetites, the deepest appetite of man, one finds that all the efforts of man made to satisfy these appetites seem to be in vain for[70]. And how can these five desires be satisfied? They can be satisfied by spiritual attainment, for that is the only thing which answers these five different appetites.

And now[71] to explain how these five a.[72] are only[73] answered by spiritual attainment. The desire to live can only be satisfied when the soul realizes its eternal life. [74]For mortality exists rather in conception than in reality[74] from a spiritual[75] p.o.v.[76] M.[77] is the lack of soul's[78] understanding of its own self. For instance, a person always thought that his coat was himself; he lived all his life in that conception and when that coat was torn[79] he thought that he died. The same one experiences in life. It is a kind of illusion that the soul gets from this physical body and identifies itself with this mortal being. It is just like identifying oneself with one's overcoat. And by the loss of the coat one thinks that: I am lost.

Nevertheless an intellectual knowledge of this is but of a little use. Because when the inner self has identified itself with the body and when in

66. Sk.sh.: "studied" crossed out, "learned" inserted in sh. in front of "studied"; "learned" in a.o.d.
67. A.o.d.: "that" instead of "this"
68. Sk.sh.: "Himalay." abbr. in lh. for "Himalaya", and written out in a.o.d.
69. Er.tp., Sk.tp.: "whole" omitted ; (er.tp., Sk.tp.)Sk.cr.: reinstated; Sr.Sk.: confirms "whole" omitted
70. A.o.d.: "for" omitted
71. Fm.hw.: "And now" omitted
72. Sk.sh.: "a." in lh. abbr. for "appetites", and written out in a.o.d.
73. A.o.d.: "only" omitted
74. Fm.hw.: The following words omitted: "For mortality exists rather in conception than in reality"
75. Er.tp., Sk.tp.: "spirituality" instead of "spiritual"; (er.tp.)Sk.cr.: "spiritual" reinstated
76. Sk.sh.: "p.o.v." abbr. for "point of view", and written out in a.o.d.
77. Sk.sh.: "M." in lh. for "mortality"; written out in a.o.d.
78. Hq.tp.: "soul" instead of "soul's"; (Hq.tp.)Sk.cr.: "soul's" reinstated; (Hq.tp., er.tp., Sk.tp.)Sk.cr., Sr.Sk.: "the" inserted before "soul's"
79. Sk.sh.: "torn" crossed out, then restored in lh., and included in a.o.d.

imagination the person thinks: No, no, the body is but my overcoat[80]. It is therefore that the meditations are done by the wise people of all times in order to give a chance to the soul to find itself independent of the physical body. Once the soul has begun to feel itself, its own life [81] independently of its outer garb, it is beginning to have confidence of its[82] life, it is no longer afraid of what is called death. No sooner these phenomena once[83] vouchsafed[84], a person[85] no longer calls death a[86] death, he calls death[87] a change.

And now coming to[88] the idea of the[89] power. The true power is not in the,[90] in trying to gain the[91] power. The true power is in becoming power[92]. But how to become it? It requires an attempt to make a definite change in oneself and that change is a kind of struggle with one's false self and[93] when that false self is crucified, then the true self is resurrected. Apparently before the world that[94] crucifixion is the lack of power; in truth, all power is attained by that[94] resurrection.

As to the knowledge, there are two [95] aspects. One knowledge is that which one learns by knowing the names and forms of this life, what we call learning. This[96] cannot be the answer of that[96] appetite. [97]This is only a step-[98]stone to that appetite, it cannot satisfy this appetite.[97]

[99]

This, only the outer learning helps one to go[100] to the inner learning, but this[101] inner learning is quite different from the outer learning, and how is it learned? It is learned by studying self. One finds that all the knowledge that

80. (Er.tp.)Sk.cr.: "?" in lh. in margin next to "overcoat"; Sk.tp.: "coat . . ." instead of "overcoat"; (Sk.tp.)Sk.cr.: "overcoat" reinstated
81. Sk.sh.: a blank
82. Sk.sh.: "its" crossed out, and omitted in a.o.d.
83. A.o.d.: "this phenomenon is" instead of "these phenomena once"
84. Sk.sh.: apparently Sk. understood "watch safe" which she wrote in lh., probably due to unfamiliarity with the English "vouchsafe"; Hq.tp., er.tp., Sk.tp.: "watch safe" instead of "vouchsafed"; Fm.hw.: "watch has safed"; (er.tp., Sk.tp.)Sk.cr.: changed to "vouch safe"; Sr.Sk.: confirms "vouch-safed"
85. Fm.hw.: "he" added
86. Ibid.: "a" omitted, then reinstated;
87. Ibid.: "it" instead of "death"
88. Ibid.: "And now coming to" omitted
89. Er.tp., Fm.tp., Sk.tp.: "the" omitted
90. Sk.sh.: "in the," crossed out, and omitted in a.o.d.
91. Fm.hw.: "the" omitted
92. Ibid.: first wrote "powerful", then crossed out "-ful"
93. Ibid.: "and" omitted
94. Er.tp., Fm.hw., Sk.tp.: "this" instead of "that"
95. Sk.sh.: a partially written symbol in lh., illegible
96. Er.tp., Fm.hw., Sk.tp.: "This" and "that" reversed in this sentence
97. Sk.sh.: later the sentence was reordered to read: "It cannot satisfy this appetite, this is only a step-stone to that appetite."; a.o.d.: sentence reads: "It cannot satisfy that appetite; this is only a stepping stone to that appetite."
98. Sk.sh.: "step" changed to "stepping", and "stepping" in a.o.d.
99. Sk.sh.: a blank line
100. Hq.tp.: "get" instead of "go"
101. A.o.d.: "the" instead of "this"

one strives to learn and all that exists to study, it is all in oneself. Therefore one finds a kind of universe in one's self and by the study of the self one comes to that spiritual knowledge which is [102] the soul's appetite.

And[103] then comes the question of happiness. One thinks, that: If my friend is very kind to me then I will be very[104] happy; when people respond to me, or when I will get my[105] money I will be happy. But that is not the way of becoming,[106] being[107] happy. It is a mistake, because the lack of happiness makes one blame others, because they are in the way of[108] that person to be happy. But really speaking, that[109] is not so. True happiness is not gained; it is discovered. Man's way himself[110] is happiness. That is why he longs for happiness. What keeps happiness out from one's life is the closing of the doors of their[111] heart. When the heart is not living, then the happiness is not living there. Sometimes the heart is not fully living, but a little living. But[112] it expects the life from the other heart. But the real life of the heart is to live independent[113] in its own happiness. And that is gained by spiritual attainment. The person who has found his peace within himself, that person may be in a cave of the mountain or amidst the crowd; in every place he will experience his peace.

Now[114] the question is how these five things can be gained. As I have said, the first necessary thing is for the person to accomplish the object which is immediately standing before him. However small, it does not matter. It is by accomplishing it that one gains the power. As one goes on further through this way in this life, always seeking for the real, one will come to reality. Truth is attained by the love of truth.

The person who runs away from truth, truth runs away from him. If not,
truth is more near to the person than what is without truth. There is nothing more precious in life than truth itself, and in loving truth and in attaining to the truth, one attains to that religion which is the religion of all people and[115]

102. Sk.sh.: a blank; Hq.tp.: "is" omitted, blank included; (Hq.tp.)Sk.cr.: "satisfies" inserted in the blank; Er.tp., Fm.hw., Sk.tp.: blank omitted; (er.tp.)Sk.cr.: "is" crossed out, and "satisfies(?)" inserted above; (Sk.tp.)Sk.cr.: "is" crossed out and "satisfies" inserted above, then "is" reinstated
103. Fm.hw.: "And" omitted
104. Sk.sh.: "very" crossed out, and omitted in a.o.d.
105. Fm.hw.: "my" omitted
106. Fm.hw.: "to become" instead of "of becoming,"
107. Sk.sh.: "being" added, crossed out and and written again, then crossed out again; omitted in a.o.d.
108. Hq.tp.: "for" instead of "of"
109. Er.tp., Sk.tp.: "it" instead of "that"
110. Fm.hw.: "(soul) itself" instead of "himself"
111. A.o.d.: "the" instead of "their"
112. Fm.hw.: "and" instead of "But"
113. Ibid.: "independent(ly)" instead of "independent"
114. Ibid.: "Now" omitted
115. A.o.d.: "of" added

all churches. It does not matter then [116]what church he belongs[117], what religion he professes, what race or nation he belongs[118]; when once he realizes the truth, he is with all[119], all because he is with all. [120] [121]It is[122] the disagreem.[123] and misunderstanding, is[121] before a person has attained[124] the truth. When once a person has attained to the truth there is no misunderstanding. It is[125] those who have learned the outer knowledge, the disputes come among them. But those who have attained to the truth, whether he comes[126] from [127]north pole or the south pole, what country, it does not matter. When they have it[128] understood, the truth, they are atonement. And it is this object that we should keep before us in order to unite the divided section[129] of humanity. For the real happiness of humanity is in that unity which can be gained by rising above barriers which divide man.

[130]Thank you all for the most sympathetic and patient[131] response. May God bless you.[130]

---

116. Fm.hw.: "to" added before "what"
117. Er.tp., Sk.tp.: "to" added after "belongs"
118. A.o.d.: "to" added
119. Sk.sh.: "with all" crossed out, and omitted in a.o.d.
120. Sk.sh.: a blank
121. Fm.hw.: "It is the agreement and understanding which is" instead of "It is the disagreem. and misunderstanding, is"; Sk.tp.: reads: "It is the disagreement and misunderstanding is, (There is disagreement and misunderstanding),"; apparently Sk. was trying to work out the problem with the wording; (er.tp., Sk.tp.)Sk.cr.: changed to read: "There is disagreement and misunderstanding" instead of "It is the disagreem. and misunderstanding, is"
122. Hq.tp.: "when" typed above the space between "is" and "the"
123. Sk.sh.: "disagreem." in lh., abbr. for "disagreement"; written out in a.o.d.
124. Hq.tp.: "he has not attained" instead of "has attained"; er.tp., Sk.tp.: "has attained to"; Fm.hw.: "who has attained"
125. Fm.hw.: "is" crossed out and "are" written above, same hw.
126. Fm.hw.: "they come" instead of "he comes"
127. A.o.d.: "the" added
128. A.o.d.: "it" omitted
129. Hq.tp.: "sections" instead of "section"; (er.tp.)Sk.cr.: "section" changed to "sections"
130. Er.tp., Fm.hw., Sk.tp.: last two sentences omitted
131. Hq.tp.: "and patient" omitted

Sakina's shorthand reporting

[1]
[3]

Rue de Loxum, May 23rd [2]

Beloved ones of God,[4]

[5]This afternoon I wish to, and[6] speak [7] same subject which I have spoken last evening. This reason is that when a subject is spoken before a large public you cannot very well touch upon the intimate points. For that I ask your indulgence to make remarks or[8] rather to go into the detail for[9] of the same subject. I had said that there are five aspects in which the appetite

---

Documents:

Sk.sh.	=	Sakina Furnée's shorthand reporting, newly transcribed by B.v.d.B.
Sk.er.tp.1	=	an early typescript, with a handwritten note at the top by Munira van Voorst van Beest (see List): "copy of Sakina's steno-type". Sakina also made corrections, indicated in the notes as "(Sk.er.tp.1)Sk.cr."
Sk.er.tp.2	=	a typed copy of "Sk.er.tp.1", incorporating the corrections "(Sk.er.tp.1)Sk.cr.", on which Sakina wrote "compared with steno - Sakina". She also made further corrections to this document, indicated in the notes as "(Sk.er.tp.2)Sk.cr."
er.tp.	=	an early typescript of unknown origiin. A few corrections by Sakina are indicated in the notes as "(er.tp.)Sk.cr."
Sk.tp.1	=	a typed copy of "Sk.er.tp.2" made later by Sakina or under her direction, with a few corrections indicated in the notes as "(Sk.tp.1)Sk.cr."
Sk.tp.2	=	a later typed copy of "er.tp.", identical, and therefore not mentioned after note 1. A few corrections made by Sakina to this document, but not to "er.tp.", are indicated in the notes as "(Sk.tp.2)Sk.cr."
Sk.an.	=	a list of corrections prepared by Sakina when working on "Sk.tp.1". It refers to the "steno-type" and to communications with Sirdar van Tuyll and a typist.

Notes:

1. Sk.sh.: "Private Lecture", "the Aim of Life (cont)" in lh. added later; Sk.er.tp.2: "Private Lec" inserted in unknown hw.; Sk.tp.1: "MUREEDS AND FRIENDS" added, then crossed off; "Private Lecture" inserted in lh. above; Sk.tp.2: "Private Lecture" added
2. Sk.er.tp.1, Sk.er.tp.2: "1924" and "Bruxelles. for mureeds and friends. The lecture on the previous day had been on 'The Aim of Life'." added; er.tp.: date and location missing; Sk.tp.1: "1924", "Brussels" and "The lecture on the previous day had been on: 'The Aim of Life'." added
3. Er.tp.: title added: "Five Aspects in which the Appetite of the Soul shows itself."; Sk.tp.1: title added: "Cont. The Aim of Life"
4. Er.tp.: "Beloved ones of God," omitted
5. Er.tp.: several sentences omitted: "This afternoon . . . . shows itself."
6. Sk.sh.: "and" crossed out; omitted a.o.d.
7. Sk.sh.: a blank
8. A.o.d.: "or" omitted
9. A.o.d.: "for" omitted

of the soul shows itself. And those five aspects were[10]: [11]the desire, desire to live, [12]for knowledge[11], the desire for power, the desire for happiness, and the desire for peace. One person perhaps shows one desire more than another person; nevertheless, every person has these five aspects of the soul's appetite just the same.

The desire to live, if we study it profoundly we shall find that we cannot have a desire,[13] desire it is[14] if it were not in our nature. And if there is a desire, it is[14], there is an answer for it. Desire to live continually is a desire of the spiritual person as well as of the material person. [15]Spiritual person perhaps[16] hopes for the next life. A[17] material person is pessimistic against his own desire, but the desire is there all the same. Now how to attain to this continuity of life? It does not depend only upon a belief. But no doubt belief helps a person to the realization of that experience. And when there is no belief, then the way is not found by a person.

Nevertheless, the continuity of life is possible logically, because every man desires to live. For it is natural that no one will desire what is not possible. A natural desire has its possibility there already. If there was no possibility one would not desire. Yes, by this I do not say about a mad person. A mad person can desire anything, but a person with a reason will only desire what is possible to be accomplished. The secret of this question can be found by analyzing oneself. By studying the self one will find that one's body is only a cover upon one's real self. But by a still more profound study, one will find that even one's mind is a cover upon one's real self. As soon as one finds this, one will become independent of the body to live. Also one will become independent of the mind to live. But one might ask that if there is no body, then what is life? But this happens because man has limited himself by experiencing life through the body and he has not tried to experience life without its help. When man is not conscious of his body, then he is conscious of his mind. When one's[18] eyes are open he is looking at things beyond[19] him. When he is,[20] his mind is[21] closed, then he is pondering upon what his mind has gained.

In both cases he is dependent either upon his body or upon his mind,

---

10. Er.tp.: "These five aspects are" instead of "And those five aspects were"
11. Sk.sh.: the first "desire," crossed out; a.o.d.: "the desire to live, the desire for knowledge" instead of "the desire, desire to live, for knowledge"
12. Sk.sh.: above "for" the word "desire" is added again in sh.
13. Sk.sh.: this first "desire," crossed out, and omitted in a.o.d.
14. A.o.d.: "it is" omitted
15. Er.tp.: "The" added
16. Sk.er.tp.1: "he" instead of "perhaps"; (Sk.er.tp.1)Sk.cr.: "perhaps" reinstated
17. Sk.er.tp.1, Sk.er.tp.2, Sk.tp.1: ", and" instead of ". A"
18. A.o.d.: "his" instead of "one's"
19. Sk.er.tp.1, Sk.er.tp.2, Sk.tp.1: "before" instead of "beyond"
20. Sk.sh.: "he is," crossed out; omitted a.o.d.
21. (Sk.er.tp.1)Sk.cr.: dots under "mind is" and "(eyes are)" inserted above; (Sk.tp.1)Sk.cr.: "(eyes are??)" inserted in margin next to "mind is"; (Sk.tp.2)Sk.cr.: "mind is" changed to "eyes are"

that he is living. This dependence makes the soul limited. It does not only limit it, but it mortalizes the soul. I do not mean by this that the soul is mortal, but even for the soul to believe in mortality is like being mortal.

Now another question: the desire for power. Man desires for power because it is natural for him to gain. There is somewhere the power is hidden in him. He cannot help it. Man is powerless, in spite of a power which is hidden in him. The powerlessness, the experience of being powerless, is his ignorance of the power which is in him. Now in order to open the doors, in order to see the power he has in store, what is necessary is to seek the kingdom of God, as it is said in the Bible[22], because then one will find one's divine heritage, which is all-powerful[23].

And the third thing is the knowledge. In order to secure[24] that knowledge which cannot be studied, one must try to meditate and to become,[25] dive into the sea of knowledge [26]to get it. It is by diving deep into the water one gets the knowledge[26], which cannot be caught[27] by study. In this way we divide two aspects of the knowledge. One aspect is intellect. The other aspect is wisdom. Therefore wise man is not a clever man nor a clever man is not[28] a wise[29].

And now coming to the explanation of happiness. Happiness comes by digging deep into one's own heart. It is our great mistake when we look for happiness in the outside world. The true happiness is our own self, our deepest self. The more conscious we become of our real self, the true happiness comes from that.

And now we come to the question of peace. What happens is this, that in order to get a peace we always blame the others, up[30] other persons who walk[31] upon our nerves. But really speaking, the true peace can come[32] by being so firm against all influences around us that nothing can disturb us.

Now with this I shall close my speech and shall ask you all to ask your[33] any questions you may.

----

22. See Matthew 6:33
23. Sk.er.tp.1: "powerful", then "-ful" crossed out in type
24. A.o.d.: "get" instead of "secure"
25. Sk.sh.: "become," crossed out; omitted a.o.d.
26. Sk.er.tp.2, Sk.tp.1: words omitted: "to get it . . . . gets the knowledge"; (Sk.er.tp.2, Sk.tp.1)Sk.cr., Sk.an.: reinstated, probably a typographical error
27. Sk.sh.: "caught" in sh., retraced to read "got"; (Sk.er.tp.1)Sk.cr.: "caught" changed to "taught"; Sk.er.tp.2, Sk.tp.1: "taught" instead of "caught"; er.tp.: "conquered" instead of "caught"
28. (Sk.er.tp.2)Sk.cr.: "not" circled; er.tp., Sk.tp.1: "not" omitted
29. A.o.d.: "man" added
30. Sk.sh.: "others, up" crossed off; omitted a.o.d.
31. A.o.d.: "person who walks" instead of "persons who walk"
32. Sk.er.tp.2, Sk.tp.1: "only" added
33. A.o.d.: "me" instead of "your"

Question: *Do you believe in the immortality of the soul?*

Answer: Well, my whole lecture has been on the same subject.

Question: *On which basis,* [34]*your belief of the immortality*[35]*?*

Answer: There cannot be better basis than one's own realization.

Question: *I am believing, but I want to be fortified in my ideal*[36]*. I would like to get*[37] *reason for the immortality of the soul.*

Answer: What I mean to say is that all the religions of the world support this idea. Therefore, for a believer, there is everything to support it.

Question: *Is there in his*[38] *instruction for* [39] *? What can fortify that idea,*[40] *belief?*

Answer: Yes, our whole instruction is to realization[41] this, not only to fortify it. Our work, the work of the Sufi philosophy, is not to strengthen a person's belief only, but to make his belief his conviction. Therefore we do not teach people any belief.

Question: *How Murshid proposes to realization*[42] *the knowledge of one's self?*

Answer: There are four ways by which one comes to the realization of the self- knowledge: by the way of knowledge, by the way of good action, by the way of meditation, by the way of devotion. Whatever be your[43] temperament, whatever[44] of these four things are[45] near to your nature to walk in that path, and in the end you will find the answer of your soul.

---

34. Er.tp.: "is" added
35. Sk.er.tp.1, Sk.er.tp.2, Sk.tp.1: "of the soul is founded" added
36. Sk.sh.: "ideal" worked over to read "ideas", and "ideas" in a.o.d.
37. Sk.sh.: "the" inserted above between "get" and "reason"; Sk.er.tp.1, Sk.er.tp.2, Sk.tp.1: "the" omitted; er.tp.: "the" included
38. Sk.er.tp.1, Sk.er.tp.2, Sk.tp.1: "the" instead of "his"; er.tp.: "your" instead of "his"
39. Sk.sh.: a blank; Sk.er.tp.1, Sk.er.tp.2, Sk.tp.1: "of" instead of "for", followed by a blank; er.tp.: no blank; (Sk.er.tp.2, Sk.tp.1)Sk.cr.: "Sufism" inserted in the blank, confirmed in Sk.an.
40. Sk.sh.: "idea" crossed out; omitted in a.o.d.
41. A.o.d.: "realize" instead of "realization"
42. A.o.d.: "realize" instead of "realization"
43. Sk.er.tp.1, Sk.er.tp.2, Sk.tp.1: "the" instead of "your"
44. Ibid.: "when one" instead of "whatever"
45. Ibid.: "is" instead of "are"

Question: *The meditation is the principle[46], I think. The three others are interesting, but please explanation of the fourth again[47].*

Answer: Devotion is the original nature of man. Because as the Bible says: "God is love"[48], and therefore the person in whom there is love, there is God.

Question: *If perhaps an atheist has devotion, love, how can one reconcile that[49]?*

Answer: He cannot be any longer[50] an ath.[51] when he has a[52] devotion or love, because that[53] love principle in its development will make him believe. If not in God, then in a person he loves. And if a person truly loves one person, he must in the end love all persons. [54] When a person says: I love a[55] person, but hate another person, he does not yet know what love is. Because love is not limited, it is divine and it is unlimited. By opening the love element in oneself, one opens divine element in oneself. And when the divine fountain begins to rise from the heart, then all realizations which are divine must rise as a fountain. The great saints who had love, even for the smallest insect and living being, they had divine realization without great study or meditations, only their love taught them so.

Question: *How to conceive divine element?*

Answer: Love is divine from its beginning in all its aspects. The great poet of Persia, Rumi[56], he[57] says: "If you love a hu.[58] person or if[59] you love God, if you journey all through the way of all[60] love, in the end you will arrive in the presence of the sovereign of love".

---

46. (Er.tp.)Sk.cr.: "principle" changed to "principal"; a.o.d.: "principal"
47. Sk.er.tp.1, Sk.er.tp.2, Sk.tp.1: "give an explanation of the fourth" instead of "explanation of the fourth again"; er.tp.: "explain the fourth"
48. See I John 4:8
49. Er.tp.: "this" instead of "that"
50. Er.tp.: "anywhere" instead of "any longer"
51. Sk.sh.: "ath." abbr. for "atheist" in lh.; written out in a.o.d.
52. Sk.er.tp.1, Sk.er.tp.2, Sk.tp.1: "a" omitted
53. Er.tp.: "this" instead of "that"
54. Sk.sh.: a blank space which may indicate a pause in speaking
55. A.o.d.: "one" instead of "a"
56. Jelal-ud-din Rumi (see List)
57. (Er.tp.)Sk.cr.: "he" crossed out
58. Sk.sh.: the sound "h-u-" written, perhaps for "human", then crossed out; omitted in a.o.d.
59. Sk.er.tp.1: "of" instead of "if"
60. Sk.sh.: "all" crossed out; omitted in a.o.d.

Question: *The realization of the knowledge of one's self is the realization of the spirit or of the soul?*

Answer: Self is the soul. Therefore it is the realization of the soul as well as of the body and mind of the whole being. Even in the realization of [61]self, God-realization comes.

Question: *Every one in life had*[62] *to have a* but[63], *object; every one has to find his way. And in finding one's way, one must put all one's*[64] *intelligence. Is there a self*[65], *a means, of finding one's why*[66] *in life?*

Answer: Yes, if one lives a straight life, a natural life, intuitively one finds the straight way to go. Besides that, when a[67] person has got his object which is for him, then he feels himself, then he feels at home. Then he feels that everything helps him and he feels hopeful and courageous.

Question: *Is there a* [68] moyen[69] *to find the object? I have not yet found an object in life.*

[70] He[71] must develop intuition.

Question: *How can one develop the intuition in somebody who has not possessed this?*

Answer: Self-confidence. And in the first place a person must be ready to risk mistake[72]. Because he may not always have the right intuition and if he disbelieves in the intuition, then he will not have it at all.

Question: *Then it is a great risk?*

---

61. A.o.d.: "the" added
62. (Sk.er.tp.2, Sk.tp.1)Sk.cr.: "had" changed to "has", confirmed in Sk.an.
63. Sk.sh.: "*but*" crossed out; however "*but*" in French means "goal"; a.o.d.: "an object" instead of "*but*"
64. Sk.er.tp.1, er.tp.: "his" instead of "one's"
65. Sk.sh.: "a self" crossed out; omitted in a.o.d.
66. Ibid.: "why" changed to read "way", and "way" in a.o.d.
67. Ibid.: "a" crossed out, but included in a.o.d.
68. Ibid.: an illegible sh. symbol crossed out
69. Sk.sh.: "*moyen*" written in French, meaning: "means"or "way"; a.o.d.: "a means"
70. Sk.sh.: a blank; "A" for "answer" omitted; no new sentence begun; a.o.d.: answer starts here
71. Er.tp.: "One" instead of "He"
72. Er.tp.: "mistakes" instead of "mistake"

Answer: Nothing is attained without a risk. When people say that in something there is a risk, I often tell them that in not taking a risk, there is a greater risk still.

Question: Does[73] the in[74] Hindu belief admit the[75] reincarnation?

Answer: Certainly it does not except[76] reinc.[77] But it is the belief which[78] has given to the world this belief.

Question: But the reincarnation without distinction[79] of races?

Answer: The souls must have a freedom to reinc.[80]

Question: Is intuition superior to intelligence?

Answer: Superiority and inferiority are relative terms. Of[81] course, intuition sometimes comes from a deeper source as intellect. But besides it is difficult to translate in French language the difference of intellect and intelligence. Because if I were to explain what I mean by intelligence, I only mean capacity of knowing, and by intellect I mean what one knows. Intelligence is the [82] and intellect is the knowledge. Therefore intelligence is a pure substance, something most pure. And therefore the intelligence is the divine substance that one can trace in one's self. If there is any sign of soul in a person, it is the intelligence. Therefore for me, the more intelligent [83]person, the more brilliant soul that person has. But by this I do not mean that an intellectual person is intelligent[84].

---

73. Sk.sh.: "Does" in sh. altered to "But"; "Does" in a.o.d.
74. Sk.sh.: "in" altered to "belief", then both crossed out, and omitted in a.o.d.
75. Sk.er.tp.1, Sk.er.tp.2, Sk.tp.1: "the" omitted
76. A.o.d.: "accept" instead of "except"; (Sk.er.tp.2)Sk.cr.: "only" inserted before "accept"; Sk.tp.1: "only" added, and confirmed in Sk.an.; (Sk.tp.1)Sk.cr.: "only" crossed out, thus reinstating the sh. text
77. Sk.sh.: "reinc." abbr. in lh. for "reincarnation", and written out in a.o.d.
78. Er.tp.: "people which" instead of "belief which"; (Sk.er.tp.2)Sk.cr.: "the belief which" is circled and "the Hindoo" inserted before the circle and "who" inserted after, in an unknown hw.; (Sk.tp.1)Sk.cr.: "the" underscored, then crossed through the underscore; "(Hindu who)" inserted above "belief which"; Sk.an.: "the Hindu belief which"
79. .Sk.sh.: "distinction" in sh. retraced for clarity, and so in a.o.d.
80. Ibid.: "reinc." abbr. in lh. for "reincarnate", and written out in a.o.d.
81. Ibid.: "Of" crossed out, but included in a.o.d.
82. Ibid.: a blank and an illegible, minute marking; a.o.d.: "capacity" added in place of blank
83. Er.tp.: "a" added
84. Sk.sh.: "intelligent" crossed out, "intelligence" in sh. added; Sk.er.tp.1, er.tp.: "is intelligence";
(Sk.er.tp.1)Sk.cr.: "is" changed to "has"; Sk.er.tp.2, Sk.tp.1: "has intelligence"; (Sk.er.tp.2, Sk.tp.1)Sk.cr.: "(no)?" inserted after "has"; (Sk.tp.2)Sk.cr.: "is intelligence" changed back to "is intelligent"

Question: *Is the will not the nearest*[85] *to the divinity?*

Answer: Yes, if I were to give a definition of will I would call it love. I will to do it, means I love to do it. It is poetic.

Question: *I have done many things, which I did not like to do.*

Answer: Then he does not will to do it. Then he is a machine. Then there is no will there. When a person wills to do, then he loves to do. For them[86] the will-power and the love-power is one thing.

Question: *Still it is a way of developing one's will, by doing what one does not like to do?*

Answer: Yes, we develop our power of doing it. We develop a power over a part of our self which is [87] willing. That only means that a part of our self[88] and a[89] part of our self loves[90] to do it. And therefore the part which controls, we call it[91] will.

Question: *If I forgive*[92] *good for bad? The first impulse is not to do it.*

Answer: I would call it love, love in the form of forgiveness or[93] tolerance.

[94]

If you are not willing to do it, it is another thing. I would rather a man loved to do a certain virtue, or else not do it. But doing it unwillingly is not good. For instance, if a guest,[95] if someone came and visited[96] a person and then that person[97] went out and said: Shall I borrow their[98] raincoat? And you said: All right.

---

85. Sk.sh.: an illegible symbol added above "nearest"
86. A.o.d.: "me" instead of "them"
87. Sk.sh.: a space, "in dark" in sh. added above, followed by "willing" in sh. altered to "unwilling"; a.o.d.: "unwilling" instead of "[blank] willing"
88. Sk.er.tp.1, Sk.er.tp.2, Sk.tp.1: a blank with dotted lines; er.tp.: "is unwilling" added
89. Sk.er.tp.2, Sk.tp.1: "an" instead of "a"; (Sk.tp.1)Sk.cr.: "a" reinstated
90. Sk.er.tp.1: "love" instead of "loves"
91. A.o.d.: "conquers we call it the" instead of "controls, we call it"
92. Ibid.: "give" instead of "forgive"
93. Ibid.: "of" instead of "or"
94. Sk.sh.: an entire line left blank; Sk.er.tp.1 leaves a partial line; a.o.d. continue on with next sentence
95. Sk.sh.: "For instance if a guest," crossed out; a.o.d.: "if a guest," omitted
96. A.o.d.: "to visit" instead of "and visited"
97. Sk.sh.: "person" crossed out, "man" inserted; Sk.er.tp.1, Sk.er.tp.2, Sk.tp.1: "this man" instead of "that person"; er.tp.: "man" instead of "person"
98. Sk.sh.: this sh. symbol has a short down stroke, without curve; first choice for reading is "their" instead of "your"; a.o.d.: "your" instead of "their"

But then you have to go out also and then[99] say: What a bad man, he took my raincoat. I would have preferred that man would not have[100] given it, and would have said: I am very sorry, I cannot give it, sir. Every good action we do, if it comes by our love, then only it has its virtue. If not, it is a dead action. It is not living.

Question: *Does the Sufi philosophy in its essence believe in reincarnation?*

Answer: The philosophy of the Sufis does not give any belief and does not oppose against any belief. What it does is that it interprets to its best ability, every belief as favorable[101] as[102] the followers[103] of this[104] belief. For instance, if a person asks a question about Buddh.[105] to a Sufi, about Brahm.[106], Christian religion, the Sufi stands for this[107] person as the lawyer[108] would stand in the tribunal, to give his argument before the law. But Sufism does not give any belief; all[109] its own belief. And therefore there is one Sufi, he believes perhaps in one doctr.[110], another does not just now understand. In order to become Sufi it is not necessary to have this belief or that belief, this doctrine or that doctrine. The only what a[111] Sufi helps, is for the person to rise above things and to look at [112]life from a higher p.o.v.[113] [114] Sufism follows exactly this[115] idea, which is in the Bible: "Seek ye the kingdom of God first[116] and all these things will be

99. Er.tp.: "if you would" added
100. (Sk.er.tp.2)Sk.cr.: "man would not have" changed to "I had not" in unknown hw., and then changed back
101. Sk.er.tp.1: "favorable" changed to "favorably" in type; Sk.er.tp.2, Sk.tp.1: "favorably"
102. (Er.tp.)Sk.cr.: "as" crossed out and "to(?)" inserted in the margin; (Sk.tp.2)Sk.cr.: "as" in parentheses and "to" inserted above
103. Er.tp.: "follower" instead of "followers"
104. A.o.d.: "that" instead of "this"
105. Sk.sh.: "Buddh." in lh. abbr. for Buddhism", followed by Sk.er.tp.2, Sk.tp.1; Sk.er.tp.1: "Buddha" instead of "Buddhism", then changed to "Buddhism" in type; er.tp.: "Buddha" instead of "Buddhism"
106. Sk.sh.: "Brahm." in lh. abbr. for "Brahmanism" (see List), followed by Sk.er.tp.1,2; er.tp., Sk.tp.1: "Brahma, about the" instead of "Brahmanism"
107. A.o.d.: "that" instead of "this"
108. Er.tp.: "latter" instead of "lawyer"
109. Sk.er.tp.1, Sk.er.tp.2, Sk.tp.1: "as" instead of "all"; er.tp.: "for" instead of "all"
110. Sk.sh.: "doctr." in sh. abbr. for "doctrine"; written out in a.o.d.
111. Sk.sh.: "a" crossed out; omitted in a.o.d.; Sk.er.tp.1, er.tp.: "way" instead of "what"; (Sk.er.tp.1)Sk.cr.: "what" reinstated; Sk.tp.1: "thing" added before "what"; (Sk.tp.1)Sk.cr.: "thing" crossed out then reinstated
112. Er.tp.: "the" added
113. Sk.sh.: "p.o.v." in sh. abbr. for "point of view"; written out in a.o.d.
114. Sk.sh.: a blank
115. A.o.d.: "that" instead of "this"
116. Er.tp.: "first the kingdom of God" instead of "the kingdom of God first"

added to you"[117]. Instead of troubling about these beliefs[118], every[119] Sufi wants to go first straight to that central idea and when he stands there, hence[120] he sees the truth of all things. Because the mystery of life is that when the divine lantern is taken in the hand, then whenever[121] you take that lantern[122] in the hand, all things become clear to you. Therefore Sufism gives freedom to every member, to every member[123] to believe for himself to[124], to find out things for himself.

Now, in order to finish the meeting I wish to say one word. And that is: that our life's greatest need is God. And to our great disappointment we find that very ideal being lost. Whether it is a spiritual gain or material gain, all the inspiration and power is in the love of God, in the knowledge of God and in the realization of the relation of the self of[125] God.

[126]

---

117. See Matthew 6:33
118. Sk.er.tp.1: typed "this belief", then changed to "these beliefs" in type; er.tp.: "this belief" instead of "these beliefs"
119. A.o.d.: "the" instead of "every"
120. Sk.sh.: "hence" crossed out; omitted in a.o.d.
121. (Sk.er.tp.2)Sk.cr.: "whenever" changed to "wherever"; Sk.tp.1: typed "whenever (wherever)"; (Sk.tp.1)Sk.cr.: crossed out "(wherever)"
122. Sk.er.tp.1: "that lantern that lantern" (repeated)
123. Sk.sh.: the second: "to every member" in sh. crossed out, and omitted in a.o.d.
124. Sk.sh.: "to," crossed out; a.o.d.: "and" instead of the first "to"
125. Sk.er.tp.1: "and" instead of "of", changed to "of" in type; SK.tp.1: "of(and?)" instead of "of" (Sk.er.tp.2, Sk.tp.2)Sk.cr.: "of" changed to "and"; (Sk.tp.1)Sk.cr.: "of (and?)" changed to "with"
126. Sk.er.tp.1, Sk.er.tp.2, Sk.tp.1: "God bless you." added

Sakina's shorthand reporting

[1]

Mme de Stürler's
May 24th, 1924 [2]

[3]

[4]Beloved ones of God,

I[5] will be about the revelation, when awake and when asleep.[4] It wants a certain amount of spiritual progress in order[6] to believe in such a thing, in order[6] to believe that there is such a thing as R[7]. Life is revealing, its nature is revealing and so is God. Therefore in the Persian language God is called *Khuda*[8] which means self-revealing[9]. All the[10] science and art and all culture[11] known to man has originally come by revelation and not only originally, but even today every invention, every improvement in the[10]

Documents:

Sk.sh. = Sakina Furnée's shorthand reporting of the lecture, newly transcribed by B.v.d.B.

Hq.tp. = a typescript made at Headquarters, Geneva from an unknown source. A few corrections by Sakina are indicated in the notes as "(Hq.tp.)Sk.cr."

Fm.hw. = a handwritten copy of the text made by Murshida Fazal Mai Egeling (see List) from an unknown source.

er.tp. = an early typescript of unknown origin. Her corrections are indicated in the notes as "(er.tp.)Sk.cr."

Sk.tp. = a typed copy of "er.tp." prepared later by Sakina or under her direction. It is identical in wording, and therefore not mentioned after note 2 except for a few corrections by Sakina which are indicated in the notes as "(Sk.tp.)Sk.cr."

Sk.an. = a separate list of a few corrections prepared by Sakina while working on "Sk.tp."

Notes:

1. Hq.tp.: "N.81" in unknown hw. at upper left; (er.tp.)Sk.cr.: "compared with steno - Sakina" inserted at top; (Sk.tp.)Sk.cr.: "Public Lecture" inserted upper left, then "Public" changed to "Private"
2. Hq.tp.: "for mureeds and friends" added; Fm.hw., er.tp.: date and location omitted; "Brussels, May 24, 1924" inserted later in unknown hw.; Sk.tp.: "Mme de Stürler's" omitted and "Brussels" added; (Sk.tp.)Sk.cr.: "at Mme de Stürler's" inserted
3. Sk.sh.: "Revelation, when awake and when asleep." added in lh., above the text; Hq.tp.: "REVELATION, WHEN AWAKE AND WHEN ASLEEP" from the first sentence underlined as the title; Fm.hw.: title omitted; er.tp.: title included: "Revelation When Awake and When Asleep"
4. Fm.hw., er.tp.: opening words omitted: "Beloved ones . . . when asleep."
5. Hq.tp.: "My subject this afternoon" instead of "I"
6. Er.tp.: "in order" omitted
7. Sk.sh.: "R." in sh. abbr. for "revelation"; written out in a.o.d.
8. Sk.sh.: Sk. wrote "*Khuddhe*" (in lh.) for Persian "*Khuda*" (see Glossary)
9. Fm.hw.: "revelation" instead of "-revealing"
10. Er.tp.: "the" omitted
11. Hq.tp.: "cultured" corrected to "culture," in type

science or art comes by the[12] revelation. Man does not learn the[10] art or science by study. He learns it[13]; but there is much that he learns by revelation. A scientist, an[14] artist who may only learn[15] by study, he[16] is not a true scientist or artist, he is only a machine. No doubt the[10] modern life seems to have covered the[17] revelation side of culture by pushing forward the culture which is mechanical. Now[18] [19]putting this in more plain words, I should like to say that[19] a person does not only learn by one's[20] own study, but one[21] also draws so to speak knowledge from the multitude. [22] In other words I may say that[23] a child does not only inherit his father's or his ancestors' qualities, but also the qualities of his nation. If this is true, then this can be also true, that man inherits the qualities[24] of his race, also that man inherits the qualities of the whole human race. Therefore if one realized[25] profoundly that storehouse of knowledge that exists behind this veil, one will find that he[26] has a right to this heritage. And this gives one a key, a key to understand the secret of life: that knowledge is not only gained from outside, but also from within. Therefore, knowledge that one learns from outside life, one calls it[27] learning, but the knowledge that one draws from within, it is this[28] knowledge which is called revelation.

There are different degrees of revelation. In the first place one sees to a small[29] or greater extent in every person a capacity of impression. Every person more or less feels in the presence of a new person he[30] meets, whether[31] to trust that person[32] or not to trust that person. If you ask this person[33]: What makes you think like this?, he has not always got a reason to tell you, but he can only tell you: I feel that way. Women sometimes are more impressionable than men for[34] the reason is that woman by nature is

12. Fm.hw., er.tp.: "the" omitted
13. Er.tp.: "them" instead of "it"
14. Fm.hw.: "or" instead of ", an"
15. A.o.d.: "has only learned" instead of "may only learn"
16. Er.tp.: "he" omitted
17. A.o.d.: "that" instead of "the"
18. Fm.hw.: "Now" omitted
19. Er.tp.: "to put this in plainer words," instead of "putting this in more plain words, I should like to say that"
20. Ibid.: "his" instead of "one's"
21. Ibid.: "he" instead of "one"
22. Sk.sh.: a blank
23. Er.tp.: "I may say that" omitted
24. Hq.tp., er.tp.: "quality" instead of "qualities"
25. Ibid: "realizes" instead of "realized"
26. Er.tp.: "one" instead of "he"
27. Ibid.: "it" omitted
28. A.o.d.: "that" instead of "this"
29. A.o.d.: "smaller" instead of "small"
30. Hq.tp.: "one" instead of "he"
31. Fm.hw.: "with" instead of "whether"
32. Er.tp.: "that person" omitted
33. Ibid.: "this person" omitted
34. Ibid.: "for" omitted

respondent[35]. But then among two[36] men, the more respondent[37] man, he is[38] the more impressionable[39]; but besides the impression of a person, there are some who easily get an impression of a place[40]. Any place[41] they walk or they sit, they feel whether there is something agreeable or disagreeable, if there has happened something sad or something joyful. There are some so very impressionable that they can see not only the condition of a few years back but even of many years back. And very often in the East they take a person, an impressionable person, to find out where they can easily get water and that person begins to feel where the water is closest and after digging that place, they find out that it was true. This I am not telling as[42] a great spiritual power, but as[43] an ordinary simple thing of everyday life. Because impression only depends upon that respondent[44] attitude and a person gets an impression from everything that he responds to.

And now[45] going a little further one finds another aspect of revelation and that[46] may be called intuition. Before beginning to start a business or a certain affair one feels a kind of feeling. One may go against it. One may not believe in it. But one feels a feeling that: I may not have a success in this; or, when joining forces with another person in business, one might feel that it may not endure long. Also sometimes a person feels that[47]: I might see a friend, a particular friend, and then he sees that [48] friend has come to see him, without any [49] . It is intuition. [50] are many intuitive people, but they do not know it, because intuition is the portion of a person with gentle feelings. As one goes a little further into the subject one finds that there is another aspect of it and that aspect is vision. A vision is more clear in the sleeping state than in wakeful[51] state. The reason is that when a person is asleep, then he lives in the[52] world of his own, but when a person is awake he is partly in that world, but mostly in the outer world. Every

35. Ibid.: "responsive" instead of "respondent"
36. Fm.hw.: "two" omitted; er.tp.: "of two" instead of "among two"
37. Fm.hw.: "responsive the" instead of "respondent"; er.tp.: "responsive" instead of "respondent"
38. Sk.sh.: "he is" crossed out; Hq.tp., Fm.hw.: ", he is" omitted; er.tp.: ", he" omitted, to read "responsive man is"
39. Fm.hw.: "he is" added
40. Hq.tp.: "person" instead of "place"
41. Er.tp.: "In any place where" instead of "Any place"
42. Ibid.: "is not" instead of "I am not telling as"
43. Ibid.: "as" omitted
44. Fm.hw., er.tp.: "responsive" instead of "respondent"
45. Fm.hw.: "And now" omitted
46. Er.tp.: "this" instead of "that"
47. Er.tp.: "that" omitted
48. Sk.sh.: original sh. illegible due to "the" in sh. traced over it; Hq.tp., er.tp.: "the" added; Fm.hw.: no word here - reads "that friend"
49. Sk.sh., Hq.tp.: a blank; Fm.hw.: "without" crossed out and "any" omitted; continues on to read: "to see him it is intuition"; er.tp.: "arrangement between them" added
50. Sk.sh.: an unclear sh. symbol: either "great" or "there" may be read here; "There" in a.o.d.
51. Fm.hw.: "the" added before "wakeful"; er.tp.: "the waking" instead of "wakeful"
52. Er.tp.: "he lives in a" instead of ", then he lives in the"

phenomena[53] wants accommodation. It is not only the sound that[54] is audible, but it is the ears also that make it possible to hear the sound. The mind therefore is the accommodation to receive the impression[55], just like[56] the ears are the accommodations[57] to receive[58] the sound.

Therefore a natural state of sleep is like a profound concentration, like a deep meditation. And therefore what comes like a dream has a significance to[59] it. But one might ask: Are all dreams significant of something? Yes, I should say[60] everything in the world has a significance. Why must [61]dream not have its significance? There is nothing without meaning; it is our lack of understanding[62] its meaning that keeps us in a[63] darkness. But, one might ask[64]: There are sometimes quite meaningless dreams[65] one sees, what about that? It is the condition of mind. If the condition of mind is not harmonious, if the rhythm of mind is not regular, then the real thing is so mixed up that you yourself cannot read it. It is just like a letter written in darkness [66]that a[67] person did not see it while writing. But at the same time it is a letter written, it has an idea behind it. Even if the very person who has written it in a dark room may not be able to read it, yet it is a letter. When man cannot understand the meaning of his dream, it is not that his dream has no S.[68] It only means that his letter has so[69] become[70] so mixed up that man[71] cannot read his own letter. But the most interesting thing to study in the dream is its symbolical expression. As subtle be[72] the mentality of the person, so more[73] symbolical will be his dreams. The dreams of the poets, the dreams of the prophets have been so S.[74] that they are just like a beautifully written novel.

Sometimes the symbology is so subtle that it seems an art in itself, a[75] nature's art that produces such a dream. No doubt, if a simple person has

---

53. Sk.sh.: P-o-M. characteristically used only the plural of this word; "phenomenon" in a.o.d.
54. Er.tp.: "that sound" instead of "the sound that"
55. Er.tp.: "for receiving impressions" instead of "to receive the impression"; a.o.d.: "impressions" instead of "impression"
56. Fm.hw., er.tp.: "as" instead of "like"
57. Fm.hw.: "accommodation" instead of "accommodations"
58. Er.tp.: "for receiving" instead of "to receive"
59. Ibid.: "in" instead of "to"
60. Ibid.: "I should say" omitted
61. Fm.hw., er.tp.: "the" added
62. Er.tp.: "of" added
63. A.o.d.: "a" omitted; (Hq.tp.)Sk.cr.: "a" inserted
64. Er.tp.: "say" instead of "ask"
65. Ibid.: "that" added
66. Ibid.: "so" added
67. Fm.hw.: "the" instead of "that a"
68. Sk.sh.: "S." in sh. abbr. for "significance", and written out in a.o.d.
69. Sk.sh.: "so" crossed out, and omitted a.o.d.
70. Fm.hw.: "becomes" instead of "has so become"
71. Er.tp.: "he" instead of "man"
72. Fm.hw.: "The more" instead of "As subtle be"; er.tp.: "As subtle as" instead of "As subtle be"
73. Er.tp.: "is, so" instead of ", so more" to read "person is, so symbolical"
74. Sk.sh.: "S." abbr. in lh. for "symbolical", and "symbolical" in a.o.d.
75. Er.tp.: "a" omitted

a silly dream it is not to be surprised[76]. But furthermore one reads from the dream something of the past, something[77] of the present, something[77] of the future, and[78] one might ask when does cease[79] the past and when the future? And[80] the answer is: when a person's mind is focused [81]he sees the both. The future, the future.[81] If his mind is concerned[82] with the present, he sees the present. But [83]still greater phenomena[84] of [85]dream is that sometimes [86]dream proves to be a medium or[87] communication between two souls. And those,[88] this[89] communication is not limited only[90] to this world, but this communication[91] extends even to the next world.

Then there is another side of revelation which is expressed[92], but[93] by a poet, by[94] a musician, and[95] by[94] a philosopher, but by[96] a thinker. And this is called inspiration. A person may try to write a piece of music perhaps for the whole year and may not succeed in what he wanted to create. And there might come one[97], in one moment a whole symphony that the writer has no power[98], it is perfect in itself. By altering[99] he would be committing[100] a fault to[101] the harmony of the inner life, because it is given to him as something already made. No real poet, no real composer, no true thinker will deny for one moment if[102] it is not his own experience. It seems that these things he cannot create from his brain; that there is a factory already creating these things. By his communication with this factory, he gets things ready made. Once I[103] asked a poet who had written a most beautiful poetry and he

---

76. Ibid.: "a thing to be surprised at" instead of "to be surprised"
77. Ibid.: "something" omitted
78. Fm.hw.: "and" omitted
79. Sk.sh.: "cease" rewritten in lh. also, then crossed out and "sees" added in lh.; a.o.d.: "one see" instead of "cease"
80. Sk.sh.: "And" crossed out; included in Hq.tp., but omitted in other documents
81. Hq.tp., er.tp.: "on the past he sees the past, when on the future he sees the future." instead of "he sees the both. The future, the future."; Fm.hw.: "on the past he sees the past, if upon the future he sees the future."
82. Fm.hw.: "(concentrated)" added before "concerned"
83. Fm.hw., er.tp.: "a" added
84. Sk.sh.: P-o-M. characteristically used the plural of this word; "phenomenon" in a.o.d.
85. Er.tp.: "the" added
86. Ibid.: "a" added
87. Ibid.: "of" instead of "or"
88. Sk.sh.: "those," crossed out, and omitted in a.o.d.
89. Fm.hw.: "that" instead of "this"
90. Hq.tp., er.tp.: "only" omitted
91. Er.tp.: "it" instead of "this communication"
92. A.o.d.: "experienced" instead of "expressed"
93. Er.tp.: "only" instead of ", but"
94. Er.tp.: "by" omitted
95. Sk.sh.: "and" altered into "but"; Hq.tp.: "but" instead of "and"; Fm.hw., er.tp.: neither word included
96. Fm.hw.: "but" omitted; er.tp.: "but by" omitted
97. Sk.sh.: "one" crossed out, and omitted in a.o.d.
98. Fm.hw., er.tp.: "to alter" added
99. Er.tp.: "it" added
100. Fm.hw.: "commit" instead of "be committing"
101. Fm.hw.: "towards" instead of "to"; er.tp.: "against" instead of "to"
102. Fm.hw., er.tp.: "that" instead of "if"
103. Er.tp.: "a mystic" instead of "I"; (er.tp.)Sk.cr., Sk.an.: "I" reinstated

brought[104] to show [105]it to me. I asked him[105]: "Will you kindly explain to me the meaning of a certain line in that poem?" The radiance of the poet's face became pale because he had not thought about it, but after seeing this[106] line, he found he did not know himself the meaning. I[107] said: "I,[108] you need not trouble about it". It is that[109] which is called inspiration, and[110] it is this phenomena[111] that makes the creative soul like [112]a poet, like[113] a prophet, like[113] a composer to bow his hand[114] to something high, to something beyond comprehension. Unless[115] a poet, an artist or a thinker has not come to this stage[116], when his own creation surprises him so much that he no longer can own his creation, so long he has not really been the[117] real genius. Besides, inspiration does not want pleading, [118] diamond does not want bugles and trumpets to call it a diamond. Its light calls it a diamond. And so is true inspiration, that[119] great composers, the poets who have written real[120] inspirational things, the world never will be tired of them[121]. It may be[122] *milj.*[123] of years it[124] will still be alive, it will still have[125] the same impression upon[126] the world.

And[127] when we go[128] further than this, we find that[129] the highest aspect of revelation, which alone can be called a revelation, that comes from within. It makes the heart self-revealing. It is just like a new birth of the soul. It is just like the waking[130] of the heart. And when such a thing has begun in a person, he begins to feel a communication with all things and all

---

104. Fm.hw.: "brought it" instead of "he brought"; er.tp.: "had brought" instead of "he brought"
105. Fm.hw.: "to me" instead of "it to me. I asked him"; er.tp.: "it to me. I asked him" omitted; (er.tp.)Sk.cr., Sk.an.: reinstated
106. A.o.d.: "that" instead of "this"
107. Er.tp.: "The mystic" instead of "I"; (er.tp.)Sk.cr., Sk.an.: "I" reinstated
108. Sk.sh.: "I," crossed out, and omitted in a.o.d.
109. Hq.tp., er.tp.: "this" instead of "that"
110. Fm.hw.: "and" omitted
111. Sk.sh.: P-o-M. characteristally used only the plural of this word; "phenomenon" in a.o.d.
112. Er.tp.: "that of" added
113. Ibid.: "like" omitted
114. Sk.sh.: "hand" in sh. retraced to read "head"; a.o.d.: "head" instead of "hand"
115. Fm.hw., er.tp.: "until" instead of "unless"
116. Ibid.: "state" instead of "stage"
117. Er.tp.: "a" instead of "the"
118. Sk.sh.: a blank; Fm.hw.: "a" added; er.tp.: ". The" added
119. A.o.d.: ". The" instead of ", that"
120. Er.tp.: "really" instead of "real"
121. Ibid.: "them" omitted
122. Ibid.: "after" instead of "It may be"
123. Sk.sh.: "*milj.*" in lh. (Dutch for "*miljoen*") abbr. for "millions"; Hq.tp., er.tp.: "millions" Fm.hw.: "thousands" instead of "millions"
124. Er.tp.: "what they have written" instead of "it"
125. Ibid.: "and it will still make" instead of "it will still have"
126. Fm.hw.: "on" instead of "upon"
127. Ibid.: "And" omitted
128. A.o.d.: "come" instead of "go"
129. Sk.sh.: "that" in sh., traced over to read "comes"; omitted a.o.d.
130. A.o.d.: "wakening" instead of "waking"

beings. Every person he meets[131] before he has spoken a[132] word with him[133], he begins to communicate with his soul. Before he has asked anyone a question to answer[134], there he,[135] the soul, before that[136], begins to speak its own history. Every person stands before him as an open letter, and every object before him is like an open book. No longer then exists in that person that continual "why?" that you see in the[137] different people. "Why?" no longer is there because he finds the answer of[138] every question in himself, and as long as that answer is not created, [139]all the learning [140]exists in the world and was[141] taught to man, that continual "why?" will exist.

Now the question is that[142]: How one arrives to[143] this revelation? And the answer is that there is nothing in the whole, whole[144] universe which is not to be found in man. Only if[145] he cared[146] to find it out. But if he will[147] find[148] out, no one will give[149] him. For truth is not learned. The[150] truth is discovered. It is with this belief that the sages of the East went in the[151] all[152] solitude and sat with[153] their meditations in order to give that revelation an opportunity to come up, to rise. Of course[154] as the[155] life is at the present day, there is hardly time for a man today to give to such solitudes[156]. But that does not mean that man must keep ignorant of the best that is in himself. For when we compare with this great bliss which may be called revelation, all other treasures of the earth, they cannot be compared. And there is[157] everything that [158] occupies man, to earn[159] the things of the

---

131. Er.tp.: "Every person he meets" omitted
132. A.o.d.: "one" instead of "a"
133. Er.tp.: "a person he meets" instead of "him"
134. Fm.hw., er.tp.: "to answer" omitted
135. Sk.sh.: "there he," crossed out, and omitted in a.o.d.
136. Fm.hw., er.tp.: ", before that" omitted
137. Er.tp.: "the" omitted
138. Fm.hw.: "on" instead of "of"
139. Fm.hw., er.tp.: "with" added
140. A.o.d.: "that" added
141. Er.tp.: "has been" instead of "was"
142. Fm.hw., er.tp.: "that" omitted
143. Sk.sh.: an illegible pencil mark is written above "to"; Fm.hw., er.tp.: "at" instead of "to"
144. A.o.d.: the second ", whole" omitted (Fm.hw. has a partial, illegible word here)
145. Fm.hw., er.tp.: ", if only" instead of ". Only if"
146. Er.tp.: "cares" instead of "cared"
147. Hq.tp., er.tp.: "not" added
148. Er.tp.: "it" added
149. Ibid.: "it" added
150. Fm.hw.: "The" omitted
151. Er.tp.: "into" instead of "in the"
152. Sk.sh.: "all" in sh. crossed out, and omitted a.o.d.
153. Er.tp.: "in" instead of "with"
154. Ibid.: "No doubt" instead of "Of course"
155. Fm.hw., er.tp.: "the" omitted
156. Ibid.: "solitude" instead of "solitudes"
157. A.o.d.: "therefore" instead of "there is"
158. Sk.sh.: a blank
159. Er.tp.: "in earning" instead of "to earn"

world, cannot be too[160] important as[161] to[162] sacrifice that privilege of having revelation.

[163] Considering this now[164] the Sufi Movement gives a facility to those who wish to take[165] the path of meditation. There is no pretence on the part of this Movement to teach[166] anyone. For God alone is the teacher and God alone can teach, and it is the grace of God by which[167] revelation comes and not by the teaching of man. The service that mankind[168] can give[169] to his brother, [170]in helping him to prepare for that bliss which can only come by the grace of God.

[171]Thank you all for your sympathetic response. May God bless.[171]

---

160. Ibid.: "so" instead of "too"
161. Hq.tp.: "as" omitted; (Hq.tp.)Sk.cr.: reinstated
162. Er.tp.: "that he must" instead of "as to"
163. Sk.sh.: a space, apparently Sk. missed words, or a sentence
164. Fm.hw.: "now" omitted
165. A.o.d.: "try" instead of "take"
166. Er.tp.: "of teaching" instead of "to teach"
167. Ibid.: "by the grace of God that" instead of "the grace of God by which"
168. Fm.hw.: "man" instead of "mankind"
169. Er.tp.: "render" instead of "give"
170. A.o.d.: "is" added (inserted in type in Hq.tp. above the space before "in")
171. Fm.hw., er.tp.: closing omitted: "Thank you . . . . May God bless."

Sakina's shorthand reporting

Rue de Loxum
25 May '24 [1]

[2]

[3]Beloved ones of God,

I would like to speak a few words on the idea of sacredness.[3] The feeling of sacredness comes from that profound depth of the heart, which may be called [4]divine chamber; and therefore it is the religious feeling which is to be valued, rather than the outward form. The[5] people have called, in all ages, those who did not worship in the same form as themselves, heathen or pagan. And this hatred has caused all the wars and disagreements between the religions of the world. However high, beautiful or wonderful the religious form may be, if there is no sincerity of the heart it is nothing. Therefore the true religion is that sentiment which is to be found in the deepest depth of our being. And when once that [6]form is taken, when once that[6] sentiment has become real, one naturally begins to respect the same sentiment in another person.

[7] I have very often seen the sign of [8]true religious person, a person who is truly religious; if he sees another person, whatever religion he belongs, occupied in his way of worship, he respects him, because he feels the same feeling in his heart. It is just like the language of the mother, that the sentiment that a mother has for her child. She may go in[9] the North pole

---

Documents:

Sk.sh. = Sakina Furnée's shorthand reporting of the lecture newly transcribed by B.v.d.B.

Hq.st. = a stencilled copy made at Headquarters, Geneva, for the Religious Gatheka series, to be distributed to the Sufi Centres.

Sk.tp. = a typescript made by Sakina from "Hq.st.", identical in wording and therefore not mentioned in the notes. A copy of this tp. has one editing change, shown in note 9.

Notes:

1. Hq.st.: location and date omitted
2. Sk.sh.: the titles: "The Idea of Sacredness" as well as "Religious Gatheka" were added later above the discourse; Hq.st.: "Religious Gatheka." and "Number 38" added, followed by the Sufi Invocation (see List), then the title: "The Idea of Sacredness."
3. Hq.st.: sentence omitted: "Beloved . . . sacredness."
4. Ibid.: "the" added
5. Ibid.: "The" omitted
6. Ibid.: "form is taken, when once that" omitted
7. Sk.sh.: a blank
8. Hq.st.: "the" added
9. Sk.tp.: "in" put in parentheses and "to" written above, in unknown hw., on a copy of Sk.tp.

and see a mother from quite a different part of the land, but she will know her feeling; she may not, may not[10] know the language. Therefore the[11] religion is the religious sentiment, sacred sentiment. Religion is not a form. [12] And if that[13] sentiment is there, then one respects that sentiment in every form that[14] may be. There is a saying,[15] story: that Moses[16] was passing through a[17], around, an isle[18], and he saw there a young farmer, a young boy who had perhaps for the first time heard a religious sermon and who[19] heard the name of God. This farmer, sitting there, leaning against a tree in the[20] nature, was calling to the God whose name he had heard in the sermon. He said to God:[21] "If I ever saw you, if you came near[22], you cannot imagine what I would not do for you. I would take you home and give you all the nice food I can make for you, and my best clothes I would give you and I would take such great care of you. If the wolf came, I would first give my life to the wolf before it could touch you. If you only knew how I love you, you would certainly come to me." Here Moses happened to pass that way and heard this discourse of the young man. M.[23] said to [24]lad: "What are you saying? God who is the protector of all, you cannot protect. No danger can touch him, he is above all danger. Wolf and tiger and lion, all are his, he[25] made them. He does not depend upon our earthly food". The boy felt such a feeling of despair that he did not know where to go and what to say and what to think. And as Moses went further he received[26] as he, he used[27] to receive[28] the voice, the message of God. [29] The voice said: "Now[30] what have you done Moses? We sent you to the earth to bring closer those who love us. You have separated them. Every lover of ours pictures us according to his mentality. We do not concern ourselves in what way he approaches us. For we know his deepest feeling towards us." It is to learn this, to understand

---

10. Hq.st.: this second ", may not" omitted
11. Ibid.: "the" omitted
12. Sk.sh.: a blank
13. Hq.st.: "this" instead of "that"
14. Ibid.: "it" instead of "that"
15. Ibid.: "a saying," omitted
16. Moses (see List)
17. Sk.sh.: "a" crossed out
18. Hq.st.: although in her sh. book, Sk. wrote "around, an isle" in lh., a.o.d. have "countryside" instead
19. Ibid.: "had" instead of "who"
20. Ibid.: "the" omitted
21. Ibid.: ": 'O God'," instead of "to God:"
22. Ibid.: "here" instead of "near"
23. Sk.sh.: "M." abbr. in lh. for "Moses"; written out in a.o.d.
24. Hq.st.: "the" added
25. Hq.st.: "has" added
26. Ibid.: "perceived" instead of "received"
27. Sk.sh.: "he used" in sh. with "used" in lh. added above; a.o.d.: "he used" instead of "he, he used"
28. Hq.st.: "perceive" instead of "receive"
29. Sk.sh.: a blank
30. Ibid.: "Now" crossed out, and omitted in a.o.d.

this idea that the Sufi Movement has this U.W.[31] that in this Universal Worship, whatever form a person has, it does not matter, as long as he believes in God. He may come[32] with other human beings, without thinking he believes[33] in this or that. This worship does not take away anyone from his [34] own way, it only presents before every,[35] everyone his own scripture. In this service one begins to train oneself to love one's own religion and to tolerate the religion[36] of the others.

At this time when the world is divided into so many sections one working against another, it is most necessary that humanity must at least unite in God. For whatever difference there may be among human beings, before God there is no difference. He is the Father of all humanity and we all go before him as his children. This Universal Worship inspired[37] us of this. And this Universal Worship prepares us to sympathize with one another and to be blessed by all forms of wisdom which have come to us by different great teachers of humanity.

There is one God. There is one truth, so,[38] reality, there cannot be many religions, there is only one religion. And it is by the realization of this truth that we shall be truly benefited by what is called religion.

God bless you.

[39]

---

31. Ibid.: "U.W." abbr. in lh. for "Universal Worship" (see List); written out in a.o.d.
32. Hq.st.: "together" added
33. Ibid.: "his belief" instead of "he believes"
34. Sk.sh.: an illegible cross out
35. Hq.st.: "every," omitted
36. Ibid.: "religions" instead of "religion"
37. Ibid.: "reminds" instead of "inspired"
38. Ibid.: "in" added and comma after "so" omitted
39. Ibid.: "To be read at the Service of the Universal Worship" added

Sakina Furnée's typescript

---

[1]

The Hague, May 29, 1924
Anna Paulownastraat, 78.[2]

Beloved Ones of God,

[3]I ask your indulgence to the subject of this evening: The Church of All.[3] The religious side of the Sufi Movement is named: Church of All. Why do we call it Church of All? Because it contains all churches. It is likened to the League of Nations—it does not stand for one nation, but for all nations. This is the same ideal which the Church of All holds.

Now coming to the subject of religion. The less spoken of it, the better it is. For religion is something which touches the depths of the heart, and every person has a certain conception of religion. And it is that conception which he holds as something sacred. By expressing freely, one can easily hurt that conception which another one is holding as sacred. Nevertheless, the need of the Church of All has been felt in all times. In ancient times it has been the ideal of the great prophets to bring the whole humanity in one religion. But as humanity has variety of conception, it has not always been easy.

Now I should like to explain what religion consists of. Of five principal things: belief in God, adoration of the spiritual ideal, moral conception, the form of worship, and the philosophy of life. When we come to the variety of religions in the world, some believe in one God, some in many gods. Some are monotheists, some pantheists. In this way the conception of God changes among the civilized people of the world. It is to be thankful that the time does not exist any longer in which every family had its own God.

Documents:

Sk.tp. = a typescript prepared by Sakina Furnée or under her supervision. Two words were added in ink, indicated by "(Sk.tp.)Sk.cr."

Hq.st. = a stencil prepared at Headquarters, Geneva, and included in a collection of *Addresses to Cherags and Sirajs* (though this address was not given as such).

A large part of this lecture, further edited, was included in a later edition of *The Unity of Religious Ideals* as part of an added chapter on "The Universal Worship" for Volume IX (1963) of *The Sufi Message* series. This in not included in the notes.

Notes:

1. Sk.tp.: "ADDRESS ON THE CHURCH OF ALL" added at top, and "Inner Teachings of Sufi Inayat Khan (1882-1927)" below, and the Sufi Invocation (see List)
2. Hq.st.: date included, but city and address omitted
3. Ibid.: this sentence omitted

Now how does the Sufi look at the question about God? Does he believe in one God? If he believes in one God, how can he tolerate the belief in many gods? The answer is that the point of view of the Sufi is to bring peace among the different believers. He does not differ from them; he sees their point of view. He sees that those who have many gods also worship[4] God. They worship the different attributes of God. The great ones, in order to make God intelligible to man, have given him different names. They make man see clearly the divine manifestations. It is therefore that the wise ones have given different gods. As there is a saying: "To understand all is to forgive all"[5]. It is according to this saying that the Sufi looks upon life. Even he is willing to tolerate the conception of many gods, having the realization of one God.

Then arises the question: but one is or[6] a pantheist or a monotheist. Yes, many who look at theology from outside say they are two distinct ideas upon God. And they would be willing to take up one idea, not two. But in reality it is of great necessity that these two opposing ideas should exist. When you look at the centre it is one line; when you look at the ends, there are two. Monotheism is as important in life as pantheism. No one can be pantheist if he was not once a monotheist. And if one began to be pantheist, one would never understand one God. One may say: Yes, the idea of pantheism I can understand. God is in every being. Another says: It is too abstract for me. I cannot find God in such an idea. I want to have God before me exclusive, separate, remote. In reality the monotheistic idea is necessary in order to realize fully the beauty of the pantheistic idea.

Then there is the idea of God being personal. Some say: It is very difficult for me to imagine God as a person. It is like limiting God. Another says: If God is not a person, he no longer exists. He might just as well be air, space, time. Both of these have reasons. The Sufi makes himself ready to look at both from the point of view of those who hold them. And he finds from it that the natural way is that from the personal ideal you can rise to the complete ideal, the complete ideal embracing the seen and unseen, within and without, the Absolute.

Therefore the Sufi has no difficulty either with the worshipper of one God or of many gods, because he sees from their point of view. He gives their point of view a place in his life; he sees the natural development of human conception; from the small perception it expands to the highest ideal. But if one asks the Sufi, Yes, you tolerate different conceptions, but what is

---

4. Sk.tp.: "one" added in ink; Hq.st.: "one" not included
5. The well-known saying in English appears to have originated from Mme de Staël, *Corinne* (1807), 18:5: "Tout comprendre rend très indulgent" (of which the English form is a very inexact translation). See Burton Stevens, ed., *The House Book of Quotations*, (10th ed., New York, 1967).
6. P-o-M. sometimes used the construction "or . . . or" instead of "either . . . or"

your conception? Well, he says, there is no such a thing as the Sufi conception, but I have my personal conception. The God who is considered by people as the judge and creator, as the Lord of heaven, to me he is my beloved. He is my beloved ideal who only deserves all my devotion. He is all the beauty that is to be loved. Therefore as the relation of beloved the Sufi establishes his relation with God. His worship of God is his expansion of heart. His love for all beings, for every being, is his love for God. He cannot find anyone to love except God because in all he sees God. If it is shown in devotion to parents, to wife, to children, if it is shown to neighbours, to a friend, or in tolerating enemies, the Sufi considers this action of his towards God. In this way he fulfills in life the teaching of the Bible: "We live and move and have our being in God"[7].

Now coming to the second ideal of religion, the spiritual ideal in man. If man has ever found God manifest on earth, he is manifest in the godly. Whenever humanity has touched the height of civilization, they see divine manifestation in a human being, a human being who in his life expressed God the most. Before some that great ideal has appeared and they have called him Jesus Christ. In other parts of the world, in other races, the same manifestation they have called Buddha. At the same period, in a certain race, this manifestation who impressed human beings with the divine was called Moses. In another period, before certain people, the same manifestation they knew as Mohammed. People followed them, loved them, adored them, helped them in their difficulties. Through them a certain manner of living a harmonious life was given to their followers. The world has always had different manifestations whenever it was needed. But it is the limitation of mankind that made them dispute the great personalities they themselves adored. They have tried to question the greatness, the goodness of the teacher of the other community. In this way humanity has become divided into sections. The Sufi looks at it from a tolerant point of view. He says: To have devotion for a spiritual ideal, for a human personality, is an individual outlook. One has to leave it to him. A person who esteems Buddha, let him; who holds Moses in high esteem, let him; one who has devotion for Jesus Christ, let him. The Sufi says: It is too sacred to interfere with the sacred ideal of the teacher one holds in esteem. In this way he unites with them all. If one asks the Sufi: What is your ideal, which ideal do you hold?, he says: One teacher, the only one who has always been there, who claimed to be alpha and omega, the first and the last. All these different names which the world holds in high esteem are the name of one personality. Whatever name it is, the Sufi feels exaltation. He sees one personality behind all those names. In other words, he calls his divine ideal with all

7. Acts 17:28; St. Paul, speaking in Athens, cites the words "In him we live and move and have our being", sometimes attributed to Epimenides (c. 600 B.C.E.) of Crete

those names.

Now coming to the third idea, the idea of morals. The followers of one religion dispute with the followers of the other religion for not having the same moral, the same standard of moral. But it is presumption on the part of mankind to judge[8] by his own standard of moral. It is not just to try to judge another community from their point of view. There is no such action which one can point out as sin or virtue, nor right or wrong. Things become right or wrong according to the place or the right or wrong time. Good and evil are understood by a natural insight of the soul. The soul is beautiful and it looks out for beauty. What is lacking beauty, it is that which may be called evil. What is beautiful, it is that which is called virtue. One may preach all through life: It is not this, it is not that, and one will always find to be mistaken. No doubt, for a certain time a certain rule of life was given. But on that rule of life it is not right to judge the religions of different people. Therefore the word of the Sufi is to wake in his heart sensitiveness which will make him able to distinguish right for[9] wrong, good for evil. And with the ever increasing wakening of this spirit of sensitiveness, the Sufi builds his character. The Sufi is ready to tolerate another, to forgive another. He takes himself to task if he lacks beauty in expression, in thought, in speech, or in action.

Now coming to the fourth question, the form of worship. The form of worship of all different religions must be different. But it depends upon what one is accustomed to, what is akin with one's nature. One cannot make a common rule and say: This form is wrong and that form is right. One person will perhaps feel more exaltation in the form of worship if there is some art in it; it excites his emotional nature. Music, pictures, sculpture, perfumes, colours, light, all these make an effect upon a person. Another person can concentrate better if there is nothing in the room, if nothing strikes his attention. It is all a matter of temperament. There is nothing wrong if one prefers the first thing or the next thing. The Sufi sees the variety of forms as different ideals. He does not give importance to the outer expression. If there is a sincere spirit behind it, if a person has a feeling of worship, it does not matter what form of worship it is. In the church, in an open place, everywhere there is an answer to the feeling of worship. In order to make a facility to people of all different religions, this Universal Worship has been inaugurated, which is called the Church of All. It is not a church included among the variety of churches as an additional church. It is a church which gives facility to those belonging to different religions to worship together. Also it is a practice of respecting the great ones who have come from time to time to serve humanity. Those who have taught wisdom

8. (Sk.tp.)Sk.cr.: "another" inserted in ink; Hq.st.: "another" included in type
9. Both typescripts have "for", although "distinguish . . . from" is the usual construction

in different scriptures are read at the altar of the Church of All. Nevertheless, no Sufi is compelled to even attend this Church of All. A Sufi, to whatever church he goes, is a Sufi. Sufi is a point of view, a certain outlook on life. It is not necessarily a particular church.

And now we come to the fifth idea, the idea of the philosophical side of religion. Through Universal Worship what one gathers is that there is one source from which all scriptures have come, and that it is by one spirit that all great persons have come, and that in spite of the beliefs of many gods, there is only one God. And by this we come to the realization we seek through worship, through devotion: that there is one only truth. If ever anyone reached it or will reach it, it is one and the same truth. Truth can be traced in all the great scriptures of the world and is taught by all the great ones who have come from time to time. Nothing, a community, a church, or a belief, should keep one back from that realization in which resides the purpose of life. Verily truth is the seeking of every soul and it is truth which can save.

God bless you.

A typescript prepared under Sakina Furnée's supervision

June, 1st, 1924
Anna Paulownastraat 78, The Hague

Class-Lecture [1]

This evening I should like to speak a few words to my *mureeds*[2] on the subject of mureeds' obligations. There are five necessary obligations for a mureed who conscientiously realizes mureedship as something sacred and worth-while in his life.

The first obligation is devotion: devotion first to truth, to the cause which brought you that, to the teacher whom you have given your confidence, and to humanity for whom you prepare yourself to be best servants. If this first obligation is lacking, then a great deal is lacking. When this first step is rightly taken, then the whole journey is right. When there is weakness, the safety of the[3] journey is not secure.

The second obligation is contemplation. Contemplation upon ideas which you will read in *Gathas*[4] and in *Gathekas*[4]; for it is not only once going over them, but going over them often and often which opens communication with the owner of the idea, and where you come in touch with the creative spirit of wisdom, rather than the words which you read in the Gathas. If one reads them once and thinks: I have understood, one may remain in the thought of satisfaction, but thereby one gains little. It is the contemplation on an idea which works as seeds sown in a fertile ground and will bear in the soul the desired fruit. But when the seed is sown and is not watered, it will die out. And so is contemplation upon ideas which are not only[5] simple ideas as words outwards suggested, but creative in nature and character.

And the third thing necessary is meditation. Whatever be the exercise prescribed to you of holding a thought in mind or breathing

---

Documents:

Sk.tp.1 = a typescript prepared under Sakina Furnée's supervision, double-spaced on fine paper, from an unknown original.

Sk.tp.2 = a later typescript, also prepared by Sakina Furnée or under her supervision, showing a few differences, mostly copying errors. Some of these were later corrected by Sk., indicated by "(Sk.tp.2)Sk.cr." in the notes.

Notes:

1. Sk.tp.2: "Class-Lecture" omitted
2. Sk.tp.1,2: *mureed* is a word used for a Sufi initiate (see Glossary)
3. Sk.tp.2: "the" omitted
4. Sk.tp.1,2: a category of the teachings of P-o-M. (see Glossary)
5. Sk.tp.2: "only" omitted

rhythmically or of repeating a phrase a certain number of times, this all comes under the heading of meditation. If it is not the last meditation, it is perhaps the first. If you will do the exercise at a certain appointed hour regularly every day, it will become a part of your nature. It may seen apparently mechanical. But what is our life in the world? What it is maintained by? By mechanism. In spite of all goodness and sincerity [6]we may have, if we do not maintain rightly the mechanism of our being, we cannot be happy, we cannot accomplish anything. The value of goodness and sincerity[6] is great, but the value of mechanism is not any less. When you practice in meditation you only wind the subconscious mind. After this winding it goes on working along the same line, the same idea. In spite of all you do outwardly, inwardly your subconscience[7] is continuing upon the same idea and is sure thereby to bring about desired results. It is therefore an error to ever think that this is something mechanical and to say: I cannot go on with it. One might just as well say: This body is mechanical, I no longer must live in it.

When a person is unaccustomed to these practices, they seem new and strange and it is likely that a person thinks: All these things belong to another world. It is not so. All belong to this human world. These are artificial methods, but we are artificial people. If our lives were not artificial, there would be no need of artificial methods. We would have been blessed as birds are in nature with that freedom, happiness and peace. But we human beings with our evolution have made ropes to tie our hands and feet. Now it is necessary to break them and set ourselves free. This is the meaning of meditation; an artificial method adopted to discern our natural being.

The fourth thing to remember is exaltation. If a person has no imagination, he cannot reach exaltation if life will not help exaltation. Why a person is a poet, an artist, a musician is through imagination. Lack of exaltation comes by [8]pessimistic attitude in life, a hopeless condition where one has made a wall of hopelessness. I expect from my mureeds to rise above this paralysis, to be hopeful every day, in whatever condition; to keep the imagination active in spite of all bad experiences and failures. Failures are only to teach us to make a success. Besides, thinking about the hopeless side of our own nature keeps away that exaltation. We must open the door to exaltation which is the most sacred. For an instance, a little silence, an offered prayer is a natural exaltation that comes to you. If you deny it, if you think: I feel nothing, then you mar it. Every spiritual tendency has a natural

6. Sk.tp.2: this entire passage inadvertently omitted in the typing; (Sk.tp.2)Sk.cr.: the passage carefully added in ink at the bottom of the page on one copy
7. Sk.tp.1,2: this word, “subconscience”, is typed in both typescripts, which is not an established usage; the standard noun form in P-o-M.’s day was “subsconsciousness”, although now “subsconscious” is the commonly used noun.
8. Sk.tp.1: “a” added in pencil; Sk.tp.2: “a” included in type

exaltation, it turns the key of the fountain of exaltation which is called in Sanskrit *wajd*[9], which means "secret of joy". Even the simple things of life: food and walk, swimming and running give joy to a person. And more is coming out of prayer. Silence is most precious in itself. Of course, in spite of all shortcomings, falls and infirmities, we must hold on to that sacred side of life, not be drowned and pulled down, but allow ourselves to be lifted. Sacred feeling is always to be found: if we touch it, never to lose it. All things that pull us asunder are[10] like storms. It is still to cling to that vow of a sacred idea in which is all virtue, religion, piety and exaltation, one's life's safety and security.

Besides this is another ideal for a mureed to consider: that is to express in life all that benefit which he derives from his practices and studies. Not by correcting people of their faults, nor by disputing about right or wrong, nor by pretending to be wiser than others, but in a most humble way bringing to others benefit even without their knowing; they must only realize some benefit not knowing from where. In this way to try to help our fellow-men is the fulfilment of our life's purpose.

God bless you.

---

9. Sk.tp.1,2: the Sufi term for ecstasy (see Glossary), actually Arabic rather than Sanskrit
10. Sk.tp.2: "are" omitted; (Sk.tp.2)Sk.cr: "are" added in ink

Sakina Furnée's typescript

Sunday, June 1st, 1924
The Hague, Anna Paulownastraat 78

[1]

[2]

Beloved ones of God,

I would like to say a few words on the subject of [3]the need of religion in the life of man[3]. Religion is of the greatest need at whatever period in the past or future. No doubt, according to the evolution of man, the form of religion has changed. Because the form depended upon customs, upon the manner of the country, also on the psychology of the followers of that religion. These different changes made in different religions, have they sprung from the intellectual spirit of man? No, not at all. For there is another part of man's spirit, the divine part. It is the wakening of that part which raises a fountain, and that fountain is religion. In the ancient history of India there are a great many examples where people with stately position[4] wanted to bring another religion. But they never succeeded, for religion does not come from that source. Its source is divine.

If truth and falsehood are distinct and different, then what is the difference between them? Truth is God, and unreal is all this nature which

Documents:

Sk.tp.1 = a typescript prepared by Sakina Furnée or under her supervision, offering at several points alternative readings in parentheses, apparently comparing two documents (one of which was very similar to AP.tp., the other no longer to be found in the archives). Even though this may not be the oldest document, it is presented here as it contains the fullest evidence as to what P-o-M. may have said.

AP.tp. = a typescript probably from the Sufi Centre at the Anna Paulownastraat, 78, The Hague, where the lecture was given. Later, Sakina made corrections on a copy of this typescript, probably working from the Sk.tp.1, indicated by "(AP.tp.)Sk.cr." in the notes.

Sk.tp.2 = a double-spaced typescript on fine paper made by Sakina Furnée or under her supervision, mostly the same text as AP.tp.

Er.tp. = another typescript, of unknown origin, possibly from the Anna Paulownastraat, which presents an abbreviated version or summary of the lecture. As it provides no further evidence of what P-o-M. may have said, it is not included in the notes.

Notes:

1. Sk.tp.1: later "(Probably given during a service)" added in ink
2. Sk.tp.2: "Devotional-Service" added top centre
3. Sk.tp.1: "the need of religion in the life of man" later underlined by hand, apparently indicating the title
4. Sk.tp.2: "positions" typed, but the "s" crossed out in type

we see before us. Therefore all that is from God is real.

But one might ask: Has man's mentality done something in religion? Yes, it has done something. Every religion has come [5](through man, when a new religion was needed.)[5] [6](in [7]that colour by which the mentality[7] was expressed.)[6] But religion itself is from divine source. Therefore the outside may be different, but the depth is the same.

At this age it seems that science is on one side, and politics on the other side, and that education is working to (supply) (substitute)[8] religion. But nothing can (supply) (replace)[9] religion.

There is a touching story of a scientist in France who did not believe all through life, who did not admit any belief in God, soul, or hereafter. But as he lived longer in the world, the need of religion was felt. But he could not accept it, as all his life he did not accept it. The wife, on the other hand, was devote[10] and religious. One day, stirred by a profound sentiment, they were talking heart to heart on the question of religion. The wife was anxious that he should accept it, and she asked him: "Do you ever feel that need of religion, of devotion which alone is (happiness) (worth-while)[11]?" The most touching answer was, "I do not admit it, yet I believe in your belief, I enjoy your sentiment. That is my religion, my only religion in life." We do not know under what guise a person keeps his religion. It may be somewhere hidden in his heart; it does not show outward perhaps. No doubt, if everyone had had his religious sentiment unexpressed, there would be no communication. Therefore there is the greatest necessity in society that we communicate our deepest religions sentiments.

Now one might ask: What is religion? What does it consist of? The answer will be: The main thing on which religion is based is belief in God ideal. And what belief in God ideal is[12]? It is belief in the incomprehensible which is even found in a child's soul. As man enjoys greatly to look at the wide space, to fix his gaze on the horizon, so there is a benefit to think on[13] the incomprehensible, to have the desire to go in its pursuit. [14](The man who

---

5. AP.tp., Sk.tp.2: "(through man, when a new religion was needed.)" omitted; (AP.tp.)Sk.cr.: at bottom of page in ink, "alternative: through man, when a new religion was needed."
6. AP.tp., Sk.tp.2: no parentheses
7. Sk.tp.1: later "that colour by which the mentality" altered in ink to "the colour of the mentality by which it"
8. Sk.tp.1: later "(substitute)" crossed out in ink, and the parentheses around "(supply)" removed; AP.tp., Sk.tp.2: "(substitute)" omitted and no parentheses around "(supply)"; (AP.tp.)Sk.cr.: "substitute for?" added in ink
9. Sk.tp.1: later "(replace)" crossed out in ink, and the parentheses around "(supply)" removed; AP.tp., Sk.tp.2: "(replace)" omitted and no parentheses around "(supply)"; (AP.tp.)Sk.cr.: "(replace)" added in ink in margin, and "for" written after "supply"
10. All the typescripts have "devote", though it should probably read "devout" or "devoted"
11. Sk.tp.1: "is" and "(worth while)" crossed out, and "brings" added in ink in the margin; AP.tp., Sk.tp.2: "(happiness)" omitted; (AP.tp.)Sk.cr.: "happiness" added in ink in margin
12. Sk.tp.1: later in ink "is" moved to before "belief" and "the" added before "God ideal"
13. Sk.tp.1: later "on" changed to "of" in ink
14. Sk.tp.1: later the whole sentence in parentheses crossed out, but then reinstated by a broken line underneath; AP.tp., Sk.tp.2: this sentence omitted

cannot perceive the soul seeks for that which he cannot attain.)[14] To supply this need, what the wise of the world have done? They have made the incomprehensible intelligible, limited in what man can easily grasp. Instead of telling of God, the Nameless, the Formless, who is beyond time and space, beyond comprehension, they made for man a form, as an artist makes a picture. They said the King, the Judge, because man knows what justice is; most Merciful and Compassionate, for man knows what is mercy and compassion. There is nothing wrong in what they have spoken to man, only God is beyond it. God cannot be spoken of. In fact, God is greater than thought can conceive, higher than ideal.

Another aspect of religion, most necessary for man, is to humble himself. For it is humility that tunes, that makes selfless. And the more selfless one becomes, the nearer one comes to reality. And before whom shall we be[15] humble? Where is the one who deserves it as much as God? [16](Man, by repeating his prayers to God, becomes selfless.)[16] [17](Therefore by the performance of religious surrendering before God, man practises humility, and in this way he becomes selfless.)[17] For in selflessness the secret of life is hidden, the pearl of immortality is (formed) (found)[18]. On the other hand, the harder the spirit of self, the more man goes wrong, and even becomes capable of cruelty. It is [19]this that Jesus Christ hints by saying: "Blessed are the poor in spirit."[20]

But besides God, man needs something else in a human being, (yet answering)[21] the fine and spiritual attributes that the soul seeks for. That he finds in man who, so to speak, is godly, who reflects God. By thinking of that person, realizing that person who is so close to his heart, man rises above limitation, and comes nearer to the divine attributes. Jewish people see in Moses[22] that godly man, Christians see him in Jesus Christ, Buddhists in Buddha, the followers of Krishna see him in Krishna. When men dispute[23] over the ideal, giving supremacy of one ideal over the other, they are like children who say[24]: My mother is more loving[25] than yours. It is nothing, it

---

15. Sk.tp.2: "be" omitted, but later added in ink
16. AP.tp., Sk.tp.2: sentence omitted; (AP.tp.)Sk.cr.: sentence written in ink
17. Sk.tp.1: later the parentheses around this sentence crossed out in ink; AP.tp., Sk.tp.2: no parentheses
18. Sk.tp.1: later in ink "(formed)" crossed out and the parentheses around "(found)" removed; AP.tp., Sk.tp.2: "(formed)" omitted and no parentheses around "(found)"
19. Sk.tp.1: later "at" added in ink
20. Matthew 5:3
21. AP.tp., Sk.tp.2: no parentheses; (AP.tp.)Sk.cr.: parentheses added in ink
22. For Moses and the other teachers who follow, see List
23. AP.tp., Sk.tp.2: "Man disputes" instead of "When men dispute"; (AP.tp.)Sk.cr.: "When" inserted in ink
24. AP.tp., Sk.tp.2: "If two children say" instead of "they are like children who say"; (AP.tp.)Sk.cr.: "If two" crossed out, "they are like" added in ink before "children" and "who" after
25. AP.tp., Sk.tp.2: "affectionate" instead of "loving"; (AP.tp.)Sk.cr.: "affectionate" crossed out and "loving" written in ink

is most childish, for each mother is good to her child. If the child understood, if he were grown up, he would consider that mother is loving[25] because of her motherhood. At the same time at the back of all these great ones, is one and the same spirit, called divinity. This spirit of divinity which was, is, and will always be, will always manifest when the need is there to look after the children of the earth.

We all, human beings, partake of the divine spirit in our heart. What exaggeration to say that Christ is in the one and not in the other. This dispute, which has lasted for a long time, is answered by Universal Worship, where all teachers are respected. This was in reality the hope of Muhammad, the wish[26] of Christ, and of Moses, that the whole humanity under one roof should pray to God. The Sufi Movement in this way is bringing Universal Worship as the future religion of the world, realizing without doubt that truth alone is successful and that success belongs alone to truth.

God bless you.

---

26. AP.tp., Sk.tp.2: "the wish" omitted; (AP.tp.)Sk.cr.: "the wish" added in ink

3 *Juni*, A.P.str. [1]

2

[3] Beloved ones of God,

My subject of this evening is The inner Life[3]: the inner life, which is represented by our inner school, which[4] is one of the three activities of the Sufi Movement. Really speaking this activity is the most important of all three.

When speaking about the inner life, in the first place I wish to say that though this is the desire of every soul, each soul is not ready to attain to this desire. Every soul does not feel the need of it. In order to feel the need of that[5], there is something required in the life of a person. Some great blow in life, a great suffering in life opens up the eyes and that which was still,

---

Documents:

Sk.sh.	=	Sakina Furnée's shorthand reporting of the lecture, newly transcribed by B.v.d.B.
Sk.tp.1	=	a typescript prepared by Sakina Furnée or under her direction, from an early unknown source.
Hq.tp.	=	a typescript made at Headquarters, Geneva, for the Religious Gatheka series.
Hq.st.	=	a stencilled copy made at Headquarters, Geneva, for distribution of the Religious Gatheka series to the Sufi Centres. It closely follows "Hq.tp." in wording. A copy of "Hq.st." has a few ink corrections in unknown handwriting.
Sk.tp.2	=	a typed copy of "Hq.st." prepared by Sakina or under her direction, nearly identical in wording, and therefore only mentioned in a few notes.
Sk.an.	=	a separate list of corrections prepared by Sakina with a note about the publication of this lecture in *The Sufi Quarterly* (see note 206).
SQ.	=	This lecture was later published in *The Sufi Quarterly*, June, 1928, Vol. IV, No. 1, pp. 28-37.

Notes:

1. Sk.sh.: "3 *Juni*", "A.P.str.", abbr. for "Anna Paulownastraat", written in lh. at very top of page ("*Juni*" is Dutch for "June"); Sk.tp.1: "The Hague" added; "June" instead of "Juni"; a.o.d.: date and location omitted
2. Sk.tp.1: title, "THE INNER LIFE" added; Hq.tp.: "Gatheka" and "Number 27" added, followed by the title, "The four pathes [sic] of the inner life." Hq.st.: "Gatheka" and "Number 27" added, followed by the Sufi Invocation (see List); later, on a copy of Hq.st., the title, "The Four Pathes [sic] of the Inner Life" inserted in unknown hw.; SQ.: title: "THE INNER SCHOOL" followed by "the late Pir-o-Murshid Inayat Khan, Founder of the Sufi Movement in the West."
3. Sk.sh.: The opening words "Beloved ones of God, my subject of this evening is" appear in sh. at the very top of the page, followed by the title and date in lh.; Hq.tp., Hq.st., SQ.: opening sentence omitted: "Beloved . . . Life."
4. A.o.d.: "which" omitted
5. A.o.d.: "this" instead of "that"

becomes moving. When the soul was still, there was its longing, but it was not felt, but since the soul begins to move, the longing is then felt. Whose soul is not longing for it? You may implore him, you may induce him a thousand times, he will not come. But the soul who is seeking for it, even if it was running from him[6], he will follow it even to the ends of the world. This is the last appetite that wakens in the innermost being of man and this is the longing for spiritual realization. After this appetite is wakened, there is no other appetite to waken. After this is[7] satisfaction, all satisfied,[8] there is no other appetite to satisfy.

And now asking[9] to the metaf.[10] side of the subject. What is it that the soul wishes to seek in the inner culture? When a person begins to realize the limitation of life, the [11] which comes at the moment when the soul feels sober, free from the intoxication of worldly life, then it begins to wonder, wonder as to the[12] life.

To one person perhaps this moment of sobriety comes once in the year, to another person once in a month, to another person once in the day, to another person it is a craving going on, continually on[13] in the mind,[14] heart. There is one person after he has gone through his busy life in the world, in his last days of the[15] age, he begins to waken to it. There is another person, perhaps he has suffered in his middle age; there is another person, perhaps quite young,[16] who begins to wonder, quite young like Buddha.

This appetite cannot be wakened in someone in whom there[17] is not wakened yet. Many people feel anxious about the dear ones, about those near to them, if they[18] will not waken. But they do not know that it is not something that you can give,[19] teach. It is something that must come by itself. It is not therefore necessary to worry about one's dear ones,[20] that they must waken to this realization. If their time is[21] not come, it is better for them not to waken. For in the East there is a belief that it is a great fault to waken

---

6. Hq.tp., Hq.st.: "it" instead of "him"
7. Sk.sh.: "this is" crossed out (see next note)
8. A.o.d.: "satisfaction is satisfied" instead of "is satisfaction, all satisfied,"
9. A.o.d.: "Now coming" instead of "And now asking"
10. Sk.sh.: "metaf." in lh. abbr. for "metaphysical", and written out in a.o.d.
11. Sk.sh.: an illegible sh. symbol, possibly "realization"; "realization" in a.o.d.
12. A.o.d.: "the" omitted
13. A.o.d.: "on" omitted
14. Sk.sh.: "mind," crossed out, and omitted in a.o.d.
15. A.o.d.: "the" omitted
16. Hq.tp., Hq.st., SQ.: "perhaps quite young," omitted
17. Sk.sh.: the structure of this sentence in the sh. appears to be irregular, but there is no gap shown for a lost word; a.o.d.: "it" instead of "there"
18. Sk.sh.: Sk. appears to connect "they" and "it" into one word, whereby she composed the word "till" inadvertently; Sk.tp.1: "it" instead of "they"; a.o.d.: "they"
19. A.o.d.: "or" added and comma omitted
20. Sk.sh.: "those near to us" in sh. added in the margin, and included in a.o.d.
21. Sk.tp.1: "has" instead of "is"

a person who is fast asleep. The[22] reason is that the very fact that he's sleeping fast shows that he needs sleep. He is not to be pitied; one must be glad that he is sleeping. Therefore those who show impatience to wake[23] their friend, their dear ones[24] in life, they must have patience. They must know that the time has not yet arrived. It would not be the right thing to wake[23] him.

What this wakening is,[25] how does it manifest? It manifests in the form of wondering. One begins to wonder: Why do I exist? Did I exist before? Shall I exist afterwards? One begins to wonder [26]on things that one has depended[26], such as [27] position, rank, environment, conditions, dear ones around one, whether they will last. If everybody wonders[28] about it, it would be very difficult; the world would not go on as it is going on now. It is just as well that few wonder about it and many sleep. What this sleep comes[29] from? It comes from the intoxication which is brought about by being absorbed in this life of the world, morning and evening, every moment. Only a few moments[30] perhaps, by sadness they are caused[31], or perhaps by a disappointment, or heart breaking[32], a moment comes when a person wonders that[33]: What I depended upon was not worth depending[34]. Now is there anything I can depend upon?

At the time when a person is wakening, if one thing has disappointed him, if one thing has shown him the false side of life, he begins to see the same thing in all things. And it can even go so far that he cannot then[35] even rely upon himself, seeing the nature of this body, [36]which he called himself, subject to death and decay; the nature of mind,[36] which he called himself, subject to change with every mood of the day. He then wishes to seek for something reliable, [37]dependable to build his hope upon; something which will not deceive him in the end. He then begins to seek a spiritual path. He then wants to find out a secret of life. He wishes to look into the mystery of

---

22. Sk.sh.: "The" in sh. crossed out and then written in the margin; included in a.o.d.
23. A.o.d.: "waken" instead of "wake"
24. Ibid.: "one," instead of "ones"; (Sk.tp.1)Sk.cr.: that comma is crossed out
25. Ibid.: "is this wakening?" instead of "this wakening is,"
26. Ibid.: "about things that one has depended on" instead of "on things that one has depended"
27. Sk.sh.: "possession," in sh. inserted above and between "as" and "position", and included in Sk.tp.1; Hq.tp., Hq.st., SQ.: "possession," is included after "position"
28. Sk.tp.1, SQ.: "wondered" instead of "wonders"
29. A.o.d.: "does this sleep come" instead of "this sleep comes"
30. Hq.tp.: "moment" instead of "moments"
31. Hq.tp., Hq.st., SQ.: "they are caused by sadness" instead of "by sadness they are caused"
32. A.o.d.: "a heart break" instead of "or heart breaking"
33. Ibid.: "that" omitted
34. Ibid.: "on" added
35. Hq.tp.: "then" omitted, then inserted in type above
36. Sk.tp.1: "which he called himself subject to death and decay. The nature of mind," omitted
37. Sk.sh.: "something which" in sh. added, apparently omitting a verb; a.o.d.: "something which is" added

religion. In whatever way he approaches, he comes to the same channel, that one channel, this[38] leads to the knowledge of truth and this[38] channel is the knowledge of self.

Now how does he acquire it? Does he acquire it by himself? Even if man acquired the spiritual knowledge by himself, there is everything in life to contradict it. And he cannot be supported unless there was another one by his side to tell him that that is right. If not, a person with the highest truth in his mind, if not confirmed by someone in whom he has trust, he[39] will not be able to realize even for himself if it is right or wrong. For truth is something to which everyone is opposed. It is not that everyone is intentionally opposed, but everyone is looking at something quite different that:[40] What is truth? And therefore it is quite natural that [41]a seeker of truth, if he finds[41] truth, that[42] the first thing is that he will begin to doubt: Am I right or am I mad? It is therefore that a mystery was made out of the truth. It is therefore this[43] was called mysticism. It is therefore that [44]initiation was given. That the teacher told to[45] his pupil: This[46] is the truth. Speak not to anyone about it. It was not selfish on the part of [47]teacher, nor [47]pupil. It was not a desire, not[48] their part to monopolize for themselves, but because the world will ridiculize[49], will laugh at it. Only I,[50] the world will look at the north when it is at the south.

There are four paths, so to speak,[51] which may be called royal roads that the mystics have taken from time to time. The one path is the path of knowledge. The other[52] path is the path of action. The other[53] path is the path of meditation, and the other[54] path is the path of devotion.

It is not necessary that one might[55] take all four paths, but they all join in the end into one path, the only path there is to tread in order to arrive at the spiritual realization. Each of these paths are[56] suited to certain personalities. The personality which is attracted to one of these paths may

---

38. A.o.d.: "that" instead of "this"
39. Sk.tp.1, SQ.: "he" omitted
40. Sk.tp.1, SQ.: "from" instead of "that:"; Hq.tp., Hq.st.: "than" instead of "that:"
41. Hq.tp., Hq.st., SQ.: "if a seeker of truth found" instead of "a seeker of truth, if he finds"
42. A.o.d.: "that" omitted
43. Ibid.: "that it" instead of "this"
44. Ibid.: "an" added
45. Ibid.: "to" omitted
46. Hq.tp., Hq.st., SQ.: "That" instead of "This"
47. Hq.tp., Hq.st., SQ.: "the" added
48. A.o.d.: "on" instead of ", not"
49. Sk.sh.: the Oxford English Dictionary has an attestation from 1615 of this verb, meaning "to make ridiculous", perhaps based on the French verb *ridiculiser*; Sk.tp.1, SQ.: "ridicule"
50. Sk.sh.: "I," crossed out, and omitted in a.o.d.; SQ.: "Only I," omitted
51. Hq.tp., Hq.st., SQ.: ", so to speak," omitted
52. Sk.tp.1, SQ.: "second" instead of "other"
53. Ibid.: "third" instead of "other"
54. Ibid.: "fourth" instead of "other"
55. Sk.tp.1, SQ.: "should" instead of "might"; Hq.tp., Hq.st.: "may" instead of "might"
56. A.o.d.: "is" instead of "are"

not be attracted to another of these paths. This[57] path of knowledge is reached by the intellectual path. It is analyzing and synthesizing at the same time. The difference between the intellectual pursuit of a scientist and of the mystic in the path is, [58]when the[59] scientist goes on with his analysis, the mystic analyses together with synthesis. And therefore what happens is this, that perhaps a scientist has taken one atom. And perhaps his whole life, he has been busy to[60] this one a.[61] and perhaps after his whole life he has not found the last to say about this one atom.

Another scientist has come and he says [62]no, not at all, this is not a kind of atom. It is radium. It is[62] quite a different thing [63]what the scientist said fifty years before. [64]Another is still discovering and says, it is not atom nor r.[64,65] After fifty years another scientist says electron, that[66] is again another thing I have discovered. The idea is that as a person goes[67] in the observation of things limited in their real[68] nature and character, of necessity, he will work[69] to make his observations[70] limited to that particular atom[71]. Whereas the mystic path is quite on[72] the contrary. He[73] is analyzing, at the same time synthesizing. The one who is guide[74] in this path, the mystic tells him one, but he knows that one will not satisfy him. He says two halves, four quarters is one, and three, thrice[75] is one. When in all these ways he understands about one, the mission of the mystic is finished. Now one might ask that[76]: What knowledge is it that [77]mystic gives? Does he bring before mankind the analysis of heaven or of [78]divine spirit? No, the mystic opens the eyes of a person to the analysis of himself. It is not the anatomy of his being[79], but the a.[80] of his mind and that which is hidden behind his mind, an anatomy which brings man to a knowledge which contradicts every other

---

57. Ibid.: "The" instead of "This"
58. Ibid.: "that" added
59. Hq.tp.: "a" instead of "the"
60. A.o.d.: "with" instead of "to"
61. Sk.sh.: "a." in lh. abbr. for "atom", and written out in a.o.d.
62. SQ.: "no, not at all, this is not a kind of atom. It is radium. It is" omitted
63. A.o.d.: "from" added
64. SQ.: "Another is still discovering and says, it is not atom nor r." omitted
65. Sk.sh.: "r." in sh. abbr. for "radium", and written out in a.o.d.
66. Sk.tp.1: "this" instead of "that"; SQ.: ": Here" instead of "electron, that"
67. Sk.tp.1, SQ.: "on" added
68. A.o.d.: "real" omitted
69. Ibid.: "have" instead of "work"
70. Ibid.: "observation" instead of "observations"
71. Sk.tp.1, SQ.: "thing" instead of "atom"
72. A.o.d.: "on" omitted
73. Sk.tp.1, SQ.: ": it" instead of ". He"
74. A.o.d.: "guided" instead of "guide"
75. Ibid.: "thirds" instead of ", thrice"
76. Ibid.: "that" omitted
77. Sk.sh.: "the" in sh. inserted and included in a.o.d.
78. Hq.tp., Hq.st., SQ.: "the" added
79. Hq.tp., Hq.st., SQ.: "body" instead of "being"
80. Sk.sh.: "a." abbr. in lh. for "anatomy", and written out in a.o.d.

knowledge which stands outside, a knowledge that proves to an intelligent person[81] victorious over all other aspects, a[82] knowledge he had hitherto learned. The distinctions, difference to[83] various meanings[84] of all things fall flat before that one knowledge which rises up just as[85] the sun is[86] rising, a knowledge which answers this[87]: the continual "why?" which is rising at every moment in the wondering mind. There remains no question. All questions are answered, for it is[88] the absence of the sun that the, [89] are not clear. It is in their[90] darkness that the[91] things do not shine.

A knowledge which answers what relation you have with your fellow-creatures, what realization[92] with every atom of this world, with the soul, with God: the blessing of this knowledge is great. For the consciousness of the relation with all things, which I have just explained, established[93] that relation which before was only in a kind of unconscious state. [94] Once such knowledge[95] received, any religion he[96] will find to be teaching the same truth that he has realized now by this knowledge; he disagrees with no one, for he understands the p.o.v.[97] of everyone.

Now coming to the other[98] aspect, and that aspect is the path of action. When a person is conscious of[99] his action towards his fellow-man[100], when one thinks of his obligations to the others, his duties to those to whom he is indebted, he begins to tread in[101] this path. A person who lives a life of righteousness, whether he is a businessman, a professional man, whatever work he does[102] in this he acts rightfully, seeks harmony, certainly he will find a[103] straight way open before him. For the reason is that they,

---

81. SQ.: "to be" added
82. A.o.d.: "of" instead of "a"
83. A.o.d.: "and differences of" instead of ", differences to"
84. Hq.tp., Hq.st., SQ.: "meaning" instead of "meanings"
85. Hq.tp., Hq.st., SQ.: "like" instead of "as"
86. A.o.d.: "is" omitted
87. Sk.sh.: "this" in sh. crossed out, and omitted in a.o.d.
88. Sk.tp.1, Hq.tp., SQ.: "in" added; (Hq.st.)Sk.cr.: "in" inserted above
89. Sk.sh.: an illegible correction; Sk.tp.1, SQ.: "things" instead of "the, [blank]"; Hq.tp., Hq.st.: "things" added in place of the blank
90. A.o.d.: "the" instead of "their"
91. Sk.tp.1, SQ.: "the" omitted
92. A.o.d.: "relation" instead of "realization"
93. A.o.d.: "establishes" instead of "established"
94. Sk.sh.: a blank
95. Sk.tp.1: "is" added after knowledge; Hq.tp., Hq.st, SQ.: "such knowledge once" instead of "Once such knowledge"
96. Sk.tp.1, SQ.: "man" instead of "he"
97. Sk.sh.: "p.o.v." abbr. in sh. for "point of view", and written out in a.o.d.
98. Sk.tp.1, SQ.: "second" instead of "other"
99. A.o.d.: "conscientious of" instead of "conscious of"; SQ.: "conscientious about" instead of "conscious of"
100. A.o.d.: "men" instead of "man"
101. Hq.st.: "in" modified to "on", then crossed out
102. SQ.: "if" added
103. Hq.tp., Hq.st.: "a" omitted; on a copy of Hq.st., an insertion line appears in lh. but no word

as[104] it is a natural desire to realize spirit[105] life, it is not something foreign that one has to earn[106], it is something that opens before one, if one was straight in one's life. But it must be understood that it is not the[107] the world does not permit, the life does not always allow one who leads[108] a straight life. It is, it makes[109] such zigzag ways made by man for his convenience and for his benefit that one finds oneself in a puzzle; one does[110] know where to go[111] out of this, where is the door. Nevertheless there are simple souls perhaps, they know very little about the knowledge of[112] metaphysics or philosophy. Perhaps they are very little seen as religious people praying, and yet they are far beyond the average man; only by living and[113] simple, right, modest life. The very fact that a man is allowed to keep straight through his life shows the proof that the[114] heaven has opened its door to that person. The way for that person is clear and open and there is nothing in the way of the path of this person. [115]Man who consults his conscience at every move[116] he makes, at every [117] is simple, who does not doubt everyone, who is easy to deal with and[118] his action, to that person the way is open. Instead of him[119] seeking God, God seeks him.

Now coming to the third path, the path of meditation. This[120] is the path of assurance. This path assures a soul of all that is in the hereafter. He does not need to experience the hereafter; he is sitting here[121] knows over[122] what it is. All one may learn intellectually about the mystery of life, by the help of meditation, [123]begins to realize for himself; he does not need to learn what heaven means, what God means, what soul means, what will come after this life. He is sitting there[124] and he can feel every sphere, every plane[125], sitting in the same place where he is. No barriers stand before him, either earthly or heavenly, for he is above barriers. He sees it all, as one

---

104. A.o.d.: "as" instead of "they, as"; (Hq.st.)Sk.cr.: "as" crossed out
105. A.o.d.: "spiritual" instead of "spirit"
106. Sk.sh.: "urn" in lh. retraced to read "earn"; Sk.tp.1: "earn"; Hq.tp., Hq.st., SQ.: "learn"
107. Sk.sh.: "it is not the" in sh. crossed out, and omitted in a.o.d.
108. A.o.d.: "to lead" instead of "who leads"
109. Ibid.: "has" instead of "is, it makes"
110. Ibid.: "not" added
111. Ibid.: "get" instead of "go"
112. Hq.tp., Hq.st., SQ.: "the knowledge of" omitted
113. A.o.d.: "a" instead of "and"
114. Hq.tp., Hq.st., SQ.: "the" omitted
115. A.o.d.: "The" added
116. Hq.tp.: "movement" instead of "move", then "-ent" crossed out
117. Sk.sh.: an illegible sh. symbol; a.o.d.: "at every" omitted and "who" added in place of the blank
118. A.o.d.: "humble in" added
119. Hq.tp.: "him" omitted; Hq.st., SQ.: "his" instead of "him"
120. Hq.tp., Hq.st., SQ.: "That" instead of "This"
121. Sk.tp.1: "and" added; Hq.tp., Hq.st.: ", he" added; SQ.: "and he" added
122. Sk.sh.: "over" in sh. crossed out, and omitted in a.o.d.
123. A.o.d.: "he" added
124. A.o.d.: "here" instead of "there"
125. Sk.sh.: the sh. symbols for "plane" and "plain" are identical; a.o.d.: "plane"

could see the earth by rising in the air.

Besides this, that great longing of[126] peace that an evolved[127] soul continually has, that great yearning of[126] that inner joy that an evolved[127] soul always is seeking; all these things are accomplished by my[128] meditation. By the help of meditation one attains power which is beyond words to explain. Besides that, health of body and strength of mind is[129] gained by it. Inspiration and power then becomes human's[130] natural possessions.

And now one might ask how is one to meditate. Many will wonder but very few will have patience to go[131] with it. The reason is that the absorption in[132] this worldly life is so great that man becomes so accustomed to the everyday activities[133] that the state of meditation becomes[134] a foreign experience to them[135]. And he[136] cannot feel at home in meditation, unless one had long patience in order to make the world of meditation his home. The great sages and the masters of humanity, they have[137] had meditation as their greatest experience and help. The great power and inspiration they did have[138] showed[139], the religion they have given, the knowledge that were not[140] brought. They all have come from meditation, they have not been poured out from a brain. Even great musicians who even[141] left living things in the world; the great poets, even without knowing, naturally they were meditative. Great things have come from them, that after[142] the world will value for ever and ever. It is not only[143] the sages, the saints and the great masters and prophets have been meditative, but even the[144] great kings, such as Solomon[145], Alexander[146], and even in[147] the life of Napoleon[146], [148]who

---

126. A.o.d.: "for" instead of "of"
127. Ibid.: "evolving" instead of "evolved"
128. Ibid.: "my" omitted
129. SQ.: "are" instead of "is"
130. Sk.sh.: "human's" in sh. crossed out; a.o.d.: "become" instead of "becomes human's"
131. Sk.tp.1, SQ.: "on" added
132. A.o.d.: "of" instead of "in"
133. Ibid.: "activity" instead of "activities"
134. Ibid.: "quite" added
135. Ibid.: "him" instead of "them"
136. Ibid.: "one" instead of "he"
137. Sk.tp.1: "they" instead of "they have"; Hq.tp., Hq.st., SQ.: "have" instead of ", they have"
138. A.o.d.: "that they have" instead of "they did have"
139. Sk.tp.1, Sk.tp.2: "shown" instead of "showed"; (Hq.st.)Sk.cr.: "showed" crossed out in lh. on a copy of Hq.st.
140. Sk.sh.: sh. distinctly reads "were not", contrary to a.o.d. which read "they have" instead of "that were not"
141. A.o.d.: "have" instead of "even"
142. Sk.sh.: "after" in sh. crossed out, and omitted in a.o.d.
143. A.o.d.: "that" added
144. Hq.tp.: "the" omitted, then typed above
145. Sk.sh.: Sk. actually used the Dutch spelling in lh.: "*Salomon*" (see List)
146. Solomon, Alexander, Napoleon (see List)
147. Sk.tp.1, Hq.tp., Hq.st.: "in" omitted (included in SQ.)
148. Hq.tp., Hq.st., SQ.: "who went so far as Russia" omitted

went so[149] far as Russia[148], had[150] a glimpse of meditative life. [151]It is said of Nap.[152] that at such times, when[153] hours together he was at the battlefield and the energy of most of them was exhausted, this [154]king who had always been in luxuriousness[155] would[154] be most exhausted, but no[156], he would close his eyes for a moment[157], go in a condition[157] and then after that he would be as energetic as before.[151]

[158]

By the help of meditation one connects oneself to[159] that storehouse of inspiration, power, energy, life, happiness, peace that one can get any amount of it and yet it is not lacking in that store.

The examples that one has seen of the[160] meditative people are beyond expression. After the age of eighty, or even more, the memory is as brilliant as their youth's[161], their health perfect and their mind in proper rhythm, working in [162]proper balance. It is a great pity that we happen to, of those[163] claim to be meditative people, seems to be so unbalanced[164] that they alone[165] give a kind of bad name to the mystical life. But what is the reason of it? The reason is that, some of them are seeking to communicating[166] with the spirits to work wonders, to pride themselves[167] how much they know. This[168] is not the work of the meditative person. The person of meditation must show balance in every side of life. In the common sense of the[169] life, in the understanding in the[170] life above and also in seeing the life below as clearly or even more so than the average person. As a person has mastered meditation, in everything he does, he will express it. People think of a

---

149. Sk.tp.1: "as" instead of "so"
150. SQ.: "one has" instead of "had"
151. Ibid.: sentence omitted: "It is said of Nap. that . . . he would be as energetic as before."
152. Sk.sh.: "Nap." in lh. abbr. for Napoleon, and written out in a.o.d.
153. Sk.tp.1: "for" added
154. Hq.tp., Hq.st.: "emperor could" instead of "king who had always been in luxuriousness, would"
155. Sk.tp.1: "luxury" instead of "luxuriousness"
156. Sk.tp.1: "but no," omitted
157. A.o.d.: "for a moment" moved to after "go in a condition"
158. Sk.sh.: one entire line left blank
159. A.o.d.: "with" instead of "to"
160. Hq.tp.: "the" omitted, then typed above
161. A.o.d.: "in youth" instead of "their youth's"
162. Ibid.: "a" added
163. Ibid.: "what we happen to know of those who" instead of "we happen to, of those"
164. Sk.tp.1: "unbalanced" typed over a word no longer legible; SQ.: "show such lack of balance" instead of "be so unbalanced"
165. A.o.d.: "only" instead of "alone"
166. Ibid.: "communicate" instead of "communicating"
167. Ibid.: "on" added
168. Ibid.: "That" instead of "This"
169. Ibid.: "the" omitted
170. Ibid.: "of" instead of "in the"

meditative person, perhaps sitting in the caves of the mountains of Himalay[171] or in solitude, who sees no one. It is all unnatural. Why must one go to the H.[172] in the solitude; anywhere[173] one is, whatever all[174] one's occupation, the one who it[175] knows how to meditate, can meditate. Wherever he is, or what[176] he does [177] the truly meditative person must prove[178] to us in all earthly things, in art, science, in whatever profession or work, he must do it to a great fullness in that way, he must show the power and inspiration and bliss of meditation. The little meditation one does for half an hour or a quarter of an hour, it is only a kind of winding, but one[179] has mastered it, it[180] must go on night and day[181] and[182] everything he does, everything[183] must express it.

And when we come to the fourth path, the path of devotion, so little can be said about it because it is beyond all things. As the Bible says: "God is love"[184] and therefore if there is anything divine in man, it is the love element, and in order to attain to the divine knowledge there is nothing so great as the expansion of [185], as the development of [186]love element and the three paths said before, they all come in it, they all join in[187] it. A person who is most intelligent[188] and has no spark of love in him and[189] with all his intellect, he is like [190]dead. But what is love? Is love a pleasure? Love is sacrifice. And one might ask whose love[191]? Is it the love of God that I mean by devotion, and one might reason also that one loves, when one sees something beautiful, something lovable. When one does not see God, how can one love God? And that is true; also[192] many imagine that they love God.

---

171. Sk.sh.: "Himalay" in lh. for "Himalaya", and written out in Hq.tp., Hq.st.; Sk.tp.1, SQ.: "the Himalayas";
172. Sk.sh.: "H." in lh. abbr. for "Himalaya", and written out in Hq.tp., Hq.st.; Sk.tp.1, SQ.: "Himalayas"
173. Sk.tp.1: "wherever" instead of "anywhere"
174. A.o.d.: "is" instead of "all"
175. Ibid.: "it" omitted
176. Ibid.: "whatever" instead of "what"
177. Sk.sh.: a blank
178. Sk.tp.1, SQ.: "it" added
179. Sk.tp.1, SQ.: "in the one who" instead of "one"; Hq.tp., Hq.st.: "the one who" instead of "one"
180. Sk.sh.: "it" in sh. crossed out, but included in a.o.d.; in the left margin Sk. added: "night and day, it must be conscious of it" without an indication of where it was to be inserted (see next note)
181. Sk.tp.1: "; night and day he must be conscious of it" added; Hq.tp., Hq.st., SQ.: "he must be conscious of it night and day" added
182. Hq.tp., Hq.st., SQ.: "and" omitted; semicolon added
183. Ibid.: "everything" omitted
184. See I John 4:8
185. Sk.sh.: the sh. symbol is unclear, perhaps "heart"; "heart" in a.o.d.
186. Sk.tp.1, SQ.: "the" added
187. Sk.tp.1, SQ.: "into" instead of "in"
188. A.o.d.: "intellectual" instead of "intelligent"
189. Sk.sh.: "and" crossed out, and omitted a.o.d.
190. SQ.: "the" added
191. Ibid.: "Whose love of whom" instead of "who's love"
192. A.o.d.: "; so" instead of ", also"

Many may profess that they love God, but[193] to love God is a question which is not easily to be answered. But there is a verse of Rumi[194] which explains this most beautifully. R.[195] says: "If you love man or if you love God, in the end of your journey of[196] the path of love you will be brought before the sovereign of love". There is so much said about what they call *karma*[197], the action, but is there anything that can destroy K.[198], that can wipe away? There is only one thing, the after[199] power of love. It is that power alone that can wipe[200] the stains of the past and can make them[201] mirror-clear. No scriptures call[202] God a law. The scriptures call God love, which means, law is under love; love rules the[203] law. [204] God apart, when[205] an ordinary person, limited human beings like us, when a child comes to his mother with every fault that he might[206] have done against it, shall[207] and says: Mother, I am sorry for my fault; you are my mother, I am sure that you will forgive me. [208]She cannot judge him. Love rules there. The mother instantly will forgive. It is this love element.[209] When this [210]element is developed in the heart, when the heart has become a living entity, what happens: It links in[211] with the highest heaven, with God himself. What then happens, as everyone is linked with God, so everyone becomes linked with that person which he,[212] whose heart has become love. The soul becomes communicate[213] with all souls, with all he meets. That soul goes out with[214] everyone. With[214] the virtuous, with[214] the sinners[215], the wise, the fools,[216] foolish, with open heart with love. The presence with[217] that soul, the contact with that soul is purifying for others also. [218]The path which is so easy and yet so difficult to

---

193. Sk.tp.1, SQ.: "how" added
194. Jelal-ud-din Rumi (see List)
195. Sk.sh.: "R." in lh. abbr. for "Rumi", and written out in a.o.d.
196. Sk.tp.1, SQ..: "on" instead of "of"
197. *karma* (see Glossary)
198. Sk.sh.: "K." abbr. for "*karma*" and written out in a.o.d.
199. Sk.sh.: "after" in sh. crossed out, and omitted in a.o.d.
200. Sk.tp.1, SQ.: "away" added
201. A.o.d.: "the" instead of "them"
202. Hq.tp.: "scripture calls" instead of "scriptures call"; Hq.st.: "scriptures calls"
203. Sk.tp.1: "the" omitted
204. Sk.sh.: a blank
205. Hq.tp., Hq.st., SQ.: "—" instead of "when"
206. A.o.d.: "may" instead of "might"
207. Ibid.: "her" instead of "it, shall"
208. Sk.sh.: in the margin, "the mother will not judge", then crossed out; omitted in a.o.d.
209. A.o.d.: "It is this love element." omitted
210. Ibid.: "love" added
211. Ibid.: "up" instead of "in"
212. Sk.sh.: "which he," in sh. crossed out, and omitted in a.o.d.
213. A.o.d.: "communicative" instead of "communicate"
214. Ibid.: "to" instead of "with"
215. Sk.tp.1, Sk.tp.2, SQ.: "sinner" instead of "sinners"; Hq.tp., Hq.st.: "sinner" instead of "the sinners"
216. Sk.sh.: "the fools," in sh. crossed out; "fools," omitted in a.o.d.
217. Sk.tp.1: "of" instead of "with"
218. A.o.d.: "It is" added

tread. No one can teach one how to serve[219], how to develop [220]love element. It must come by itself. Only what one can do is to point out to a person that element of beauty which has the charm to create love.

The Sufi school, therefore, in the Western World is the child of that school and traditions,[221] which has always been known mostly as the Sufi school. Therefore the initiation that is given in this school is no doubt traditional, an initiation which is linked up with[222] the teachers who existed for thousands of years one before another, that those who follow these teachings may benefit themselves[223] the experiences of the meditative, devotional people, the people of knowledge who have lived centuries before us. Now[224] doubt the teaching of these schools are interpretations to the souls in a modified way to answer the need of the[225] modern times. Nevertheless, the truth is never old; it is always new. All things will change, but there is only one thing that will not change and that is the truth, the secret of life, and one will learn many doctrines, forms and many ways, but that which will save[226] is only one thing, and that is truth.

[227]

---

219. Ibid.: "love" instead of "serve"
220. Sk.tp.1, SQ.: "the" added
221. Sk.tp.1, SQ.: "a tradition of" instead of "and traditions,"; Hq.tp., Hq.st.: "a tradition" instead of "and traditions,"
222. SQ.: "that of" added
223. A.o.d.: "by" added
224. Sk.sh.: "Now" in sh., inadvertently for "No", and "No" in a.o.d.
225. Sk.tp.1, SQ.: "the" omitted
226. A.o.d.: "live" instead of "save"; (Sk.tp.2)Sk.cr.: on a copy of Sk.tp.2, Sk. inserts in lh. "save" under "live", and indicates on Sk.an. that "live" instead of "save" was printed in the *Sufi Quarterly*
227. Hq.st.: "To be read before Candidates for Initiation in the Sufi Order." added

---

2 Classes, 8 o'clock[1]

[3]I would like to speak to my mureeds on the subject of the attitude that a *mureed*[4] should have.

A mureed's attitude towards life must be hopeful; towards his motives must be courageous; towards *Murshid*[5] faithful; towards the cause sincere; toward[6] that object which he has to accomplish earnest, without the slightest doubt. In every aspect of life it is our attitude that counts and attitude in the end proves to be creative of phenomena. Success, failure, all

---

Documents:

Sk.sh.	=	Sakina Furnée's shorthand reporting of the second half of the lecture, newly transcribed by B.v.d.B.
Sk.tp.1	=	a typescript of the second half of the lecture, prepared by Sakina, or under her supervision, perhaps from her shorthand as they are nearly identical. A typed copy of this document is also in the file. Sk. made corrections to both documents, indicated in the notes as "(Sk.tp.1)Sk.cr.
er.tp.1	=	an early typescript, prepared as a Class Lecture, from an unknown source. It includes the complete lecture, and is the source for the first half of the text shown here. A few corrections by Sakina are indicated in the notes as "(er.tp.1)Sk.cr."
Sk.tp.2	=	a typed copy of er.tp.1, made by Sakina or under her supervision, identical in wording, and therefore only mentioned in notes 1, 2 and 12. One copy of this document was later corrected by Sakina, indicated in the notes as "(Sk.tp.2)Sk.cr." See also "Sk.an." below.
er.tp.2	=	a typescript with a note at the top: "From legacy Fatah v. Seters". It contains major editorial revisions which do not pertain to the text of the lecture, and is therefore not included after note 2.
Sk.an.	=	a separate list of corrections to Sk.tp.2 made by Sakina in 1967. It includes her note about the two different dates assigned to this lecture.

This lecture was published in a highly edited form in *The Sufi Message* series, vol.X (London, 1964), ch. ix (pp. 110-114) of "The Path of Initiation and Discipleship", not mentioned in the notes.

June 3, 1924, has been assigned as the date of this lecture. Although Sk. indicates in "Sk.an." that May 5 is the correct date, P-o-M. was in Paris on that date but apparently Sk. was not, and in the Hague on June 3, as was Sk. Also, the "er.tp.2", from another collection, is dated June 3.

Notes:

1. Sk.sh.: date is missing: "missed the beginning May 5th 1924" added in lh. above the first phrase; Sk.tp.1: same as sh. above, plus "The Hague, at Baron van Tuyll's." added; er.tp.1, Sk.tp.2: "3rd June 1924 Anna Paulownastraat 78, The Hague"; er.tp.2: "3 June 1924"; Sk.an.: cross references Sk.'s internal numbering system: "no. 15 as May 5, 1924" and "no. 270 as June 3, 1924"; her no. 15 is Sk.tp.1 above and 270 is Sk.tp.2.
2. Sk.sh.: title is missing; Sk.tp.1: "Class For Mureeds." added; "Private Lecture" added and crossed out; er.tp.1: "Class Lecture." added as the title, followed by the Sufi Invocation (see List); Sk.tp.2: "Mureeds' Class" added.
3. The first half of the lecture is taken from "er.tp.1" as the sh. of the first part is missing
4. Sufis use the word *mureed* to indicate an initiate (see Glossary)
5. Sufis use the word *murshid* to indicate a spiritual guide (see Glossary)
6. (Er.tp.1)Sk.cr.: "toward" changed to "towards"

depend upon it. As there is a Hindu saying that: if the attitude is right, all will come right.

There is a natural tendency in the seeker on the spiritual path to wonder if he is really progressing. And very often he begins to wonder from the day he begins the path. It is like wrong digestion. It is like asking while eating is not finished: Shall I be able to digest? The spiritual path leads to selflessness. The more we worry about ourselves, the less progress we make because the whole striving is: to forget the self. Mostly it is the self which hinders the path. The path is made for the soul; it is natural and easy for the soul to find it. Therefore know that while a person is wondering about his progress, he is wasting time; it is standing on the path on which one must go forward. It is like a person who has gone on a path and stands, wondering: Am I walking? He is really standing, he is not walking; it is the wondering which makes him stand. If he did not wonder, he would go on. What does it come from? It comes from the lack of faith. Faith we need more than anything in life and if faith is tore[7] aside, all is tore[7] aside. I always remember my murshid's blessing every time I took leave: "May your faith be strengthened" were his words. As a young man I wondered: "Is this the only thing my murshid wished for me? There are so many other things: health, success, liberation, illumination". Many years after that I realized the value of that blessing. In the strengthening of faith all benefit is included. As Christ has said: "If there were faith, it would remove mountains".[8] This will always prove true. It might seem at times that faith is for the simple person who wants to walk blindly; but one does not know that faith is the life of the simple person, but the soul of the wise person.

Does anyone distinguish how he changes day after day in his face and form? No. For there is no distinct mark of change to point out one day after the other. If in the external self one cannot distinguish change properly, then how can one distinguish change in the inner process? It is not something you can weigh on a scale just like after coming from the seaside one has gained ten pounds. There is no such gain in spiritual progress.

Then there are some who see that some time, who imagine that some time they are progressing and then go backwards. Then they are discouraged and say: I thought I had reached some place where I was, but it is an illusion. Life is like the sea. The sea is not always calm. There are times when the sea is rough that the boat naturally will move downwards and then again upwards. And while the boat is moving downwards, to think that it goes down is mistaken, is deceiving. It is going down in order to go up; it is its

---

7. (Er.tp.1)Sk.cr.: "tore" changed to "torn"; Sk.tp.2: "torn" instead of "tore"; (Sk.tp.2)Sk.cr., Sk.an.: "destroyed?" inserted at bottom as an alternate reading for "torn aside"
8. See Matthew 17:20

movement, it is natural. A mureed in the path of life is subject to such experiences. Life will take its own course. The one who sails will have to meet many times rough sea; he has to be prepared, not to be frightened, not to be discouraged. He has still to go on through life. If life's journey were soft and smooth, there would be no necessity of spiritual development. He has to take the reins in hand more wisely to go through calm sea and storms both.

Then the mureed wonders what others say, if they are displeased or pleased. If they are displeased he thinks: I am not progressing. But this has nothing to do with progress. Those who are displeased would even be displeased with Jesus Christ. Those inclined to be pleased would be pleased with the worst person. It does not mean that one does not progress.

Then if the condition is adverse, the mureed thinks that he is not on the right path. But does it mean that the ship is not on the right line if the storm meets it? It is on the right line. Neither Murshid nor God are responsible if the conditions are adverse. The best thing is to meet them, to be more brave, and courageously to make your way through them.

Ghazali[9], the great Sufi writer of Persia, says that spiritual progress is likened to shooting at a target in darkness. You do not know where, you do not see, but you are doing the action just the same.

The true ideal of the spiritual person is not a great power, nor a great amount of knowledge; his true ideal stands beyond power and knowledge—that which is limitless, incomprehensible, nameless and formless. There are no milestones to count; one cannot say: So many miles I have gone and so many there are still before me. This would not be spiritual journey. The pursuit of the limitless is limitless, of the formless is formless; one cannot make it tangible. The question is: What is it that insures progress, on what evidence have we to go on? There is only one evidence, that is your belief. There is one insurance, that is your faith. If you believe, you can go[10] on; if you are convinced you will reach, you must reach. Are there any outer signs? Yes, there are innumerable signs. But you need not think in the absence of signs that you are not progressing. What are these signs of progress? That you feel inspiration. That[11] things you could not understand yesterday are easy today. Yet, if there are things for[12] which you are not ready to understand them[13], you must have patience till tomorrow. As soon as one is agitating against the lack of inspiration, that means closing the doors of inspiration. Agitation is not allowed in this path. Agitation

9. (Er.tp.1)Sk.cr.: "Ghizali" typed and corrected to "al-Ghazali" (see List)
10. Sk.tp.2: "go" omitted; (Sk.tp.2)Sk.cr.: reinstated
11. Sk.tp.2: "(you)" added; (Sk.tp.2)Sk.cr., Sk.an.: crossed out
12. (Sk.tp.2)Sk.cr., Sk.an.: "for" crossed out
13. (Sk.tp.2)Sk.cr., Sk.an.: "them" crossed out

disturbs one's rhythm and makes one paralyzed; and then one proves in the end to be one's own enemy. But this one will not admit and one will blame others. And if one has kind feelings towards others, one blames the conditions. But very often it is lack of patience rather than others or conditions.

[14]The other sign of progress is that one begins to feel power. It might manifest physically to some extent, mentally also, and later the power could manifest as a[15] power on[16] one's affairs in life. A[17] spiritual pursuit is endless, so the[18] power has no end.

The third sign of the[18] progress is that one begins to feel a joy, a happiness.

But in spite of that feeling it is possible that clouds of depression and despair may come from without. And one might think for[19] that moment that: All the happiness and joy which I gained spiritually was snatched away from me. But it[20] was not so. If spiritual joy could be snatched away, it cannot be then the spiritual joy. It is[21] like all material comforts, when they are taken[22] from you, you have lost them. Spiritual joy is yours. It is your property. No death nor decay can take it away from you. Changing clouds, as they surround the sun, so they might surround your joy, but once[23] they are scattered you will find your own[24] property in your own heart. It is something you can depend upon, that[25] nobody can take[26] from you.

There is another sign of progress that[27] makes one fearless. Nothing seems to frighten one. Whatever, by[28] the situation of life, even that [29] a fearlessness comes to a person against all things in life that might seem frightening and a brave spirit develops out of it. A spirit which gives one patience and strength to struggle against all adverse conditions, however terrible they seem to be. It can even develop so[30] that one would like to fight

---

14. The shorthand begins here. Sakina indicated she "missed the beginning". In Sk.tp.2, Sk.writes "15" next to this paragraph and at the end of the text, a cross-reference to Sk.tp.1
15. Er.tp.1: "a" omitted
16. Ibid.: "in" instead of "on"
17. Ibid.: "As" instead of "A"
18. Ibid.: "the" omitted
19. A.o.d.: "at" instead of "for"
20. Er.tp.1: "that" instead of "it"
21. A.o.d.: "not" added
22. Er.tp.1: "away" added
23. Ibid.: "as" instead of "once"; (Sk.tp.2)Sk.cr., Sk.an.: "once" reinstated
24. Ibid.: "own" omitted; (Sk.tp.2)Sk.cr.: reinstated
25. Ibid.: "something" instead of "that"
26. (Sk.tp.1)Sk.cr.: "away" inserted on one copy; er.tp.1: "away" added
27. Er.tp.1: "it" added
28. A.o.d.: "be" instead of "by"
29. Sk.sh.: a blank; (Sk.tp.1)Sk.cr.: "(death?)" inserted in margin on one copy; er.tp.1: "death" instead of "that [blank]"
30. Er.tp.1: "to such an extent" instead of "so"

with death. Nothing seems to him too horrible before which he[31] would feel helpless.

The other side[32] of progress is that one begins to feel peaceful; at moments it[33] might increase; a kind of[34] restful feeling comes in the heart. One may be in the solitude, even[35] in the crowd, and[36] yet one feels restful. Life in the world is most exciting and[37] has a very[38] tiring effect upon a sensitive person. When a person is restful[39], the condition in life could make him experience the greatest discomfort, for there is no pain greater than restlessness and if there is any remedy for the lack of peace it is spiritual progress. Once peace is developed in a soul, that soul feels such a great power and has such a great influence upon those who approach that soul, and if[40] conditions which are upsetting[41] against all; jarring influences coming from all sides, that as water makes the rising dust sink down, so all the jarring influences are settled down under [42]feet of the peaceful.

[43] the story of Daniel in the Bible[44], who went in[45] the lions'[46] cave. What does this story teach us, what does it suggest? Was it Daniel's hypnotism? If it was h.[47] let the lions'[48] hypnotisers go to the lions today[49]. No, it was[50] the inner peace; that[51] influence of that[52] is so powerful upon all passions that even it[53] calms the lions and makes them sleep. One may make excuses[54]: that my surroundings are worrying me. My friends are terrible, or my enemies are horrible. But before the[55] peace awakes[56] in the heart, nothing can stand. They all must calm down, they all must settle down, just

---

31. Er.tp.1: "one" instead of "he"
32. (Sk.tp.1)Sk.cr.: "side" changed to "sign"; (er.tp.1)Sk.cr.: parentheses inserted around "side" and "sign" in margin
33. Er.tp.1: "this" instead of "it"
34. Ibid.: "so much that a" instead of "a kind of "
35. Ibid.: "but even if one were" instead of "even"
36. Ibid.: "and" omitted
37. Ibid.: "it" instead of "and"
38. Ibid.: "very" omitted; (Sk.tp.2)Sk.cr., Sk.an.: reinstated
39. A.o.d.: "restless" instead of "restful"
40. A.o.d.: "upon" instead of "if"
41. Er.tp.1: "and" added
42. A.o.d.: "the" added
43. Sk.sh.: a blank
44. See Daniel 6:17-25
45. Er.tp.1: "to" instead of "in"
46. Sk.tp.1: typed "lions's"; (Sk.tp.1)Sk.cr.: crossed out last "s" to read "lions'"; a.o.d.: "lion's" instead of "lions'"
47. Sk.sh.: "h." abbr. in lh. for "hypnotism", and written out in a.o.d.
48. Sk.tp.1: "lion" instead of "lions'"; a.o.d.: "lion's" instead of "lions'"
49. Er.tp.1: "and experience" added
50. Sk.tp.1: "is" crossed out, followed by "was", all in type; er.tp.1: "is" instead of "was"
51. Sk.sh.: "that" crossed out; a.o.d.: "the" instead of "that"
52. Er.tp.1: "peace" added
53. Er.tp.1: "it even" instead of "even it"
54. Sk.tp.1: "excuse" instead of "excuses"; er.tp.1: "the excuse"
55. Er.tp.1: "the" omitted
56. Sk.tp.1: "wakened" instead of "awakes"; er.tp.1: "that is wakened" instead of "awakes"

like[57] dust, after the water is[58] sprinkled [59] .

But suppose[60] this power did not come to my mureeds in one day, would they[61] be disappointed? Do they expect all this journey to be made in one[62] week? I would not be surprised if you[63] did it. But it[64] is the life-long journey and those who have really accomplished this journey, they are the ones who have not for one moment[65] doubted that: I shall not progress. They have never allowed such a[66] doubt to come in their mind, that: I[67] shall be hindered. They do not[68] even concern themselves with that[69] question. They only know that: I am going[70]; I must reach there, and[71] I shall reach there[72]. That is the attitude that they must [73]take. He must never leave,[74] let his[73] mind feel, after having taken four steps, that[75] I must go to the right or left. If[76] man has one strength, and this[77] is the[78] faith, this[77] is all the power he needs in the path, he can go along, and nothing will [79]
at the end[80] will accomplish.

[81]

---

57. Er.tp.1: "like the" instead of "just like"
58. Er.tp.1: "has been" instead of "is"
59. Sk.sh.: a blank; Er.tp.: "on it" added
60. Er.tp.1: "that" added
61. Ibid.: "let them not" instead of "would they"; (Sk.tp.2)Sk.cr., Sk.an.: "would they" reinstated
62. Ibid.: "a" instead of "one"; (Sk.tp.2)Sk.cr., Sk.an.: "one" reinstated
63. A.o.d.: "they" instead of "you"
64. Er.tp.1: "this" instead of "it"
65. Ibid.: "for one moment" omitted; (Sk.tp.2)Sk.cr., Sk.an.: reinstated
66. Ibid.: "this" instead of "such a"
67. Ibid.: "they" instead of "I"
68. Sk.sh.: "they do not" in sh. written across illegible sh., and included in a.o.d.
69. Er.tp.: "this" instead of "that"
70. Ibid.: "I am going" omitted; (Sk.tp.2)Sk.cr., Sk.an.: reinstated
71. Ibid.: "and" omitted
72. Ibid.: "if I do not reach today, tomorrow I will reach" added
73. Ibid.: "never let their" instead of "take. He must never leave, let his"
74. Sk.tp.1: "leave," omitted
75. Er.tp.1: "that" omitted
76. (Er.tp.1)Sk.cr.: "If" crossed out
77. A.o.d.: "that" instead of "this"
78. (Er.tp.1)Sk.cr.: "the" crossed out
79. Sk.sh., Sk.tp.1: a half sentence left blank; (Sk.tp.1)Sk.cr.: "hinder" inserted, and included in a.o.d.
80. (Sk.tp.1)Sk.cr.: "at the end" changed to "And in the end he"; er.tp.1: "And in the end he"
81. A.o.d.: "God bless you." added

The Hague, June 6, 1924
Anna Paulownastraat, 78[1]

Class - Lecture

The Path of Initiation

I would like to speak a few words to my mureeds on the subject of the path of initiation[2]. The esoteric school in the Sufi Movement is the most important factor, although it is not the most important activity for the reason that this school has to do with some few, not with the multitude. The esoteric school is not for all, will never be for all; it only is for the few.

Often people have asked me why Sufis of past ages have not tried to spread Sufism. I have always answered that there has only been one factor of Sufism existing for ages, and that has been the inner school, which in all ages kept exclusive and will always be kept in the same way. Propaganda is not for the school, it is for the betterment of humanity; it is for the brotherhood- message, not for the inner school. The inner school is for the few who seek for truth earnestly, steadily and with patience, who are awake to the voice of truth and will have patience all along the journey. The inner school is not something man follows, a form, a dogma, or a belief. The inner school has not got a dogma, neither a belief; the work of the inner school is to tune the soul, to raise the individual from the plane where he stands, to uplift the soul. This is a school where one learns to know himself, where one comes to understand life. It is as the picture is given in *diwan*[3] in a poetry: once a lion was wandering in the woods and found among the sheep a cub of lion. He gave it a great surprise by saying to it, "Cub of lion"; but it also ran away with the sheep. The lion followed the cub and when he approached, it

---

Documents:

Sk.tp.1 = a typescript prepared under Sakina Furnée's supervision, double-spaced on fine paper, apparently the closest to the original text. No reporting or older typescript has been found in the archives.

Sk.tp.2 = another typescript prepared by Sakina Furnée or under her supervision, showing only two small differences from Sk.tp.1, one of which was later corrected, indicated by "(Sk.tp.2)Sk.cr.)".

Notes:

1. The Sufi Centre in The Hague where the class was given
2. Sk.tp.1,2: "Path of Initiation" capitalized and put in quotation marks to indicate the title
3. A word for a collection of poetry in Arabic, Persian or Urdu; probably P-o-M. refers to the *Diwan* of Hafiz (see List)

was much frightened. "Why?" the lion said, "you are a lion too". "No, no", was the answer. "I am a sheep; I am no lion, I am frightened, I tremble". But the lion said: "I will not let you go among the sheep, you are a lion". The cub was very much frightened but followed the lion. They came near a pool of water; the sun was clear, the water still. The lion said: "While you drink this water, see your reflection and look at me". And it saw for itself: "I am the same as this lion. Why do I run among the sheep? Let the sheep go, and do the works of lion".

That is the work of the inner school. Initiation which *Murshid*[4] gives to the *mureed*[5] is as the call of the lion. The lake is the heart. When in the heart one begins to seek, one finds self, the secret of which one had not known fully. Therefore know that you have to expect nothing by initiation, that it does not give a new power, a great power or visions. No, this school does not pretend to give things of that sort. It is a school of tradition of thousands of years, to which belonged saints and sages whose names are found in manuscripts of the past, whose names are not imaginary names, whose lives can be found in the history of the past. Therefore know that behind us is a backbone of tradition of masters, prophets, wise men, and sages who have proved to have understood the secret of life. We do not work for worldly success; our movement aims at something greater. We shall keep conscious of the dignity of the tradition behind us. We shall not pretend to be on this side or on that side; we shall not try to be popular or to attract the masses. We do not mind how few we are. If only we are earnest in the task we have before us. Success in this school does not belong to the great number, does not depend upon worldly things, but upon the unfoldment of those who belong to it. Knowing this, we shall be conscious of the dignity of the path of initiation in the school of the Sufi Movement.

How can this dignity be observed? First by closing the lips. It is the light-hearted who throw all out what[6] is given to them, who speak of spiritual matters to anyone. This should not be your manner. You must show the lion's heritage, keeping the lips closed on sacred matters. Mind not if another has a different belief, a different conception. The Sufi is above the differences of opinions. The whole secret of this path is to journey with the lips closed. No discussion, no argument, not too much talking on the subject of the soul which is too sacred to be talked about with everyone. Besides, if you disagree, if you feel contempt for another custom, another manner, it shows your limitation. By tolerance, by understanding, by forgiving one shows that the heart is large enough to assimilate all things. The ordinary

4. *Murshid* is a word used by Sufis to refer to a spiritual teacher (see Glossary); it was commonly used as a form of address for P-o-M.
5. The word *mureed* is used by Sufis to refer to an initiate (see Glossary)
6. Sk.tp.2: "that" instead of "what"

mentality respects certain things and other things it does not like. The more one becomes spiritual, the more one is assimilating, understanding. The higher one is spiritually evolved, the greater is the willingness, the readiness to forgive. "To know all is to understand all."[7]

One might ask: Through the school of initiation, what does one learn? No principle? What principle has one to adopt? And I say: There is only one principle and that is the largeness of your heart. And who will judge it? You yourself. Every thought, word and feeling you must weigh, you must find out whether it is large or small, or whether it shows lack of evolution, imperfection.

Man has an earthly body but a heavenly soul. His earthly parentage is apparent; his real parentage is God's parentage. The more aristocratic and noble, the more conscious, the more there is the expression of the divine. Then whatever one thinks or feels or does, one expresses the divine. This is the right principle. There is no need for Murshid to tell you what is small or large. As the eyes can discriminate, so the heart can discriminate whether what we think, say or do is small or[8] large. A person may be in a high rank or position, he may have a great wealth; if his heart is small, he is a small person. Whatever he does is small. Another may be void of all that belongs to the world and yet if his heart is large, he is great. In this way, by struggling with the self one will find nobility, which is a divine heritage. Thus life will become harmonious, an expression of the divine.

Besides, there is another thing and that is meditation. By that is not meant to pray on Sunday, or every evening, or to close the eyes for a few minutes. That is the beginning. That is not what I mean. But our whole life we must be in meditation, with everything we do; not one single moment should pass without. By this one accomplishes a task which is the only yearning of the soul: to seek perfection. Remember in which boat you are travelling—in the boat of responsibility. Keep before you the dignity of your ideal. And by persevering faithfully, you can be sure of the desired result, without doubt.

God bless you.

---

7. Sk.tp.1,2: this saying appears in quotation marks in both typescripts; however, no reference for it has been discovered, nor is it a saying familiar to most speakers of English; it may be that P-o-M. was thinking of the saying "To understand all is to forgive all", for which see the lecture of 29 May
8. Sk.tp.2: "of" typed, probably by mistake; (Sk.tp.2)Sk.cr.: "of" changed back to "or" in ink

Sakina's shorthand reporting

Anna Paulownastraat
8 Juni 1924[1]

2

[3]I would like to speak a few words on the subject of attaining to the inner life through religion.[3] Very often people divide the esoteric or the inner part of life from [4]exoteric, or [4]outer form of religion. But[5] to divide them in a conception is possible, but[6] to divide them in reality is as separating the head from the body.

As head linked with body make[7] the form complete, so religion with inner life makes the spiritual ideal perfect. Nevertheless thoughtful[8] wise of all ages with their philosophical minds, with their scientific tendencies, with their intellectual strife, often thought of separating religion from the inner life. But if they are separated, it is just like a[9] bread without butter. It is like [10]milk without sugar. It is like[10] food without salt. But there has been one[11] reason why this tendency has come, very often especially among the thoughtful people. The reason is that it is natural that such a tendency should

---

Documents:

Sk.sh. = Sakina Furnée's shorthand reporting of the lecture, newly transcribed by B.v.d.B.

Hq.st. = a stencilled copy of the lecture prepared at Headquarters, Geneva, as part of the Religious Gatheka series for distribution to the Sufi Centres. Later a new stencil was made, identical in wording and therefore not mentioned further.

Sk.tp. = a typescript prepared by Sakina or under her direction, from "Hq.st.", identical in wording and therefore not mentioned in the notes except for two corrections by Sakina shown as "(Sk.tp.)Sk.cr."

bk. = part of this lecture was later published in *The Unity of Religious Ideals* (1929), Part VII, Chapter III, pp. 311-313.

Notes:

1. Sk.sh.: "Juni" in lh., Dutch for "June"; a.o.d.: date and location omitted
2. Hq.st.: "Religious Gatheka." and "Number 40" added at the top, followed by the Sufi Invocation (see List); then the title: "ATTAINING to the INNER LIFE through RELIGION."; bk.: title: "III. ATTAINING TO THE INNER LIFE THROUGH RELIGION"
3. A.o.d.: opening sentence omitted: "I would like . . . through religion."
4. Bk.: "the" added
5. Bk.: "though" added
6. A.o.d.: "but" omitted
7. Ibid.: "makes" instead of "make"
8. Ibid.: "the thoughtful and" instead of "thoughtful"
9. Bk.: "a" omitted
10. Sk.tp.: "milk without sugar, it is like" omitted; (Sk.tp.)Sk.cr.: the omitted passage inserted in hw. in the margin
11. A.o.d.: "a" instead of "one"

come. When the body becomes a corpse as[12] life leaves [13]body, even the dear ones, those who loved the person, begin to think, that[14] as soon as possible we should clear away[15] this body, for the one whom they loved is gone from it. The body is left as a corpse and so when the inner life, which is just like a breath in the body of religion, when that life[16] departs from it, then the religion becomes like a c.[17] Then the most faithful adherents begin to feel that it is a corpse. In all ages and in all periods of history we shall trace this, that there has been a limit of years for a religion. During that the religion prospered and it gave benefit to humanity. Why? Because it has[18] the breath in it. It had the spiritual aspect in it. But when that inner life departed it was left like a corpse. Still, the faithfuls[19] kept it, but those with intelligence could not keep it any longer. Still there is a necessity: like[20] the rain falls year after year and gives to the earth a new life, a new sustenance.

So it may be[21] necessary then create[22] new message of spiritual upliftment should come. Whenever it came people have fought against it, not knowing that it is the same truth, breath, soul of religion[23] has come again [24] not knowing the secret of religion. The rainfall of last year is not different from this year's. It is the same water, the same substance[25], the same energy. As vapours it goes above and as raindrops it falls and[26] Solomon[27] has said therefore [28]. It has always been the same old message, only brought in different bottles and[29] new labels.

[30]Now coming to the philosophical point; at that[31] what is the necessity of religion, which is the most most[32] important? That[33] is one: Besides all the moral principles that religion teaches, besides all the ethics that religion gives, there is one[34] central theme which can be traced as the

---

12. Ibid.: "and" instead of "as"
13. Ibid.: "the" added
14. Sk.sh.: "that" in sh. crossed out, and omitted in a.o.d.
15. Bk.: "bury" instead of "clear away"
16. A.o.d.: "when that life" omitted
17. Sk.sh.: "c." abbr. in sh. for "corpse", and written out in a.o.d.
18. A.o.d.: "had" instead of "has"
19. Ibid.: "faithful" instead of "faithfuls"
20. Ibid.: "as" instead of "like"
21. Ibid.: "has been" instead of "may be"
22. Sk.sh.: "create" in sh. crossed out; a.o.d.: "that the" instead of "create"
23. A.o.d.: ": that" added
24. Sk.sh.: a blank
25. Sk.sh.: "substance" in sh., retraced for clarity; a.o.d. read "sustenance"
26. A.o.d.: ". As" instead of "and"
27. Solomon (see List)
28. Sk.sh.: a blank, unfinished sentence; a.o.d.: "there" instead of "therefore", and "is nothing new under the sun" added (Ecclesiastes 1:9)
29. Bk.: "with" added
30. A.o.d.: "And" added
31. Ibid.: "at that" omitted
32. Ibid.: this second "most" omitted
33. Bk.: "There" instead of "That"
34. A.o.d.: "a" instead of "one"

nature of life, of spirit. And what is it? It is to make that perfect being intelligible to the limited mind of man. And what is done for it? The ideal of God is preached. The prophets[35] who have brought from time to time a religion, which[36] central theme of this was that they have brought the ideal of God, and every one of them have tried their[37] best to make the picture of that ideal, in order that the people of their time,[38] of that period when they lived, could grasp it easily and benefit by it, to fulfill the purpose of spiritual perfection. But one thing,[39] that the different picture[40] that the great prophets of the world have made, very often they[41] differ from one another. But one finds that in order to make one photo[42] clear, there have to be so many different developments of it. A plate to be made as from this[43] plate; a development has to be made and then brought and[44] the paper. Then dozens are made on it.[45] Different processes to make a photo[46] complete. And so has it been with those who have made the picture of [47]deity. A picture here may be made newly[48], which is beyond man's[49]. They have done their best. Artists have painted that picture. Three artists painting[50] the portrait of one person, they are all three different,[51] [52] they only differ because they are different artists; so with the prophets: for one and the same motive, in order to make that picture intelligible to the limited mind of man, who knows nothing better than what he knows of himself, and of his brother man. Therefore the best that man can[53] think of God, the best picture he can make of God is that of man. Therefore in the ancient religions of the East one says: This[54] God was pictured in man. Then the picture of the later days was that man was pictured as God. After that a reform followed, [55]in order to separate them, in order to break away[56] with that confusion caused by these

---

35. Bk.: "Messengers" instead of "prophets"
36. A.o.d.: "– the" instead of ", which"
37. Ibid.: "has tried his" instead of "have tried their"
38. Ibid.: "of their time," omitted
39. Hq.st.: "is" added and comma omitted; bk.: "It is true" instead of "But one thing,"
40. A.o.d.: "pictures" instead of "picture"
41. A.o.d.: "they" omitted
42. Sk.sh.: "*foto*" written in lh. (Dutch for "photo"); "photograph" in a.o.d.
43. A.o.d.: ", and from that" instead of "as from this"
44. Ibid.: "on" instead of "and"
45. Ibid.: "it is retouched up, –" instead of "dozens are made on it."
46. Ibid.: "photograph" instead of "photo"
47. Ibid.: "the" added
48. Ibid.: "which cannot be made fully" instead of "here may be made newly"
49. Ibid.: "power to make" added
50. Ibid.: "When three artists paint" instead of "Three artists painting"
51. Ibid.: "the three are different." instead of "they are all three different,"
52. Sk.sh.: a blank, several lost words; omitted in a.o.d.
53. A.o.d.: "what that man can best" instead of "the best that man can"
54. A.o.d.: "it is said that" instead of "one says: 'This"
55. Bk.: this is the last sentence in the chapter: "In order to separate . . . . yet God is God and man is man."
56. A.o.d.: "away" omitted

two opposite ideas that God was God, as[57] man was man. But the present message, which comes of necessity, is that God is in man and man in God and yet God is God and man is man.[55] If it would have been[58] possible a thousand years before[59], this Church of All[60] with all scriptures and with the candles' light[61] in the name of all the great ones, would have existed. It was the longing of the awakened souls. It was the ideal of the wise ones in all ages. What prevented them? The multitude. The childlike followers of a certain religion, who would stick to their own and would not wish to listen to another, yet not knowing what is their own and what is another. When there is one Father, and all human beings his children, coming from him, going to him, where lies the difference? Where is the other? The other comes by the faults man makes before his own intelligence. Was it not the desire of Moh.[62]? Was it the wish of J.Chr.[63]? Was it not the task of Mos.[64]? Was it not the wish of Krn.[65] or of Bud.[66]? That the[67] wisdom in all its aspects may be understood? That all those who have sacrificed their life[68] and energies in the[69] service for man, that the service may be too[70] fulfilled and humanity blessed and benefited by what they brought. Was it not the wish of Rama[71] that all the men of the world should come together in understanding that there is only one religion? [72]Cannot the evolution of man here, today[72] allowed us, and we must be thankful that what gathers[73] together, even some few souls who can tolerate such an idea, and[74] try to understand, that behind all religion there was[75] one, and be patient[74]. That there can only be one truth. The,[76] there is only one truth.

That we are willing to listen to the words of all the great souls who have come perhaps thousands of years before us, and what is left of them, is in their words; we can see the glimpses of their feelings in the[77] words. Why

---

57. A.o.d.: "and" instead of "as"
58. Hq.st., Sk.tp.: "had be" instead of "would have been"; (Sk.tp.)Sk.cr.: "be" changed to "been"
59. Hq.st.: "ago" instead of "before,"
60. Church of All (see List)
61. Hq.st..: "candles lighted" instead of "candles' light"
62. Sk.sh.: "Moh." in lh. abbr. for "Mohammed", and written out in a.o.d. (see List)
63. Ibid.: "J.Chr." in lh. abbr. for "Jesus Christ", and written out in a.o.d. (see List)
64. Ibid.: "Mos." in lh. abbr. for "Moses", and written out in a.o.d. (see List)
65. Ibid.: "Krn." in lh. abbr. for "Krishna", and written out in a.o.d. (see List)
66. Ibid.: "Bud." in lh. abbr. for "Buddha", and written out in a.o.d. (see List)
67. Hq.st.: "the" omitted
68. Ibid.: "lives" instead of "life"
69. Ibid.: "the" omitted
70. Ibid.: "too" omitted
71. Rama (see List)
72. Hq.st.: "The evolution of man today has" instead of "Cannot the evolution of man here, today"
73. Hq.st.: "we can gather" instead of "what gathers"
74. Sk.sh.: "and be patient" inserted here in sh.; included here in a.o.d (without the second "and"), with the phrase omitted at end of sentence
75. Hq.st: "is" instead of "was"
76. Ibid.: ", that" instead of ". The,"
77. Ibid.: "their" instead of "the"

should we not be benefited by them? The Church of All[78] therefore is the religion of the future, which brings to humanity the ideal of manifestation[79] of religion. The ideal of going[80] above the sectarianism, the limitedness of communities, of groups. And we must remember that any effort made by political or socials[81] will not be complete unless the uniting in God, the only source in which humanity must unite, is held fast in[82] truth.
[83]

---

78. Ibid.: "Universal Worship," instead of "Church of All" (see List)
79. Ibid.: "unification" instead of "manifestation"
80. Ibid.: "getting" instead of "going"
81. Ibid.: "social efforts" instead of "socials"
82. Sk.sh.: "in" in sh. crossed out, but included in a.o.d.
83. Hq.st.: "To be read at the Service of Universal Worship" added

Supplement 1923

The following lecture had been erroneously filed with the material from 1924; upon examination, a date in December 1923 has been assigned to the lecture. Since the material from 1923 has already been published, this lecture is included here until a new edition is required for 1923.

Sakina's partial shorthand reporting and
Murshida Sherifa Goodenough's typescript

1 Rue du Dragon
2 Dec. 8th, 1923[3]

4

I wish to speak on the subject of life's mechanism[5]. By the word mechanism I mean environments. It is not unknown to the individuals who think that life's m.[6] has a great deal to do with one's success or a[7] failure. Nevertheless, everyone does not think about it far enough to know to what extent it has effect upon one's life. A[8] mystic always teaches about treating oneself as a patient and curing oneself of one's weaknesses. But condition

---

Documents:

Sk.sh. = Sakina Furnée's shorthand reporting of part of the lecture, newly transcribed by B.v.d.B.

Sk.tp. = an early typescript made by Sakina or under her supervision, perhaps a transcription of Sk.sh. It contains the same part of the lecture which her shorthand copy book contains.

Gd.tp. = Murshida Sherifa Goodenough's typescript of the entire lecture, made on her large-lettered typewriter. On the typescript, Gd. made editorial alterations, indicated by "(Gd.tp.)Gd.ed." in the notes.

Hq.tp. = a typescript made at Headquarters, Geneva "N. 95", closely following "(Gd.tp.)Gd.ed."

Note: The date of this lecture is unclear (see note 3). Although it is included in Sakina's shorthand copy book chronologically as December 8, 1923, it has been filed under May, 1924 folder since the Gd.tp. is dated May, 1924. It was not included in *Complete Works* 1923 II and is therefore included here in *Complete Works* 1924I.

Notes:

1. Sk.tp.: "Private Lecture" added upper left; (Gd.tp.)Gd.ed.: "N.95" inserted later in lh., upper left, and so in Hq.tp.
2. Sk.sh.: "Goodenough" written in lh. above the lecture apparently as a reminder to Sakina herself that Mda. Goodenough reported part of this discourse, although in earlier instances such mentioning of Mda. Goodenough's name may indicate a practice dictation to Sakina
3. Sk.tp.: "Paris." added and "Rue du Dragon" omitted; Gd.tp.: no location or date included; (Gd.tp.)Gd.ed.: "Paris. rue du Dragon, May 1924, Reported by: Sherifa Goodenough" inserted lh.; Hq.tp.: "Aug. 1924" instead of "Dec. 8th, 1923", otherwise follows (Gd.tp.)Gd.ed.; later "Aug." was crossed out and "May" inserted lh.
4. Sk.sh.: the title "Life's Mechanism" added later in lh.; Gd.tp., Hq.tp.: title: "Life's Mechanism" included
5. Sk.tp.: "life's mechanism" underlined and capitalized, presumably as the title; Gd.tp., Hq.tp.: this sentence: "I wish . . . mechanism." omitted
6. Sk.sh.: "m." abbr. for "mechanism"
7. Gd.tp., Hq.tp.: "a" omitted
8. Gd.tp., Hq.tp.: "The" instead of "A"

is something which is wanted[9] to be thought of also from a practical p.o.v.[10] But[11] this practical point of view I do not give you only as a practical ideal, but [12]has with it as a[13] support the words of Christ. One would not wonder if man cannot accomplish soon enough what he wishes to accomplish in life, when it was even difficult for the Creator. It is to teach that[14] philosophy and secret that Christ has said that[15]: "Thy will be done on earth as [16]in heaven"[17]. What is its meaning? Its meaning is this[18]: Thy will is easily done in heaven and I wish that people will help this[18]: [19]Thy will be done easily not[20] only there,[19,21] on the earth. [22]When one has to swim and[22] journey by swimming, it would take a great courage, great perseverance and great faith to make a journey; and yet one will[23] not know when one will[24] arrive at the destiny[25]. But when the ship is made, it is made convenient; then one does not need to exhaust one's faith and patience and [26] to that extent. But there is a fact before one: to attain the object. Mechanism therefore is the most necessary thing for the attainment of every object. In the home, if one wishes comfort one wants a mechanism for it. If one has a business or [27]an industry, a certain organ.[28] makes conditions[27] better. [29]Where there is a state or[29] government[30] answers the purpose to keep order and peace. As well[31] when there is cold one needs warm clothes, and in the summer one needs different environments.

Now this is easy to understand, but it is the most difficult thing to make the right mechanism. For in the first place there are so many who have not an object clear in their mind. They will go on day after day not knowing

---

9. Sk.sh.: "wanted" in sh. crossed out and omitted in a.o.d.
10. Sk.sh.: "p.o.v." abbr. for "point of view"
11. (Gd.tp.)Gd.ed.: "But" crossed out and omitted in Hq.tp.
12. A.o.d.: "it" added
13. Gd.tp., Hq.tp.: "in" instead of "as a"
14. Gd.tp., Hq.tp.: "this" instead of "that"
15. Ibid.: "that" omitted
16. Ibid.: "it is" added
17. See Matthew 6:10
18. A.o.d.: "that" instead of "this"
19. Sk.tp.: "Thy will be done easily also" instead of "Thy will be done easily not only there,"; Gd.tp., Hq.tp.: "it will be done as easily"
20. Sk.sh.: "not" in sh. crossed out (see note 19)
21. Sk.sh.: "there" in sh. crossed out (see note 19)
22. Gd.tp., Hq.tp.: "If one had to swim in the sea, to" instead of "When one has to swim and"
23. Gd.tp., Hq.tp.: "does" instead of "will"
24. Ibid.: "would" instead of "will"
25. Ibid.: "destination" instead of "destiny"
26. Sk.sh.: a blank; Gd.tp., Hq.tp.: "perseverance" instead of "patience and [blank]"
27. Gd.tp., Hq.tp.: "industry, in that a certain organization makes the condition" instead of "an industry, a certain organ. makes conditions"
28. Sk.sh.: "organ." in sh. abbr. for "organization"
29. Gd.tp., Hq.tp.: "When there is a state a" instead of "Where there is a state or"
30. Sk.sh.: "mechanism" in sh. inserted above the space after "government" and included in Sk.tp., but excluded in Gd.tp. and Hq.tp. (see note 29)
31. Gd.tp., Hq.tp.: "well" omitted

what really they want; thinking every day differently what they do[32] want. [33]Well, that in the first place[33] deprives them[34] of that[35] mechanism which can only be produced after knowing one's definite object in life. Very often by too much enthusiasm, by too much arranging of the mechanism, one spoils one's affair, one[36] defeats one's purpose. At other times[37], at[38] the lack of mechanism, one falls short because[39] the mechanism does not answer their[40] purpose that that mechanism[41] holds. Never[42] one can say that he has sufficient knowledge on this subject, for in treating oneself one has to have one's own knowledge, but in arranging mechanism one has to deal with many different natures. And how much more knowledge of human nature, [43]of life one must possess in order to make a right mechanism in life. Often people have come to me and said: I have been able to manage myself as I have been instructed and[44] I have been able to keep up my concentrations and meditations as I have been told, but yet the purpose is not near to be[45] reached. But what is lacking there is not the lack of practice or lack of self training, what is lacking is the mechanism which is another necessity. For instance, if a person will say, "I have been able to discipline myself, and now I can fairly well make a meditation. Shall I sit at the seaport? Shall I meditate that I am in New York? Shall I reach there?" Or a person with self discipline will meditate that "All the wealth that is in the Credit Lyonnais[46] will come in my house," will it come? Even if he continued for a thousand years to meditate on the Credit Lyonnais Branch[47] he will not have it. There is a necessity in this objective world of an objective mechanism to produce certain results, and people going in the spiritual path, if they will not see this side of it, they with all[48] their goodness and spirituality, will prove to the others lack of balance, and then the practical man has a reason to laugh at the mystically[49]-minded person. Therefore the work of the Sufi Movement is not

32. Gd.tp., Hq.tp.: "do" omitted
33. (Gd.tp.)Gd.ed.: "Well, that in the first place" changed to "That", and so in Hq.tp.
34. Sk.tp.: "them" omitted, then inserted lh.
35. Gd.tp., Hq.tp.: "the" instead of "that"
36. Gd.tp., Hq.tp.: "one" omitted
37. Sk.tp.: "time" instead of "times"
38. Gd.tp., Hq.tp.: "by" instead of "at"
39. Gd.tp., Hq.tp.: "for" instead of "because"
40. A.o.d.: "the" instead of "their"
41. Gd.tp.: Hq.tp.: "the purpose which one" instead of "that that mechanism"
42. Sk.tp.: "No" instead of "Never"
43. Gd.tp., Hq.tp.: "and" added
44. Sk.sh.: Sakina's reporting of the lecture in her shorthand copy book ends here; Sk.tp.: also ends here and "Unfinished; lecture must have been interrupted here." typed at bottom of page; Gd.tp.: the balance of the lecture shown here is taken from Gd.tp.
45. (Gd.tp.)Gd.ed.: "to be" changed to "being" and so in Hq.tp.
46. Credit Lyonnais: a major bank in France; (Gd.tp.)Gd.ed.: "Credit Lyonnais" changed to "bank" and so in Hq.tp.
47. (Gd.tp.)Gd.ed.: "Credit Lyonnais Branch" changed to "bank" and so in Hq.tp.
48. Hq.tp.: "all" omitted, then inserted lh.
49. Hq.tp.: "mystical" instead of "mystically"

only to guide souls to the higher ideal, but also to keep their eyes open on the way, that they may see the way with open eyes. We shall only give an example to the people who have no belief in spiritual ideas by striking a balance through our lives. A person may take good care of himself and may concentrate upon good health, and yet the environments would cause him an illness. That cannot be helped; it is not the lack of spirituality in that person, it is the lack of materiality. Does this not show that we ought to have the balance of both? There is no great exaltation if a person has become so spiritual that he is levitating in the air, if he is no better than a balloon. If one can very well stand on earth that person has accomplished something. It is not in connection with every man that we can say that he stands on his own feet. Nothing is worse in this world than to be dependent, and if spirituality will make man more dependent, in other words at the mercy of other people in the practical things of life, then spirituality is not to be hoped[50] for. Spirituality is mastery, materially and spiritually both, to be able to manage oneself and to be able to keep the mechanism right.

Now, what I have to say to my *mureeds*[51] is this: that it is very easy to make your *murshid*[52] contented and pleased even with as small a number as we are just now, only by knowing that this is our sacred duty and our spiritual responsibility to make ourselves as much as we can an example of the teaching that the Sufi Movement wishes to spread. And in order to become examples of this I do not ask you to work wonders, or to be so good that you are difficult[53] to live in the world, too good to live in the world. Only in the[54] example you should strike a balance, [55]you will talk about the higher things standing on the earth, (you will stand on your feet). It is then that people will listen to you, and then they will trust the Movement at this time when a reconstruction of the world is necessary and our humble service at this juncture is to contribute that what is mostly needed for this reconstruction. Therefore we should all consider ourselves as the soldiers of the cause, each in [56], and discipline ourselves and make that mechanism in life which is necessary for the attainment of our object. For the very reason that we are few we are more responsible for our existence. We must stand by one another, we must do for one another in every way we can that we may not be easily blown away by the blowing of the wind. In order to get to that balance and force and stability, we must not only meditate but we must

---

50. (Gd.tp.)Gd.ed.: "hoped" crossed out and "wished" inserted, and so in Hq.tp.
51. The word "*mureed*" is used by Sufis to indicate an initiate: see Glossary
52. The word "*murshid*" is used by Sufis to indicate a spiritual guide; here it refers to P-o-M. himself; see Glossary
53. (Gd.tp.)Gd.ed.: "you are difficult" changed to "it is difficult for you", and so in Hq.tp.
54. (Gd.tp.)Gd.ed.: "in the" changed to "as an", and so in Hq.tp.
55. Ibid.: opening parenthesis inserted before "you" and new sentence begins here; Hq.tp. follows this and omits the opening parentheses later in the sentence
56. (Gd.tp.)Gd.ed.: "each in [blank]," crossed out , and so in Hq.tp.

practise these things in our everyday life.[57]

57. Mda. Goodenough's reporting of the lecture ends here; see note 44 also

Appendix A

Publication and Classification of Lectures

In the left-hand column appears the title of the lecture as originally given (or, in the absence of a title, a few words from the first sentence), followed by the date and the page on which the lecture begins in the present volume. In the far right-hand column appears the journal and date for the material published in the Sufi magazines, or the classification by series and number for the material privately circulated to Sufi centres. In general, the Gathekas, Social Gathekas, and Religious Gathekas were intended for use in meetings open to the public. The Gathas and Sangathas were used in classes in the centres for the training of initiates. However, some of that same material was published in the early days, so no unwarranted assumptions should be made about the intended use of any particular lecture. In any case, the Gathas were published in 1982, and much of the other formerly reserved material has made its way into print. Material published in *The Sufi Message* series is not noted, since generally the wording was changed considerably and passages were mixed from different lectures given in different years. Likewise, material included in the "Supplementary Papers" (also known as the "Dutch Papers") is not noted, as that collection has had a very limited circulation.

Articles

Title of Article:	Date:	Page:	Journal:
Divine Impulse	26 Jan.	59	*Sufism* (June 1924, 3-7)
Spiritual Circulation through the Veins of the Nature	28 Jan.	65	*Sufism* (Sept. 1924, 4-7)
The Law of Life	28 March	187	*The Sufi Record* IV, 3 (1932)
The Mystery of Breath	? March ?	193	*Sufism* (March, 1924, 9-11)

Gathekas

Title:	Date:	Page:	Series and number:
Mysticism	15 Jan.	15	Gatheka 7
Sufi Mysticism II	16 Jan.	23	Gatheka 10
The Method by which a Mystic Prepares his Heart to Tread the Spiritual Path	19 Jan.	41	Gatheka 11
Initiation Mureeds	20 Jan.	50	Gatheka 33
Mureeds' Class	22 Jan.	55	Gatheka 33 (continued)
"...initiation."	23 Feb.	128	Gatheka 26
"...faith..."	27 Feb.	151	Gatheka 31
The problem of the Day	March ?	197	Gatheka 35
The Doctrine of Karma	16 May	253	Gatheka 9
"...things...necessary for a mureed."	22 May	262	Gatheka 34
"The Inner Life"	3 June	319	Gatheka 27
Faith	20 Jan.	46	Religious Gatheka (not included in series)
The Kingship of God	30 Jan.	71	Religious Gatheka 41
"...the idea of sacredness."	25 May	304	Religious Gatheka 38
"...attaining to the inner life through religion."	8 June	344	Religious Gatheka 40
The Persian Poets	18 Feb.	103	Social Gatheka (not

"...intellect and wisdom."	25 Feb	140	included in series) Social Gatheka 53

Gathas

"...breath is a light..."	12 March	170	*Pasi Anfas*. Series III. Number 5.
"Innocence..."	15 March	172	*Takua Taharat*. Series III. Number 4.
"Why is breath called prana?"	17 March	174	*Pasi Anfas*. Series III. Number 6.
"He alone is capable..."	18 March	176	*Takua Taharat*. Series III. Number 6.
"Breath is likened to water..."	24 March	183	*Pasi Anfas*. Series III. Number 7.
"Exaltation..."	26 March	185	*Takua Taharat*. Series III. Number 7.
"...bad impressions..."	? March	201	*Takua Taharat*. Series III. Number 5.
"The inspiration comes…"	26 Sept.	364	*Pasi Anfas*. Series III. Number 2.

Sangatha

Attitude towards the Murshid and towards the Cause	18 Jan.	37	Nasihat (pp. 61-3)

Appendix B

Illustration of Documents

On the following pages appear photocopies of a few typical documents, most of which have not been illustrated in previous volumes of this series. For previous illustrations, see Appendix B in the volumes 1922 I and 1923 II, and Appendix D in 1923 I.

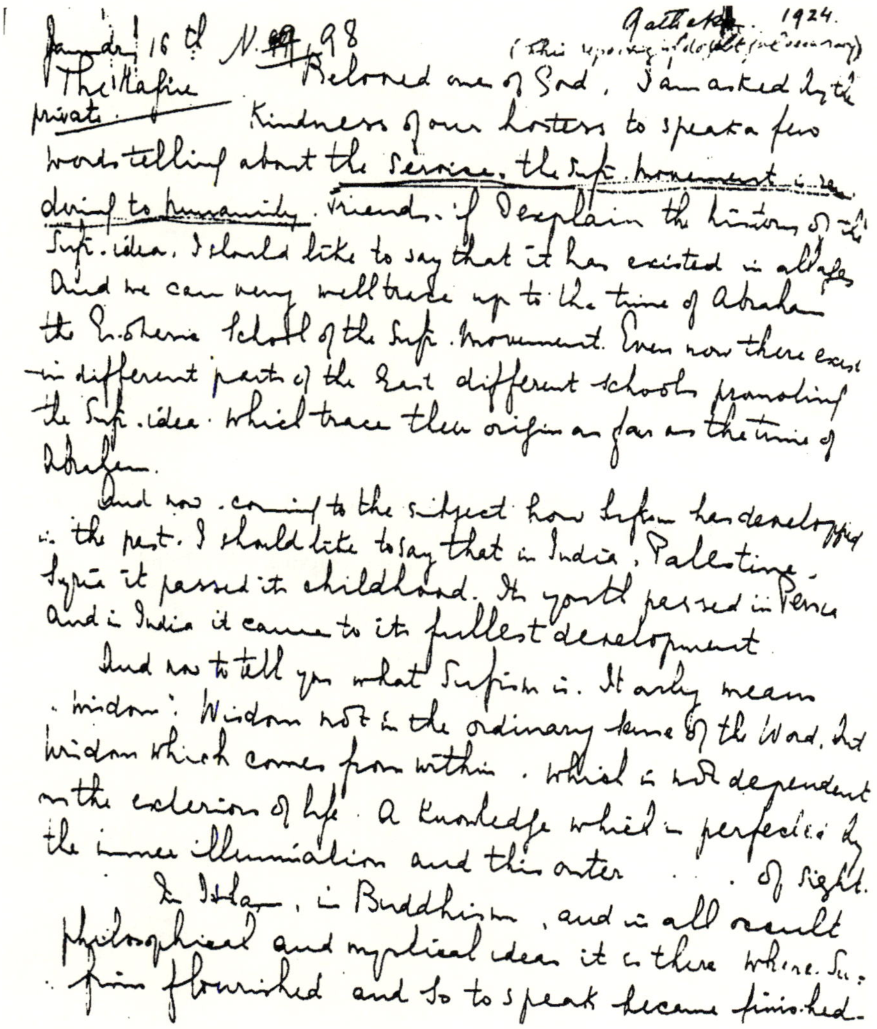

January 16th N. 98 Gatheka. 1924.
([illegible])
The Kafira
private
Beloved ones of God, I am asked by the kindness of our hostess to speak a few words telling about the service the Sufi Movement is doing to humanity. Friends, if I explain the history of the Sufi idea, I should like to say that it has existed in all ages. And we can very well trace up to the time of Abraham the Esoteric School of the Sufi Movement. Even now there exist in different parts of the East different schools promoting the Sufi idea which trace their origin as far as the time of Abraham.

And now coming to the subject how Sufism has developed in the past, I should like to say that in India, Palestine, Syria it passed its childhood. Its youth passed in Persia and in India it came to its fullest development.

And now to tell you what Sufism is. It only means wisdom; Wisdom not in the ordinary sense of the word, but wisdom which comes from within, which is not dependent on the exterior of life. A knowledge which is perfected by the inner illumination and this outer . . . of sight.

In Islam, in Buddhism, and in all occult philosophical and mystical ideas it is there where Sufism flourished and so to speak became finished.

Miss Toni de Ridder's handwritten text of 16 January 1924

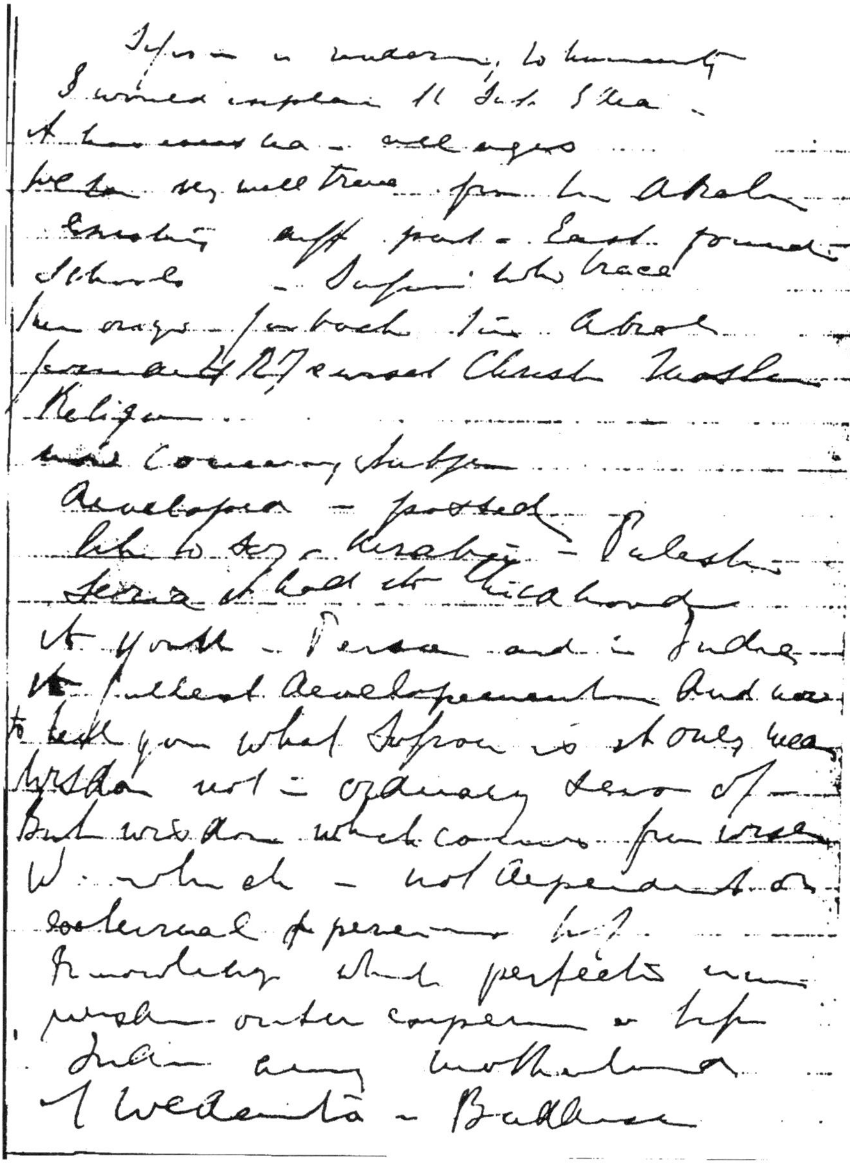
Sufism is endeavouring to humanity
I wished explain the Sufi Idea -
A human idea - all ages
We can very well trace from the [illegible]
[illegible] past - East found
Schools - Sufism who traced
the ages - far back [illegible]
[illegible] Christ Moslem
Religion
[illegible] Common subject
development - [illegible]
like to say - Arabia - Palestine
Persia it held the [illegible]
its youth - Persia and in India
its fullest development And now
to tell you what Sufism is it only means
Wisdom not ordinary sense of
But wisdom which comes from within
[illegible] - not dependent on
external [illegible]
[illegible] which perfects man
[illegible] outer experience of life
India [illegible]
of Vedanta - Buddhism

Mrs. E. Leembruggen's handwritten text of 16 January 1924

GATHEKA. Number 11.

Toward the One, the Perfection of Love, Harmony and Beauty, the Only Being, united with All the Illuminated Souls, who form the Embodiment of the Master, the Spirit of Guidance.

SUFI MYSTICISM III.

The method by which a mystic prepares his heart to tread the spiritual path.

In the first place one asks, " What is the heart? Where is the heart ?" And man is accustomed to say that the heart is in the breast. Yes, that is true. There is a nerve centre in the breast of man which has so much to do with the feelings that always the heart is pictured in the breast, that centre which is most sensitive to our feelings. When a person is feeling a great joy it is in that centre that one feels something lighted up, and by the lighting up of that centre the whole person seems light. The person feels as if he flew, there is a great joy in his life. And again, if depression or despair has come into his life this has an effect upon the centre. Man feels his throat choked and his breath is laden heavily with a load, it again means that it is that centre that feels.

But it is not that only which is the heart. It is like a mirror standing before the heart, focussed to the heart, and every thing, every feeling is reflected in this mirror in the physical being of man. As man is ignorant of his soul, so he knows not where his heart is, nor where the centre is where his feelings are reflected. This is a fact which is known by the scientists, as well as that it is the heart which is the beginning of the formation of a child. But if one comes to a mystic's conception one will see that it is in the heart, which is the beginning of form, which is also the beginning of the spirit, which makes man individual. The depth of that spirit is in reality what we call the heart. By this we understand that there is some such thing as a heart which is the deepest depth of man's being, and if one knows something of it first, it is from the impression which he receives in this nerve centre, which is in the breast of man, and therefore man calls it the heart.

In these days people give less importance to sentiment. They rely more upon the intellect. The reason is that when they meet two sorts of people, the intellectual and the sentimental people, they find in an intellectual man greater balance than in the one with sentiment. This is no doubt true. But the lack of balance is for the very reason because there is a greater power than the intellect, which is the sentiment. The earth is fruitful, but not so living and powerful as the water. The intellect is creative, yet not so powerful as the water. The intellect is creative, yet not so powerful as the heart and the sentiment. In reality the intellectual man in the end will prove unbalanced too if he has no sentimental side attached to it.

Are there not many people of whom their surroundings

Headquarters stencil of lecture of 19 January 1924

Mureeds' Classes II

340 a 6

-9-

Brighton,
February 6th 1924
In handwriting.

MUREEDS' CLASS.

The Religion of the Sufi.

I wish to speak a few words to my mureeds on the subject of the religion of the Sufi. The religion of the Sufi is the religion of the heart.

The principal moral of the Sufi is to consider the heart of others, so that in the pleasure and displeasure of his fellow- man he sees the pleasure and displeasure of God.

It is so simple, and yet so difficult to practise. This teaching is the central theme of all religions. It is the thing which no-one in the world does not know, and yet the practise of it is never enough.

What generally happens is that there are three intoxications which cover the tendency for considering the feelings of others and keep man ignorant of that which is his own.

The first intoxication is produced by oneself, it is the consideration of one's own interest which covers the feeling of consideration for another. One is so absorbed in one's own interests in life that one is intoxicated by them and so does not see the importance of considering the feelings of others.

The second intoxication is that which comes from another person. If a person does not come up to one's ideal, if he does not act towards one as one wishes, if he does not answer one's expectation, if he jars upon one's fine feelings, if he is irritable, disagreeable, or of coarse vibrations, all this causes another intoxication, which keeps one from feeling for another and sets one against him.

The third intoxication comes from conditions. There are conditions which offer temptations or which cause anxiety, fear, doubt, or confusion. Then there are conditions which promise profit or benefit, things which one desires in life, and under these circumstances another intoxication comes, as a third cover over the heart.

A person may be wise, learned and thoughtful and yet these covers may keep him from seeing clearly the way of seeking the pleasure of every person he meets. This is the tragedy which causes much pain, even though it appears to have come from this or that source.

It matters little what church, faith, or religion a person belongs to, what doctrines or principles he believes in, what counts is that man is sincere. If he thinks and feels sincerely, he certainly is religious. The world does not need so much regilious or philosophical people, it needs living hearts ready to serve and to feel the pain of others. If there is a religion, it is the religion of the heart. This religion is best lived if one offers prayers at every moment in the form of thoughtfulness and consideration towards our fellow-men.

The question is, " how are we to learn this "? Whatever be the condition in our home or outside, we are always presented with op-

portunities to

Miss Sakina Furneé's typescript for her collection known as "the set" of the lecture of 6 February 1924

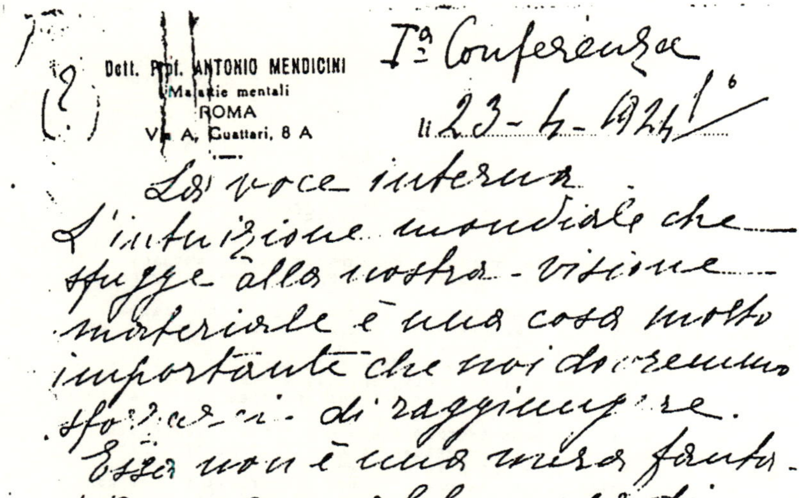
Dott. Prof. ANTONIO MENDICINI
Malattie mentali
ROMA
Via A. Guattari, 8 A

I^a Conferenza

li 23-4-1924

La voce interna

L'intuizione mondiale che sfugge alla nostra visione materiale è una cosa molto importante che noi dovremmo sforzarci di raggiungere. Essa non è una mera fantasia ma qualche cosa di reale. La logica può essere seguita in ciò che noi chiamiamo istinto. Molti credono che il torto e il giusto si siano imparati dopo esser venuti in questo mondo e non già prima. Questo è un errore che può essere scoperto quando andiamo alle radici del giusto e

Dr. Mendicini's handwritten reporting of Prof. Formichi's simultaneous translation into Italian of the lecture of 23 April 1924 in Rome

Appendix C

Missing Lectures

The Netherlands:

The Sufi Message	Nijmegen	January 4
Lecture (title unrecorded)	Nijmegen	January 5
The Life of the Sages and Saints in India	Deventer	January 6
Sermon at Universal Worship (no title noted)	The Hague	January 7
The Teachings of Sufism in Daily Life	Hilversum	January 8
The Solution to the Problem of Today	Amsterdam	January 9
Class for Candidates (no title noted)	Amsterdam	January 10
The Lost Word	Amsterdam	January 11
Class for Candidates (no title noted)	Amsterdam	January 12
Sermon at Universal Worship (no title noted)	Amsterdam	January 13
The Essence of Religion	Haarlem	January 14
The Wisdom of the Sufi School	The Hague	January 18
Mureeds' Class (no title noted)	The Hague	January 19
The Coming Civilization	The Hague	January 20
Sufi Mysticism, Class for Candidates	The Hague	January 21
The Spiritual Life	Leiden	January 22
Sufi Mysticism, Class for Candidates	The Hague	January 23

	Italy:	
The Purpose of Life	Florence	April 12
The Power of the Spirit	Florence	April 15
Intuition	Florence	April 17

Glossary of Foreign Words

The original language is indicated following each word in parentheses:

Arabic = A
French = F
Gujarati = G
Hindustani, Hindi = H
Persian = P
Sanskrit = S
Urdu = U

The usual (dictionary) meaning of the word is given first; if the word has a special use in Sufi terminology, this meaning is given second, indicated by (Suf); if the word seems to be used in some special sense by Pīr-o-Murshid 'Ināyat Khān, this is indicated by (IK).

Transliterations were made according to the following systems:

for Arabic:	*The Encyclopedia of Islam* (New edition, Leiden, 1960-), except "k" and "dj" which have been replaced by "q" and "j".
for Persian:	F. Steingass, *Comprehensive Persian-English Dictionary*, (8th edition, London, 1977).
for Sanskrit:	M. Monier-Williams, *Sanskrit-English Dictionary*, (New Delhi, 1976; originally published in 1899).

---

compris (F) - understood; included, 87

dhikr (A), the (zikar, H, G) - remembering, memory; recital; reading or reciting the praises and names of God;
- (Suf) the praise and glorification of God, a certain spiritual practice to induce awareness of the divine Presence, 145

diwān (P) - a collection of poems, or of sheets of records, 98, 303

gāthā (S) - verse, song, metre; part of the scripture of the Parsis;
- (Suf) the name Pīr-o-Murshid 'Ināyat Khān gave to a series of his teachings, including several categories, 51, 153, 161, 236, 278

gāthaka (S)	-	chanting of a sacred poem;
	-	(Suf) the name Pīr-o-Murshid 'Ināyat Khān gave to a series of his teachings, including several categories, spelled *gatheka*, 236, 278
gāyan (S)	-	singing;
	-	(Suf) one of the books of Pīr-o-Murshid 'Ināyat Khān containing sayings and prayers, called *Notes from the Unstruck Music from the Gāyan of Inayat Khan*, 183
Ḥadraṭ (A)	-	title, literally meaning "presence", popularly given to important Sufi figures, often after their death, as an indication of great respect. Pīr-o-Murshid 'Ināyat Khān was generally called "Murshid" by his followers during his lifetime, and used the title Pīr-o-Murshid on publicity; later, however, he became generally known as Hazrat (English form of Ḥadraṭ, based on Persian/Urdu pronunciation) Inayat Khan, and this title is often assumed to be part of his name, title page
īmān (A)	-	faith, belief in God, security, trust;
	-	(Suf) self-confidence, 132
jalāl (A)	-	majesty, power, divine greatness;
	-	(Suf) positive power, energy, 127, 150, 161
jamāl (A)	-	beauty, elegance;
	-	(Suf) beauty, responsiveness, 127, 150, 161
jinn (A, P/U)	-	a fire spirit, inhabitant of an intermediary world between the angelic and the human, 92
kamāl (A)	-	completion, perfection;
		(Suf) inertia, moment between jalāl and jamāl, 162
karmā (S)	-	act, work, result, the rhythm of past actions; law of action and the consequences it produces in the present or future, 227, 230, 295
Khudā, Khodā (P,U)-		God, Lord, the self-revealing God, 262
Muqtadir, al- (A)-		name of God (no. 70 in some traditional lists), meaning "Creator of all power", "the One Who determines everything", 160
murīd (A, P/U)-		willing; aspiring, aspirant, follower, disciple of a murshid, passim (see Index)

murshid (A, P/U)	-	guide, spiritual teacher;
	-	(Suf, capitalized) Pīr-o-Murshid 'Ināyat Khān (L), passim, or Abū Hāshim Madani (L), see Index
nirvāṇa (S)	-	extinguishment, annihilation, literally "blowing out", as of a candle; the indescribable state of fulfilment, in which all thought of individual ego ceases to exist, not thought of negatively, but as a transcendent state;
	-	(IK) perfect peace, 230
pasī anfās (A, P)	-	literally "watching breath";
	-	(Suf) the name Pīr-o-Murshid 'Ināyat Khān gave to a category of his teachings, translated as "Breath", 149, 153, 161
prāṇa (S)	-	breath, vitality, life, 6, 153, 171
qadr (A)	-	greatness, dignity, power; one of the names of God, 193
qaḍa (A)	-	divine decree, divine will, 193
rāga (S)	-	root meaning: to colour; that which creates feeling; a theme or a mode in Indian music; a fixed arrangement of notes, around which a musician improvises, 85
rajas (S)	-	energy, action; one of the three forms of energy, 56
salat (A)	-	formal prayer;
	-	(Suf) title given by 'Ināyat Khān to one of his prayers, 49
sama' (A)	-	hearing (of music);
	-	(Suf) music session, especially known in the Chishtiya Sufi schools, 90
sangām (S)	-	union, coming together, the confluence at Allahābād of the sacred rivers Ganga and Yamuna, one of the holiest sites in Hinduism, 162
saṅgīta (S)	-	general word for the arts of singing, playing musical instruments, and dancing, 87
sattva (S)	-	being, goodness, virtue; one of the three forms of energy, 56

ṣaum (A)	-	fasting;
saum, soum	-	(Suf) a play on the above and the word "psalm", title given by 'Ināyat Khān to one of his prayers, 49
sophia (G)	-	wisdom;
	-	(IK) often mentioned in association with the word ṣūfī, 21
ṣūfī (A)	-	usually derived from ṣūf (A), wool (woollen garments were worn by certain groups of ascetics as a sign of renunciation); applied to individuals and groups devoting their lives to inwardness and asceticism, eventually applied to the mystics generally, with the term *taṣawwuf* ("Sufism" in English) becoming the technical term for mysticism as such. An initiate does not traditionally refer to him- or herself as "a ṣūfī", but rather *mutaṣawwif*, one who is searching, or reaching out toward Sufism, passim (see Index).
sūra (H)	-	from svara (S), "heaven": sound, voice, tone, note; music, 88
sūra (A)	-	one of the 114 chapters or units of the Qur'an;
	-	(Suf) the name of a category used by Pīr-o-Murshid 'Ināyat Khān (a play on the Hidaustani and Arabic words) in classifying a part of the sayings in his books: *Notes from the Unstruck Music from the Gāyan*, *The Divine Symphony or Vadan*, and *Nirtan, or The Dance of the Soul*, 96
tāmas(S)	-	darkness, error, ignorance; one of the three forms of energy, 56
taqwā ṭahārat (A)	-	piety is purity, God-consciousness as the means of purifying the self;
	-	(IK) the name Pīr-o-Murshid 'Ināyat Khān gave to a category of his teachings, translated as "Everyday Life", 151, 155
Vedānta (S)	-	end (complete knowledge) of the Veda; name of the most important part of the third of the three great divisions of Hindu philosophy, 84
wajd (A)	-	literally, finding; ecstasy, rapture, 76, 279

yaqīn (A)	-	confidence, certainty, firm faith, conviction, 132
zikar (H,G)	-	see dhikr, 145

List of Persons, Places, Works, etc.

All dates are C.E. (A.D.) except where designated B.C.E. (B.C.)

Abraham, Ibrāhīm (A, P, U, flourished ca. 1750 B.C.E.): Patriarch and prophet,, regarded as the ancient founder of their religious tradition by Jews, Christians and Muslims, the three "Abrahamic Religions", 18, 104

Abū Hāshim Madanī, Sayyed Muhammad: 'Ināyat Khān's murshid, or spiritual guide, whom he met in Hyderabad, India, in 1903 or 1904, and under whom he studied Sufism intensely until the murshid's death in 1907 (his birth year appears not to have been recorded), 96, 149, 211

Ādam: in the Hebrew Bible and the Qur'an, the first man, human being, 127

Aladdīn: character in the Arabian Nights who obtains a magic lantern inhabited by a jinn, 138

Alexander the Great (Iskander, S(h)ikander, 356-323 B.C.E.): Macedonian conqueror who subdued much of the world, including parts of the Indian subcontinent, during his brief career, 208

Amīr Khusrau (1253-1325): poet and musician, who decisively influenced the northern (Hindustani) style (for a fuller entry, please see 1922 I), 117

Anna Paulownastraat: a street and square in The Hague, Netherlands, on which is located a building, formerly a tram station, which Sirdar van Tuyll (q.v.) transformed into a Sufi Centre, 195, 198, 200, 203, 211, 215, 217

Asaf: pen name of Mir Mahbub Ali Khan, sixth Nizam of Hyderabad (1869-1911), a poet himself (pupil of the poet Dagh) and a patron of poets (as well as musicians, including 'Ināyat Khān), 111

'Aṭṭar, Muḥammad ibn Ibrāhīm Farīd-ud-Dīn: celebrated Persian Sufi poet from Nishapur, traditionally said to have been born in 1119' and to have been killed by the Mongol invaders in 1230 at the age of 110 (now disputed by some scholars). 'Aṭṭar means perfumer, a profession he is said to have followed. Many of his writings are well-known, including the *Mantiq-ut-Tair* (Conference of the Birds), *Tazkirat-ul-Auliya* (a prose work of the lives of Sufi saints), the *Ilahi Nama* (an epic), and others, 70

Bible, the: from the Greek *ta biblia* (ultimately from the Lebanese port of Byblos, from which Egyptian papyrus was exported to ancient Greece), title given to the combined collection of the Jewish Hebrew scriptures, known to Christians as the *Old Testament*, and the Greek Christian scriptures, the *New Testament*, 48, 52, 136, 196, 209

Bose, Sir Jagadis Chandra (1858-1937): Indian plant physiologist and physicist who did pioneering work in demonstrating the movements and reactions of plants, 43

Brahma (S): God, the Creator in the Hindu religion, 38

Brahmins: Sanskrit *brāhmaṇa*, the highest social class in Hindu India, including the priests, philosophers, and scholars, 43, 164

Buddha: from Pāli, Sanskrit, meaning the old, the seniormost, the enlightened one. Title of Siddhartha Gautama (ca. 563-ca. 483 B.C.), 204

Burbank, Luther (1849-1926): plant breeder who attained astonishing results in his garden in Santa Rosa, California, where Pīr-o-Murshid 'Ināyat Khān visited him in the spring of 1923, 43

Church of All: original name given by Pīr-o-Murshid 'Ināyat Khān to what later became known as the Universal Worship (q.v.), 30, 195, 219

Coué, Émile (1857-1926): French pharmacist who popularized the idea of autosuggestion, especially the phrase "Every day, and in every way, I am becoming better and better", 6

Daniel: Jewish prophet, putative author of one of the last books to be included in the Hebrew Bible (partly in Aramaic), 8, 214

Divan of Shams-i Tabriz: the first book of poetry of Jalāl-ud-Dīn Rūmī, written after the assassination or disappearance of his teacher Shams-i Tabriz, expressing his longing, 70

Ecclesiastes: book in the Hebrew Bible traditionally attributed to Solomon, 55, 218

Edison, Thomas Alva (1847-1931): American inventor and creator of the first industrial research laboratory, 99

Egeling, Fazal Mai (Egeling-Grol, Nelly, 1861-1939): Dutchwoman who became a *mureed* in 1921, and later a Murshida in the Sufi Order, known by her Sufi name Fazal Mai; she became a member of Pīr-o-Murshid 'Ināyat Khān's household in Suresnes, France, from 1922 on. (For further information, please see 1923 II), 171, 184

Eurydice: in the myth of Orpheus (q.v.), the beloved wife of Orpheus who was killed by a serpent's bite, 99

Firdausī, Abdul Qāsim Mansūr (935-1020 C.E.): Persian poet, author of the *Shāh Nāmeh (Book of Kings)*, 69

Furnée, Jeanne E.D. (Sakīna, Nekbakht, 1896-1973): Dutchwoman who became one of Pīr-o-Murshid ‘Ināyat Khān’s three personal secretaries in 1921, and who took down most of his lectures from 1922 on in shorthand, forming the basis for the texts of these *Complete Works*. Her spiritual name Sakīna was changed by ‘Ināyat Khān to Nekbakht not long before he left for India in 1926; she continued to use the name Sakīna, but gave the name Nekbakht to the foundation she created in 1950 to preserve ‘Ināyat Khān’s teachings and distribute them, *passim*

Ganga, the Ganges: great river of north India, held sacred by the Hindus. It flows from the Himalayas to the south-east, joined by the river Brahmaputra. The sacredness of its water plays an important part in the lives of those who follow the Hindu religion, 115

Gathas: lessons given by Pīr-o-Murshid ‘Ināyat Khān for beginning students of Sufism, consisting of three series of ten lessons each on seven different topics. These short lessons were dictated by ‘Ināyat Khān (often to Murshida Sherifa Goodenough, who compiled them) from 1918 to 1925, 36, 110, 115, 168, 198

Gathekas: talks and lessons given by Pīr-o-Murshid ‘Ināyat Khān which were designated for use in classes for candidates, for use in the brotherhood work (Social Gathekas), or as sermons in the Universal Worship (Religious Gathekas), 169, 198

Gāyan: a collection of sayings by Pīr-o-Murshid ‘Ināyat Khān, originally published in 1923, based on notes written in various notebooks (full title *Notes from the Unstruck Music from the Gāyan of Inayat Khan*), 132-3

Ghazālī, Abū Hāmid Muḥammad al- (1058-1111): a native of Ghazal, a village near Tūs in Khūrāsān (Persia), Muslim jurist, theologian and mystic, whose work formed the basis of reconciliation between the orthodox religious establishments and the Sufis. He was a man of brilliant gifts, and his sceptical nature and his restless mind at times led him to complete agnosticism. Neither the study of theology and religious law nor of philosophy satisfied him. He went through many stages of intellectual and religious experiences, and the influence thereof reflects in his many works, among which the *Iḥyā’u’l ‘Ulūm-id-Dīn* (*The Revivification of Religious Sciences*) and his *Mishkātu’l Anwār* (*The Niche for Lights*), besides works on canon law, on logic and many other subjects. He is mainly known as one of the greatest theologians and mystical scholars of Islam. Sufism with him finds a place in orthodox Islam, 212

Goodenough, Lucy (Murshida Sherifa, (1876-1937): Englishwoman who became a *mureed* in London during the First World War, and was known by her Sufi name, Sherifa. She became one of Pīr-o-Murshid ‘Ināyat Khān’s secretaries and the principal editor of his work for publication, and was initiated as a Murshida in 1923, *passim*

Hāfiz̤, Shams-ud-Dīn (1325?-1389): widely-known Persian poet, whose proverbial verses are quoted throughout the Muslim East and India (for a fuller entry, please see 1922 I), 67, 70-1, 118, 215

Headquarters: The International Headquarters of the Sufi Movement, established in Geneva in the early 1920s, and remaining there (officially) until the early 1980s, *passim*

Hebrew: the language of the ancient Jews, a Semitic language (like Arabic), 103-4

Himalayas: the mountain range separating India and Nepal and China (Tibet), including the highest mountains in the world, 176

Hindu: a word meaning Indian, applied to the system of various but related native religions of the Indian sub-continent, all accepting the sacred revelatory character of the earliest scriptures, the *Veda*s, and held together by the caste system as social structure and the ideal of asceticism, renunciation, and finally liberation from the human condition, 104, 162

In an Eastern Rose Garden: a book of Pīr-o-Murshid 'Ināyat Khān compiled and edited by Dr. O. C. Grüner, containing lectures on various subjects, first published in England in 1921, 171

'Ināyat Khān, Pīr-o-Murshid Ḥadraṭ (1882-1927): Indian gentleman-musician and mystic who came to the West in 1910, where he taught Sufism and established the Sufi Order (from October 1923 called Sufi Movement). Traveling widely, he lived in London during World War I, thereafter in France, where he and his family eventually settled at Suresnes (near Paris) in 1922. In 1913 he had married Ora Ray Baker, an American, from then on known as Amina Begum; they had four children. He died while on his first return tour through India on February 5th, 1927, *passim*

Jalāl-ud-Dīn Rūmī (1207-1273): widely considered the greatest poet of the Persian language (for a fuller entry, please see 1922 I), 64-5, 71

Jesus Christ (4 BCE?-29 CE?): founder and central figure in the Christian religion, believed by Christians (and Muslims) to have been the Messiah, 1, 11, 13, 28, 31, 40, 44, 53, 55, 72, 77, 83, 104, 139, 186, 212

John the Baptist: maternal relative of Jesus Christ who founded a movement of purification within Judaism which required ritual immersion (baptism), 83

Jumna: English name for one of the principal rivers of India; see Yamuna

Koran, see Qur'an

Kṛṣṇa (Krishna): widely-worshiped god in India, considered the eighth incarnation of Vishṇu. He appears in art often blue and carrying or playing a flute, 138, 201, 219

League of Nations: international organization founded by the victorious Allies after World War I to solve political problems and foster cooperation; its headquarters were in Geneva; after World War II, it was replaced by the United Nations, 195

Maṣnawī (fully *Maṣnawī-ye ma'nawī, The Spiritual Couplets*), major poetical work of Jalāl-ud-Dīn Rūmī (q.v.), a vast compendium of Sufi lore conveyed in fables and anecdotes, with the love of God as its principal theme, 71, 171

Mercury: Roman god, equated with the Greek Hermes, who acted as a messenger for Jupiter (Zeus), 99

Moses [Moshe (H), Musa (A)] (13th century BCE): Hebrew prophet who received the Torah on Mount Sinai (for a fuller entry, please see 1922 I), 31

Muḥammad, the Prophet (570-632 CE): Arab prophet whose messages from God constitute the sacred scripture of Islam, the *Qur'ān* (q.v.; for a fuller entry, please see 1922 I), 202

Murshid: title used in Sufism for a spiritual guide; often a substitute for the name of Pīr-o-Murshid 'Ināyat Khān, and used by him to refer to his own spiritual guide, Abū Hāshim Madanī (q.v.),2, 3, 24-5, 34-6

Napoléon Bonaparte (1769-1821): French military leader, originating from a Corsican family of minor nobles, which enabled him to enlist as a French officer cadet. He became emperor, extending French domination over a large part of Europe, and over Egypt, and from there sought to re-establish French influence and interests in southern India in alliance with Tipu Sultān, the then powerful ruler of the vastly extended kingdom of Mysore, 208

Nizāmī, Ilyās ibn Yūsuf (d. 1209): Sufi romantic poet, 70

Orpheus: ancient legendary Greek god-hero with extraordinary skill in music and song. Many stories about Orpheus emphasize his ability to control situations through his music, but his attempt to take his wife Eurydice out of the underworld ended in failure when he forgetfully looked back, 99

Pīr-o-Murshid 'Ināyat Khān: see 'Ināyat Khān, Pīr-o-Murshid

Qur'ān: the sacred scripture of Islām, the record of the revelations received by the Prophet Muḥammad (q.v.), 38, 70

Rumi: see Jalāl-ud-Dīn Rūmī

Sa'dī of Shīrāz, Muṣlih-ud-Dīn (1184-1291): an important Persian poet and writer who, after his studies, spent many years of his life traveling. On the mystic path he received instruction from Abdu`l Qādir Jīlanī, founder of the Qādirī Sufi Order. Sa`dī's *Būstān* and *Gulistān* became extremely popular, and well-known even in the West, 50, 71

Satan: English form of the Hebrew śāṭān (Arabic shaitan), accuser, the proper name of the Devil,38, 150

Shams-i Tabriz, see Divan of

Solomon [Shlomo (Hb), Suleymān (A)] (flourished 10th c. B.C.): third king of Israel, successor to his father David, and builder of the Temple in Jerusalem. He was famous for his wisdom, and several books in the Jewish scriptures are attributed to him, 55, 208, 218

Sorbonne: the best-known college of the University in Paris, founded c. 1257, where Pīr-o-Murshid 'Ināyat Khān sometimes lectured, 59, 65, 87

Sufi Invocation, the: spoken by Pīr-o-Murshid 'Ināyat Khān at the beginning of the Universal Worship service and certain lectures, and also used at the beginning of each paper in the series of Sufi teachings prepared at International Headquarters, Geneva, and on other occasions: "Towards the One, the Perfection of Love, Harmony and Beauty, the Only Being, united with All the Illuminated Souls, who form the Embodiment of the Master, the Spirit of Guidance", *passim*

Sufi Message, the: name used by Pīr-o-Murshid 'Ināyat Khān to designate his universal teachings (for example in the title of his first book in English, *A Sufi Message of Spiritual Liberty*), later sometimes called just the Message, 23

Sufi Movement, The: official name after October, 1923, of Pīr-o-Murshid 'Ināyat Khān's Sufi organization, see Index

Sufi Order, The: the organization founded in 1910 by Pīr-o-Murshid 'Ināyat Khān, formalized in 1916 in London, to give Sufi teaching; in 1923 the organization was renamed the Sufi Movement (q.v.), and the Sufi Order was defined as the Esoteric School of Inner Culture, central among the activities of the Movement, see Index

Sufi Quarterly: journal instituted in Geneva in 1925, edited first by Ronald. A. M. (Mumtaz) Armstrong, an English *mureed*, and then by Miss Margaret Skinner, which continued until 1940, presenting the teachings of Pīr-o-Murshid 'Ināyat Khān and articles by many others, often not Sufi *mureed*s, on related topics, 203

Suresnes: a suburb west of Paris, France, on the Seine river; in the hills above the river, Pīr-o-Murshid 'Ināyat Khān gave his Summer Schools from 1922 to 1926, and there he lived with his family in a mansion with grounds, known as Fazal Manzil (house of blessing), situated in the Val d'Or, originally part of the municipality of St Cloud, but then annexed to the rapidly expanding Suresnes, 228

Theosophical Society, the: an organization founded in 1875 by Mme Helena Petrovna Blavatsky (1831-91), which did much to promote interest in Eastern thought in Europe and America; in Pīr-o-Murshid 'Ināyat Khān 's day, the Society in Europe was led by Miss Annie Besant (1847-1933), whom 'Ināyat Khān is said to have met in Geneva in 1921. Many persons who became followers of 'Ināyat Khān had previously been associated with the Theosophical Society, 4

Tuyll van Serooskerken, Baron Sirdar van (1883-1958): Dutch mureed of Pīr-o-Murshid 'Ināyat Khān, known as Shaikh Sirdar van Tuyll, 171, 177, 208

Unity of Religious Ideals, The: a book posthumously published in 1929 of 'Ināyat Khān's teachings on various religious traditions, edited and compiled by Murshida Sherifa Goodenough, 2 73

Universal Worship: a formal worship service, incorporating the scriptures of various religions, initiated by Pīr-o-Murshid 'Ināyat Khān in 1921 in London, see Index

*Upanishad*s: scriptures of the Hindu religion, later than the *Veda*s, 96

Vedānta: the main system of Hindu philosophy, based on the interpretation of the *Upanishads*, themselves elaborations on the most ancient scriptures, the *Vedas*, 84

Voorst van Beest, Munira van (1916-1990): founding editor of these *Complete Works*, xiv

Yamuna: one of the principal rivers of India, originating in the Himalayas, which merges with the Ganges, 161

Yoga: Hindu system of spiritual training on all levels, aiming at union with ultimate reality, highly esteemed by Sufis as well, referred to from al-Bīrūnī (d. 1048) on, 87, 145

Zarathushtra: the Avestan original form of the Greek name Zoroaster, a prophet who lived in the north-east of Old Iran (Bactria), flourishing probably in the 6th c. B.C.E. or earlier. He is the founder of the religion which bears his name, also known as *Parsi*ism in India, meaning of Persian origin, where it mainly survives among a community of about 100,000 Gujarātī speakers in the States of Gujarāt and Mahārashtra (i.e. around Bombay). They emphasize the beneficent rôle of Ahura Mazda (Wise Lord), promising immortality and bliss in the afterlife to the faithful. This religion had a profound, if now mostly unacknowledged influence on the development of the moral and theological tradition of Judaism, Christianity and Islam. Thus, e.g., the word and conception of Paradise (*Firdaus*) is of Zoroastrian origin. The anglicized *Parsi* community had a considerable influence on 'Ināyat Khān during his earlier years, 94-96

Index

Entries followed by (G) appear also in the Glossary, and those followed by (L) appear also in the List of Persons, etc.